The
Handbook
for the
New Legal Writer

SECOND EDITION

ASPEN COURSEBOOK SERIES

The
Handbook
for the
New Legal Writer

SECOND EDITION

JILL BARTON
Professor of Legal Writing
University of Miami School of Law

RACHEL H. SMITH
Professor of Legal Writing
St. John's University School of Law

Published by Wolters Kluwer in New York.

Wolters Kluwer Legal & Regulatory U.S. serves customers worldwide with CCH, Aspen Publishers, and Kluwer Law International products. (www.WKLegaledu.com)

Cover art by HunyFuny/Shutterstock.com

To contact Customer Service, e-mail customer.service@wolterskluwer.com, call 1-800-234-1660, fax 1-800-901-9075, or mail correspondence to:

Wolters Kluwer
Attn: Order Department
PO Box 990
Frederick, MD 21705

Printed in the United States of America.

1 2 3 4 5 6 7 8 9 0

ISBN 978-1-5438-0214-6

Library of Congress Cataloging-in-Publication Data

Names: Barton, Jill (Professor of Legal writing) author. | Smith, Rachel H.,
    1976- author.
Title: The handbook for the new legal writer / Jill Barton, Professor of
    Legal Writing, University of Miami School of Law; Rachel H. Smith, Asst.
    Professor of Legal Writing, St. John's University School of Law.
Description: Second edition. | New York : Wolters Kluwer, [2019] | Series:
    Aspen coursebook series | Includes bibliographical references and index.
Identifiers: LCCN 2018034318 | ISBN 9781543802146
Subjects: LCSH: Legal composition—United States.
Classification: LCC KF250 .B378 2019 | DDC 808.06/634—dc23
LC record available at https://lccn.loc.gov/2018034318

About Wolters Kluwer Legal & Regulatory U.S.

Wolters Kluwer Legal & Regulatory U.S. delivers expert content and solutions in the areas of law, corporate compliance, health compliance, reimbursement, and legal education. Its practical solutions help customers successfully navigate the demands of a changing environment to drive their daily activities, enhance decision quality and inspire confident outcomes.

Serving customers worldwide, its legal and regulatory portfolio includes products under the Aspen Publishers, CCH Incorporated, Kluwer Law International, ftwilliam. com and MediRegs names. They are regarded as exceptional and trusted resources for general legal and practice-specific knowledge, compliance and risk management, dynamic workflow solutions, and expert commentary.

To our anchors:
Lucy, Rudy, Lipkin, and Eric

Summary of Contents

Contents

Preface

Welcome to the second edition of *The Handbook for the New Legal Writer*—a legal writing textbook that is grounded in the realities of modern law practice.

We were thrilled by the positive response to the first edition of the *Handbook*. Legal writing students and professors told us that they appreciated the *Handbook's* step-by-step instructions and annotated examples. In this second edition, we have added more examples of effective legal writing from recently decided cases and more examples of the types of documents students write in first-year legal writing courses.

The *Handbook* begins with objective writing in the form of law school exams and office memos. Later, we move to persuasive writing through trial motions and appellate briefs. Then, we cover other forms of legal communication, including correspondence via letter, email, and instant message. We also describe how to draft judicial opinions and prepare for oral argument.

At every step, the *Handbook* uses annotated examples of realistic legal documents prepared by the authors, skilled practitioners, and judges to show—rather than tell—students how to be successful legal writers. Because it is designed to be the only textbook students need to excel in their first-year legal writing programs, the *Handbook* also includes chapters on legal research, *Bluebook* citation, and writing tools, including grammar, punctuation, plain language, and style.

The *Handbook* uses the term "anchors" throughout the text to show students how to analyze legal questions. If the best answer in law school is, "It depends," then we finish the answer by stating, "It depends on the anchors." Anchors are the facts, rules, and reasons that the answer to a legal question depends upon. We coined this term as a tool to help students understand how to read and synthesize legal authorities and how to analyze a client's legal problem. We have enjoyed watching as students and professors adopt this term over the last five years, and we think that this new edition offers even more detailed instruction in using anchors to conceptualize and organize legal documents.

We hope that by offering clear direction and pertinent examples, the *Handbook* will be an accessible, trustworthy, and valuable guide for the new legal writer.

Anchors aweigh!

Jill and Rachel
November 2018

Acknowledgments

We are grateful for the support of our creative and talented colleagues at the University of Miami School of Law and St. John's University School of Law. We especially appreciate the feedback and support from our earliest adopters—Alyssa Dragnich, Christina M. Frohock, Pete Nemerovski, Shara Kobetz Pelz, Rachel Stabler, Annette Torres, and Cheryl E. Zuckerman—who helped us refine the first edition before its publication.

We also owe a great debt to our colleagues in the national legal writing community. Their encouragement and enthusiasm for the first edition inspired us and helped us make this second edition a more effective teaching tool. We especially appreciate the more recent collegiality and kindness of Shakira Pleasant, Renee Schimkat, and Marcia Narine Weldon at Miami Law and Kelly Alexander, Rosa Castello, Larry Cunningham, Robin Boyle Laisure, Patricia Montana, Bob Ruescher, Jane Scott, and Kayonia Whetstone at St. John's.

We also owe thanks to our students, whose thoughtful questions over the past six years have helped us make the *Handbook* more helpful for our primary audience. We cannot forget the efforts of our research assistants for the first edition: Olivia Kelman, Candice Manyak, Christine Tudor, and Daniel Zailskas. And we greatly appreciate the efforts of our research assistants on this second edition: Caitlin Emling, Elisabeth Rabin, Stephanie Rosner, and Bianca Velikopoljski at Miami Law and Kevin Hale, Jacqueline Mancini, Anthony Nania, Michael Pitre, and especially Daniel Lynch, at St. John's. Additionally, we are grateful to our supportive administrators: Dean Patricia D. White and Acting Dean Osamudia James at Miami Law and Dean Michael Simons and Associate Dean Anita Krishnakumar at St. John's.

We also appreciate the efforts of everyone at Aspen Publishers, especially Donna Gridley, David Herzig, Richard Mixter, and Dana Wilson, for once again turning our vision into a reality. Their attention to detail in designing the abundant examples, annotations, and illustrations in this book is unsurpassed.

Finally, we want to express our admiration and appreciation for the legal writers whose excellent work provided examples for this book. First, our thanks go to U.S. Supreme Court Chief Justice John G. Roberts; Associate Justices Clarence Thomas, Ruth Bader Ginsburg, Stephen Breyer, Samuel Alito, Sonia Sotomayor, Elena Kagan, and Neil Gorsuch; former Associate Justices Robert H. Jackson, John Paul Stevens, Sandra Day O'Connor, Antonin Scalia, and Anthony Kennedy; U.S. Seventh Circuit Court of Appeals Judge Richard Posner, U.S. Fifth Circuit Court of Appeals Judge Don R. Willett; U.S. District Judge Steven D. Merryday;

Minnesota Supreme Court Justice Natalie Hudson; Judge G. Alan Blackburn of the Court of Appeals of Georgia; Judge Kevin G. Ross of the Minnesota Court of Appeals; and Judge Vance E. Salter of the Florida Third District Court of Appeal.

Second, we want to thank and credit attorneys Michelle R. Bennett, Howard K. Blumberg, Matthew A. Fitzgerald, Bryan A. Garner, Gregory G. Garre, Nathaniel P. Garrett, Charles L. Hobson, Neal K. Katyal, Brian Koukoutchos, James R. Layton, Ria Tabacco Mar, Theodore B. Olson, Mitchell L. Rothman, Sarah J. Ryan, Carolyn M. Snurkowski, Kenneth W. Starr, Kathleen Sullivan, Laurence H. Tribe, Lindsey N. Ursua, Seth P. Waxman, and Frederick R. Yarger. We know their words will continue to inspire our students, as they have inspired us.

The
Handbook
for the
New Legal Writer

SECOND EDITION

Reading and Writing Like a Lawyer

Introduction to Legal Writing

To be a lawyer is to be a writer. Most lawyers write every single day that they practice law. On a given day, the average attorney can be expected to write or edit any number of documents that vary widely in form, style, and purpose. Even a new lawyer is responsible for understanding how to prepare a vast range of documents, including memos, briefs, letters, and emails. This book guides you with step-by-step instructions for how to prepare each of these common legal documents.

Legal documents can generally be divided into two categories: (1) objective documents and (2) persuasive documents. Objective and persuasive documents serve different purposes, have different audiences, and require the legal writer to adapt to different formats and writing styles. The type of document that you will prepare in a given situation depends upon the purpose of the document and its intended audience.

1. OBJECTIVE DOCUMENTS

The purpose of an objective legal document is to inform and counsel. An objective document analyzes a legal issue to predict the most likely outcome.

The typical objective document is an office memorandum that applies the relevant law to the client's facts. Objective memos are used to analyze the legal consequences of particular facts, the potential success of a legal claim, the advisability of a legal strategy, and many other legal questions. The conclusion of an objective legal document is usually similar to the following statement:

The court will likely hold that _____ because _____.

The most common objective documents are office memos, judicial opinions, and advice letters and emails. Because readers expect an objective document to accurately advise them, the analysis must be scrupulous, balanced, and reliable.

2. PERSUASIVE DOCUMENTS

The purpose of a persuasive legal document is to argue, convince, and induce action. A persuasive document analyzes a legal issue to persuade the reader of the correct outcome.

The typical persuasive document is a motion that asks the court to grant some particular relief to the writer's client. The conclusion of a persuasive legal document is usually similar to the following statement:

> The Court should grant the requested relief because _____.

The most common persuasive documents are trial motions, responses, replies, and appellate briefs, which the writer directs to the court. Opposing counsel reviews and responds to persuasive documents filed with the court, and both sides typically draft persuasive letters and emails to opposing counsel. Because a persuasive document is intended to persuade the reader, the analysis in a persuasive document must be logical, credible, and compelling.

Law students and lawyers write both objective and persuasive documents. Both types of documents require a careful legal analysis. The next chapter shows you how to approach your legal analysis, beginning with how to read and understand the authorities that will allow you to analyze your legal question. Then, Chapter 5 introduces you to the common formats for both objective and persuasive documents. And Chapter 6 shows how to use these formats to write successful answers on essay exams.

Reading and Understanding Authorities

1. READING CONSTITUTIONS AND STATUTES

The right to speak freely, the right to bear arms, the right against unreasonable searches and seizures—all are rights guaranteed by the U.S. Constitution—with some carefully worded limitations. These limitations have been subject to debate for centuries. While some argue that the Constitution is a living, breathing document with a meaning that evolves over time, others advocate for a plain language interpretation. But even the most careful reader will strain to understand the plain meaning of the Constitution. As an example, consider the meaning of the Second Amendment, which citizens have argued over since before it was ratified in 1791:

> A well regulated Militia, being necessary to the security of a free State, the right of the people to keep and bear Arms, shall not be infringed.

The centuries-old language raises some questions: What is a well-regulated Militia? Why is the clause "being necessary to the security of a free State" offset by commas? And what does the term "Arms" include?

When reading constitutions and statutes, every word, every comma, and every clause matters. You will need to carefully consider the meaning of each term and punctuation mark. Take care to look for terms that impact the meaning of the words around them, including "and," "or," "unless," "except," "not," "if," "may," "must," "shall," and "provided that."

When reading statutes, you also need to consider the overall organization of the body of laws. Statutes are typically organized by topic into numerical titles or subject codes. For instance, federal statutes contained within the U.S. Code are organized into 51 titles, from Title 1—General Provisions to Title 51—National and Commercial Space Programs. Some state statutes are organized into subject codes organized alphabetically. For example, the California statutes contained within the California Code are arranged into 29 subject codes, from Business and Professions to Welfare and Institutions. Federal and state statutes are then divided within the titles or subject codes into subtitles, chapters, sections, and subsections.

When you search for a statute on a particular legal question, keep in mind that more than one statute or statutory section might apply. For instance, suppose you need to defend a client against a littering charge in Arizona. To find the littering statute(s), you would begin by reviewing the list of titles in the Arizona Revised Code. Your search would reveal the following hierarchy:

Title 13 Criminal Code
→ Chapter 16 Criminal Damage to Property
→ 13-1601 Definitions
→ 13-1602 Criminal damage; classification
→ 13-1603 Criminal littering or polluting; classification
→ 13-1604 Aggravated criminal damage; classification
→ 13-1605 Aggregation of amounts of damage

You will likely quickly recognize that Section 1603 applies:

A. A person commits criminal littering or polluting if the person without lawful authority does any of the following: 1. Throws, places, drops or permits to be dropped on public property or property of another that is not a lawful dump any litter, destructive or injurious material that the person does not immediately remove.[1]

A careful reading shows that Section 1603 describes the littering conduct prohibited. You would notice that the statute criminalizes "any" of the listed actions and repeatedly uses "or." You would also notice that the statute appears to include exceptions if the person acts with "lawful authority" or "immediately remove[s]" the litter. But a few terms in the statute, including "litter" and "destructive or injurious material" are open to interpretation. Section 1601 helpfully provides a definition of "litter" that you would use in interpreting the statute.

In this chapter, unless the context otherwise requires:
3. "Litter" includes any rubbish, refuse, waste material, offal, paper, glass, cans, bottles, organic or inorganic trash, debris, filthy or odoriferous objects, dead animals or any foreign substance of whatever kind or description, including junked or abandoned vehicles, whether or not any of these items are of value.[2]

But because Section 1601 does not define "destructive or injurious material," you would have to use case law to see how courts have interpreted the term. You would also want to use case law to understand how courts have interpreted the definitions in Section 1601 and how they have applied the language of Section 1603 to the actions of defendants in specific cases.

This reading of an Arizona statute shows that you must consider the context of each statute you analyze because related statutes often define key terms. It also shows that legislative bodies regularly use dense, complicated

---

1. Ariz. Stat. § 13-1603(A)(1) (2018).
2. *Id.* § 13-1601(3).

language that might leave room for debate. Your task as a new legal reader is to carefully analyze the language in a constitutional or statutory provision so you can understand its precise meaning.

2. READING AND BRIEFING A CASE

Reading a case is different than reading a novel or news article. You might have to read a case several times before you understand it. Cases often involve complex legal issues, archaic language, unfamiliar terms, and confounding analyses. Your job as a lawyer when reading a case is to figure out how and why the court reached its decision. You can start by identifying the eight key parts of a case:

1. Case name and citation
2. Procedural history
3. Issue(s)
4. Facts
5. Rule(s)
6. Reasoning
7. Holding(s)
8. Order or disposition

These eight key parts of a case form the basis of a "case brief." A case brief is a document you create for your own use where you identify each of these key parts. Preparing a case brief allows you to read the case carefully and record your analysis. This record guarantees that you will have noticed and extracted the most important parts of the case, and it preserves your understanding of the case so you can come back to it later and not have to analyze the case from scratch. As a law student, you will write countless case briefs. As a lawyer, you will probably develop your own shorthand for briefing cases, but you will always need to identify the following key parts of any case you read.

A. Case Name and Citation

The case name identifies the parties in the case. The citation provides the volume, case reporter, and page where the case was published, the court that decided the case, and the year of decision. The citation is the primary information a lawyer uses to locate a case. See Chapter 43 for details on how to write citations according to the preferred format in *The Bluebook: A Uniform System of Citation*.

B. Procedural History

The procedural history describes the case's progress through the legal system. The procedural history will tell you how the case arrived at the court that wrote the opinion you are reading.

C. Issue(s)

The issue is a summary of the legal question that the opinion is intended to answer. It is usually a combination of the law and facts that gave rise to the dispute before the court. Some cases address multiple issues.

D. Facts

The facts are those facts that are legally significant to the issue that the court is deciding. Facts are legally significant if they impact the court's decision or, if changed, might alter the outcome of the case.

E. Rule(s)

The rules are the legal principles that the court applies to the facts of the case to reach its decision. Usually, the rules come from statutes or other cases.

F. Reasoning

The reasoning is the analytical process the court follows to reach its decision. The reasoning describes how the court applied the rules to the facts to determine the appropriate outcome. Identifying the reasons that support the court's resolution of the issue is crucial to understanding a case.

This book identifies these reasons as "anchors." Anchors are the grounds or bases of a court's decision. The court might state the anchors explicitly, or the court might use wording that is less direct. As a result, you will need to carefully read and understand an opinion to fully identify the anchors that motivated a court's decision. Chapter 3 describes anchors in more detail and discusses how to use the anchors from multiple cases to answer new legal questions.

G. Holding(s)

The holding is the court's answer. It states the court's resolution of the specific issues before it. The holding briefly describes how the court applied the rule to the specific facts of the case. Cases that address multiple issues will have multiple holdings: one for each issue.

H. Order or Disposition

The order or disposition is the court's instruction for what should happen in the case procedurally in light of the court's holding.

When you write a case brief, it's important to begin to digest the information you read and highlight in an opinion. Case briefs need to be concise, even for opinions that are dozens of pages long. The case brief should summarize and synthesize the information from the opinion. Although most cases include all eight key parts, cases rarely (if ever) describe each part concisely and in order. Moreover, cases often include information that is not directly relevant to the court's decision or the reason you are reading the case.

In the following case, the plaintiff sued a circus company for negligence after a circus bear frightened the plaintiff's horse while on a public street. The eight key parts of the case and the anchors are identified in the margin. A sample case brief follows on page 13.

BOSTOCK-FERARI AMUSEMENT CO. v. BROCKSMITH
73 N.E. 281 (Ind. App. 1905) [3]

This is the **case name and citation.** Bostock-Ferari Amusement Co. is the defendant, and Brocksmith is the plaintiff. The citation abbreviates the North Eastern (N.E.) Reporter and includes the volume (73) and page number (281). Ind. App. is the correct *Bluebook* abbreviation for the Appellate Court of Indiana. 1905 is the year the case was decided.

Opinion

The complaint alleges that the plaintiff, while driving in his buggy, was injured in consequence of his horse taking fright from the sight of a bear walking along a public street of the city of Vincennes. The action was begun in the circuit court of Knox county, and, upon change of venue, tried in the circuit court of Sullivan county. The court rendered judgment upon the verdict of the jury in favor of appellee for $750.

The complaint was in three paragraphs. The first was dismissed, and the cause was tried upon the amended second and third paragraphs, to which a general denial was filed. The errors relied upon are the action of the court in overruling demurrers to the said second and third paragraphs, respectively, of the complaint, and overruling appellant's motion for a new trial. Among the reasons set out in the motion for a new trial are that the verdict was contrary to the law, and was not sustained by sufficient evidence.

The first two paragraphs describe the case's **procedural history**—the legal steps that led to this appeal.

The question of the sufficiency of the second paragraph of complaint is not entirely free from doubt, but we conclude that each of said paragraphs is sufficient to withstand a demurrer.

It is sought to maintain an action for damages resulting from the fright of a horse at the sight of a bear, which its keeper and owner was leading along a public street for the purpose of transporting it from a railroad train by which it had been carried to Vincennes to the point in Vincennes at which the bear was to be an exhibit, as a part of appellant's show. It is not claimed, either by allegation or proof, that the show was in itself unlawful; and there is no pretense that the transporting of the bear from one place to another for the purpose of exhibition was unlawful, or in itself negligence. The case is therefore one of the fright of a horse merely at the appearance of the bear while it was being led along the street, was making no noise or other demonstration, and was in the control of its keeper. It appears without contradiction from the evidence that when the horse took fright the bear was doing nothing except going with his keeper. He was muzzled. He had a ring in his nose, to which a chain was attached. It was strong enough to hold and control him. He had

These three sentences describe the central **issue** in the case. A good case brief will concisely summarize the legal question and reference the relevant facts and law.

This section includes most of the key **facts**. A case brief should summarize the key facts, focusing on the facts that are legally significant.

---

3. Note that the citations in this opinion and the citations in the examples provided throughout this book have been edited to conform to *Bluebook* style.

around his neck a collar about two inches wide and one-half inch thick, to which also was attached a chain. The keeper had both chains in his hand when the accident occurred. The chain connected with the ring in his nose was small. The one connected with his collar was large. It was for the purpose of chaining him at night when he was alone. The chains were strong enough to control the bear. The animal was characterized by the witnesses who knew him as "gentle," "kind," and "docile." His keeper testified that he had never known him to be mean or growl. He testified, also, that he never knew of a bear scaring a horse; that shortly before the accident the keeper met two ladies in a buggy, and their horses did not scare. He was described as of pretty good size and brown. One witness said he was a "large, ugly looking brown bear." When a person is injured by an attack by an animal ferae naturae, the negligence of the owner is presumed, because the dangerous propensity of such an animal is known, and the law recognizes that safety lies only in keeping it secure. 2 Am. & Eng. Ency. Law 351(2d Ed.). In the case before us the injury did not result from any vicious propensity of the bear. ⚓ He did nothing but walk in the charge of his owner and keeper, Peter Degeleih. He was being moved quietly upon a public thoroughfare for a lawful purpose. ⚓

*This is the first of two major **rules** from the case.*

*The most important parts of the court's **reasoning** are highlighted in gray throughout this opinion. Most courts detail step-by-step the rationales for their decisions.*

We have given the facts that are not controverted. There is also evidence tending strongly to support the claim made by appellant that appellee was guilty of negligence proximately contributing to his injury. Appellant also earnestly argues—supporting its argument with references to recognized authorities—that the owner and keeper of the bear was an independent contractor. But the disposition which we think should be made of the appeal makes it unnecessary to consider these questions. The liability of the appellant must rest on the doctrine of negligence. The gist of the action as claimed by appellee is the transportation of the bear, with knowledge that it was likely to frighten horses, without taking precaution to guard against fright. An animal ferae naturae, reduced to captivity, is the property of its captor. 2 Black. Comm. 391, 403; 4 Black. Comm. 235, 236. The owner of the bear had the right to transport it from one place to another for a lawful purpose, and it was not negligence per se for the owner or keeper to lead it along a public street for such purpose. *Scribner v. Kelley*, 38 Barb. 14 (N.Y. Sup. Ct. 1862); *Macomber v. Nichols*, 34 Mich. 212 (1876); Ingham on Law of Animals, 230. The conducting of shows for the exhibition of wild or strange animals is a lawful business. The mere fact that the appearance of a chattel, whether an animal or an inanimate object, is calculated to frighten a horse of ordinary gentleness, does not deprive the owner of such chattel of his lawful right to transport its property along a public highway. *Macomber v. Nichols*, supra; *Holland v. Bartch*, 120 Ind. 46 (1889); *Wabash, etc., Co. v. Farver*, 12 N. E. 296 (Ind. 1887); *Gilbert v. Flint, etc.*, 16 N. W. 868 (Mich. 1883); *Piollet v. Simmers*, 106 Pa. 95 (1854). One must use his own so as not to unnecessarily injure another, but the measure of care to be employed in respect to animals

*This is the first part of the court's two-part **holding**. The holding may look like a rule, but the rules are general legal principles and the holding is the specific application of the rules to the facts of this case.*

*This is the second major **rule**.*

and other property is the same. It is such care as an ordinarily prudent person would employ under similar circumstances. ⚖ This is not inconsistent with the proposition that, if an animal ferae naturae attacks and injures a person, the negligence of the owner or keeper is presumed. The evidence is that the horse was of ordinary gentleness, but this fact would not deprive the appellant of the right to make proper use of the street. If the bear had been carelessly managed, or permitted to make any unnecessary noise or demonstration, it would have been an act of negligence. It is not uncommon for horses of ordinary gentleness to become frightened at unaccustomed sights on the public highway. The automobile, the bicycle, the traction engine, the steam roller, may each be frightful to some horses, but still they may be lawfully used on the public streets. King David said, "An horse is a vain thing for safety." Modern observation has fully justified the statement. A large dog, a great bull, a baby wagon, may each frighten some horses, but their owners are not barred from using them upon the streets on that account. Nor, under the decisions, would the courts be warranted in holding that the owner of a bear, subjugated, gentle, docile, chained, would not, under the facts shown in the case at bar, be permitted to conduct the homely brute along the public streets, because of his previous condition of freedom. In *Scribner v. Kelley*, supra, the court said: "It does not appear that the elephant was at large, but, on the contrary, that he was in the care and apparently under the control of a man who was riding beside him on a horse; and the occurrence happened before the passage of the act of April 2, 1862, regulating the use of public highways. There is nothing in the evidence to show that the plaintiff's horse was terrified because the object he saw was an elephant, but only that he was frightened because he suddenly saw moving upon a highway crossing upon which he was traveling, and fully 100 feet from him, a large, animate object, to which he was unaccustomed. Non constat that any other moving object of equal size, and differing in appearance from such as he was accustomed to see, might not have inspired him with similar terror. The injury which resulted from his fright is more fairly attributed to a lack of ordinary courage and discipline in himself than to the fact that the object which he saw was an elephant." ⚖

It is alleged in the complaint that the bear was an object likely to frighten a horse of ordinary gentleness, which fact the appellant well knew. There is no evidence that the bear was an object likely to frighten horses of ordinary gentleness, nor that the appellant knew that the bear was an object likely to frighten horses of ordinary gentleness. ⚖ The evidence shows, so far as the observation of the keeper and the appellant is stated and gave information, that he had not frightened horses.

The learned counsel for appellee insist that the appellant was negligent in not having had the proper number of persons in charge of the bear to give warning of the danger; citing *Bennett v. Lovell*, 12 R. I. 166 (1878).

In that case the plaintiff and his wife were thrown from their wagon and injured in consequence of their horse taking fright from some tubing and machinery which had been left upon a public highway by the defendant, who was carrying the same for the use of the city waterworks. The court held that one who left such an object on the highway without proper precaution cannot be said to be using the due care he ought to use. The court indulges in dicta by way of illustration to the effect that a person moving an animal which, from its appearances, noise, or offensiveness, is calculated to frighten human beings, without taking precautions by having a sufficient number of persons in charge of it to warn others of the danger, and, if need be, to aid them in passing it, or who leaves such an object on the highway without proper precaution, cannot be said to be using that due care he ought to use, etc. The facts are not analogous with those in the case at bar. The appellant used the public highway. The animal was gentle, was securely in the control of his keeper, and is — This sentence is the second part of the court's **holding**. not shown to have been an animal which, from its appearance, noise, or other offensiveness, was calculated to frighten horses. The facts upon the question of negligence are undisputed, and that question is therefore to be determined by the court as a matter of law.

The judgment is reversed, with instruction to sustain appellant's motion — This is the court's **order**. for a new trial.

1. **Case name and citation:** *Bostock-Ferari Amusement Co. v. Brocksmith*, 73 N.E. 281 (Ind. App. 1905).

2. **Procedural history:** The plaintiff sued the bear owner for negligence and won $750 at the trial court. The defendant appeals the denial of its motion for a new trial.

3. **Issue:** Is the owner of a wild animal, like a bear, liable for negligence if the injury suffered is not the result of any vicious propensity of the wild animal?

4. **Facts:** The plaintiff was injured while driving a horse-drawn buggy after his horse was scared when it saw a bear being walked along a public street. The bear's owner was lawfully transporting the bear from the train to an exhibit where it would be on display. The bear was muzzled, chained, and controlled by its owner. The bear was characterized by those who knew it as "gentle," "kind," and "docile."

5. **Rules:**
   a. When a person is injured in an attack by a wild animal, the negligence of the owner is presumed.
   b. An owner must employ a measure of care that an ordinarily prudent person would employ under similar circumstances so that he does not unnecessarily injure another.

6. **Reasoning:** The fact that the appearance of a wild animal may frighten a horse of "ordinary gentleness" does not mean that the owner of the animal does not have the "lawful right to transport its property along a public highway." The bear in this case was like an automobile, bicycle, traction engine, steam roller, large dog, great bull, or baby wagon—all of which may frighten a horse, but are allowed on public streets. The holding fits with the rule that the owner of a wild animal that attacks and injures a person is presumed to be negligent because this bear did not attack anyone. The court compared this case to *Scribner v. Kelley*, where a horse was frightened by the sight of an elephant, not because it was an elephant, but because it was a large object moving ahead of the horse that the horse had never seen before. The court distinguished a case where a horse had been frightened by tubing and machinery that had been left by the side of the road, because in leaving the tubing and machinery by the road, the defendant in that case had not exercised due care.

7. **Holding:** The defendant was not negligent because it had the right to transport the bear "from one place to another for a lawful purpose," and the bear was gentle, under the control of his keeper, and not the type in "its appearance, noise, or other offensiveness" that would frighten horses.

8. **Order:** The judgment was reversed with an instruction to sustain the defendant's motion for a new trial.

It Depends on
the "Anchors"

The law typically doesn't offer easy answers. The best answer to a legal question is often, "It depends." The *Handbook* uses the term "anchors" to describe the facts, rules, and reasons that your answer depends on. Now, you can start your legal analysis with this simple answer to your legal question: "It depends on the anchors."

> **Anchors**
>
> - The reasons why a court decided a legal question
> - The grounds of a court's decision on a specific issue
> - The relevant parts, key facts, or minor rules

The anchors are the reasons why a court decided a legal question the way it did—they are the grounds of a court's decision on a specific issue. Anchors can be the relevant parts of a constitution or statute, or they can be key facts or minor rules from case law. Your job as a lawyer is to figure out what anchors will impact the resolution of your legal question. By identifying the anchors and applying them to your facts, you can effectively analyze most legal questions.

As you read cases to help answer your legal question, carefully consider how the court addressed your issue. To identify the anchors, consider which facts, rules, or reasons were especially relevant. The court might state the anchors explicitly, or the court might use wording that is less direct—especially if your legal question is not the primary issue in an opinion. So you'll need to carefully read and understand an opinion and hone in on your issue to fully identify the anchors that motivated a court's decision.

Reading, briefing, and analyzing cases to identify the anchors requires more than just note taking. As you read multiple relevant cases, you will be able to compare the anchors among them to gain a deeper understanding of your legal question—and what's most important to reach the answer. Effective legal analysis requires you to achieve a sophisticated understanding of a relevant area of law. This process requires you to synthesize and summarize your understanding of multiple authorities, rather than merely regurgitating and repeating your notes and case briefs.

1. IDENTIFYING THE ANCHORS

The case about the bear and the horse has five anchors—listed here in the order that they appear. The anchors are noted throughout the opinion with the ⚓ symbol.

1. The bear did not have a "vicious propensity."
2. The bear was under its keeper's control as it "moved quietly upon a public thoroughfare for a lawful purpose."
3. The bear was securely under its keeper's control, showing that the owner employed a "measure of care" that an ordinarily prudent person would employ under similar circumstances.
4. A lack of ordinary courage and discipline in the horse can be more to blame than the fact that the horse was surprised to see a large animal on the street.
5. There was no evidence that the owner knew that the bear was likely to frighten horses of ordinary gentleness.

This list summarizes the reasons that motivated the court's decision making. As you reread the list of anchors and compare it to the opinion on pages 9–12 where the anchors are marked, you will notice that the anchors appear throughout the court's opinion. Further, the court states some anchors more than once—sometimes using different language—and combines its discussion of some of the anchors.

2. SYNTHESIZING THE ANCHORS

After you identify the anchors in a case, you should understand how the court reached its decision in that case. When you are asked to analyze a legal question to solve a client's problem, you will likely need to read more than one relevant case. You will, therefore, need to create a list of anchors synthesized from multiple cases. In addition, to answer the client's question, you will need to tailor your list of anchors to address the client's specific situation.

For instance, suppose your client was bicycling down a neighborhood sidewalk at dawn when a rooster crowed from a fence post a few feet away and frightened her, causing her to fall. She wants to know whether she can recover damages from the rooster's owner for negligence because the rooster was on a neighbor's fence when it scared her. The *Bostock-Ferari* case will help you answer her question, along with *Scribner*,[1] which it cited. In your search for more recent cases, you also find *Thompson v. Lee*,[2] which affirmed a verdict against a motorcyclist who collided with an escaped cow on a highway.

---

1. 38 Barb. 14 (N.Y. Gen. Term. 1862).
2. 402 N.E. 1309 (Ind. Ct. App. 1980).

To answer your client's question, you should start by reading and briefing each case. Next, you should review each case to identify the anchors that are relevant to the legal question before you. Here, the question is whether the owner of a noisy rooster that flew to a neighbor's fence is negligent.

Start by listing the anchors from each case that address your legal question:

BOSTOCK-FERARI AMUSEMENT CO. v. BROCKSMITH

1. The bear did not have a "vicious propensity."
2. The bear was under its keeper's control as it "moved quietly upon a public thoroughfare for a lawful purpose."
3. The bear was securely under its keeper's control, showing that the owner employed a "measure of care" that an ordinarily prudent person would employ under similar circumstances.
4. A lack of ordinary courage and discipline in the horse can be more to blame than the fact that the horse was surprised to see a large animal on the street.
5. There was no evidence that the owner knew that the bear was likely to frighten horses of ordinary gentleness.

SCRIBNER v. KELLY

6. The defendants did not know their elephant was dangerous and would frighten the plaintiff's horse.
7. The horse was not injured by any action of the elephant; instead, the horse was frightened because it lacked ordinary courage when it saw a large, unfamiliar object traveling 100 feet in front of it.

THOMPSON v. LEE

8. Cows are not normally dangerous or ferocious.
9. The owner did not have any reason to believe that this cow was abnormally dangerous or vicious.
10. The owner did not know the cow had escaped.

Once you have a list of the anchors from each of the relevant cases, you can develop a synthesized list, combining common anchors from different cases. A review of the anchors above reveals that the courts had two broad reasons for their decisions. First, the courts examined the nature of the animal that allegedly caused injury, and second, the courts analyzed whether the animals' owners exercised the necessary level of care. From this understanding, you can create a synthesized list of the anchors to help answer your client's question about the rooster owner's negligence:

1. Whether the animal had a propensity to be vicious or frightening (Anchors 1 and 8) and whether the injured party had the propensity to frighten easily (Anchors 4 and 7).

2. Whether the owner took care to keep the animal contained and did not know of a vicious propensity or escape. (Anchors 2, 3, 5, 6, 9, and 10).

These anchors are referenced in different ways throughout the courts' opinions. Each reference to an anchor gives you new insight into how the courts made their decisions, and it helps you identify what is most relevant in answering your legal question. By identifying the anchors and synthesizing the list of anchors that address your legal question, you will reach the level of understanding that is necessary for you to effectively analyze and write about a legal question.

Understanding Hierarchy of Authority

When you are presented with a legal question, the first step is to identify the sources of authority for resolving that question. Some sources are law, and some sources comment on the law. The sources that make up the governing law are called "primary" authorities. The sources that comment on the law are called "secondary" sources. This chapter explains how to understand the sources of authority that will help you answer your legal question by describing the hierarchy of authority.

Principles of Hierarchy of Authority

- Primary authorities are law; secondary sources comment on the law.
- Primary authorities in the U.S. judicial system are either federal or state law.
- The hierarchy of authority is (1) constitutions, (2) statutes, (3) case law, and (4) regulations.
- The hierarchy of case law determines whether a case is binding or non-binding on a legal issue.
- Whether a case is binding or non-binding on a new legal issue depends on (1) what jurisdiction's law applies to the issue and (2) which courts from that jurisdiction have the power to bind other courts.

---

1. PRIMARY AUTHORITIES

Primary authorities include constitutions, statutes, cases, regulations, ordinances, and other government rulings. All of these authorities will not apply to every legal question, so understanding the differences between primary authorities and their relative rank or hierarchy is important.

Primary authorities in the U.S. judicial system fall into one of two categories: federal law or state law. For example, an opinion from the U.S. District Court for the District of Massachusetts is a federal authority because it comes from a federal court. Likewise, the Constitution of the Commonwealth of Massachusetts is a state authority because it is the governing document for the state government of Massachusetts.

A. The Hierarchy of Primary Authorities

In both federal and state law, a simple hierarchy applies (see Figure 4.1). First, constitutions are the highest authority and preempt all other law. A county government cannot enact a regulation that conflicts with the state constitution—and if a county does so, a court would overturn the regulation.

Statutes enacted by Congress and state legislatures are second in the hierarchy of primary authorities. Case law—at the third level—includes the opinions from courts of all levels. Courts will often be called upon to interpret constitutional and statutory provisions and determine whether statutes conflict with the constitution. Finally, the lowest level includes government regulations, rulings, and ordinances. Local environmental regulations and traffic ordinances are included in this fourth level.

B. The Hierarchy of Case Law

Case law is the type of primary authority that lawyers most often use to analyze legal questions. Even if a constitution or statute applies, lawyers will use case law to interpret the provisions. The impact of a particular case on your legal question is determined by the hierarchy of case law, which depends on what type of court issued the opinion and where that court is situated in the judicial system.

Figure 4.1

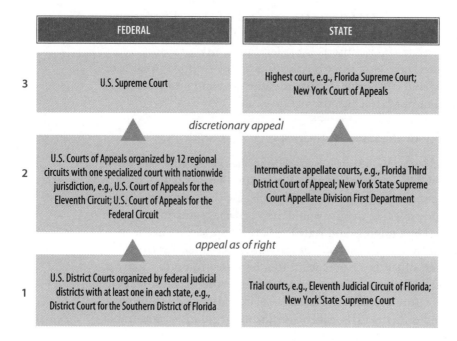

Figure 4.2

i. Court System Structure

United States courts are broadly divided into two systems: federal courts and state courts. There is one system of federal courts, and every state has its own system of state courts. The federal and state court systems share a similar tiered structure, although the names that states use to describe the courts at each level vary.[1]

To understand the differences between the courts, consider how a lawsuit usually progresses through the federal court system. First, a lawyer files a lawsuit in a trial court, called a U.S. District Court, before a single judge. Next, the losing party in the trial court can appeal as of right to an intermediate appellate court, called a U.S. Court of Appeals, where the case will be decided by a panel of judges. Then, the losing party can ask the highest court—the U.S. Supreme Court—which has a panel of justices, to exercise its discretion to review the case.

Many states have a three-tiered structure like the federal courts, but some states have no intermediate, appellate-level court. Some states have specialized courts for certain cases based on subject matter, a tier below the trial court level that handles small claims, or a combination of these structures. Figure 4.2 depicts the typical three-tiered court structure.

Some trial courts and most of the intermediate appellate and highest courts issue written opinions explaining their reasoning and decisions.

---

1. Refer to the courts' websites to learn the specific names for the courts in your state. You may also consult Table 1 in *The Bluebook*.

Those opinions are the cases that you will read and rely upon to do your legal analysis.

ii. Jurisdiction

The term "jurisdiction" means the authority of a court to exercise its power over the subject matter and parties in a case. Jurisdiction also describes the geographic area over which a court exercises its power. Both of these meanings are important for understanding the hierarchy of case law.

a. Authority

Federal courts have the authority to decide cases that raise a federal question or satisfy the requirements for diversity jurisdiction.[2] Under diversity jurisdiction, a federal court can decide a case that doesn't raise a federal question—meaning a case that requires the application of state law—when the parties are from different states and the amount in controversy exceeds $75,000.[3] A federal court can also use its discretion to exercise supplemental jurisdiction over a state law claim that is closely related to a claim over which it has jurisdiction.[4]

Most state trial courts have the authority to decide cases that arise within their borders, including disputes governed by state and federal law. Some state courts, however, are limited by subject matter, including courts that decide only criminal, probate, or family law cases.

b. Area

All federal courts do not apply the same law, just as all state courts do not apply the same law. Instead, courts apply the law of a specific geographic area or jurisdiction. The federal courts are divided into 94 judicial districts,[5] organized into 13 circuits.[6] Each regional circuit has a court of appeals that decides cases appealed from the district courts in that circuit. The federal courts within a circuit apply the law of that circuit to federal law issues. For example, the District Court for the Southern District of Florida is in the Eleventh Circuit, so it applies Eleventh Circuit law to federal law issues.

Figure 4.3 (on the next page) shows the geographic division of the federal circuits. In addition to the 11 numbered circuits, the D.C. Circuit covers the District of Columbia, and the Federal Circuit Court of Appeals has jurisdiction based on subject matter, including patents, trademarks, and international trade.[7]

State courts usually apply their own law to state law issues. State courts, however, may apply the law of another state in certain situations, including a contractual agreement by the parties to be bound by the law of another state.

---

2. In addition, the federal system has courts that specialize by subject matter, including courts that handle bankruptcy or tax cases.
3. 28 U.S.C. § 1332(a)(1) (2018).
4. 28 U.S.C. § 1367(a) (2018).
5. 28 U.S.C. §§ 81-131 (2018).
6. 28 U.S.C. § 41 (2018).
7. 28 U.S.C. § 1295 (2018).

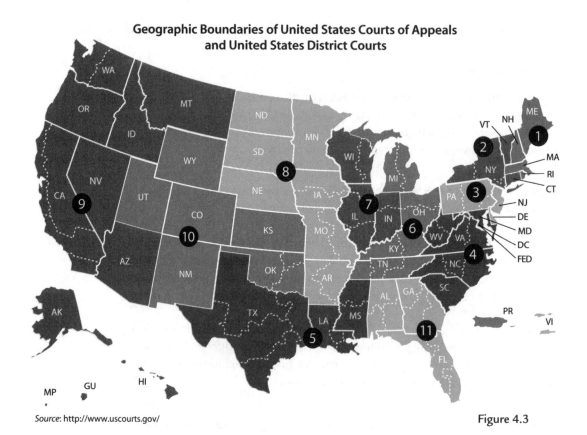

Geographic Boundaries of United States Courts of Appeals and United States District Courts

Source: http://www.uscourts.gov/   Figure 4.3

iii. Binding and Non-Binding Cases

Stare decisis is a Latin phrase that means "to stand by things decided."[8] In practice, stare decisis describes the policy of American courts to follow the precedents established by earlier cases.

The precise impact that an earlier precedent will have on a later case depends on whether it is binding or non-binding. A binding precedent is one that a court is required to follow. These cases are also referred to as "mandatory" authorities. A non-binding precedent is one that a court may consider but is not required to follow. These cases are also called "persuasive" authorities.

Before you can decide the outcome of a legal question, you have to determine which precedents are binding and which are not. Determining whether a case is binding for your particular legal issue requires you to answer the following two questions:

1. What jurisdiction's law applies to my legal issue?
2. Which courts from that jurisdiction have the power to bind the court in my case?

---

8. *Black's Law Dictionary* (10th ed. 2014).

a. What Jurisdiction's Law Applies?

First, you need to identify the specific jurisdiction that is the source of the law that governs your issue. If your legal question is one of federal law, any case that applies the law of the governing federal circuit is potentially binding. Similarly, for state law questions, any case that applies the law of the governing state is potentially binding.

When trying to identify the specific jurisdiction that governs your issue, keep in mind that a federal court can hear a case involving a state law issue and a state court can hear a case involving a federal claim. For instance, suppose a California resident wants to sue someone who lives in Nevada to quiet title (or defeat another's ownership claim) on a piece of land in California. On the basis of diversity jurisdiction, the California resident may sue the Nevada resident in federal court on a state adverse possession claim. Because the adverse possession claim will be decided under California law, any case that applies California state law is potentially a binding case. Thus, the governing law may not be from the jurisdiction of the court where your case will be heard.

b. Which Courts Are Binding?

Next, you will need to determine which particular courts have the power to bind the court in your case. A court is bound by the decisions of higher courts from the jurisdiction that supplies the governing law. This is known as "vertical stare decisis."

For example, if you are dealing with a state law issue in a case in a state trial court in Florida, decisions of the Florida intermediate appellate courts[9] and the Florida Supreme Court are binding because those courts are within the governing jurisdiction and higher than the Florida trial court where the case is being heard. Decisions of the Florida trial courts are non-binding because they are at the same level as the trial court deciding the case. And decisions of the federal courts and other states' courts are non-binding because they are not within the governing jurisdiction (see Figure 4.4 on the next page).

Similarly, if you are dealing with a federal law issue in a case in the District Court for the Southern District of Florida, decisions of the Eleventh Circuit Court of Appeals and the U.S. Supreme Court are binding because those courts are within the governing jurisdiction and higher than the district court. Decisions of the district courts in Florida, federal courts in other circuits, and state courts are non-binding because they are outside the governing jurisdiction of the Eleventh Circuit (see Figure 4.5 on the next page).

In addition to the obligation to follow the decisions of higher courts from the governing jurisdiction, many courts also have a policy that they follow their own previous decisions. This policy is known as "horizontal stare decisis." Horizontal stare decisis operates differently depending on the level and jurisdiction of the court.

---

9. In some states, a trial court is bound only by the decisions of the appellate court to which its decisions are appealed. *See, e.g., In re Quirk*, 705 So. 2d 172, 181 n.17 (La. 1997).

Figure 4.4

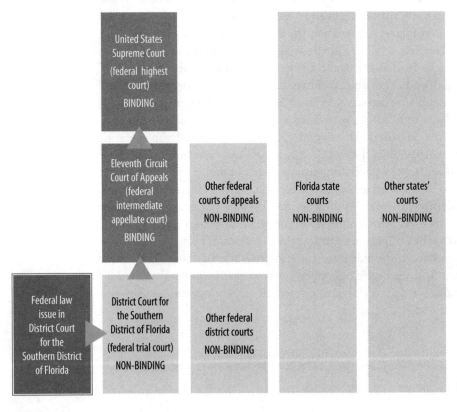

Figure 4.5

A highest-level federal or state court will usually follow its own decisions, but it can overrule itself. For instance, the U.S. Supreme Court famously overruled its 1896 decision in *Plessy v. Ferguson* with the landmark decision of *Brown v. Board of Education* in 1954.

The federal courts of appeals are bound by their own previous decisions under the "law of the circuit rule."[10] Decisions of a federal court of appeals bind horizontally later panels of that court in addition to binding vertically the district courts in that circuit. A federal court of appeals' decision can be overruled by the U.S. Supreme Court or that same court of appeals sitting en banc, which is when a case is reheard by all (or most) of the judges of that court, rather than the typical three-judge panel. Thus, if you are dealing with a federal law issue in a case that has been appealed to the Fourth Circuit Court of Appeals from the District Court for the Eastern District of Virginia, decisions of the U.S. Supreme Court and the Fourth Circuit Court of Appeals are binding. Decisions of federal district courts, other federal courts of appeals, and state courts are non-binding (see Figure 4.6).

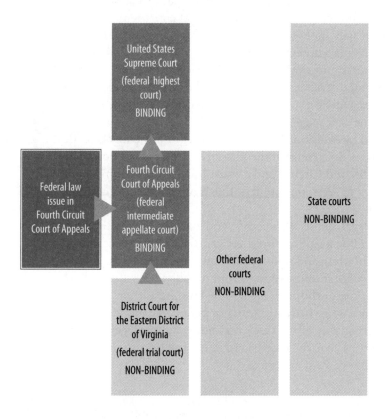

Figure 4.6

10. *See, e.g.,* Amy E. Sloan, *The Dog That Didn't Bark: Stealth Procedures and the Erosion of Stare Decisis in the Federal Courts of Appeals,* 78 Fordham L. Rev. 713, 718-19 (2009) ("In the federal appellate courts, the law of the circuit rule implements the policy of horizontal stare decisis. The law of the circuit rule provides that the decision of one panel is the decision of the court and binds all future panels unless and until the panel's opinion is reversed or overruled, either by the circuit sitting en banc or the Supreme Court. Every circuit follows the law of the circuit rule.").

States vary in whether their intermediate appellate courts follow a policy of horizontal stare decisis. For example, in Wisconsin a decision from one court of appeals binds all other intermediate appellate courts in the state.[11] In contrast, an Illinois intermediate appellate court is bound only by decisions of the highest court; it is not obligated to follow a decision by another state intermediate appellate court.[12]

Federal and state trial courts are not bound by their previous decisions under horizontal stare decisis. So the federal district courts do not follow a "law of the district rule," which means they are not bound by their own previous decisions or decisions of sister district courts in the same jurisdiction.[13] In practice, however, federal district courts may treat their own prior decisions as "highly" persuasive—meaning that they are not binding but are given more consideration than other non-binding authorities.

When a federal court applies state law or a state court applies federal law, only decisions of the highest court from the governing jurisdiction are binding.[14] Consider the adverse possession case, where the California resident wants to sue the Nevada resident in federal court in California. When the California resident files suit, the case will be at the trial court level. Because the federal district court will apply state law, the only binding authority will be decisions of the California Supreme Court. Decisions of the California intermediate appellate courts and trial courts will be persuasive, but they are not binding on the federal district court. Also, federal court decisions, even if they apply California law, will be non-binding, but they may be highly persuasive (see Figure 4.7 on the next page).

A court is not bound by decisions from lower courts or any court outside the governing jurisdiction. So a court in the Eleventh Circuit is not bound by court rulings from the Second Circuit, and a court in New Hampshire is not bound by court rulings in Vermont (unless the New Hampshire court is applying Vermont law).

When analyzing a legal question, identify and use binding authorities when they are available. But keep in mind that your legal analysis could involve a combination of binding and non-binding precedent. And if your legal question involves a case of first impression in your jurisdiction, you will have to rely entirely on persuasive authorities because no binding authorities exist. Finally, before using any case—whether binding or persuasive—as an authority, you must analyze the quality of the case's reasoning and the legal, factual, and procedural similarities that the case has to your situation to determine how useful the case will be to your analysis.

---

11. *Cook v. Cook*, 560 N.W.2d 246, 256 (Wis. 1997); *see generally* Andrew T. Solomon, *A Simple Prescription for Texas's Ailing Court System: Stronger Stare Decisis*, 37 St. Mary's L.J. 417, 476 (2006).

12. *O'Casek v. Children's Home & Aid Soc'y*, 892 N.E.2d 994, 1006 (Ill. 2008).

13. Joseph W. Mead, *Stare Decisis in the Inferior Courts of the United States*, 12 Nev. L.J. 787, 800 (2012) (citing *Threadgill v. Armstrong World Indus., Inc.*, 928 F.2d 1366, 1371 (3d Cir. 1991)).

14. The issue of how much weight state courts applying federal law should give to the decisions of federal intermediate appellate courts is unresolved. *See* Amanda Frost, *Inferiority Complex: Should State Courts Follow Lower Federal Court Precedent on the Meaning of Federal Law?*, 68 Vand. L. Rev. 53, 62–64 (2015).

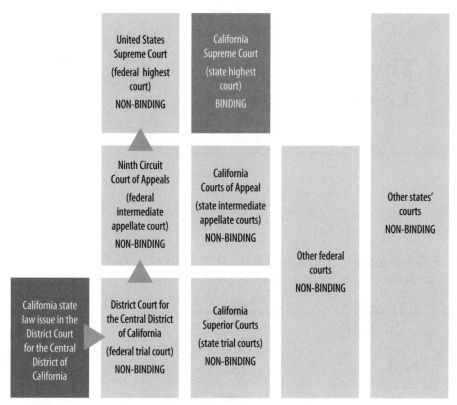

Figure 4.7

2. SECONDARY AUTHORITIES

Primary authorities are the law, while secondary sources comment on the law. Secondary sources include legal encyclopedias, treatises, Restatements, and law review articles. Secondary sources are often the best place to start your research of a legal issue because you can read them to gain an understanding of the particular area of law relevant to your legal issue. In general, you will not cite secondary authorities in a legal memorandum or a persuasive document because they are not law. But secondary sources will point you to helpful primary authorities because secondary sources contain citations, annotations, and explanations of the law. And on occasion, you may need to cite secondary sources in your legal documents because they express ideas that you cannot find in primary authorities.[15]

---

15. Indeed, the U.S. Supreme Court cites secondary sources in its opinions, and secondary sources are often cited in briefs submitted to the Supreme Court. *See, e.g., Whole Woman's Health v. Hellerstedt*, 136 S. Ct. 2292, 2305 (2016) (citing Restatement (Second) of Judgments § 24); *Ariz. State Legislature v. Ariz. Indep. Redistricting Comm'n*, 135 S. Ct. 2652, 2662 (2015) (citing Peter Miller & Bernard Grofman, *Redistricting Commissions in the Western United States*, 3 U.C. Irvine L. Rev. 637, 661, 663–64, 666 (2013)).

The Format for Legal Analysis

1. CREAC

Written legal analysis is organized using a format known as "CREAC."[1] Each letter of CREAC stands for a necessary component of legal analysis:

> C = Conclusion
> R = Rule
> E = Explanation
> A = Analysis, Application, Argument
> C = Conclusion

Using this structure, the legal writer begins and ends the analysis with the Conclusion on a particular legal issue. The beauty of the CREAC format is that it assures the reader that there will be no surprises because the writer provides the Conclusion at the outset. Further, the CREAC format requires the writer to identify and fully explain the relevant legal authorities before applying those authorities to the facts from the legal question. After doing so, the writer walks the reader through the law and analysis so that the reader understands the logical progression of the writer's thinking. CREAC thus helps guarantee that the writer's legal analysis is logically sound and meticulously supported.

CREAC is the preferred structure for most analytical legal documents, including memos, motions, briefs, and judicial opinions. Judges, lawyers, and legal writing professors all expect these documents to follow the CREAC format. This book describes in detail and provides examples and instructions for how to write each of the CREAC components.

---

1. This structure for legal analysis can be identified in other ways, including BaRAC or BRAC (starting with a bold assertion) CRAC, CREXAC, and TREAT (starting and ending with a thesis). These names all identify the same organizational format.

The following is an excerpt of a judicial opinion that is organized using the CREAC format. The annotations reflect each CREAC component. In the opinion, the plaintiffs' daughter was injured by a dog, and they sought damages from the dog's owners. After the trial judge granted summary judgment in favor of the dog owners, the plaintiffs appealed, arguing that the owners should have known that their dog was likely to harm someone. The appeals court affirmed, finding a lack of evidence of the dog's propensity to bite.

HAMILTON V. WALKER
510 S.E.2d 120 (Ga. Ct. App. 1998)[2]

In this "dog bite" tort action, Sarah B. Hamilton, on behalf of her daughter, Sarah E. Hamilton, appeals the trial court's grant of summary judgment to Richard and Evelyn Walker, contending that the Walkers should have known that their dog had vicious propensities prior to its attack on Sarah, and, as such, the Walkers should be liable for Sarah's injuries. — *The opinion begins with a short introduction stating the legal issue, basic facts, and procedural history.*

Because there is no evidence that the Walkers' dog ever bit anyone prior to biting Sarah, we affirm the trial court's decision which comports with Georgia's "first bite" rule. — *This is the court's **Conclusion**.*

Georgia's first bite rule holds that a dog owner is liable for damages only if he has knowledge that his dog has the "propensity to do the *particular act* [biting] which caused injury to the complaining party." *Smith v. Culver*, 322 S.E.2d 294 (Ga. Ct. App. 1984) (punctuation omitted; emphasis supplied); *Fitzpatrick v. Henley*, 269 S.E.2d 60 (Ga. Ct. App. 1980). The test requires two determinations: (1) whether the dog has the propensity to do the act which caused the injury (biting), and (2) if so, whether the owner had knowledge of that propensity. *Rowlette v. Paul*, 466 S.E.2d 37 (Ga. Ct. App. 1995). — *This is the **Rule**. Here, the court identifies the legal rule that governs the issue. The court cites the relevant legal authorities so the reader knows where the rule comes from. This is a rule with a two-part test.*

With regard to the first prong, this Court consistently has held that the dog must have, on a prior occasion, done the same act which resulted in the injury comprising the tort action. *E.g.*, *Johnson v. Kvasny*, 495 S.E.2d 651 (Ga. Ct. App. 1998). Thus, where a dog was known to chase people, but had never chased a car or motorcycle, the owner had no knowledge that the dog might chase a motorcyclist causing him to wreck. *McNair v. Jones*, 223 S.E.2d 27 (Ga. Ct. App. 1975). But summary judgment granted to the dog owner was reversed where the dog was known to chase people and the plaintiff was injured when she fell while being chased by the dog. *Evans-Watson v. Reese*, 372 S.E.2d 675 (Ga. Ct. App. 1988). Likewise, where a dog had on several occasions grabbed or nipped people, or ripped their clothes without actually biting, there was sufficient evidence — *This is the **Explanation**. Here, the court explains how the two parts of the test have been interpreted and provides examples of earlier cases where the test was applied.*

---

2. Disapproved of by *Steagald v. Eason*, 797 S.E.2d 838, 841 (Ga. 2017). This is an edited version of the case. The citations lack pinpoint citations because they were omitted in the original.

to support a verdict that found the owner should have had knowledge of the dog's propensity to bite. *Torrance v. Brennan*, 432 S.E.2d 658 (1993).

Acts of aggressive or menacing behavior have not been found to show a dog's propensity to bite. A dog's attacks on other animals were insufficient to put an owner on notice that the dog might attack people. *Carter v. Ide*, 188 S.E.2d 275 (Ga. Ct. App. 1972). Additionally, a startled dog that had bitten a strangely dressed visitor had not shown a propensity to bite. *Rowlette*, 466 S.E.2d at 37. In *Thomas v. Richardson*, 201 S.E.2d 653 (Ga. Ct. App. 1973), the plaintiff was bitten when she entered the fenced yard of a playmate whose family owned the dog. In that case, the evidence of the dog's propensity to bite consisted of a prior incident where a neighbor's child decided to "test" the dog to see if it would defend the owner's child. The dog attacked the neighbor's child, although it was disputed whether the dog bit the child. *Id*. This Court held these facts did not present a genuine issue regarding the dog's propensity to bite. *Id*.

Likewise, the facts in this case do not present a genuine issue regarding the dog's propensity to bite. Menacing behavior is all that the Hamiltons have shown. This Court has specifically declined to establish a rule that a dog's menacing behavior should put an owner on notice of a dog's propensity to bite. "[I]nsofar as *Carter* suggests that a dog's menacing behavior would alone be sufficient to apprise its owner of the animal's vicious propensities, we decline to follow it as controlling precedent, noting the well-recognized adage that a dog's bark is often worse than its bite." *Banks v. Adair*, 251 S.E.2d 88 (Ga. Ct. App. 1978) (citing *Carter*, 188 S.E.2d at 275). There is no evidence of the dog's propensity to bite, the particular act which caused injury here, so the first prong of the test is not met. Accordingly, the trial court appropriately granted summary judgment in favor of the Walkers.

— This is the **Analysis**. Here, the court analyzes the facts of this particular case by applying the law and explaining the reasoning that led to the court's Conclusion.

— This is the **Conclusion**. Here, the court repeats the Conclusion it has reached on the legal issue before it. Conclusions in opinions can be very brief or they can restate a reason in support.

2. IRAC

A close relative of the CREAC format, known as IRAC, is a common format for law school exams and the essays on the bar exam. IRAC includes the following components:

> I = Issue
> R = Rule
> A = Analysis, Application, Argument
> C = Conclusion

CREAC is merely an evolution of IRAC, and IRAC reflects the fact that the writer has not had time to think through the legal question and provide a conclusion at the start. The fundamental difference between IRAC and CREAC is that under IRAC, the writer begins the analysis with an objective statement of the Issue to be addressed, rather than the specific Conclusion the writer has reached after completing the analysis.

For example, in the case excerpt from *Hamilton v. Walker*, the court begins its analysis with the Conclusion:

> Because there is no evidence that the Walkers' dog ever bit anyone prior to biting Sarah, we affirm the trial court's decision which comports with Georgia's "first bite" rule.

Under the IRAC format, the writer would instead state the Issue being analyzed without reaching a conclusion:

> The issue before the court is whether the trial judge correctly decided that the Walkers were not liable to Sarah because there was no evidence that their dog had a propensity to bite.

Because the IRAC format allows the writer to outline the analysis before reaching a conclusion, it is useful when planning, organizing, and outlining documents that will ultimately follow the CREAC format. That's why many writers use the IRAC format for first drafts or for law school or bar exam essays. But aside from this difference between the initial Conclusion and an objective Issue statement, the analysis under CREAC or IRAC is the same.

The CREAC format explicitly builds in a more detailed explanation of the rules, identified as the Explanation section, than the IRAC format. But in practice, the level of rule explanation required in a particular document depends on the nature of the legal issue being analyzed, not whether the writer is using CREAC or IRAC. With these structures in mind, the next chapter shows how to use the IRAC and CREAC formats to write an essay answer for a law school or bar exam question. Then, the following chapters describe how to write each CREAC component for both objective and persuasive documents.

chapter 6

The Format for Exam Essays

Every semester in law school ends with exams. And law school ends with the biggest exam of all—the bar exam. These exams might appear intimidating, but with preparation, you can approach each exam with confidence. The four-step approach described in this chapter will help you successfully tackle the essay exams in your future.

> **Approaching Essay Exam Answers**
> 1. Read twice.
> 2. Identify issues.
> 3. Write in IRAC or CREAC.
> 4. Proofread.

1. READ TWICE

This first step is a familiar one—read everything—and read it at least twice. Most essay exam questions will start by telling a story and then ask one or more specific legal questions, often at the end. Start by reading the precise question—also called the call of the question. The question is key to understanding what you are looking for in the story, and it will point you to the topic and issue being tested. On the bar exam, for example, the question might narrow your focus to contracts versus torts. On an exam for your torts course, the question might guide you to think about one or two intentional torts instead of the broad issue of negligence. Knowing the specific question will help you hone in on the topics being tested as you read the facts.

The facts in the story will give rise to one or more legal issues, and your goal is to identify each legal issue and then describe three things: (1) the relevant rules, (2) your analysis, and (3) your conclusion. You'll do all of this while focusing on the precise call of the question.

Here's an example of what a short essay question on a torts exam could look like:

Emil, an employee at the "It's a Ruff Life" store in Cincinnati, Ohio, became suspicious of a customer who was walking around the shopping cart collection area of the store's parking lot. Emil asked the customer if she needed help. The customer, Camille, then asked Emil to put two large bags of dog food that she had in a shopping cart into her car. Emil did so, and Camille then placed her large purse next to them in the trunk. The purse sat wide open, and Emil noticed at least two "It's a Ruff Life" dog-food bowls jutting out from the top of the bag. Emil asked Camille if she had receipts for the bowls, and when she said no, Emil ordered Camille to go inside to the store office with him. Camille followed Emil inside to the office, where she immediately picked up the two bowls and turned toward the exit. "I want to leave. This is nonsense," Camille said. "I paid for these bowls earlier." Emil moved to stand in front of the exit and responded, "That's not happening. This store is cracking down on shoplifting. Now sit here while I call the police!" Emil took Camille's arm and guided her back toward a chair. Camille hesitantly sat down, and Emil called the police while Camille waited. When two police officers arrived about 40 minutes later, Emil opened the office door and pointed to Camille, "I've caught the thief right here," he told them. The police officers made a written report, recording Emil's and Camille's versions of events. But they did not detain or arrest Camille. The next day, she emailed copies of her receipt for the dog bowls, which she had purchased a week earlier but left in her purse.

Camille has come to you for advice. Discuss her potential causes of action against Emil, their likelihood of success, and any potential defenses for Emil.[1]

Even if you haven't taken a torts course yet, you'll recognize on your first reading the key players, and you may notice some "rights" and "wrongs." In other words, as you read you can ask yourself: What legal rights do the characters have? And how were they wronged? These rights and wrongs are the basis of the legal issues that the exam question was designed to explore. The story will not hide them, but instead, it will reveal these issues using one or more key facts. The key characters are Emil, the store, and Camille. And the story shows that Emil is trying to protect the store's right to guard against shoplifters—but he acts in a way that may have wronged Camille.

Before you read the story a second time, refer again to the precise question you've been asked. The question here requires you to identify potential causes of action for Camille against Emil and Emil's potential defenses. Camille is

---

1. This essay question is adapted from the Florida Board of Bar Examiners, Florida Bar Examination Study Guide and Selected Answers February 2012–July 2012, at 13, https://www.floridabarexam.org/__85257bfe0055eb2c.nsf/52286ae9ad5d845185257c07005c3 fe1/f78b141ea0b950bc85257c0c0066c839 (last visited June 12, 2018). Reprinted with the permission of the Florida Board of Bar Examiners.

the potential plaintiff, and Emil is the potential defendant. (The store is a potential defendant, too, but the question asks only about Emil.) Keep in mind that plaintiffs can have multiple claims and defendants can have multiple defenses.

Then, read the story a second time. Consider the fact pattern broadly to check whether you missed any key issues. Consider the rights and wrongs—which will point to the potential causes of action—and identify the specific facts that support your theories. For the torts question, reading a second time helps you hone in on key words:

- Emil "ordered" Camille inside.
- Camille said, "I want to leave."
- Emil blocked the exit and told Camille, "That's not happening" and "sit here."
- Emil took Camille by the arm and called her a "thief."
- Camille then waited 40 minutes.

Look hard on the second reading for any details you might have mistaken or missed. Skimming the story too quickly can cause a reader to skip a word like "not" that changes the story or a single phrase like "took Camille's arm." That single phrase is the only supporting detail for a potential battery claim. Keep an open mind as you read so that you don't accidentally ignore important details. Stay focused on the question so that you don't start identifying unrelated issues. And any time you feel unsure of what happened in the story, go back and read it again.

2. IDENTIFY ISSUES

After you read the story and exam question—at least twice—you will begin to recognize the relevant legal issues. This question asks you to identify Camille's potential causes of action against Emil and Emil's potential defenses. Consider again the rights and wrongs:

- What legal rights do Camille and Emil have?
- How were they wronged?

Even if you haven't studied torts yet, you'll probably recognize that Emil should have a right to protect the store against shoplifters. You'll also recognize that Emil acted improperly by confining Camille in the store office, taking her arm, and calling her a "thief."

If you have studied torts, you should recognize three potential claims and one potential defense. First, Camille's right against being confined in the office is covered by the intentional tort known as "false imprisonment." Second, her right against being touched—or taken by the arm—is covered by the intentional tort called "battery." Third, her right against being falsely labeled a "thief" in a police report is covered by the tort of "defamation." And finally, Emil's right to guard against shoplifters gives rise to the potential defense known as the "shopkeeper's privilege."

Identifying these legal issues and defenses—false imprisonment, defamation, battery, and shopkeeper's privilege—sets you up to write a successful essay exam answer. As you read a second (or third) time, underline or circle key words and key players, and make notes in the margin about the potential causes of action.

Emil, an employee at the "It's a Ruff Life" store in Cincinnati, Ohio, became suspicious of a customer who was walking around the shopping cart collection area of the store's parking lot. Emil asked the customer if she needed help. The customer, Camille, then asked Emil to put two large bags of dog food that she had in a shopping cart into her car. Emil did so, and Camille then placed her large purse next to them in the trunk. The purse sat wide open, and Emil noticed at least two "It's a Ruff Life" dog-food bowls jutting out from the top of the bag. Emil asked Camille if she had receipts for the bowls, and when she said no, Emil ordered Camille to go inside to the store office with him. Camille followed Emil inside to the office, where she immediately picked up the two bowls and turned toward the exit. "I want to leave. This is nonsense," Camille said. "I paid for these bowls earlier." Emil moved to stand in front of the exit and responded, "That's not happening. This store is cracking down on shoplifting. Now sit here while I call the police!" Emil took Camille's arm and guided her back toward a chair. Camille hesitantly sat down, and Emil called the police while Camille waited. When two police officers arrived about 40 minutes later, Emil opened the office door and pointed to Camille, "I've caught the thief right here," he told them. The police officers made a written report, recording Emil's and Camille's versions of events. But they did not detain or arrest Camille. The next day, she emailed copies of her receipt for the dog bowls, which she had purchased a week earlier but left in her purse.

> The parties
> —Defense against shoplifting
> False imprisonment
> Battery
> Defamation

Camille has come to you for advice. Discuss her potential causes of action against Emil, their likelihood of success, and any potential defenses for Emil.

3. WRITE IN IRAC OR CREAC

Consider who reads your exam answers. Whether it's your professor or a bar exam grader, the person evaluating your exam likely has a teeming pile of papers to assess. Professors might feel pressure to finish grading because of deadlines set by their law schools, and adjunct professors are busy balancing teaching with their law practices. Bar exam graders also might feel both time and financial pressures. In California, for example, graders work in groups to compare scores in a set time frame and receive a mere $3.25 for each essay exam they evaluate.[2]

Because your reader is busy, your goal should be to make your answer easy to follow and easy to score. The best way to do that is by following one of the common—and expected—organizational frameworks known by the acronyms IRAC and CREAC.[3] As the last chapter detailed, these abbreviations stand for Issue-Rule (and Explanation)-Analysis-Conclusion and Conclusion-Rule-Explanation-Analysis-Conclusion.

These formats are basically the same. IRAC reflects that writers start drafting their answers before thinking through the analysis and reaching an answer, so they begin with an Issue statement rather than a Conclusion. CREAC is an evolution of IRAC and indicates that the writer has considered the analysis and counteranalysis and can begin with a Conclusion instead of an Issue statement. While the IRAC acronym doesn't include the "E" for Explanation, both frameworks should include a long and detailed rule statement.

With the modern practice of typing exams on a laptop, writing an essay in the CREAC format instead of the IRAC format takes just one extra step—copying and pasting the Conclusion you write at the end of your essay over the Issue statement you wrote at the start. Your professor might state a preference for one format over the other, or the question might explicitly ask you to state the issue at the start. But if not, follow the format that feels more appropriate for you.

A. Emphasize Your Legal Issues with Headings

You've done a lot of studying and thinking to correctly identify the legal issues. So make sure your reader can easily see this step. Use headings—bolded, underlined, or set apart on a separate line—to emphasize the issues.

Organize the headings in a way that makes sense. And if the exam provides an instruction about organization, make sure to follow it. In general, you can analyze the claims and defenses chronologically, in a way that mirrors the organization of the story in the essay question. Or when dealing with multiple claims and defenses, you might want to analyze each of the plaintiff's potential claims first, followed by the defendant's potential defenses. The organization of the sample essay answer on pages 41-42 is chronological. The headings identify the issues in order: "False Imprisonment," "Shopkeeper's Privilege Defense," "Battery," and "Defamation."

---

2. The State Bar of California, *Becoming a Grader*, http://www.calbar.ca.gov/Admissions/Examinations/Exam-Administration/Becoming-a-Grader, and *California Bar Exam Grading*, http://www.calbar.ca.gov/Admissions/Examinations/California-Bar-Exam/Description-and-Grading-of-the-California-Bar-Exam (last visited April 30, 2018).

3. This structure for legal analysis can be identified in other ways, including BaRAC or BRAC (starting with a bold assertion) CRAC, CREXAC, and TREAT (starting and ending with a thesis). These names all identify the same organizational format.

B. Write Every IRAC or CREAC Part for Every Issue

Once you identify the issues, you can write a complete IRAC or CREAC for each. These organizational structures are designed to help you think through legal questions. So address each section in order.

Consider how you can make each part of your answer easy to read and understand. You can identify each section of the IRAC or CREAC by starting your sentences with key phrases or transitions. For longer answers, you can separate each part of the IRAC and CREAC into its own paragraph with a heading for "Issue," "Rule," and so forth. The next chart gives some examples of key phrases and transitions for your essay answer.

Key Phrases to Start Each IRAC or CREAC Part	
Issue	The issue is The question is whether This question analyzes if….
Rule	The rule is New York law requires In Ohio, Negligence [or insert the name of a different cause of action here] requires….
Explanation	This claim requires Establishing intent [or insert the name of a different element here] requires….
Analysis	Here, In this case, All the elements of the claim are likely/likely not met.
Conclusion	In conclusion, Thus, In sum,….

Use these phrases as you draft each IRAC or CREAC part. For the "I" or the Issue statement, summarize the legal question, name the parties, and identify the potential cause of action using precise legal terms. For the "R" or Rule section, state the controlling legal principle. Begin with the broadest rule statement from the highest authority. If a federal or state constitutional provision is relevant, describe that first. If not, a federal or state statute is second in the hierarchy of authority. If no constitutional or statutory provision applies to the legal issue, then use common law, which comes from case law, to define your Rule statement.

For the "E" or Explanation section of the CREAC, explain each part of your Rule. If your Rule has elements or factors, explain each one. If your Rule has a balancing test, illustrate how the parts of the test work. If your Rule has exceptions, define how each exception limits the Rule. If your Rule is especially complex, consider providing an illustration of how the Rule works in practice. Use your best judgment to tailor your Explanation with the appropriate level of detail. Depending on the question, you probably don't need to define commonly understood terms like "intent" or "reasonable person standard," but more complicated concepts, like "Miranda waiver" or "spendthrift trust," likely deserve more explanation. Essay exam graders typically are looking for long and detailed Rule and Explanation sections.

The "A" or Analysis section of the IRAC/CREAC is a crucial part of every essay answer—and typically worth half the points on a bar exam question. To succeed here, follow this well-known writing tip: "Show; don't tell." You can show your work in the Analysis section by describing in as much detail as possible how the relevant law applies to the facts in the story. Try to identify every fact in the essay question that's relevant to your legal issue. Then, apply the law to those facts. Avoid simply restating the facts and telling your reader the conclusion. Instead, show your reader exactly how you reached that conclusion, by detailing how the facts connect to the law. Describe how your facts meet—or don't meet—each part of the rule. Follow a logical organization. If your Rule has three elements, then analyze how each element applies to the facts in order using clear transitions, like "first," "second," and "third."

Then, consider if any counterarguments—those analysis points that do not support your conclusion—are obvious. If so, show your thinking on these points too by describing how the law applies to the facts. Use key transitions to indicate counterarguments like "but," "conversely," "however," "instead," or "yet."

Finally, briefly summarize your Conclusion. The best Conclusion statements will have three parts: They will (1) provide an answer on the legal issue, (2) indicate a level of certainty, and (3) describe a reason. The answer will tell the reader whether the party has a successful claim or defense. The level of certainty will tell the reader just that—often using a qualifying term like "probably" or "likely." And the reason will summarize the best legal argument.

The following chart briefly summarizes what each part of an IRAC or CREAC should describe. It also provides examples of the IRAC parts for an essay analyzing whether a fireworks company was negligent when its fireworks shells exploded and flew into a crowd of spectators. The legal and factual context for the essay is explained in more detail as you read through the chart.

IRAC and CREAC Parts	
Issue	• Summarizes the precise legal issue • Names the parties • Pinpoints the specific cause of action using precise legal terms **Example:** The issue is whether PyroCo is liable to Sawyer in negligence for mishandling the fireworks.
Rule	• States the controlling legal principle • Uses the highest relevant authority: constitutions > statutes > case law/common law **Example:** To succeed in a negligence cause of action, Sawyer would have to prove four elements: duty, breach, cause, and harm.
Explanation	• Explains each element, factor, or part of the Rule • Provides illustrations for complex Rules • Defines uncommon terms • Tailors the level of detail to the complexity of the Rule **Example:** First, the defendant must have a duty or a legally recognized obligation to protect the plaintiff against unreasonable risks by conforming to a specific standard of care. The standard of care is that for a reasonable person under the circumstances. Second, a breach occurs when the defendant fails to exercise the duty of reasonable care that's required, meaning that the defendant fails to act as a reasonable person would under the same or similar circumstances. Third, liability in negligence requires proof that the defendant's conduct was the actual or proximate cause of the harm. Proximate cause requires a reasonable connection between an act or omission of the defendant and the harm suffered by the plaintiff. In analyzing this element, courts look to whether the harm and risks are foreseeable. And fourth, negligence requires proof of some legally recognized harm or damages.
Analysis	• Applies the law to the facts • Shows the reader how the facts connect to the law • Describes how the facts meet—or don't meet—each part of the rule • Avoids simply restating the facts or law **Example:** Here, PyroCo likely was negligent because all four elements are met. First, a fireworks company setting off explosive devices owes a duty to those watching the fireworks show. By providing a large truckload of dangerous fireworks, setting them up, and igniting them over a 30-minute period, PyroCo would be bound to exercise a high degree of care to prevent injury to those watching the show. Second, PyroCo likely breached its duty of care. Even if PyroCo had complied with the applicable industry regulations and standards as it alleges, it failed to exercise reasonable care when a technician insisted that "the show go on" even after the shells malfunctioned during an early round of fireworks. Any reasonable person who is responsible for igniting a large fireworks display would exercise caution after some of the fireworks malfunction. But instead, the PyroCo technicians continued the show, without any further checks or precautions, and a second shell malfunctioned and propelled horizontally "directly into the crowd," striking a spectator's cooler and detonating.

> Third, Sawyer will likely be able to prove that the defendant's conduct was the proximate cause of her injury. Sawyer is a foreseeable plaintiff because she came to watch the fireworks, along with many others, based on the company's promotions, as the company intended. She was in a foreseeable zone of harm because she was sitting in the ball field, where spectators were expected, about 700 feet from where the firework shells were launched. She sat with her children "so close" to where the exploding shell landed that sparks landed around her group.
>
> Finally, the harm element is satisfied because Sawyer's eye and arm injuries and related medical bills amount to a legally recognized harm.[4]
>
> **Conclusion**
> - Provides an answer on the legal issue
> - Indicates a level of certainty
> - Describes a reason in support
>
> **Example:** PyroCo likely is liable in negligence for Sawyer's injuries because PyroCo breached a duty that it owed to Sawyer and its conduct caused her harm.

4. PROOFREAD

Time presents one of the biggest challenges when writing an essay exam answer. While you should devote the bulk of the time allotted to reading the question and writing your IRAC or CREAC, you can improve your final score if you take a few moments to check your work.

Because of the time constraint, your professor (or bar exam grader) might overlook a few spelling or grammar issues in your answer. But repeated errors detract from a writer's credibility. Try to win over your reader by presenting a polished, readable document. You can do this by breaking up long paragraphs of text and especially long sentences. The average sentence should be about 20 words.[5] That doesn't mean you should spend your time counting words, but if you can't see the end of a sentence in a particularly long paragraph, try to add a period—or two.

Also, check that you have clearly identified each of the IRAC or CREAC parts. Add headings or key transitions, and skip a line or start a new paragraph to set each section apart. If you're following CREAC, check that the Conclusions at the beginning and end of your document give the same answer. And finally, if you have time, proofread quickly to catch and fix any obvious grammar, style, or punctuation errors. This final check just might set your mind at ease as you await your grade or results.

---

4. This analysis example is loosely based on the facts and reasoning in *Evarts v. Pyro Eng'g, Inc.*, 117 A.D.3d 1148, 1150–51 (N.Y. App. Div. 2014).

5. *See, e.g.,* Bryan A. Garner, *LawProse Lesson #269: Average Sentence Length,* (April 18, 2018, 10:35 AM), http://www.lawprose.org/lawprose-lesson-269-average-sentence-length/.

The following is an example answer for the torts essay question (on page 33) that's discussed throughout this chapter. Note that your professors might have more specific instructions for your essay answer. For example, professors might ask you to include references to key cases (without citations) so your answer is more like the formal legal memorandum on page 105. Or professors might ask you to incorporate policy arguments throughout your analysis. But while specific instructions might vary, the most widely accepted form for any legal analysis is IRAC or CREAC, as shown in the example answer here.

TORTS ESSAY ANSWER EXAMPLE

False Imprisonment

Camille has a strong false imprisonment claim against Emil.

— This brief **Conclusion** pinpoints the cause of action in precise legal terms, names the parties, and gives the answer to the legal question.

The intentional tort of false imprisonment requires four elements: (1) the defendant has the intent or purpose to confine another within a limited area; (2) the defendant's affirmative conduct causes the confinement; (3) the person confined is aware of the confinement; and (4) the person confined does not consent to the confinement.[7]

— This **Rule** statement spells out the four elements derived from common law.

The tort of false imprisonment does not require the plaintiff to prove that she suffered physical or emotional harm or distress. The tort recognizes that a person has a legal right not to suffer unwanted, intentional, or substantial interference with her freedom of movement, unless the defendant is protected by an applicable privilege.[8]

— This **Explanation** elaborates on the requirements of the Rule.

Here, Camille probably could successfully prove each of the four elements. First, Emil showed the intent or purpose to confine Camille when he "ordered" Camille into the store office, which by design is a confined, limited area. He further showed this intent when he moved to stand in front of the office's exit and yelled at her to "sit here." Second, Emil's conduct caused the confinement because Camille complied with Emil's orders: She left the store parking lot to go into the office with Emil and sat within the confined space at his instruction. Finally, Camille showed both that she was aware of the confinement and that she did not consent when she stated that she wanted to leave.

— The **Analysis** section applies the law to the facts for each element — in order. It uses a transition, "here," to mark the section's start and "first," "second," and so forth for each element.

Emil's conduct showed that he caused Camille to suffer interference with her freedom of movement. Thus, unless Emil can successfully establish a valid defense, Camille has a strong claim of false imprisonment against Emil.

— The final **Conclusion** indicates the writer's level of certainty in answering the legal question.

---

7. Rule adapted from Restatement (Third) of Torts: Inten. Torts to Persons § 7 TD No. 2 (2017).
8. *Id.*

Shopkeeper's Privilege Defense

Emil probably will not be able to successfully claim the shopkeeper's privilege as a defense to Camille's false imprisonment claim.

Under Ohio law, a store employee who has reasonable cause to believe that an individual unlawfully took items offered for sale by the store is privileged to detain that individual in a reasonable manner for a reasonable length of time within the store.[9]

*Each section of this CREAC, beginning with this **Conclusion** and **Rule** statement, is set apart in its own paragraph for readability.*

Whether the employee's actions were reasonable in his suspicions, in the manner of detainment, and in the length of detainment depends on the facts and circumstances of each case. A shopkeeper cannot avail himself of this privilege if he acts reasonably in one way, such as by detaining a suspected individual for a very short time, but also acts unreasonably in another, such as by unfairly suspecting an individual or by using force to detain her.[10]

*The **Explanation** illustrates how the Rule is applied.*

In this case, Emil's actions overall were unreasonable. Both the length of detainment and manner of detainment were unreasonable. Forcing Camille to wait for 40 minutes until the police arrived is excessive, especially given Emil's unreasonable and threatening actions throughout the encounter. Taking Camille by the arm, ordering her to sit, and labeling her a thief all show that Emil easily exceeded the bounds of reasonable conduct.

*The **Analysis** shows the writer's work by detailing how the law applies to each reasonableness factor, focusing here on the second two factors because that analysis supports the Conclusion.*

However, Emil's initial suspicions might seem reasonable because a customer walking around the parking lot cart collection area would draw attention. Also, Emil's initial suspicions justifiably intensified when he spotted two of the store's bowls in Camille's bag. He further acted reasonably in assuming that Camille had purchased the bowls on that visit to the store and thus would have receipts for them.

*The writer begins a second **Analysis** paragraph to analyze the first factor: the reasonableness of Emil's suspicions. This analysis offers a counterargument.*

Nonetheless, because Emil acted unreasonably in aggressively detaining Camille for an extended length of time, he likely cannot successfully assert the shopkeeper's privilege defense to Camille's false imprisonment claim.

*The **Conclusion** resolves the counteranalysis and closes the CREAC with a decisive answer and specific reason.*

Battery

[IRAC/CREAC Analysis Omitted]

Defamation

[IRAC/CREAC Analysis Omitted]

---

9. Ohio Rev. Code § 2935.041 (2018).

10. *See, e.g., Hodges v. Meijer, Inc.*, 717 N.E.2d 806, 810 (Ohio Ct. App. 1998).

part II

Objective
Writing

Constructing CREAC in Objective Documents

Lawyers, clients, and judges need to understand both sides of a legal issue to make fair and objective decisions. Throughout your law school and legal career, you will be asked to answer legal questions that vary in scope and complexity. Clients will come to you with legal problems to solve. Supervising attorneys will call on you to assist in analyzing part or all of a legal dispute or transaction. If you work as a judicial intern or clerk, your judge will expect you to fairly evaluate both sides of a case to help resolve it.

The key to writing objectively is to fully and fairly examine both sides of the arguments surrounding your legal question and to make an accurate prediction about the most likely result. This part of the *Handbook* shows you how to prepare each part of an objective CREAC analysis for your legal problem. Whether you need to summarize your analysis in a memorandum, judicial opinion, letter, or email, you can use the CREAC format to clearly and effectively explain your legal analysis.

Writing an Objective Conclusion

The first sentence of every CREAC is a Conclusion. The Conclusion statement provides a fitting topic sentence for the discussion of your legal question. The Conclusion should convey two pieces of information: (1) your answer to the legal question and (2) a reason for your answer.

Typically, the Conclusion is a single sentence that states the answer, then the word "because," and then the reason for the answer. Occasionally, for complex legal questions, you might need to write two or even three sentences to summarize your Conclusion. Giving the reader the answer to the legal question at the start is the best way to introduce the analysis that follows.

> **Writing an Objective Conclusion**
>
> 1. Use an issue statement as a placeholder.
> 2. Develop your legal question—the Question Presented.
> 3. Develop your answer—the Brief Answer.
> 4. State your conclusion and give a reason.

1. STEP ONE: USE AN ISSUE STATEMENT AS A PLACEHOLDER

Even though the Conclusion is the first sentence of any CREAC, you usually cannot provide an educated answer to a legal question until you have written a draft of the other parts: the Rule, Explanation, and Analysis sections. Thus, the first step in reaching your Conclusion is to identify the precise legal question you have been asked to answer. Because you need to analyze the relevant law and how the law applies to your facts before you can reach your Conclusion, you should start the draft of your document with a precise issue statement that can serve as a placeholder for the Conclusion. (This is just like writing an exam answer in the IRAC organization.) For this step, be vigilant in identifying and narrowing your legal issue.

For instance, suppose you have been asked to analyze the broad question of whether your client's burglary conviction will be overturned on appeal.

After you analyze the relevant facts and law, you might realize that your client's appeal depends on only one element of burglary: whether he entered the "curtilage" of the home of the victim, Miguel Perry. Your issue statement placeholder for this document could be the following:

> The issue is whether Miguel Perry's compound qualifies as curtilage.

Similarly, in a legal memorandum on a contract dispute involving whether a business owner had the intent to sell the business even though she made a pricing mistake in her offer, the Conclusion should hone in on the precise legal issue that will determine the outcome of the case. The precise legal issue is whether the owner made a binding offer. An effective issue statement placeholder for this memorandum could be as follows:

> This case concerns whether Sandra Lee made a binding offer to sell her widget business to Graham Enterprises.

The issue statements do not include any legally significant facts yet because at this stage of the writing process, the writer has not reviewed the relevant case law to determine the relevant anchors. Without a solid understanding of the relevant law and the anchors, the writer cannot identify which facts are legally significant. As a result, an early draft of an issue statement merely states the precise legal question.

2. STEP TWO: DEVELOP YOUR LEGAL QUESTION— THE QUESTION PRESENTED

A. Identify the Anchors

At this point, you can begin unraveling the mystery behind your legal question. Review the relevant authorities and begin to list the anchors that justified the courts' decisions on your precise legal question.[1] Remember that the anchors are what the outcome depends on—they are the grounds or bases of a court's decision on your issue. The court might state the anchors explicitly or use wording that is less direct. As a result, you'll need to carefully read and understand an opinion to fully identify the anchors that motivated a court's decision on your legal question. After you identify the anchors, consider the list in its entirety. Decide whether any anchors overlap and create a synthesized list of the anchors that are relevant to your precise legal question.

For example, burglary cases typically define the "curtilage" surrounding a home according to three anchors. Your synthesized list of the anchors for your analysis of the curtilage issue could be as follows:

1. Whether the area has an enclosure;

---

1. Refer to Chapter 2, "Reading and Understanding Authorities"; Chapter 3, "It Depends on the 'Anchors'"; and Part VIII, "Research" for detailed instructions on finding relevant authorities.

2. Whether the enclosure has openings for entering and exiting the property; and

3. Whether the enclosure is irregular, like sparse shrubs, or fortifying, like a privacy fence.[2]

B. Use the Anchors to Identify the Legally Significant Facts

The anchors break down the reasoning of the relevant cases into concrete parts, so they not only help you understand the nuances of the authorities, but they also guide you to identify the facts that will help answer your question. These facts are your "legally significant facts."

With the curtilage anchors in mind, the kinds of facts that would be legally significant become obvious: (1) facts relating to the enclosure surrounding a property, (2) facts relating to openings or gaps in the enclosure, and (3) facts relating to the kind of enclosure.

Review the anchors and facts relating to your legal question. Pick out the facts that fit best with the anchors. Match up every legally significant fact to a relevant anchor. Keep in mind that you want to look at the legal question objectively, so try to identify facts that support each side of the argument for each anchor. For instance, in the curtilage analysis, that would mean identifying facts that could help you argue that the enclosure is—and is not—sufficient.

C. Follow a Common Format

A Question Presented is a formal statement of your specific legal issue and the most relevant facts. Questions Presented are common at the beginning of a legal memorandum because they give the reader an overview of your case. (See examples of legal memoranda beginning on page 105.)

Writers can frame Questions Presented in several ways. One common format follows a formula known as "under-does-when" or a variation of it. This format is written as a single sentence ending with a question mark. This type of Question Presented has three parts:

1. **Under:** The Question Presented begins with an introductory clause starting with "under," and it identifies the jurisdiction and the type of law.
2. **Does:** The Question Presented then states the precise legal question using a verb, such as "does," "did," "can," "is," or "was." Because the Question Presented gives an overview of the case, it can refer to the parties involved generally or use specific names. Terms, including "buyer" and "seller" or "plaintiff" and "defendant," are common.
3. **When:** Finally, the Question Presented states two or more legally significant facts that are typically introduced with "when" or "where."

---

2. *See, e.g., State v. Hamilton,* 660 So. 2d 1038 (Fla. 1995).

The Question Presented should be precise when stating the facts and should summarize them in a way that does not show bias toward one conclusion. It should use parallel construction to make the facts easy to understand.[3]

Another common format, known as the multisentence format, uses multiple sentences, including at least one statement and one question, to describe the law, facts, and legal issue. In this format, the law and key facts are presented as statements and the legal issue is presented as a question. You can decide whether to put the law and fact statements into one sentence together or two separate sentences. You can also decide whether the law or facts should come first. This format is often useful for more complex legal questions, where a single-sentence Question Presented would be awkward.

A third type of issue statement that begins with "whether" has a more informal format. It usually starts with the legal question and then lists some key facts, often incorporating the jurisdiction. Even though it's a phrase and not a complete sentence, the "whether" issue statement ends with a period.

For the legal issue introduced on page 47 on whether the business owner made a binding offer to sell her business when she placed an ad with a pricing mistake, the following examples show the "under-does-when" structure, the multisentence format, and the "whether" Questions Presented.

Under-Does-When Format

Under New York contract law, did the owner of a widget business make a binding offer to sell her business when she placed an ad to sell her business, but she mistakenly priced the business for a fraction of its worth?

— The first part of the Question Presented provides the jurisdiction and the type of law.

— The second part provides the specific legal question.

— The third part provides the most important legally significant facts. This Question Presented states the facts objectively, and it has facts that support a "yes" answer and a "no" answer to the question.

Multisentence Format

New York law requires a binding offer for a contract to exist. Ms. Lee placed an advertisement to sell her widget business, but mistakenly priced the business at a fraction of its worth. Was Ms. Lee's advertisement a binding offer?

— This Question Presented starts with a statement describing the relevant law.

— The second sentence is a statement describing the legally significant facts.

Notice that this Question Presented would also make sense if the order of the first two sentences was reversed.

— The third sentence presents the specific legal issue as a question.

---

3. Refer to page 143 in Chapter 20, "Grammar Principles for the New Legal Writer," for detailed instructions on parallel construction.

Whether Format

Whether the owner of a widget business in New York made a binding offer to sell her business when she placed an ad to sell her business but mistakenly priced the business for a fraction of its worth.

This Question Presented starts with the issue, incorporating the jurisdiction — New York.

— It then provides context with two legally significant facts.

Judicial opinions also may begin with an objective statement of the issue that incorporates legally significant facts. These issue statements follow varying formats to seamlessly fit in with the opinion that follows. For example, Justice Antonin Scalia began *Florida v. Jardines* with the following:

> We consider whether using a drug-sniffing dog on a homeowner's porch to investigate the contents of the home is a "search" within the meaning of the Fourth Amendment.[4]

In a similar case that also involved a drug-sniffing dog, Justice Elena Kagan began the opinion by precisely framing the issue before the Court:

> In this case, we consider how a court should determine if the "alert" of a drug-detection dog during a traffic stop provides probable cause to search a vehicle.[5]

As these examples show, a good Question Presented or issue statement will introduce the reader to the precise legal question and provide some legally significant facts to put the dispute in context.

3. STEP THREE: DEVELOP YOUR ANSWER— THE BRIEF ANSWER

The Brief Answer logically follows the Question Presented in a legal memorandum. (See an example on page 105.) It provides a formal summary of your conclusion. The Brief Answer also typically has three parts, often broken up into two to five sentences.

1. The first sentence of the Brief Answer provides a direct answer to the question asked in the Question Presented—either "yes" or "no." Your answer will often include a qualifying term, such as "probably," because no one can predict with absolute certainty how a court or jury will decide a particular case. The Brief Answer commonly begins with "probably yes" or "probably not."

---

4. *Florida v. Jardines*, 569 U.S. 1, 3 (2013).
5. *Florida v. Harris*, 568 U.S. 237, 240 (2013).

2. The next one to two sentences briefly summarize the applicable rules and anchors.

3. The final one to two sentences summarize your analysis and conclusion. Be careful not to repeat the facts from the Question Presented; instead, your Brief Answer should explain how the facts fit with the law and how you reached your conclusion.

The following example contains the answer, two sentences summarizing the relevant law and anchors, and one sentence summarizing the writer's reasoning and conclusion.

> The Brief Answer begins with a direct answer and a qualifying term.

Probably not. An advertisement is not an offer but a mere invitation to enter into a bargain. Even where a binding offer is made, the offeror — This part describes the most relevant rules and anchors. can withdraw a mistaken offer if she exercised ordinary care, the other party was aware of the mistake, and enforcement of the offer would be unconscionable. Here, a court would likely find that no offer was made — This summary of the analysis supports the conclusion, applying the relevant anchors to the specific facts from the Question Presented. because the advertisement merely invited buyers to make an offer to buy the business, and forcing the offeror to accept the low price listed in the advertisement would likely be deemed unconscionable.

4. STEP FOUR: STATE YOUR CONCLUSION AND GIVE A REASON

Once you have drafted the Question Presented and Brief Answer, you have the foundation for a strong Conclusion. All Conclusions should provide your answer to the legal question and a supporting reason. You can start with the following format:

_____[answer to legal question]_____ because _____[supporting reason(s)]_____.

A Conclusion also might include the parties' names and the jurisdiction. Depending on your level of certainty, an objective Conclusion typically includes a qualifying term, such as "probably" or "likely."

The examples of the following Conclusions identify the precise legal issues, and they reference legally significant facts and anchors when giving the reason.

For objective documents, you may use a qualifying term, such as "probably" or "likely."

The precise legal question is whether the yard is curtilage.

Miguel Perry's compound would likely qualify as curtilage because a picket fence encloses most of the yard, which supports Tom Chapman's burglary conviction.

This reason provides a specific fact that references an anchor — enclosure.

This phrase is helpful because it reminds the reader of the broad legal issue — whether Chapman will be convicted of burglary.

The Conclusion often states
the parties' names in full.
Here, both parties are named.

This legal dispute involves a
contract question. The precise
legal question is whether
Lee made a binding offer.

Sandra Lee probably did not make a binding offer to sell her widget business to Graham Enterprises under New York law because she priced the business so low that buyers would know it was a mistake.

Identifying the jurisdiction in the Conclusion is helpful.

Every good Conclusion provides a reason. Here, the reason provides a specific, legally significant fact that's tied to the anchors of whether the seller exercised ordinary care and whether buyers would be aware of the mistake.

A strong Conclusion at the start of your legal document is helpful because it introduces your reader to the legal question and your answer. On the Supreme Court, most of the justices begin their opinions with a Conclusion (to follow the CREAC format) most of the time.[6]

The Conclusions in judicial opinions are similar to those in legal memoranda. They also detail the legal issue and the answer, and they might reference the law and legally significant facts. But a judicial opinion's Conclusion will be authoritative and definite—unlike the Conclusion in a legal memorandum that may include a qualifier like "probably."

The following paragraph serves as Justice Kagan's opening Conclusion in *Florida v. Harris*, a criminal appeal centered on the Fourth Amendment. Justice Kagan's example shows that you can write Conclusions in various ways, depending on the purpose of your legal document, the complexity of the legal issue, and the certainty of your Conclusion.

The Conclusion begins
with a precise statement of
the issue.

In this case, we consider how a court should determine if the "alert" of a drug-detection dog during a traffic stop provides probable cause to search a vehicle. The Florida Supreme Court held that the State must in every case present an exhaustive set of records, including a log of the dog's performance in the field, to establish the dog's reliability. We think that demand inconsistent with the "flexible, common-sense standard" of probable cause.[7]

The second sentence provides
key facts and the procedural
history to put the dispute
in context.

The Conclusion ends with the
Court's answer and a reference to the supporting law.

---

6. Chief Justice John G. Roberts and Justice Sonia Sotomayor occasionally use the IRAC format instead. Both formats effectively introduce the law and analysis that follow. A Conclusion also gives the reader a better idea of what's coming.

7. *Harris*, 568 U.S. at 240 (citations omitted).

Checklist for your opening Conclusion
Does my opening Conclusion...

☑ State my prediction on the legal issue?
☑ Use hedging language if necessary to accurately describe my level of certainty?
☑ Answer the legal question the memo was written to address?
☑ Give a specific reason in support of my answer?

Writing an Objective Rule Section

While the Conclusion narrows your legal question, the Rule should be broad. The Rule section lays out the controlling law, beginning with the broadest and most important rule.

> **Writing an Objective Rule Section**
> 1. Organize rules from general to specific.
> 2. Include quotations of key language.
> 3. Cite correctly.

1. STEP ONE: ORGANIZE RULES FROM GENERAL TO SPECIFIC

When you write about a simple legal issue, the Rule could be a single sentence. For more complex questions, the Rule section could be a whole paragraph or more. No matter the complexity, the Rule section should start with the broadest, most general rule from the highest authority. More specific rules will follow—to complete the Rule and Explanation sections.

A. Start with Constitutions and Statutes

When constitutions and statutes govern your question, they provide a logical starting point based on hierarchy of authority. The constitutional provision or statute is the broadest statement of the rule. Typically, when the Rule section is made up of a constitutional provision or statute, the Explanation section begins with case law that interprets the provision. A legal memorandum addressing the question of whether a suspension violated a student's free speech rights could begin like this:

> The suspension of a student who held a sign promoting illegal drug use at —Conclusion
> a school-supervised event likely did not violate the student's free speech

rights. The state constitution guarantees that "[e]very person may freely — This Alaska constitutional
speak, write, and publish on all subjects, being responsible for the abuse   provision provides the
of that right." Alaska Const. § 5 (2002).   broadest Rule.

Similarly, Justice Ruth Bader Ginsburg began the Rule section in an opinion
in a death penalty case by quoting key language from the Eighth Amendment.

The Eighth Amendment prohibits "cruel and unusual punishments," — The Rule begins with key
and "reaffirms the duty of the government to respect the dignity of all   language from the highest
persons," *Hall v. Florida*, 134 S. Ct. 1986, 1992 (2014). "To enforce the   authority and a broad
Constitution's protection of human dignity," we "loo[k] to the evolv-   interpretation from a
ing standards of decency that mark the progress of a maturing society,"   leading case.
recognizing that "[t]he Eighth Amendment is not fastened to the obso- — Justice Ginsburg then adds a
lete." *Id.*[1]   second explanatory statement.

Questions governed by statutes will likewise begin with the statute—but
take note that more than one statute or statute section could apply. For
instance, in the example below, the legal question relates to burglary; more
specifically, it relates to whether the defendant entered what's known as the
"curtilage" of a home. The Rule section begins with the state burglary statute,
which does not reference curtilage, and continues with a second state statute
that defines a different key term in the statute: "dwelling."

The definition of dwelling then provides the first reference to curtilage.
The structure of the Rule section moves from the broad idea of burglary
to the specific idea of curtilage, showing the reader why the legal question
requires interpretation of the term "curtilage." The second statute would not
make sense without the first, and the answer to the legal question requires
an understanding of both. So the organization of the Rule section is logical,
beginning with the broad statute and then providing the more specific definitional statute.

Miguel Perry's compound would likely qualify as curtilage because a — Conclusion
picket fence encloses most of the yard, lending support to Chapman's
burglary conviction. Burglary means "entering or remaining in a dwell- — This Rule section begins
ing, a structure, or a conveyance with the intent to commit an offense   with the broad burglary
therein...." Fla. Stat. § 810.02(b)(1) (2017). A "dwelling" includes a   statute about a "dwelling."
"building or conveyance...which has a roof over it and is designed to be — The second statute defines
occupied by people lodging therein at night, together with the curtilage   "dwelling" and references
thereof." *Id.* § 810.011(2).   "curtilage."

Similarly, in the next example, two statutes apply. The first provides the
broad rule on adverse possession, so it begins the Rule section. The second
sentence logically follows because it defines a key part of the controlling statute: what "occupied" means under California adverse possession law.

Blackhurst can likely establish the "open and notorious" possession ele- — Conclusion
ment for an adverse possession claim. In California, adverse possession

---

1. *Moore v. Texas*, 137 S. Ct. 1039, 1048 (2017).

is defined as follows: "Where it appears that there has been an actual continued occupation of land, under a claim of title, exclusive of any other right, but not founded upon a written instrument, judgment or decree, the land so actually occupied, and no other, is deemed to have been held adversely." Cal. Civ. Proc. Code § 324 (2017). Land is "deemed to have been possessed and occupied" only where "it has been protected by a substantial enclosure" and "has been usually cultivated or improved." *Id.* § 325.

— This Rule section begins with the controlling adverse possession statute. The second sentence explains one key term: "occupied."

When no constitution or statute applies to your legal question, case law provides the starting point for the Rule section.

B. Outline Your Case Law

Rule sections that are made up of case law also should be organized from the broadest, most general rule to the more specific rules. A good place to start figuring out this organization is by reviewing your cases to see how the courts explain your rules. Courts typically reference the broadest rule first and then provide more specific illustrations and interpretations, so the structure of your Rule section will likely be similar to the structure found in the cases you are using.

Create an outline of your Rule section that follows one of your strongest cases, putting the broadest rule at the top and putting the more specific rule(s) below. Do the same outline with two more cases. The outlines should be comparable and provide you with a map for your Rule section. Here are examples of five of the most common types of Rule sections from case law.

i. Rule with Key Terms That Need to Be Defined

Your broadest rule might include legally significant terms that you need to define and interpret to answer your legal question. If so, your Rule section will begin with the general rule, followed by more specific rules that define key terms:

Zahid Villa was not malicious or grossly negligent when he failed to warn others that the old oil well was next to the party tent because he believed the well posed no danger. A landowner who offers his land for recreation loses immunity if he is malicious or grossly negligent in failing to warn others about a danger. *Lonergan v. May*, 53 S.W.3d 122, 127 (Mo. Ct. App. 2001). Under Missouri law, malice requires actions "so reckless or wantonly and willfully in disregard of one's rights that a trier of fact could infer from such conduct bad faith." *Henderson v. United States*, 965 F.2d 1488, 1494 (8th Cir. 1992). Gross negligence equals "a reckless disregard for proper conduct" and can be demonstrated by "a conscious indifference" to others' safety. *Id.* at 1493-94.

— Conclusion

— This Rule section begins with the broad rule on failure to warn. The next two sentences help define two key terms: "malice" and "gross negligence."

ii. Legal Test with Elements

Perhaps your legal question involves one element of a multipart legal test. Generally, in an elements test, every element must be present to satisfy the rule. The rule stating the legal test would be the first sentence of your Rule section, and the rule describing the specific element or elements you will analyze would be next.

> The Court will likely dismiss the Plaintiff's claim for intentional infliction — Conclusion
> of emotional distress because Prudence Jones did not act outrageously
> when she asked the Plaintiff to leave the store after he removed all of
> his clothes. The tort of intentional infliction of emotional distress has — This broad rule states the
> the following four elements: (1) extreme and outrageous conduct; (2)   legal elements.
> intent to cause, or disregard of a substantial probability of causing, se-
> vere emotional distress; (3) a causal connection between the conduct and
> the injury; and (4) severe emotional distress. *Howell v. N.Y. Post Co.*, 612
> N.E.2d 699, 702 (N.Y. 1993). Outrageous conduct is "conduct exceeding — This sentence describes the
> all bounds usually tolerated by decent society." *Id.*   specific element that the
> memo will analyze.

iii. Factors Test

Your rule might involve a set of factors that courts should consider when applying the rule. A factors test differs from a legal test with elements because in a factors test, not every factor must be present to satisfy the rule. The rule stating the purpose of the test would be the first sentence of your Rule section, and the rules describing the relevant factors would follow.

> The Court will probably find that the trademarks are so similar that the — Conclusion
> public is likely to be confused because both include the silhouette of a cat
> and the number nine. The Ninth Circuit applies the eight-factor *Sleekcraft* — This sentence states the
> test to determine whether there is a likelihood of confusion. *Jada Toys, Inc.*   purpose of this factors test.
> *v. Mattel, Inc.*, 518 F.3d 628, 633 (9th Cir. 2008). The eight factors are — This sentence lists the
> as follows: (1) the strength of the mark; (2) the proximity of the goods;   relevant factors, using
> (3) the similarity of the marks; (4) the evidence of actual confusion; (5)   parallel construction for
> the marketing channels used; (6) the type of goods and the degree of   each factor.
> care likely to be exercised by the purchaser; (7) the defendant's intent in
> selecting the mark; and (8) the likelihood of expansion of the product
> lines. *Id.*; *see also AMF Inc. v. Sleekcraft Boats*, 599 F.2d 341, 348-49 (9th
> Cir. 1979).

When listing the elements or factors for a factors test, you should state each factor using parallel construction to enhance readability.[2]

---

2. Refer to page 143 in Chapter 20, "Grammar Principles for the New Legal Writer," for more guidance on parallel construction.

iv. Balancing Test

Your main rule also might include a balancing test, where each part of the test needs to be described. The logical organization would be to start with the overall balancing test, then explain the parts of the test. Remember to use your cases as a guide to develop the organizational structure of your Rule section.

> The Court will likely hold that the evidence is admissible under Federal Rule of Evidence 403 because any potential jury confusion can be mitigated by an instruction from the Court. Rule 403 requires a district court to engage in balancing to determine whether the probative value of the evidence is "substantially outweighed" by the dangers listed in Rule 403, including unfair prejudice, confusion of the issues, misleading the jury, undue delay, waste of time, or needless presentation of cumulative evidence. Fed. R. Evid. 403. In balancing, "the proper equation places on one side the maximum reasonable probative force for the offered evidence," while "the other side of the equation should include the likely prejudicial impact of the evidence." *Coleman v. Home Depot, Inc.*, 306 F.3d 1333, 1343 (3d Cir. 2002).

— Conclusion

— This sentence describes the overall balancing test.

— This sentence further explains the parts of the test.

v. Rule with Exceptions

Your rule also might be one that is limited by exceptions. The statement of the rule would be the first sentence of your Rule section, and the later sentences would describe the relevant exceptions.

> The Court is unlikely to hold that the warrantless search was unreasonable in this case because the firefighter was probably acting within the community caretaking exception. The Fourth Amendment guarantees the "right of the people to be secure in their persons, houses, papers, and effects, against unreasonable searches and seizures." U.S. Const. amend IV. Generally, a search of private property without a warrant based upon probable cause is unreasonable. *Cady v. Dombrowski*, 413 U.S. 433, 439 (1973). There are, however, exceptions to the warrant requirement, including searches the police undertake as part of their "community caretaking" function. *Id.* at 441. The community caretaking exception applies when law enforcement officers conduct a warrantless search as part of their caretaking function, "totally divorced from the detection, investigation, or acquisition of evidence relating to any criminal statute." *Id.*

— Conclusion

— These two sentences state the rule.

— These sentences describe the relevant exception to the rule.

2. STEP TWO: INCLUDE QUOTATIONS OF KEY LANGUAGE

Once you have your rules organized in an outline from the broad to the specific, you can begin drafting the Rule section. Analyze the language of the rules to determine how much you want to quote directly and how much you want to paraphrase. You should write your Rule section in the present tense because it describes the rules that apply to your case in the present.

Generally, writers quote the key language from constitutions and statutes directly. Our legal system has spent centuries interpreting the precise language of constitutional and statutory provisions, so using the exact language in your legal documents is key.

A writer may make a stylistic choice to quote only portions of a key provision or to use an ellipsis to cut out irrelevant parts. Consider the previous examples. Note how the writers quoted the most important parts of the relevant constitutional and statutory provisions while paraphrasing a small portion for readability.

Rule sections made up of case law, though, will likely include fewer quotations. As you may have noticed in the outline you made of your key cases, courts use different language to state the same rules. Unless a court states a rule in a particularly eloquent way or uses legal terms of art that are important to the meaning of the rule, you should try to rewrite and paraphrase the rules from case law to fit your legal document.

In the next Rule paragraph, the writer quotes only key portions of the pivotal case to state the overarching rule. The Rule section starts broadly and narrows to reach the central issue: whether a state can refuse to put the names of same-sex spouses on their children's birth certificates.

> A state may not "exclude same-sex couples from civil marriage on the same terms and conditions as opposite-sex couples." *Obergefell v. Hodges*, 135 S. Ct. 2584, 2600-01 (2015). States "have throughout our history made marriage the basis for an expanding list of governmental rights, benefits, and responsibilities." *Id*. This list expressly identifies "birth and death certificates," in part because several *Obergefell* plaintiffs were challenging their state's "refusal to recognize their same-sex spouses on their children's birth certificates." *Id*.[3]

3. STEP THREE: CITE CORRECTLY

As a final step, check that you have provided a citation for each rule in your Rule section. Your readers will not be able to verify your analysis if they can't find the sources you cite. Failing to cite your sources correctly will undermine the usefulness and credibility of your Rule section.

In general, every sentence in the Rule and Explanation sections will have a citation. There are rare exceptions, such as when the writer includes a transition sentence that helps guide the reader through the Rule section but

---

3. Adapted from *Pavan v. Smith*, 137 S. Ct. 2075, 2078 (2017).

does not come from a controlling authority. Each citation should follow the preferred format detailed in *The Bluebook*. Proper *Bluebook* citation format is discussed in detail in Chapter 43.

Checklist for your Rule Section
Does my Rule section...

☑ Organize the rules from general to specific with attention to the hierarchy of authority?

☑ Follow the structure of the rule?

☑ Use present tense?

☑ Quote legally significant language?

☑ Correctly cite authority for every sentence?

Writing an Objective Explanation Section

At this point, you have identified the major rule or rules for your legal document. Whether your rule is from a statute or a case or multiple statutes or cases, your next job is to explain what the rule[1] means. Looking at different fact patterns in cases and various courts' interpretations of the rule will help you explain the rule to your reader. Rule explanation is a critical step because without it, the reader has no context for understanding how courts have interpreted and applied the language of the rule.

Consider how unhelpful your document would be if you quoted a burglary statute with a confusing term like "curtilage," but you did not explain what curtilage means. Plenty of courts have examined the boundaries of curtilage in burglary cases, and you should use relevant case law to explain burglary, curtilage, and other related rules of law.

Your job in the Explanation section is—not surprisingly—to explain the rules to the reader in the easiest possible terms. Before you explain the rules, make sure you fully understand your cases. Read and reread your cases—you will discover new, relevant details each time. As you read your cases, try to identify the issues that impact a court's decision. Every opinion has at least one anchor that is the basis for the court's decision.

Use the anchors to guide your explanation of the relevant law. In burglary cases in Florida, for example, an offender can be convicted if he enters the curtilage surrounding a home. Courts often define curtilage according to three anchors: (1) whether the area has an enclosure; (2) whether the enclosure has openings for entering and exiting the property; and (3) whether the enclosure is irregular, like sparse shrubs, or fortifying, like a privacy fence.[2] This list of three anchors is synthesized from reading multiple relevant court opinions. The answer to a new legal question involving curtilage depends on how the facts of the question line up with one or more of these anchors.

For instance, if an offender steps past a single shrub to reach a property, a court would likely determine that he did not enter the curtilage of a home.

---

1. As described in Chapter 9, your Rule section will often involve multiple rules, but in this section, we will refer to the rule as singular for the sake of simplicity.

2. *See, e.g., State v. Hamilton*, 660 So. 2d 1038 (Fla. 1995).

The facts do not fit with the anchor that requires some sort of enclosure surrounding the property. But if an offender rappels over a 10-foot brick wall and breaks into a house, he might want to explore a plea agreement. The fact that he crossed over a well-fortified enclosure means that a conviction would be solidly anchored in the law.

The structure of your Explanation section depends on your purpose and your audience. For an objective legal document, such as a client advice email, judicial opinion, or office memorandum, your task is to thoroughly explain both sides of the law so you can justify your Conclusion. If you are writing an office memorandum that predicts the outcome of a dispute for a senior attorney, the attorney will need to understand the law that is favorable and unfavorable to the client before trusting your Conclusion. In the same way, a court would not want to give a one-sided view of the law in its opinions. The parties and the public expect fairness and a complete explanation of the law.

Writing an Objective Explanation Section

1. Focus on your question.
2. Understand the big picture.
3. Use cases to describe your anchors.

---

1. STEP ONE: FOCUS ON YOUR QUESTION

Keep in mind that the Explanation should explain only the rule that applies to the question you have been asked to answer. Many cases address more than one issue, requiring you to focus your Explanation on only the relevant parts of the cases. Your legal question is the one identified in your Question Presented.

For instance, suppose your supervisor asks you to analyze whether a client made a valid offer to sell her business in a contract dispute. Relevant cases will analyze whether a party made a valid offer, but they also might analyze other elements and issues, such as whether a party accepted the offer or whether a party had the legal capacity to enter into a binding contract. Relevant cases also might address additional causes of action. Your job is to identify the parts of the cases that relate only to your precise question—whether the client made a valid offer.

2. STEP TWO: UNDERSTAND THE BIG PICTURE

To write your Explanation section, you will need to understand the applicable law so well that you feel like an expert. A good starting place is to identify and understand a seminal case that relates to your legal issue. A seminal case is usually the first case from the highest court to decide a particular issue, or it can be the first case to reverse or revise a rule. It can also be a case where the court analyzed the issue in unusual depth or explained it with particular eloquence. For instance, if you are analyzing the curtilage question in an Ohio burglary case, the earliest case from the Ohio Supreme Court stating the relevant rule is probably the seminal case. One easy way to find a seminal case is that most subsequent cases analyzing that same issue—those from the Ohio Supreme Court and lower courts—will cite the earlier, seminal case.

The next logical step is to identify, read, and digest the cases that have fact patterns comparable (or contrastable) to the facts in your legal question. Reading cases where the courts have detailed the background and reasoning that led to their decisions in depth is also helpful. Try to understand the "big picture" legal framework that relates to your legal issue.

As you read and reread your relevant cases, make sure to identify the anchors that determine the courts' decisions. Keep asking, "What did the court's decision on my issue depend on?" If you were researching the question of whether your client made a valid offer, you would want to understand why one case held there was a valid offer and why another case held there was not. Detailing examples of what did or did not satisfy the anchors for your issue will make your Explanation effective.

For most legal issues, you will rely on multiple cases to understand the big picture. One case is rarely enough to explain what a rule means, to understand how it has been interpreted, and to identify the anchors that the courts have used to apply the rule. Your task in the Explanation is to extract and synthesize this information from multiple cases.

Remember that you can think creatively when choosing applicable cases to use in your Explanation. The facts from your legal question do not have to match up perfectly to the cases. For the question of whether your client made a valid offer to sell her business, any applicable case dealing with "offer" could work well in your Explanation, even if it deals with the offer to sell a car or a circus. The key would be to identify binding cases where the courts analyzed the language and actions that demonstrated—or failed to demonstrate—an offer being made.

3. STEP THREE: USE CASES TO DESCRIBE YOUR ANCHORS

A. Start with a Broad Topic Sentence

Once you understand the body of law that relates to your legal question, think about how you can most logically explain the anchors to your reader. An Explanation section usually requires multiple paragraphs, and Explanation paragraphs should begin with a topic sentence to help guide the reader through the section. A topic sentence should provide substantive information, like a conclusion summarizing a major point or an introduction to the paragraph's subject. The purpose of a topic sentence is to help your reader understand the information you are about to convey. In the Explanation section, the topic sentence of each paragraph will usually broadly describe one or more anchors. These topic sentences either describe the anchor as a broad legal principle or as a rule derived from previous cases. If the topic sentence describes the anchor as a generally applicable principle, it should be written in the present tense. If the topic sentence describes an anchor as a principle established in prior cases, it should be written in past tense. The topic sentence should be followed by a citation to a case from which the anchor was derived.

Most Explanation sections will start with broad statements about the law and then provide more specific details, facts, and reasoning to explain the broad statements. The organization is comparable to an upside-down triangle—the broad statements are at the top, giving the big picture, and the more specific details follow. This Explanation paragraph by Chief Justice Roberts is a perfect example of an upside-down triangle.

> Our cases make clear that students do not "shed their constitutional rights to freedom of speech or expression at the schoolhouse gate." *Tinker v. Des Moines Indep. Cmty. Sch. Dist.*, 393 U.S. 503, 506 (1969). At the same time, we have held that "the constitutional rights of students in public school are not automatically coextensive with the rights of adults in other settings," *Bethel Sch. Dist. No. 403 v. Fraser*, 478 U.S. 675, 682 (1986), and that the rights of students "must be 'applied in light of the special characteristics of the school environment,'" *Hazelwood Sch. Dist. v. Kuhlmeier*, 484 U.S. 260, 266 (1988) (quoting *Tinker*, 393 U.S. at 506).[3]

The first topic sentence introduces the general principle that students have First Amendment rights. It is written in present tense and followed by a citation to a seminal case.

The second sentence uses a transition to qualify the first rule, explaining that students' rights are subject to special limits.

This final part explains a specific limitation.

B. Illustrate Your Anchors

Providing a broad summary of one of the anchors is an excellent place to start your Explanation. Then, the rest of the sentences in the paragraph should include specific facts, holdings, and reasoning from relevant cases that explain and illustrate the anchor or anchors described in the topic sentence. By illustrating the anchors in this way, you are synthesizing and simplifying the cases for the reader so she can learn everything she needs to know about the cases as they relate to your issue without having to read each one. As you illustrate the cases, consider whether they have critical language that would be helpful to quote or jargon or legalese that you can clarify.

For example, remember that Florida courts define curtilage in burglary cases according to the following anchors:

1. Whether the area has an enclosure;
2. Whether the enclosure has openings for entering and exiting the property; and

---

3. *Morse v. Frederick*, 551 U.S. 393, 396-97 (2007).

3. Whether the enclosure is irregular, like sparse shrubs, or fortifying, like a privacy fence.[4]

A student writing a memo on a curtilage question could logically organize the Explanation section into three distinct paragraphs. The first Explanation paragraph would start with a topic sentence that describes the enclosure anchor according to case law. Then, the paragraph would include specific facts, holdings, and reasoning from binding cases that explain the enclosure anchor. The second paragraph would explain the anchor relating to openings in curtilage, and so on. Depending on their complexity, some anchors can be described in a sentence or two, while others will require a paragraph or more.

The following Explanation section example (following the Conclusion and Rule sections) describes the curtilage anchors. The first paragraph explains the enclosure anchor. The second paragraph combines the explanation of the other two anchors because they are closely related. The sentences describing the facts, holdings, and reasoning of past cases are written in the past tense. And each sentence is followed by a citation to give support and credibility:

Miguel Perry's compound would likely qualify as curtilage because a picket fence encloses most of the yard, lending support to Chapman's burglary conviction. Burglary means "entering or remaining in a dwelling, a structure, or a conveyance with the intent to commit an offense therein...." Fla. Stat. § 810.02(b)(1) (2017). A "dwelling" includes a "building or conveyance...which has a roof over it and is designed to be occupied by people lodging therein at night, together with the curtilage thereof." *Id.* § 810.011(2).

— This Conclusion begins the CREAC and answers the legal question.

— This Rule section takes up two sentences because Florida has two applicable statutes: one that defines burglary and another that defines dwelling. Not all issues will be governed by statutes. Some Rule sections will include one or more rules from cases instead.

Florida courts have established that "some form of an enclosure" is required for the area surrounding a residence to qualify as "curtilage," as required by the burglary statute. *State v. Hamilton*, 660 So. 2d 1038, 1040 (Fla. 1995). Curtilage originally referred to the areas surrounding castles that were fenced in with high stone walls, but Florida courts have enlarged the modern definition to include land and structures close enough to a dwelling that they "deserve the dwelling's protection." *Martinez v. State*, 700 So. 2d 142, 143 (Fla. Dist. Ct. App. 1997). The enclosure requirement avoids "unreasonable, harsh, or absurd consequences," such as convicting a person of burglary after he innocently wanders into an open yard "in broad daylight, without the homeowner's consent, with the intent to take a piece of fruit from a tree." *Hamilton*, 660 So. 2d at 1045.

— This paragraph covering Anchor No. 1 starts with a broad topic sentence about the enclosure requirement. The sentence provides a strong transition from the statutory rules in the first paragraph by showing that curtilage is defined by case law. It describes the anchor as a principle established by prior cases so it is written in past tense. The paragraph then provides specific details to illustrate the enclosure rule. The organization of this paragraph looks like an upside-down triangle because it moves from the broad to the specific.

But curtilage does not need not to be completely enclosed. *DeGeorge v. State*, 358 So. 2d 217, 218 (Fla. Dist. Ct. App. 1978). For example,

— This topic sentence is broad enough to cover Anchor Nos. 2 and 3, which are closely related and combined in one paragraph here. These anchors are described as general legal principles so the topic sentence is in present tense.

---

4. *See, e.g., Hamilton*, 660 So. 2d at 1038.

a paved area next to a structure that was partially enclosed by a fence — This sentence provides the specific facts from one case that help show how the court defined curtilage.
and a brick wall qualified as curtilage. *Id*. Similarly, a fenced yard that had a 10- to 15-foot gap in the fencing to make room for a boat and trailer was deemed curtilage. *Chambers v. State*, 700 So. 2d 441, 442 — The next two sentences provide fact-specific holdings from additional applicable cases. They further show how the courts define curtilage.
(Fla. Dist. Ct. App. 1997). And a yard with a chain link fence around it, with an opening for the driveway, also was curtilage. *Dubose v. State*, 210 So. 3d 641, 653–54 (Fla. 2017). Courts have recognized that, as a — This sentence explains the court's reasoning for the holding in the previous sentence.
practical matter, a property owner has an interest in maintaining convenient access to his property. *Id*. But an unfenced area that is bordered only by "several unevenly spaced trees" does not have an enclosure suf- — This sentence provides an example to contrast with the previous three examples. Giving examples of what curtilage is and is not helps the reader understand the boundaries of the law. Every sentence in the Explanation section is followed by a citation to a case.
ficient to support a burglary conviction. *Hamilton*, 660 So. 2d at 1042.

C. Tailor the Level of Detail to Reflect Each Case's Importance

i. Using Multiple Case Examples

The amount of detail provided in the Explanation about a particular case should reflect the importance of that case to the outcome of your legal issue. An Explanation section should describe only those case details that are relevant to an anchor. Most anchors can be illustrated through brief case descriptions of one or two sentences per case that include only the details of the cases that are relevant to the anchor.

In the paragraph above, the *Chambers* case is described in two sentences, and the *DeGeorge*, *Hamilton*, and *Dubose* cases are each described in a single sentence. Every detail about the facts, holding, and reasoning is directly relevant to the anchors being illustrated in the paragraph. This paragraph illustrates two anchors: whether the enclosure has openings for entering and exiting the property and whether the enclosure is irregular or fortifying.

Using multiple case examples is helpful and common. In the following excerpt of an Explanation section, Justice Anthony Kennedy used four case examples to explain the law supporting the decision in the landmark case, *Obergefell v. Hodges*, which held that same-sex couples are entitled to the fundamental right to marry.

[T]he Court has long held the right to marry is protected by the Con- — Broad topic sentence
stitution. In *Loving v. Virginia*, which invalidated bans on interracial unions, a unanimous Court held marriage is "one of the vital personal — The following three sentences describe the relevant facts, holdings, and reasoning of three key cases: *Loving*, *Zablocki*, and *Turner*.
rights essential to the orderly pursuit of happiness by free men." 388 U.S. 1, 12 (1967). The Court reaffirmed that holding in *Zablocki v. Redhail*, which held the right to marry was burdened by a law prohibiting fathers who were behind on child support from marrying. 434 U.S. 374, 384 (1978). The Court again applied this principle in *Turner v. Safley*, which held the right to marry was abridged by regulations limiting the privilege of prison inmates to marry. 482 U.S. 78, 95 (1987). Over time and in other contexts, the Court has reiterated that the

right to marry is fundamental under the Due Process Clause. *See, e.g.,* ——The last sentence describes how broadly the holding applies by citing five supporting cases.
M.L.B. v. S.L.J., 519 U.S. 102, 116 (1996); *Cleveland Bd. of Ed. v. LaFleur*, 414 U.S. 632, 639–640 (1974); *Griswold v. Connecticut*, 381 U.S. 479 (1965); *Skinner v. Oklahoma ex rel. Williamson*, 316 U.S. 535, 541 (1942); *Meyer v. Nebraska*, 262 U.S. 390, 399 (1923).[5]

ii. Writing a Single Case Illustration

A longer case illustration, where a single case is discussed for an entire paragraph or more, is necessary only when a seminal case controls an issue or a single authority is particularly important and on point. For instance, if you are analyzing a state law issue, and the state's highest court has issued only one opinion on the matter, a longer case illustration paragraph may be necessary to help your reader understand the legal issue. To determine whether your issue is controlled by a seminal or particularly important case, ask the following questions:

- Is there a case that dominates the field of this legal issue due to its weight of authority or recency?
- Would the typical legal reader expect an in-depth discussion of this case?
- Would the document be incomplete without an in-depth discussion of this case?

If you answer "yes" to any of these questions, then you have a seminal or particularly important case that will require a longer case illustration.

Once you have identified a case that deserves an illustration of more than a sentence or two, create a short outline before drafting your paragraph by identifying the fundamental pieces of the case illustration: the holding, key facts, background, and reasoning. Make sure that each piece is relevant to your legal question.

After you identify and review these relevant pieces, draft a topic sentence that summarizes the main point of the case illustration. Usually, the main point will include the holding for context and broadly describe the anchor that is relevant to your legal question. After the topic sentence, describe the specific facts, background, and reasoning that explain how and why the court reached its holding. Use your judgment to explain the case in the easiest possible terms to your reader. But take care to provide the holding before the relevant facts and reasoning. A fact likely will seem out of context if its relation to the outcome of the case is not clear from the start. A simple case illustration looks like the following example:

The area surrounding a residence is curtilage when it contains "some ——Topic sentence with holding on key issue
form of an enclosure." *State v. Hamilton*, 660 So. 2d 1038, 1044 (Fla. 1995). The surrounding area in *Hamilton* did not have a fence, but merely ——Key facts with specific details for support
contained several unevenly spaced trees, which was insufficient to sup-

---

5. *Obergefell v. Hodges*, 135 S. Ct. 2584, 2598 (2015).

port a burglary conviction. *Id.* at 1046. The enclosure requirement — Key background for establishes where boundaries to a home start and end. *Id.* Florida's bur- reasoning glary law requires that curtilage be enclosed by more than sporadic trees, — More detailed reasoning but it does not require a complete enclosure. *Id.* To hold otherwise could lead to second-degree felony convictions for individuals who enter an — More reasoning, justifying open yard around a home, without the owner's consent, to merely pick a why the opposite holding piece of fruit from a tree on the property. *Id.* at 1045. is untenable

Some case illustrations will need more depth. For instance, in the free speech case *Morse v. Frederick*, Chief Justice Roberts wrote a long case illustration for the landmark decision in *Tinker v. Des Moines Independent Community School District*. Writing a description of *Tinker* was an obvious choice. The 1969 case helped define students' First Amendment rights and set forth the standard for determining when a school's disciplinary actions are unconstitutional. Any legal question that deals with students' First Amendment rights would likely warrant an explanation of *Tinker*. Chief Justice Roberts wrote two paragraphs for his *Tinker* illustration, each with a topic sentence.

Here's the first topic sentence: "In *Tinker*, this Court made clear that 'First Amendment rights, applied in light of the special characteristics of the school environment, are available to teachers and students.'"[6] The sentence introduces the case name and provides a broad summary of a major principle from the case. The sentence sets the stage for the more specific information that follows.

And here's the second topic sentence: "*Tinker* held that student expression may not be suppressed unless school officials reasonably conclude that it will 'materially and substantially disrupt the work and discipline of the school.'"[7] This sentence is more specific than the first topic sentence, and it summarizes the case's holding. A holding can be a strong opening sentence for a case illustration paragraph because it does exactly what a topic sentence should. The holding tells the reader the main point of the paragraph and provides a summary of the case's outcome that sets the stage for the facts and reasoning to come.

Take a look at the various parts of Chief Justice Roberts' complete *Tinker* case illustration:

In *Tinker*, this Court made clear that "First Amendment rights, applied — Topic sentence with broad in light of the special characteristics of the school environment, are holding available to teachers and students." 393 U.S. at 506. *Tinker* involved — Key facts listed chronologically a group of high school students who decided to wear black armbands to protest the Vietnam War. School officials learned of the plan and then adopted a policy prohibiting students from wearing armbands. When several students nonetheless wore armbands to school, they

---

6. *Morse*, 551 U.S. at 403.
7. *Id.*

were suspended. *Id.* at 504. The students sued, claiming that their — Key procedural background fact
First Amendment rights had been violated, and this Court agreed.

Tinker held that student expression may not be suppressed unless — Topic sentence, providing the
school officials reasonably conclude that it will "materially and sub- holding
stantially disrupt the work and discipline of the school." *Id.* at 513.
The essential facts of *Tinker* are quite stark, implicating concerns at the — A more specific topic sentence to
heart of the First Amendment. The students sought to engage in po- introduce the facts of the case
litical speech, using the armbands to express their "disapproval of the — Key facts with specific quotes for
Vietnam hostilities and their advocacy of a truce, to make their views support
known, and, by their example, to influence others to adopt them."
Id. at 514. Political speech, of course, is "at the core of what the First
Amendment is designed to protect." *Virginia v. Black*, 538 U.S. 343, 365 — Key background from a more
(2003). The only interest the Court discerned underlying the school's recent case that explains an
actions was the "mere desire to avoid the discomfort and unpleasant- important principle and uses
ness that always accompany an unpopular viewpoint," or "an urgent quotations to signify important
wish to avoid the controversy which might result from the expression." language
Tinker, 393 U.S. at 509, 510. That interest was not enough to justify — Reasoning, again quoting key
banning "a silent, passive expression of opinion, unaccompanied by language
any disorder or disturbance." *Id.* at 508.[8]

Notice how Chief Justice Roberts used a rule from *Virginia v. Black* in the
middle of his *Tinker* illustration. That's because an explanation of only one
case usually makes for an incomplete explanation of the law. As a result, use
case illustration paragraphs for only the most important cases. Most—if not
all—of the paragraphs in the Explanation section should use multiple cases to
explain how courts apply the anchors in different contexts.

In the next example, Minnesota Supreme Court Justice Natalie Hudson
devotes a few paragraphs to explaining the closest relevant case to support
her holding that an air-powered BB gun is not a "firearm" under a specific
Minnesota statute. Minnesota courts had not previously considered the question, and the case she illustrates, *State v. Seifert*, defines "firearm" but under a
different, related statute.

No Minnesota appellate court has defined the term "firearm" in — Topic sentence introducing case
section 609.165. We have, however, construed the word "firearm" in illustration with historical context
the context of the definition of a "dangerous weapon" under Minn.
Stat. § 609.02. *See State v. Seifert*, 256 N.W.2d 87, 87–88 (Minn. 1977).

In *Seifert*, we held that a .177–caliber CO_2 BB pistol was a "firearm" un- — Topic sentence with broad holding
der Minn. Stat. § 609.02(6) (1974). Seifert pleaded guilty to aggravat- — Key procedural background fact
ed robbery, Minn. Stat. § 609.245 (1974), which required proof that he
was "armed with a dangerous weapon or inflict[ed] bodily harm," while — Key part of controlling rule for
committing a robbery. *Seifert*, 256 N.W.2d at 88. Minnesota Statutes that case

8. *Id.* at 403-04.

Section 609.02, subdivision 6, defined "dangerous weapon" as "any *firearm*, whether loaded or unloaded, or any device designed as a weapon and capable of producing death or great bodily harm...." (Emphasis added.) At the plea hearing, Seifert admitted possessing an unloaded CO_2 BB pistol during the robbery; he also admitted that, to the best of his knowledge, his accomplice used a firearm. *Seifert*, 256 N.W.2d at 88. The district court accepted Seifert's plea and sentenced him to a minimum term of one year and one day in prison under Minnesota Statute Section 609.11 (1975), which permitted imposition of a minimum sentence in certain situations in which the offender "possess[ed] a firearm or used a dangerous weapon at the time of the offense." *Seifert*, 256 N.W.2d at 88. Seifert later challenged both his plea and the imposition of the minimum sentence on the ground that he did not possess a dangerous weapon during the robbery because his BB gun was not a "firearm." *Id*. The district court denied relief, holding that the gun Seifert admitted using was clearly a "dangerous weapon," and we affirmed. *Id*. In explaining our decision, we stated:

— Key facts and background with specific quotes to show the court's rationale

— Procedural history with the specific holding

> The gun used by defendant might also qualify as a dangerous weapon under the alternative test contained in [section] 609.02 ("any device designed as a weapon and capable of producing death or great bodily harm"). In any event, defendant also admitted at the change-of-plea hearing that to the best of his knowledge the gun his accomplice used was a firearm. In conclusion, defendant's testimony at the change-of-plea hearing provided a sufficient factual basis for the plea....

— A quote of the key reasoning

Id.[9]

This longer case description of *Seifert* was helpful and necessary because no other precedent existed. If only one or two binding cases are relevant to your legal issue, an illustration of each might make the most sense for the Explanation section of your legal document.

But for many legal issues, the body of relevant case law includes numerous cases with detailed fact patterns and in-depth reasoning. If that's the case, an Explanation with several examples from several cases makes the most sense. See the example Explanations—highlighted in pink in the memos on pages 105, 109, and 113—for more guidance.

---

9. *State v. Haywood*, 886 N.W.2d 485, 488–89 (Minn. 2016).

Checklist for your Explanation Section
Does my Explanation section...

☑ Explain the rules to the reader by identifying the anchors that were the grounds for the courts' decisions in relevant cases on my specific issue?

☑ Use an easy-to-follow organization by beginning the explanation of each anchor with a broad description of the anchor and then narrowing to describe specific facts, holdings, and reasoning?

☑ Illustrate each anchor using several cases, including examples that show both sides of the legal issue, if possible?

☑ Tailor the level of detail used to illustrate each case to that case's importance?

☑ Use only the relevant details from the cases, rather than writing long case illustrations of every case, but with sufficient clarity that the reader will understand what is important about each case without having to read it?

☑ Discuss the cases in past tense?

☑ Cite authority after every sentence?

Writing an Objective Analysis Section

The Analysis section is the most complex part of any CREAC. The Analysis is also known as the Application or the Argument, but its purpose is always the same—to describe in detail the legal reasoning that supports the Conclusion. The Conclusion is your answer, and the Analysis is the place where you show your work for how you reached that answer.

The Analysis proves that the Conclusion is correct by demonstrating how to apply the relevant law to the facts of your case. Most Analysis sections have three parts: the core analysis, the counteranalysis, and the resolution. In the first part, you predict how a court would apply the anchors by comparing your case to similar cases. This comparison, called analogizing and distinguishing, shows the reader that you have legal support for your Conclusion.

The second part, called the counteranalysis, describes the strongest counterarguments—those arguments that do not support the Conclusion. It shows the reader that you have considered the possibility that the opposite conclusion is correct. Finally, the resolution describes why the arguments in the core analysis are stronger than those in the counteranalysis and refutes the strongest counterarguments.

Because the Analysis section in a legal memorandum is objective, providing an impartial examination of the facts and law is crucial. This objective analysis allows you to make sure not only that you reach the correct Conclusion but also that you inform your reader of alternate interpretations of the facts and law.

The following two structures can serve as an outline for many objective Analysis sections. How much detail you need depends on the complexity of the question your memo addresses:

Core Analysis Section in a Short Memo

First paragraph:
- Broad thesis sentence stating answer to legal question and summarizing strongest arguments based on the anchors
- Two or more sentences describing factual and legal support for the most important argument, specifying how the argument supports the Conclusion by analogizing and distinguishing relevant cases

Second paragraph:
- Topic sentence summarizing how additional argument(s) supports the Conclusion
- Two or more sentences describing factual and legal support for the argument(s), specifying how the argument supports the Conclusion by analogizing and distinguishing relevant cases

Repeat in successive paragraphs for each argument that supports the Conclusion until all supporting arguments have been discussed.

Counteranalysis and Resolution in a Short Memo

- Topic sentence summarizing counterargument(s) regarding anchor that weighs against the Conclusion
- One or more sentences describing factual and legal support for counterargument(s), specifying how the argument is contrary to the Conclusion by analogizing and distinguishing relevant cases
- One or more sentences refuting counterargument(s) and describing why the arguments in the core analysis are stronger than the counter-argument(s)

Note: When the counteranalysis is brief, the counteranalysis and resolution can be combined in a single paragraph. The resolution may be stated in a single sentence that summarizes why the arguments overall support the Conclusion.

OR

Core Analysis Section in a Complex Memo

First paragraph:
- Broad thesis sentence stating Conclusion
- Summary of arguments that relate to anchors and support the Conclusion in the order they will be discussed

Second paragraph:
- Topic sentence summarizing how the most important argument supports the Conclusion
- Two or more sentences describing factual and legal support for the argument, specifying how the argument supports the Conclusion by analogizing and distinguishing relevant cases

Repeat in successive paragraphs for each argument that supports the Conclusion until all supporting arguments have been discussed.

Counteranalysis in a Complex Memo

- Topic sentence summarizing counterarguments regarding anchor that weighs against the Conclusion
- One or more sentences describing legally significant facts from the present case and legal support for first counterargument, specifying

how the argument is unfavorable to the Conclusion by analogizing and distinguishing relevant cases

Repeat in successive paragraphs for each argument that weighs against the Conclusion until all counterarguments have been discussed.

Resolution in a Complex Memo

- Topic sentence refuting counterarguments and describing why the arguments in the core analysis are stronger than the counterarguments
- One or more sentences describing factual and legal support for the refutation of the counterargument, including summarizing previous arguments, analogizing and distinguishing relevant cases, or both
- If needed, one or more additional sentences summarizing support for Conclusion

---

Writing an Objective Analysis Section

1. Start with a broad thesis.
2. Use topic sentences to organize your analysis.
3. Analogize and distinguish.
4. Detail counterarguments; then refute and resolve them.

---

1. STEP ONE: START WITH A BROAD THESIS

The Analysis should start with your thesis. Your thesis is a broad summary of your Conclusion and best reasoning. By making your thesis the first sentence of your Analysis, you will remind the reader exactly what your Analysis is going to prove.

The thesis in an objective memo frequently begins with the transition word "here" to signal to the reader that you are moving from the description of the anchors in the Explanation to the application of the anchors to your specific case in the Analysis. Your thesis should include your answer to the legal question and the reasons that support that answer. Those reasons will summarize the most important facts from your case and how they fit with the anchors that you identified in the relevant law. The anchors are particularly important in the Analysis section because the focus of the Analysis section is to provide specific factual and legal support for your Conclusion. By focusing on the anchors, you will focus on the most relevant facts and law.

In addition, because the anchors help you focus the Analysis, a strong thesis will summarize all your arguments, as they relate to the anchors, in the order you are going to discuss them. In this way, the thesis provides an outline of the arguments to come. For instance, the following sentence is the Conclusion in the curtilage example:

Miguel Perry's compound would likely qualify as curtilage because a picket fence encloses most of the yard, lending support to Tom Chapman's burglary conviction.

To begin your Analysis section, you can summarize this Conclusion with a similar thesis statement, adding a summary of your best reasoning and focusing on your arguments as they relate to the anchors. You could rework the Conclusion as a thesis as follows:

Here, Miguel Perry's compound would likely qualify as curtilage because the compound has a picket fence and it encloses most of the yard.

The thesis draws the reader's attention to the precise legal question, the answer to it, and two key arguments. It also tells the reader that you are going to discuss the fence first and the enclosure of the yard second. Be sure to describe the arguments in the thesis in the same order that you will discuss them in the Analysis.

The thesis statement above summarizes only two arguments, and they were closely related. But you may write an Analysis in a more complex memo with too many relevant arguments to summarize in one sentence. For a more complex memo, you should devote a paragraph to stating the thesis and listing the arguments. For instance, here is a thesis to begin an Analysis section with three arguments:

Here, Miguel Perry's compound would probably not qualify as curtilage for three reasons. First, only the front yard is enclosed; the back yard is unbounded. Second, the front yard's enclosure is provided by low, uneven shrubs. Last, three breaks in the shrubs allow for entering and exiting the yard.

Whether your thesis requires one sentence or one paragraph, it sets up the remainder of the Analysis where you will discuss each of your arguments in detail.

2. STEP TWO: USE TOPIC SENTENCES TO ORGANIZE YOUR ARGUMENTS

After the thesis, organize your arguments in order of importance. Your arguments—which are based on the anchors—often will mirror the organization of the Explanation, analyzing the anchors in the same order that they were explained in the Explanation. Or you may need to organize your arguments according to the test, elements, or factors from the Rule. Your discussion of each argument (or group of arguments if you combine your discussion of some of the arguments) should begin with a topic sentence. These topic sentences beginning each paragraph provide the backbone for your Analysis section. Each topic sentence should summarize why that argument and the relevant facts from your case support your Conclusion. Think of these topic sentences as miniconclusions that add up to the broad thesis that is the first sentence of the Analysis section.

In the previous curtilage example, the Analysis would begin with the following thesis:

> Here, Miguel Perry's compound would likely qualify as curtilage because the compound has a picket fence and it encloses most of the yard.

The next step is to write a topic sentence summarizing each of the two arguments in the Analysis. Topic sentences begin a paragraph—or complete the paragraph that starts with a thesis sentence—and are followed by detailed arguments that use facts, analogies, and distinctions:

> The compound would probably qualify as curtilage because Miguel Perry installed a picket fence that is 6-feet tall, creating a sufficient fortification.

> The compound would likely qualify as curtilage because the picket fence encloses 90 percent of the yard.

These topic sentences tell the reader how the arguments relate to the anchors and the supporting law and why they support the Conclusion in your case. They summarize the major arguments and do not reference any other cases. Following each topic sentence, the rest of the paragraph should discuss in detail the application of each anchor to the facts of your case.

3. STEP THREE: ANALOGIZE AND DISTINGUISH

After a topic sentence summarizing why an argument supports your prediction, you have to provide factual and legal support. This support comes from drawing comparisons between your case and similar cases. You can draw two types of comparisons: analogies and distinctions.

Analogies show the reader why your case is similar to relevant cases. Distinctions show the reader how your case differs from relevant cases. Analogies are usually more effective than distinctions. An analogy gives the reader an answer, while a distinction shows the reader what the answer shouldn't be. Imagine asking a friend where the pet food store is located. It would be more helpful if she replied, "it is close to your house, just a little further north," than if she replied, "it is nowhere near where you went to high school." The analogy informing you that the store is close to your house helps clarify where the pet food store is located. But the distinction establishing that the store isn't in the vicinity of your former school just removes one of many possibilities. Ideally, you will have both analogies and distinctions in your Analysis. And if you do, you usually will want to use analogies first.

A. Analogize to Similar Cases That Support Your Analysis of an Anchor in Your Case

Analogizing requires you to compare the analysis of the anchor in a relevant case to how the anchor should be analyzed in your case. This comparison involves putting the specific facts, reasoning, and predicted holding of your case next to the facts, reasoning, and holdings of relevant cases. This form of analogical reasoning explains how the anchors apply to your case and provides authority for your Conclusion.

Usually, the cases you should use for analogies are those cases that are binding authority and have an outcome similar to the outcome you have predicted in your Conclusion. There will likely be significant overlap with the cases that you used to illustrate the anchors in the Explanation section. Indeed, the purpose of the Explanation section is to prepare the reader for the legal arguments you make in the Analysis. A case that you illustrated in the Explanation, which will be familiar to the reader, is thus well suited to be the basis for an analogy in the Analysis.

To be effective, an analogy must be substantive, parallel, and specific. This means that the analogy should be tied to an anchor, should compare like with like, and should be narrowly drawn.

i. Substantive

An analogy is substantive if it is closely related to one of the anchors that you have identified. Because the anchors are the grounds or bases for the courts' decisions in relevant cases, an analogy that is not tied to an anchor will not be helpful in predicting the court's decision in your case.

Cases may have similarities that are not substantive. For instance, two cases could both involve plaintiffs named Sofia Nguyen. That similarity, however, would not be tied to an anchor (unless one of the anchors was the name of the plaintiff), so it would not be substantive.

ii. Parallel

An effective analogy must be parallel, meaning it compares apples to apples. An analogy will not succeed if it compares things that are not comparable (i.e., an entire case to a specific person). The first step in drawing a parallel analogy is to compare the same types of information from your case and the relevant case.

TYPES OF PARALLEL ANALOGIES

- **Fact to fact:** The yard in the present case is like the yard in *Chambers* because both yards were almost completely enclosed by man-made fences. The small gap in Perry's fence of 25 feet that left open the property's driveway is comparable to the 10- to 15-foot gap for the trailer and boat in *Chambers*.
- **Reasoning to reasoning:** The court here will likely find that the small gap in the fence for the driveway did not prevent the yard from being enclosed

because driveways allow for access. That reasoning follows *Chambers*, where the court noted that a small gap allowing convenient access to a property does not mean that it is not enclosed because a gap is necessary to enter and exit the property.

- **Holding to predicted holding:** Here, the court will likely hold that the picket fence, even with the small gap, provided "some form of enclosure" for Perry's property. In the same way, the *Chambers* court held that the yard, despite a gap, qualified as curtilage and satisfied the "some form of enclosure" requirement.

The next step is to present these parallel analogies as an argument about your case that uses the analogous facts, reasoning, and holding of the relevant case to support your Conclusion. If your case and the relevant case share similar facts, but the comparable case's holding and reasoning are inapplicable, your analogy will not be effective. Similarly, an analogy that compares the holding in a case to the predicted holding in your case will not be useful unless it also establishes that the underlying facts are sufficiently similar to support the same reasoning. Thus, the Analysis for the curtilage example would include all three of the analogies in the example to show the reader that Perry's yard will likely be treated as curtilage like the yard in *Chambers*.

Notice that the examples above all discuss the present case before the analogous case. Doing so makes the Analysis section, which is focused on arguments about your case, distinct from the Explanation section, which is focused on describing cases that have already been decided. Because you will likely discuss at least some (if not all) of the same cases in both the Explanation and Analysis sections, the organization of the paragraphs and sentences in the Analysis section must be focused on your case to avoid confusing the reader. This organization is a reminder to you and the reader that the purpose of the core analysis is to make arguments that support your Conclusion. Also, notice that the examples above discuss the present case in present tense as the issue has yet to be decided, and the other cases in past tense because they have already been resolved.

In the following example, adapted from *City of Erie v. Pap's A.M.*, the writer draws a detailed analogy between a nude dancing case and a key case that involved draft card burning. The analogy compares the facts, reasoning, and holdings of the two cases to support the conclusion.

Erie's ordinance banning public nudity does not violate the free speech rights of the operator of a totally nude entertainment establishment and satisfies the test in *United States v. O'Brien*, 391 U.S. 367, 377 (1968). One purpose of the ordinance was "to combat negative secondary effects," and "on its face, the governmental interest in combating prostitution and other criminal activity is not at all inherently related to expression." *See Barnes v. Glen Theatre, Inc.*, 501 U.S. 560, 585 (1991).

> This analogy compares the holding from *O'Brien* to the predicted holding to argue that the present case satisfies the test from the earlier case.

In that sense, this case is similar to *O'Brien*. Here, the ordinance prohibiting public nudity is aimed at combating crime and other negative secondary effects caused by the presence of adult entertainment establishments,

> This analogy compares the facts regarding the anti-nudity ordinance to the facts about the draft-card statute.

like Kandyland, and not at suppressing the erotic message conveyed by this type of nude dancing. Similarly, the statute that O'Brien was convicted under made it a crime to knowingly mutilate or destroy a draft card; it was not aimed at suppressing the message of draft resistance that O'Brien sought to convey by burning his draft card.

Put another way, the Erie ordinance does not attempt to regulate the primary effects of the expression—the effect on the audience of watching nude erotic dancing—but rather the secondary effects, such as the impacts on public health, safety, and welfare, which the Court has previously recognized are "caused by the presence of even one such" establishment. *See Renton v. Playtime Theatres, Inc.*, 475 U.S. 41, 47–48 (1986). That purpose lines up with the reasoning in *O'Brien*, where the Court rejected O'Brien's claim that the statute violated his First Amendment rights, reasoning that the law punished him for the "noncommunicative impact of his conduct, and for nothing else." *See O'Brien*, 391 U.S. at 382.[1]

— This analogy compares the reasoning regarding the non-expressive secondary effects of the regulated conduct in both cases.

iii. Specific

Even if an analogy is substantive and parallel, it will not be effective if it lacks specificity. Being specific makes an analogy credible because it shows the reader the comparison is analytically sound. For instance, a writer's comparison of only the outcomes of two cases would lack the detail necessary to make it effective.

- **Lacks specificity:** In *Barton v. Smith*, the plaintiff prevailed. Similarly, the plaintiff should prevail in this case.

This analogy fails because it is not specific. It does not tell the reader why the plaintiff prevailed in *Barton v. Smith*, nor does it tell the reader why that same outcome is appropriate in the present case. Indeed, it is so general that it asks the reader to assume that all of the underlying specifics are the same. Because it does not show the reader those specifics and how they are similar, it is not credible. It sounds like the writer is asserting the plaintiff should prevail in the present case simply because the writer wants it to be so. Obviously, more factual and legal support and specificity are required.

To make an analogy specific, you must harvest all the details from your case and the relevant cases that are necessary to flesh out the analogy. For instance, in the example comparing the yard in the present case to the yard in a relevant case, the more factual details you include about the yard, the more specific and effective the analogy becomes.

- **Lacks specificity:** The yard in the present case is like the yard in *Chambers*.
- **Some improvement:** The yard in the present case is like the yard in *Chambers* because both yards were almost completely enclosed, except for openings for access.
- **Very specific:** The yard in the present case is like the yard in *Chambers* because both yards were enclosed by man-made fences, except for small

---

1. Example based on *City of Erie v. Pap's A.M.*, 529 U.S. 277, 291 (2000).

gaps of 25 feet in Perry's yard and 10- to 15-feet in Chambers' yard that were necessary to enter and exit the property.

Although these examples are a single sentence, you may need multiple sentences to draw an analogy that is substantive, parallel, and specific. An effective analogy between your case and a relevant case may take an entire paragraph to describe.

For example, the following paragraphs, adapted from Justice Kagan's concurring opinion in *Florida v. Jardines*, draw a specific analogy between the facts, reasoning, and holding of the dog-sniffing case before the Court and an earlier case involving thermal-imaging technology.

> The "firm" and "bright" rule from *Kyllo v. United States* governs this case: The police officers here conducted a search because they used a "device...not in general public use" (a trained drug-detection dog) to "explore details of the home" (the presence of certain substances) that they would not otherwise have discovered without entering the premises. *Kyllo v. United States*, 533 U.S. 27, 40 (2001).

— This analogy compares facts to facts to show similarities between the use of a drug-detection dog and a thermal imager.

> The dissent's argument that the device is just a dog cannot change the equation. As *Kyllo* made clear, the "sense-enhancing" tool at issue may be "crude" or "sophisticated," may be old or new (drug-detection dogs actually go back not "12,000 years" or "centuries," but only a few decades), may be either smaller or bigger than a breadbox. Still, "at least where (as here)" the device is not "in general public use," training it on a home violates our "minimal expectation of privacy"—an expectation "that *exists*, and that is acknowledged to be *reasonable*." That does not mean the device is off-limits, as the dissent implies; it just means police officers cannot use it to examine a home without a warrant or exigent circumstance. *See Brigham City v. Stuart*, 547 U.S. 398, 403–04 (2006) (describing exigencies allowing the warrantless search of a home).[2]

— This analogy compares reasoning to reasoning to show that the use of the dog and the imager qualify as a search.

— This analogy compares holdings to show that a warrant is required in both cases.

Justice Kagan shows why the dog's actions also amounted to a search by constructing a detailed comparison between the thermal-imaging device in *Kyllo* and the drug-detection dog in *Jardines*. In the same way, the next two examples of analogies show how to support the opposite conclusion—that a low-flying drone over a rural property did not conduct a search when it took photos of marijuana plants.

> The Defendant revealed sensitive information to authorities by failing to cover the marijuana plants growing in his backyard, in the same way that the defendant in *Gabel* exposed the illegal pornographic files he owned by posting the information on a file-sharing network. Any citizen flying in an airplane or helicopter could look down with binoculars or a zoom lens to see the marijuana plants in the Defendant's

— This analogy lines up key facts from the drone case with comparable facts from a similar case. It then shows support for the conclusion that the drone did not violate the Defendant's objectively reasonable expectation of privacy by describing the analogous reasoning that applies in both cases.

2. Adapted from *Florida v. Jardines*, 569 U.S. 1, 14–15, 33 (2013) (Kagan, J., concurring) (some quotations and citations omitted).

backyard, just like any computer user could gain access to Gabel's pornographic files.[3]

The drone's viewpoint at 115 feet in the air, while somewhat lower than what a plane or helicopter would have, was still higher than the vantage point created by the camera perched on a utility pole in *Nowka*, where the court held that no search occurred because the camera's view was no different from what "any person could see from the public street." The Defendant here does not have an objectively reasonable expectation of privacy that no one could observe his marijuana growing operation from overhead, just like the defendant in *Nowka* had no reasonable expectation of privacy, even though he believed that no one could see his driveway and garage.[4]

— This analogy starts by comparing specific facts. It then shows how the holding and reasoning of both cases match up.

B. Distinguish Negative Cases to Support Your Analysis

After you have written the analogies necessary to provide legal support for each argument, you should consider whether you need to distinguish any relevant cases. Usually, the only candidates for distinction are those cases that are binding authority and have an outcome contrary to your Conclusion. Again, these cases may overlap with cases you used to illustrate the anchors in the Explanation section. To determine whether you need to distinguish a case in your Analysis, consider the following questions:

- Is the case binding authority or one of the most recent decisions on the issue from a relevant court?
- Would a memo reaching the conclusion opposite to your Conclusion likely use the case as support?
- Would not distinguishing the case hurt the credibility of your objective analysis by making it appear one sided?

If you answer "yes" to any of these questions, you should distinguish the case.

The guidelines for effective distinctions are the same as those for analogies. Distinctions should be substantive, parallel, and specific. They can be as short as a single sentence or take an entire paragraph. The first example below concisely distinguishes two cases at once. The second takes the distinction a bit further.

Unlike the plane flying at 1,000 feet in *Ciraolo* and the helicopter flying at 400 in *Riley*, the drone here dove significantly lower, to 115 feet, conducting surveillance in airspace where public navigation was not routine.[5]

— This distinction directly contrasts the specific facts about height to show that the drone was flying low enough that it was not conducting a search.

---

3. *See United States v. Gabel*, No. 10-60168, 2010 WL 3927697, at *2 (S.D. Fla. Sept. 16, 2010).

4. *See United States v. Nowka*, No. 5:11-CR-474-VEH-HGD, 2012 WL 6610879, at *5 (N.D. Ala. Dec. 17, 2012).

5. *See Florida v. Riley*, 488 U.S. 445 (1989); *California v. Ciraolo*, 476 U.S. 207 (1986).

Unlike the sophisticated thermal-imaging device in *Kyllo*, a drone with an attached camera is commonplace. While the *Kyllo* device could scan a garage roof and wall to determine the temperature, the camera attached to the drone is no more sophisticated than the one most Americans have in their cell phones.[6]

— This distinction shows why the facts in *Kyllo* are different from those in the drone case in two ways: the technology is more sophisticated and uncommon.

The next example is a bit more complex. In a dissent in *Florida v. Jardines*, Justice Samuel Alito presented a specific distinction of the same case that Justice Kagan analogized to in her concurrence quoted on page 80:

Contrary to the interpretation propounded by the concurrence, *Kyllo* is best understood as a decision about the use of new technology. The *Kyllo* Court focused on the fact that the thermal imaging device was a form of "sense-enhancing technology" that was "not in general public use," and it expressed concern that citizens would be "at the mercy of advancing technology" if its use was not restricted. 533 U.S. at 34–35. A dog, however, is not a new form of "technology" or a "device." And, as noted, the use of dogs' acute sense of smell in law enforcement dates back many centuries.[7]

C. Repeat for Each Argument

After you have fully supported your analysis of an anchor with the necessary analogies and distinctions, you should move on to the next argument. If necessary, you can write a short summary of your argument or conclusion to transition between paragraphs. You should continue to write paragraphs of this kind until you have discussed all the arguments that support your Conclusion. Each of these paragraphs should have the same structure:

- Topic sentence summarizing how the argument supports the Conclusion
- Legal support through analogy and distinction proving that the analysis of the anchor and its application to your facts are correct

Courts often analogize and distinguish cases to support their decisions. For example, Justice Ginsburg writing for the Court in *Skilling v. United States* focused on the anchors to distinguish numerous relevant cases when an Enron executive challenged his conviction on the basis, among other things, of juror prejudice.

First, we have emphasized in prior decisions the size and characteristics of the community in which the crime occurred. In *Rideau*, for example, we noted that the murder was committed in a parish of only 150,000 residents. Houston, in contrast, is the fourth most populous city in the Nation: At the time of Skilling's trial, more than 4.5 million individuals eligible for jury duty resided in the Houston area. Given this

— Topic sentence summarizing how Anchor No. 1 supports the Court's Conclusion that the jurors were not prejudiced

— Legal support for Conclusion describing comparable facts of relevant case related to Anchor No. 1

---

6. *See Kyllo v. United States*, 533 U.S. 27 (2001).
7. *Jardines*, 569 U.S. at 24 (Alito, J., dissenting).

large, diverse pool of potential jurors, the suggestion that 12 impartial individuals could not be empaneled is hard to sustain.

Support for Conclusion on Anchor No. 1 describing distinguishable facts of present case

Second, although news stories about Skilling were not kind, they contained no confession or other blatantly prejudicial information of the type readers or viewers could not reasonably be expected to shut from sight. Rideau's dramatically staged admission of guilt, for instance, was likely imprinted indelibly in the mind of anyone who watched it. *Cf. Parker v. Randolph*, 442 U.S. 62, 72 (1979) (plurality opinion) ("[T]he defendant's own confession [is] probably the most probative and damaging evidence that can be admitted against him." (internal quotation marks omitted)). Pretrial publicity about Skilling was less memorable and prejudicial. No evidence of the smoking-gun variety invited prejudgment of his culpability.

Topic sentence summarizing how Anchor No. 2 supports the Court's Conclusion that the jurors were not prejudiced

Legal support for Conclusion describing comparable facts of relevant case tied to Anchor No. 2 with parenthetical adding further support

Support for Conclusion on Anchor No. 2 describing distinguishable facts of present case

Third, unlike cases in which trial swiftly followed a widely reported crime, *e.g.*, *Rideau*, 373 U.S. at 724, over four years elapsed between Enron's bankruptcy and Skilling's trial. Although reporters covered Enron-related news throughout this period, the decibel level of media attention diminished somewhat in the years following Enron's collapse.

Topic sentence summarizing how Anchor No. 3 supports the Court's Conclusion that the jurors were not prejudiced

Support for Conclusion on Anchor No. 3 describing distinguishable facts of present case

Finally, and of prime significance, Skilling's jury acquitted him of nine insider-trading counts. Similarly, earlier instituted Enron-related prosecutions yielded no overwhelming victory for the Government. In *Rideau*, *Estes*, and *Sheppard*, in marked contrast, the jury's verdict did not undermine in any way the supposition of juror bias. It would be odd for an appellate court to presume prejudice in a case in which jurors' actions run counter to that presumption. *See, e.g.*, *United States v. Arzola-Amaya*, 867 F.2d 1504, 1514 (5th Cir. 1989) ("The jury's ability to discern a failure of proof of guilt of some of the alleged crimes indicates a fair minded consideration of the issues and reinforces our belief and conclusion that the media coverage did not lead to the deprivation of [the] right to an impartial trial.").[8]

Topic sentence summarizing how Anchor No. 4 supports the Court's Conclusion that the jurors were not prejudiced

Legal support for Conclusion describing facts and reasoning of relevant cases tied to Anchor No. 4

Support for Conclusion on Anchor No. 4 describing distinguishable facts of present case

4. STEP FOUR: DETAIL COUNTERARGUMENTS; THEN REFUTE AND RESOLVE THEM

Typically, at least one anchor, fact, or argument will not support your prediction. Indeed, most memos are assigned because the legal question is a close one—where both sides have viable arguments. An argument that is contrary to your Conclusion provides a counterargument. An Analysis section needs to include a counteranalysis and resolution where counterarguments are explained and refuted.

---

8. *Skilling v. United States*, 561 U.S. 358, 381–84 (2010).

Because the purpose of your analysis is to objectively analyze a legal question, you cannot ignore counterarguments. To be effective, an objective memo must be thorough in its analysis of all relevant arguments on both sides. Failing to include a counteranalysis and resolution hurts the credibility and usefulness of your analysis. A senior attorney or client cannot rely on your analysis if you have not considered all the possible arguments that weigh for and against your Conclusion.

Counterarguments should usually be addressed after you have discussed in your core analysis all the arguments that support your Conclusion. At the beginning of the counteranalysis, you can use a transition like "however," "but," or "in contrast" to signal to the reader that you have moved from the core analysis to the counteranalysis. The organization of the counteranalysis and resolution paragraphs should be similar to that of the other paragraphs in the Analysis section. The counteranalysis paragraphs can have the following format:

Counteranalysis and Resolution in a Short Memo

- Topic sentence summarizing counterargument(s) regarding anchor that weighs against the Conclusion
- One or more sentences describing factual and legal support for counterargument(s), specifying how the argument is contrary to the Conclusion by analogizing and distinguishing relevant cases
- One or more sentences refuting counterargument(s) and describing why the arguments in the core analysis are stronger than the counterargument(s)

Counteranalysis in a Complex Memo

- Topic sentence summarizing counterarguments regarding anchor that weighs against the Conclusion
- One or more sentences describing legally significant facts from present case and legal support for first counterargument, specifying how the argument is unfavorable to the Conclusion by analogizing and distinguishing relevant cases

Repeat in successive paragraphs for each argument that weighs against the Conclusion until all counterarguments have been discussed.

Because the counteranalysis describes the arguments that weigh against your Conclusion, you need to resolve the discrepancy between the analysis and the counteranalysis before restating your Conclusion. If you have raised a counterargument that cannot be resolved, that may be a sign that your memo needs to reach the opposite conclusion. The resolution's purpose is to show your reader why the arguments, when considered together, still support the Conclusion. This resolution may be a sentence or longer, depending on the complexity of your analysis and counteranalysis. In many memos, the resolution is brief because it is based on the arguments that were discussed fully in the core analysis. Starting the resolution with a transition like "but," "yet," or "even so" can help the reader understand the progress of the memo from counteranalysis to resolution. If the resolution requires a paragraph, use the following format as a guide:

Resolution in a Complex Memo

- Topic sentence refuting counterarguments and describing why the arguments in the core analysis are stronger than the counterarguments
- One or more sentences describing factual and legal support for the refutation of the counterarguments, including summarizing previous arguments, analogizing and distinguishing relevant cases, or both
- If needed, one or more additional sentences summarizing support for Conclusion

When the counteranalysis is brief, the counteranalysis and resolution can be combined into a single paragraph. The first few sentences can describe the counterarguments with supporting analogies and distinctions. Then, the resolution can summarize in a single sentence why the arguments overall support the Conclusion. This resolution logically flows to the final Conclusion of the CREAC.

In the curtilage example, the counteranalysis and resolution paragraphs could be as follows:

However, the defendant may argue that Perry's compound should not qualify as curtilage because the gap in Perry's fence of 25 feet is larger than the gap in the fence in *Chambers*. *See* 700 So. 2d at 441. In *Chambers*, the gap in the fence was only 10- to 15-feet wide, which is approximately half the size of the gap in this case. *Id.* — Topic sentence summarizing counterargument and introducing it with a transition — Factual and legal support, including specific reference to distinguishable facts that set up refutation

Although the gap in the present case is larger than the gap in the fence in *Chambers*, the reasoning from *Chambers* still applies. *See id.* "Total enclosure" is not required for curtilage, and the gap in Perry's fence, like the gap in *Chambers*, was necessary for "ingress or egress" to the compound. *See id.* at 442. Accordingly, the yard likely will qualify as curtilage because Perry's fence provided some form of enclosure as required. — Topic sentence refuting counterargument — Legal support for refutation, including analogizing to relevant case — Short conclusion summarizing support for Conclusion

When finalizing the Analysis section of your objective document, see the example Analysis sections in the memos on pages 105, 109, and 113 for more guidance. You can also use the checklist on the next page as a guide.

Checklist for your Analysis Section
Does my Analysis section . . .

☑ Contain the core analysis in support of the Conclusion first, then the counteranalysis, and then the resolution?

☑ Use an easy-to-follow organization, beginning with a thesis statement or thesis paragraph for the core analysis, depending on the complexity of the issue?

☑ Use a transition like "here" at the beginning of the thesis statement to signal the start of the Analysis section?

☑ Organize each argument supporting the Conclusion into paragraphs (keeping in mind that complex arguments might deserve multiple paragraphs, while simpler points can be combined into one paragraph)?

☑ Start each paragraph with a topic sentence that summarizes its main point?

☑ For each argument and in each paragraph, detail specific, substantive, and parallel analogies and distinctions to describe the support for the argument?

☑ Discuss the present case before the comparable cases to make the Analysis paragraphs focused on the present case and distinct from the Explanation paragraphs?

☑ Use a transition like "but" or "however" or "in contrast" and start a new paragraph to signal the beginning of the counteranalysis?

☑ Begin the counteranalysis with a topic sentence summarizing the best counterargument(s)?

☑ Detail the support for the counterargument(s) with specific, substantive, and parallel analogies and distinctions?

☑ Use a transition like "yet" or "still" or "even so" to signal the beginning of the resolution?

☑ In the resolution, describe why the arguments in the core analysis are stronger than the counterarguments?

☑ In the resolution, describe legal support for refutation of the counterargument(s), including summarizing previous arguments, analogizing and distinguishing relevant cases, or both?

☑ Use consistent terms and verb tenses?

☑ Use plain language?[9]

☑ Provide solid support for my Conclusion overall?

---

9. See Chapter 21, "Plain Language," for more guidance.

Writing an Objective Conclusion

A Conclusion should start and end each CREAC to keep the reader focused on your answer to the legal question. Although you will write a specific Conclusion at the start of your CREAC, you do not want to repeat the exact same sentence at the end. The reader does not want to encounter the exact same sentence twice in the same document. Instead, rephrase your Conclusion, making sure to provide a specific reason in support and to keep precise legal terminology the same.

For example, the following Conclusions could start and end a CREAC on the curtilage question.

Opening Conclusion:
Miguel Perry's compound would likely qualify as curtilage because a picket fence encloses most of the yard, lending support to Tom Chapman's burglary conviction.

Ending Conclusion:
Thus, Tom Chapman will likely be convicted of burglary because a picket fence encloses nearly all of the Perry yard, making the compound part of the curtilage of the home.

Both Conclusions should state your overall answer to the precise legal question and provide one or more specific reasons in support. They also will indicate your level of certainty, possibly using a word like "probably" or "likely" to hedge. For complex legal questions, the Conclusion could require a few sentences or take up a whole paragraph.

In *United States v. Windsor*, Justice Kennedy wrote an opinion for the Supreme Court resolving whether same-sex couples who are legally married under state law are deprived of their Fifth Amendment rights to equal protection under federal law by the Defense of Marriage Act ("DOMA"), which defined marriage as a "legal union between one man and one woman." His landmark opinion held that the Defense of Marriage Act was unconstitutional. The analysis begins and ends with Conclusions that serve as an effective introduction and closing, respectively, to the case.

Opening Conclusion in Part IV of the Opinion:

DOMA seeks to injure the very class New York seeks to protect. By doing so it violates basic due process and equal protection principles applicable to the Federal Government. The Constitution's guarantee of equality "must at the very least mean that a bare congressional desire to harm a politically unpopular group cannot" justify disparate treatment of that group.

Ending Conclusion in the Opinion:

DOMA instructs all federal officials, and indeed all persons with whom same-sex couples interact, including their own children, that their marriage is less worthy than the marriages of others. The federal statute is invalid, for no legitimate purpose overcomes the purpose and effect to disparage and to injure those whom the State, by its marriage laws, sought to protect in personhood and dignity. By seeking to displace this protection and treating those persons as living in marriages less respected than others, the federal statute is in violation of the Fifth Amendment. This opinion and its holding are confined to those lawful marriages. The judgment of the Court of Appeals for the Second Circuit is affirmed.[1]

An objective memo analyzing the same issue could similarly use opening and closing Conclusions that restate the memo's prediction in similar, but not identical, terms.

Opening Conclusion in Memo:

The Defense of Marriage Act provision that excludes a same-sex partner from the definition of "spouse" is likely unconstitutional because it violates basic due process and equal protection principles applicable to the Federal Government.

Ending Conclusion in Memo:

Because the DOMA provision excludes same-sex partners from the definition of "spouse," it deprives a person of the liberty guaranteed by the Fifth Amendment.

Checklist for your closing Conclusion
Does my closing Conclusion ...

☑ Differ stylistically from my opening Conclusion?
☑ State my prediction on the legal issue?
☑ Use hedging language if necessary to accurately describe my level of certainty?
☑ Answer the legal question the memo was written to address?
☑ Give a specific reason in support of my answer?

---

1. *United States v. Windsor*, 570 U.S. 744 (2013) (citations omitted).

Putting the Legal Memorandum Together

Incorporating Your CREAC into a Cohesive Document

The office memorandum is a common assignment for law students, new lawyers, and judicial clerks. Memoranda usually answer one or more legal questions about a specific case and make a prediction or recommendation about the outcome of that case. You will typically write a memorandum for your supervisor—whether that person is a supervising attorney, senior judicial clerk, judge, or law professor. But your memo could be shared with a client or with clerks and judges in other chambers. In a law firm where similar legal questions arise in the future, memoranda could be read and adapted for years to come.

This part of the *Handbook* details how to incorporate your CREAC analysis into a formal legal memorandum. You'll start by creating a template for your memo based on how many legal issues you are addressing. Then, you will add a section that describes the facts relating to your legal question. Finally, you will add introductory paragraphs called a roadmap to help your reader follow your analysis, and you will add transitions and headings to make sure your final document is cohesive and clear.

Writing a Legal Memo

1. Create a template for your memo.
2. Outline and draft your Facts section.
3. Draft a roadmap.
4. Create a cohesive document.

Create a Template for Your Memo

The format of an office memorandum depends on the number and complexity of the legal questions you are addressing. The following structure can serve as an outline for most memos that address a single issue, like the memo analyzing the deadly weapon on page 105:

Single-Issue Memos

1. Heading
2. Question Presented
3. Brief Answer
4. Facts section
5. Discussion section with a CREAC
6. Final Conclusion section (optional)

For memos that address more than one issue, the exact structure depends on the type of questions you have been asked, but the following structures can serve as a guide:

Multiple-Issue Memos

1. Heading
2. Question Presented addressing all legal issues
3. Brief Answer addressing all legal issues
4. Facts section
5. Discussion section that begins with a roadmap describing all legal issues and sets up the analysis to come
   a. CREAC discussion section for the first legal issue
   b. CREAC discussion section for the second legal issue
   c. Repeat for each successive legal issue.
6. Final Conclusion section summarizing the Conclusions for all legal issues and the predicted outcome for the case as a whole

Or, when your legal questions cannot neatly be summed up in a single Question Presented, write a Question Presented and Brief Answer for each legal issue, using the following structure as a guide:

Multiple-Issue Memos

1. Heading
2. Questions Presented
   a. Addressing first issue
   b. Addressing second issue
   c. Repeat for each successive legal issue.
3. Brief Answers
   a. Addressing first issue
   b. Addressing second issue
   c. Repeat for each successive legal issue.
4. Facts section
5. Discussion section that begins with a roadmap describing all legal issues and sets up the analysis to come
   a. CREAC discussion section for the first legal issue
   b. CREAC discussion section for the second legal issue
   c. Repeat for each successive legal issue.
6. Final Conclusion section summarizing the Conclusions for all legal issues and the predicted outcome for the case as a whole

1. USE A FORMAL MEMORANDUM HEADING

Once you decide on the basic organizational structure for your memo, create a template for your document. Your supervisor may have a preferred memo format. If so, follow it. If not, format your memo to look readable and professional. Begin your memo with a formal heading. The heading should contain four pieces of information: (1) the recipient's name, (2) your name, (3) the date, and (4) a "re" line that briefly describes the subject of your memo. Here's an example of a formal memo heading. (See Figure 14.1)

MEMORANDUM

To: Supervising Attorney
From: Student
Date: August 1, 2018
Re: Analysis of seller's intent to make binding offer in New York contract
          dispute for client Sandra Lee

QUESTION PRESENTED

Figure 14.1

2. CREATE THE HEADINGS FOR THE ADDITIONAL MEMO PARTS

Next, add headings for each of the additional parts of your memo: (1) Question(s) Presented, (2) Brief Answer(s), (3) Facts, (4) Discussion, and (5) Conclusion. Put into place each of the memo pieces that you have already completed—the Question(s) Presented, the Brief Answer(s), and the CREAC for each legal issue. (See Part II for a review.) Then, you can start to create and fill in the missing pieces.

Outline and Draft
Your Facts Section

The Facts section provides the story behind your legal problem. The Facts section should include all facts that are important to the Discussion section and any background facts needed to pull the story together. Because your goal in writing the memo is to be objective, the Facts section should provide an honest account of what happened. As a result, take care to include all the facts that are important to your Discussion, even if they do not support your Conclusion.

1. IDENTIFY THE IMPORTANT FACTS

Any fact connected to an anchor or included in the Analysis portion of your CREAC should be a prominent part of your Facts section. These facts are legally significant because if they changed even slightly, the outcome of the case could change as well. To identify the legally significant facts, review the anchors from your authorities. Then, review the facts for your case and highlight every fact that is connected to an anchor. Make a list of these legally significant facts; they will form the basis of your Facts section.

2. TIE THE STORY TOGETHER

Providing a list of legally significant facts would not be particularly helpful or interesting. As a result, the Facts section should provide a well-organized story that describes the legally significant facts and how they relate to each other. This story should use (1) background facts, (2) a logical organization, and (3) transitions and topic sentences to tie the story together.

A. Add Background Facts

The Facts section should use background facts where needed to provide context and describe important details. For example, in a memo about whether a yard is curtilage, the fact that the property had two entrances is legally significant. The fact that the owner used one of the entrances to take his boat and trailer out every other Tuesday might not be legally significant, but that detail could help illustrate and explain the legally significant fact about the property's entrances. And the fact that the owner bought the property six years ago is also not legally significant but could be useful to include in the Facts as context and background. In contrast, the fact that the owner had three Labrador retrievers is probably not legally significant or helpful to understanding a legally significant fact and does not provide necessary context, so it should be omitted from the Facts section.

B. Use a Logical Organization, Topic Sentences, and Transitions

Once you have a list of the legally significant facts and essential background facts, consider how to logically organize them into a story. Organizing the facts chronologically provides a good starting point. If you have multiple players or issues in a case, organizing the story by topic might work as well.

Then, break the story down into short paragraphs. Short paragraphs in the Facts section help the reader by breaking up the information into readable chunks. Each paragraph can cover a particular point in time or a specific issue in the case. To help your reader follow the story, use a topic sentence or a transition at the start of every paragraph. Often, the Facts section begins with a date, like "in November 2017" or "on June 2, 2019" and the paragraphs that follow use chronological transitions, like "then," "next," "after," "later," and "finally."

For example, for the memo focusing on curtilage, the following framework would provide a logical organization for the Facts:

¶1 Paragraph describing the alleged burglary, starting at the beginning of the chronology of events
• **Topic sentence:** In November 2017, Tom Chapman visited Miguel Perry's home on a country road in unincorporated Palm Beach County.

¶2 Paragraph describing what happened next, including the arrest
• **Topic sentence:** After receiving a phone call at 8 p.m., sheriff's deputies arrived at the Perry home and arrested Chapman in the yard behind the home.

¶3 Paragraph describing the scene of the alleged crime, including the yard that might be considered curtilage
• **Topic sentence:** The Perry property stretches across nearly two acres, and most of the yard is surrounded by either a white picket fence or shrubs.

¶4 A second paragraph providing more details about the yard
• **Topic sentence:** In addition, the parking area is protected by a 6-foot-high automatic gate.

¶5 Final paragraph describing the current state of the case or a transition to the Discussion
- **Topic sentence:** Finally, on November 18, 2017, prosecutors formally charged Chapman with burglary.

Note that paragraphs 1, 2, and 5 have topic sentences that introduce a time element. The third paragraph has a broad topic sentence describing the yard, and the fourth paragraph starts with a transition that shows the reader that the description of the yard is continuing. Paragraph markers like these make your reader's job easier and help keep your reader focused on the distinct parts of your story.

The next example of a Facts section, adapted from the opinion in Chapter 37, tells the story of a police officer finding a gun on a defendant "by accident" as she helped him by hoisting up his baggy, drooping pants.[1]

Facts

St. Paul police officer Kara Breci and her partner were on patrol on a November 2008 afternoon in a high drug-activity area when they noticed a car parked with its engine idling in a White Castle parking lot. Officer Breci had seen many drug deals, and several things in addition to the location aroused her suspicion that she was witnessing another one. The driver and a man later identified as appellant Frank Wiggins sat in the front seat, and a third man approached and entered the back seat without any food from the restaurant. No one in the car appeared to be eating. The back-seat occupant began to look down at his lap. As the officers walked to the car, they saw the rear occupant drop a plastic bag to the floor. They asked the man what the bag contained, and he replied, "Some weed." Wiggins seemed nervous to Officer Breci while her partner was questioning the rear occupant.

— The Facts section tells the story of the case chronologically. First, it sets the scene by establishing the basic facts of who, when, and where. Then, it explains why the officers stopped the defendant and asked him to step out of the car. The section sets forth the facts in an impartial and straightforward manner.

The officers ordered the men out of the car. Officer Breci directed Wiggins to raise his hands above his head. Wiggins wore loose-fitting jeans, which, when he stood, were hanging down around his knees. Officer Breci decided to pat-frisk Wiggins for weapons. But first, she pulled his pants up. As she lifted Wiggins' pants, she felt a hard object in his front pocket. She asked Wiggins what it was, and he responded that he did not know. The officer surmised that it was a handgun and removed a .380 caliber pistol from Wiggins' pocket.

— Next, the story continues the chronology by describing why and how one police officer searched the defendant.

Because Wiggins had prior violent-crime convictions, the state charged him with possession of a firearm by an ineligible person. Wiggins moved the district court to suppress the gun evidence, arguing that the seizure of

— The Facts section then details the state's criminal case against the defendant and the procedural history that led to the appeal. It also explains the legally significant reasons for Officer Breci's actions.

---

1. Adapted from *State v. Wiggins*, 788 N.W.2d 509 (Minn. Ct. App. 2010).

the car and its occupants was unsupported by reasonable suspicion and that the officer conducted an unconstitutional frisk when she hoisted his pants. The district court denied Wiggins' motion to suppress, reasoning that the officers lawfully approached the car and ordered the occupants out based on their seeing the marijuana, that Officer Breci reasonably chose not to direct Wiggins to reach for his own pants out of concerns for her own safety, and that Officer Breci did not search Wiggins but instead found the gun by accident as she was "help[ing] him get his pants into a decent position."

Wiggins waived his right to a jury trial and submitted the case to the district court on stipulated facts, preserving for appeal his challenge to the stop and alleged search. The district court found Wiggins guilty of possession of a firearm by an ineligible person. Wiggins appeals, challenging the district court's denial of his pretrial suppression motion.

The section ends with a conclusion transitioning to the question in this case: the potential of Wiggins' appeal.

Draft a Roadmap for Complex Memos

At this point, a draft of most of your memo should be complete. The heading, Question(s) Presented, Brief Answer(s), Facts, and Discussion are all in place. The next step is to tie everything together.

Memos that cover more than one issue need one more piece in the Discussion section that ties the CREACs together: an introductory roadmap of the issues. The roadmap can be one or more paragraphs that introduce your reader to the overarching legal issue in your case, the minor issues that are the focus of each CREAC, and how the issues relate to each other. Because the roadmap is an introduction, it will start the Discussion section, preceding the individual CREAC discussions of each issue. And the roadmap should work like a map—giving the reader an overview of the legal issues in the order they are addressed in the CREACs. After reading the roadmap, the reader will understand where the Discussion is headed and the route it will take to get there.

The roadmap should start with the overall Conclusion. It also should include any broad rules that govern all of the issues. These broad rules establish the legal context for the more specific rules in the individual CREACs. A rule in the roadmap should not be repeated in the CREACs that follow. Indeed, a memo rarely includes a rule more than once. Whether there are any broad rules to include in the roadmap depends on the nature of your legal issues. For example, memos analyzing multiple factors under a single legal test or multiple elements of a single statutory provision need to include the test or statutory provision in the roadmap. But some memos may address issues that are sufficiently distinct that they don't share any broad rules. For example, memos analyzing whether certain conduct qualifies as different intentional torts or whether a defendant is entitled to assert multiple affirmative defenses may not have any rules shared by both issues, so the rules would appear only in the CREACs, not in the roadmap.

The roadmap also should provide a summary of the analysis that follows, meaning it will reference the specific Conclusion for every CREAC. The roadmap can be organized with the Conclusions before, after, or on both ends of the broad rules. Organize the overall Conclusion, specific Conclusions, and general rules to prepare the reader for the CREACs to come.

In the example below, the legal question is whether Blackhurst's adverse possession claim will succeed. Adverse possession in Blackhurst's jurisdiction has five elements. This roadmap begins a memo that will address two of the five elements: notice and continuous use. This roadmap puts the overall Conclusion first, then the general rules, and then the specific Conclusions, creating a thesis for the memo.

Discussion

Blackhurst's adverse possession claim is likely to succeed because she continuously used the small parcel for more than five years and her use provided constructive notice to the owner. In California, adverse possession is defined as follows: "Where it appears that there has been an actual continued occupation of land, under a claim of title, exclusive of any other right, but not founded upon a written instrument, judgment or decree, the land so actually occupied, and no other, is deemed to have been held adversely." Cal. Civ. Proc. Code § 324 (West 2018). Land is "deemed to have been possessed and occupied" only where "it has been protected by a substantial enclosure" and "has been usually cultivated or improved." *Id.* § 325.

To establish adverse possession, a plaintiff must prove (1) actual occupation that is sufficiently "open and notorious" to give the owner reasonable notice; (2) possession "hostile to the owner's title," which includes possession that occurred through mistake; (3) a claim by the possessor that the property is "his own, either under color of title, or claim or right"; (4) "continuous and uninterrupted" possession for five years; and (5) payment by the possessor of "all taxes levied and assessed upon the property." *West v. Evans*, 175 P.2d 219, 220 (Cal. 1946). Blackhurst's adverse possession claim will likely succeed because her actions on the parcel, including erecting signs, provided the owner with constructive notice. In addition, her use was continuous because she exerted daily control over the parcel.

> This Conclusion provides a broad summary of the predicted outcome. The subsections that follow will provide more specific Conclusions for each issue.

> The roadmap then provides the broad Rules that govern both issues, beginning with the highest authority. These rules will not be repeated in the individual CREACs.

> The last two sentences provide a Conclusion for each of the legal issues, in the order that they will be discussed, creating a thesis or roadmap for the memo.

Create a Cohesive Document

Despite its many parts, a legal memorandum should be a cohesive and consistent document. A reader should be able to easily follow your analysis from beginning to end. Adding transitions, headings, subheadings, and a separate Conclusion section will help your reader understand how every part of your memo ties together.

1. ADD SUBHEADINGS FOR EACH CREAC IN MULTIPLE-ISSUE MEMOS

For memos that address multiple issues, inserting headings for each CREAC you have written will help guide your reader through your memo. The headings should be concise and straightforward, and they should reference the precise legal issue for the CREAC. Here are subheadings that could follow the roadmap in Blackhurst's adverse possession case. Note how they use similar language.

A. Blackhurst can likely establish the open and notorious possession element of her adverse possession claim.
(CREAC on open and notorious element)

B. Blackhurst can likely establish the continuous and uninterrupted element of her adverse possession claim.
(CREAC on continuous and uninterrupted element)

For short memos, a word or short phrase could suffice as the heading. A Fourth Amendment case that analyzes both "search" and "seizure" could use those single words as the headings. For the Blackhurst adverse possession case, the headings could be shortened to reference just the elements.

A. Open and Notorious Possession
(CREAC on open and notorious element)

B. Continuous and Uninterrupted Possession
(CREAC on continuous and uninterrupted element)

2. ADD A SEPARATE CONCLUSION SECTION IF IT WOULD HELP THE READER

For single-issue memos, the Conclusion that appears at the end of the CREAC provides the only Conclusion you need at the end of the memo. But if you have identified questions that require further research or analysis or have recommendations for next steps, you can note them in a separate Conclusion section at the end of the memo. The following example would work as the Conclusion section in the adverse possession memo analyzing a single element.

Conclusion

Blackhurst will likely prevail in her adverse possession claim because her use of the small parcel was continuous and open. Blackhurst will need to provide any photographs she has of the signs she posted on the property. The next step will be to assess whether Blackhurst's possession was "continuous and uninterrupted" for five years.

For multiple-issue memos, each CREAC will end with a Conclusion on the precise legal issue. Following your discussion of all the issues, you can add a separate Conclusion section that summarizes each Conclusion and includes your prediction for the case as a whole, if you think it will help the reader. A Conclusion section is necessary when the reader needs your help to see how the multiple issues relate to each other and to your overall Conclusion. This section can be a single sentence or it can include a sentence for each issue and a sentence for the overall Conclusion. The following example summarizes the overall Conclusion for the adverse possession case first and then summarizes the individual Conclusions for the two minor issues.

Conclusion

Blackhurst will likely prevail in her adverse possession claim because her use of the small parcel was continuous and open. Blackhurst continuously and consistently used the parcel of land for more than five years. In addition, her installation of the shed and "No Trespassing" signs provided constructive notice of her open use to the owner.

3. REVIEW YOUR ENTIRE MEMO

With the roadmap, headings, and Conclusion in place, the first draft of your memo is nearly complete. Because you might have written the various sections of the memo at different times, review each part and make sure it logically flows to the next section. The goal is to create one cohesive document—not a collection of disjointed parts.

New legal writers often worry that the various sections of the memo create repetition—the Brief Answer, roadmap, and Conclusions can all include similar information. When reviewing the entire memo, read these sections together and try to economize. Make sure that each part of the memo is serving the whole and helping the reader. Use the checklist below as a guide.

Single-Issue Memos

☑ Read the Question Presented and Brief Answer. Does the Brief Answer reference the question and directly answer it by explaining how the facts from the question fit with the law?

☑ Read the Facts section. Does it logically follow the Brief Answer? The Facts section should introduce the parties and describe all the legally significant facts, even those details that were in the Question Presented.

☑ Does the Facts section end with a statement about the current state of the litigation or a transition that sets up the Discussion section and Conclusion?

☑ Does the CREAC fully explain the law and analysis summarized in the Brief Answer?

☑ Do the first four parts of the CREAC—the Conclusion, Rule, Explanation, and Analysis—support and logically lead to the final Conclusion?

Multiple-Issue Memos

☑ Read the Question(s) Presented and Brief Answer(s). Does each Brief Answer reference the question and directly answer it by explaining how the facts from the question fit with the law?

☑ Read the Facts section. Does it logically follow the Brief Answer? The Facts section should introduce the parties and describe all the legally significant facts, even those details that were in the Question(s) Presented.

☑ Does the Facts section end with a statement about the current state of the litigation or a transition that sets up the Discussion section that follows?

☑ Does the Discussion begin with a roadmap that introduces the precise issues in the CREACs and that provides any broad rules?

☑ Does each CREAC begin with a concise, straightforward heading?

☑ Does each CREAC fully explain the law and analysis summarized in the Brief Answer?

☑ Do the first four parts of each CREAC—the Conclusion, Rule, Explanation, and Analysis—support and logically lead to the final Conclusion section for each CREAC?

☑ Does the memo end with a separate Conclusion section that addresses all issues and summarizes the overall Conclusion, if that would be helpful for the reader?

4. REVISE, REVISE, REVISE

With all the pieces in place, the first draft of your memo is complete—but it remains a first draft. Take care to revise and edit your document so it reflects your best work. Review Part IV "Writing Tools for the New Legal Writer" for guidance.

Putting your document aside for a day or even a few hours before you read it again can help you catch errors. Read the document critically and consider whether each section, paragraph, sentence, and word is as strong as you can make it. Reading the document aloud—slowly—is also a good way to catch grammar errors, missed words, and awkward wording. In addition, reviewing a printed copy of your memo will help you catch formatting errors and stranded headings. In a profession where a single mistake can affect your credibility, taking the time to polish your final work product will pay off.

5. REVIEW EXAMPLES

The following pages show three office memo examples. The first is a simple, single-issue memo on a criminal law question. The second example is a more complex single-issue memo addressing an adverse possession question. The third example incorporates an additional question on the same adverse possession claim to create a multiple-issue memo.

Example
Memo 17.1

MEMORANDUM

To: Supervising Attorney
From: Student
Date: June 1, 2018
Re: Whether Sara Willis' carving fork qualifies as a deadly weapon for aggravated robbery charge

---

QUESTION PRESENTED

Under Ohio law, does Sara Willis' carving fork qualify as a "deadly weapon" for an aggravated robbery charge when she swatted a competitor on the back with the 5-ounce fork more than a dozen times and scratched his neck while trying to poke him with the fork's sharp, metal tines?

— This **Question Presented** uses the under-does-when format. It identifies the jurisdiction, the precise legal issue, and the legally significant facts.

BRIEF ANSWER

Probably yes. Under Ohio law, an object qualifies as a deadly weapon when its design, contemplated use, or manner of use make it capable of causing great bodily harm or death. Here, the carving fork could qualify as a deadly weapon for aggravated robbery purposes because by swatting her competitor and poking him, Willis used the fork in a manner that could inflict great bodily harm.

— This **Brief Answer** begins with a direct response to the Question Presented above. Next, it summarizes the three anchors. The last sentence summarizes the reasoning in support of the Conclusion.

FACTS

On May 19, 2018, Sara Willis was brimming with confidence when she entered the PigMania State Championship BBQ & Music Festival in Lima, Ohio. But later that day, when organizers announced that her longtime rival Gus Bitner won the championship trophy, Willis felt cheated.

Willis followed Bitner to the parking lot and confronted him. She accused him of copying her Ruby-Red Righteous BBQ Sauce recipe and claimed he was not entitled to the trophy or the $15,000 in prize money. She was so upset that she was not aware at first that she had her 10-3/4-inch Wüsthof carving fork in her apron pocket.

When Bitner defended his recipe and his championship title, Willis became livid. She pulled the fork from her pocket and started poking the air, ranting about tomato puree, molasses, and apple cider vinegar. Bitner then told her that he uses his grandfather's recipe, and he's been using the same recipe and name for his sauce—Buckeye BBQ—for generations.

Next, Willis lunged at Bitner with the fork. He turned his back, and she swatted him more than a dozen times, all the while saying that he should give the trophy to her. Bitner said that being hit was not comfortable, but it did not cause any bruising or other marks. He turned to try to stop Willis from

— This **Facts** section begins by setting the scene with the date, the main character (the client), and the location. It then tells the story chronologically, using short paragraphs and vivid language.

— The sentences and paragraphs are linked together with temporal transitions like "when," "then," "next," and "finally."

hitting him, but she then tried to poke him with the sharp tines of the fork. She scratched his neck with the first poke and missed on a second try. By then, Bitner had turned toward his car. Finally, he drove off, calling police on his way out of the parking lot.

Bitner left in a hurry, leaving behind the 18-karat-gold trophy and a 5-gallon container of his award-winning Buckeye BBQ Sauce—both of which Willis took with her to her car. But before she could drive away, the police stopped Willis. They arrested her on aggravated robbery charges, recovered Bitner's property, and took the fork into evidence, noting that it was a "deadly weapon" under Ohio law.

The online advertisement for the fork that Willis used states that it is precision forged from a single piece of sturdy, high-carbon steel with a design that ensures a 20% sharper blade. It has two curved tines to hold meat in place for steady carving and a handle contoured for a comfortable grip. Willis bought the fork about a week before the competition.

The last paragraph centers on the issue of the fork, providing a detailed description of the object that is the focus of the memo's analysis.

DISCUSSION

The carving fork likely will qualify as a "deadly weapon" because when Willis swatted and poked her competitor with the fork, she used it as a bludgeon and in a way that was capable of inflicting death. The Ohio aggravated robbery statute states that "no person, in attempting or committing a theft offense," is permitted to "have a deadly weapon on or about the offender's person or under the offender's control and either display the weapon, brandish it, indicate that the offender possesses it, or use it...." Ohio Rev. Code § 2911.01(A)(1) (2018). Ohio law defines "deadly weapon" as "any instrument, device, or thing capable of inflicting death, and designed or specially adapted for use as a weapon, or possessed, carried, or used as a weapon." *Id.* § 2923.11(A).

*This **Discussion** begins with a **Conclusion** that states the precise legal question, gives an answer, and provides a reason.*

*The **Rule** section is organized from broad to narrow. It begins with the governing statute and then provides the statutory definition for a key term.*

An object qualifies as a deadly weapon when its nature or design is calculated to inflict death. *State v. Hicks*, 469 N.E.2d 992, 993 (Ohio Ct. App. 1984). Thus, a gun, even when unloaded, is a deadly weapon because it is designed and constructed to cause death or great bodily harm when used in its ordinary manner. *State v. Vondenberg*, 401 N.E.2d 437, 439-40 (Ohio 1980). The state does not need to prove that a gun could successfully fire a projectile to sustain an aggravated robbery conviction. *Id.*

*The five **Explanation** paragraphs explain three anchors: nature/design, contemplated use, and manner of use. The Explanation begins with a topic sentence describing the legal principle underlying the first anchor. Then, it provides examples from cases to illustrate that anchor. This anchor appears first because it is the broadest of the three anchors.*

An object also qualifies as a deadly weapon when its contemplated use as a bludgeon could cause death or great bodily harm. *Hicks*, 469 N.E.2d at 993. For example, a 3- to 5-pound metal wrench disguised as a gun qualified as a deadly weapon because its use as a bludgeon could cause death. *State v. Powers*, 667 N.E.2d 32, 36 (Ohio Ct. App. 1995). The defendant in *Powers* wrapped a wrench and brush together with two black socks to resemble a gun, and even though the object could not fire a bullet, the law "does not require that an object be used in its most lethal capacity." *Id.* (affirming aggravated robbery conviction where defendant placed object against victim and threatened her).

*The second and third **Explanation** paragraphs describe the second anchor: contemplated use. Again, the topic sentence describes the legal principle underlying the anchor.*

Also, a 5- to 6-inch piece of metal resembling a knife or a screwdriver was a deadly weapon because "if either one were plunged into the victim's neck," it would be "capable of inflicting a deadly wound." *State v. Umphries*, No. 02CA2662, 2003 WL 257410, at *2-3 (Ohio Ct. App. Feb. 4, 2003). And a toy gun made of light- to medium-weight metal that looked like a .25- or .38-caliber handgun was a deadly weapon because it could be used as a bludgeon. *Hicks*, 469 N.E. 2d at 993-94.

> Specific examples from case law illustrate the anchor. The case law examples are concise—limited to those facts relevant to the application of the anchor in each case.

Finally, an object qualifies as a deadly weapon when its manner of use is enough to inflict death or great bodily harm—no matter how innocuous the object might seem when not in use. *State v. Deboe*, 406 N.E.2d 536, 537 (Ohio Ct. App. 1977). A car, for example, could be a deadly weapon, even though it is made for another purpose and not designed to be lifted with one's hands and used as a weapon, unlike other deadly weapons. *State v. Orlett*, 335 N.E.2d 894, 896 (Ohio Mun. Ct. 1975). A baseball bat covered in a spongy material qualified as a deadly weapon when it was used to strike the victim 15 or 20 times, causing bruising on the victim that lasted for weeks. *Deboe*, 406 N.E.2d at 537. And a two-by-four thrown at a victim was a deadly weapon, even though it was not used as a bludgeon and caused only a bruise on the victim that lasted a few days. *State v. Holmes*, 53 N.E.3d 843, 848-49 (Ohio Ct. App. 2015).

> The last two **Explanation** paragraphs describe the third anchor: manner of use. Again, after the general topic sentence describing the legal principle, specific examples from case law illustrate the anchor. The examples in the first paragraph show what is a "deadly weapon," and the examples in the second paragraph show what is not a "deadly weapon," according to the cases.

But a .22-caliber blank starting pistol was not a deadly weapon where the two witnesses to a robbery testified that the defendants never indicated that they intended to strike them with it. *State v. Luckey*, 322 N.E.2d 354, 359 (Ohio Ct. App. 1974). The pistol was incapable of causing harm; it fired a blank cartridge, not a projectile, and "makes a noise and that is all that it does." *Id.* at 356. Moreover, when a defendant had "nunchakus" concealed in his car, the object was not a deadly weapon. *State v. Maloney*, 470 N.E.2d 210, 211 (Ohio Ct. App. 1984) (finding no evidence indicating the device was designed or specifically adapted for use as a weapon but instead that it was used only for lawful purposes). Similarly, an ordinary straight razor was not a deadly weapon because it was not designed, specially adapted, or used as a weapon. *State v. King*, 455 N.E.2d 1327, 1327 (Ohio Ct. App. 1982). In the same way, the car in *Orlett* was not a deadly weapon because the defendant was not using it in a dangerous manner when he started his car at a regular speed in a parking lot, hit an attendant, and carried the attendant 200 feet. 335 N.E.2d at 894.

Here, the carving fork will likely qualify as a deadly weapon because its manner of use and contemplated use mean that it could inflict great bodily harm. Willis' manner of using the carving fork as a bludgeon and stabbing device make it a deadly weapon. First, by stabbing and swatting her competitor, Willis used the carving fork to cause harm. Willis swatted her competitor more than a dozen times and stuck him with the fork, similar to the defendant swinging the bat repeatedly at the victim in *Deboe*. See 406 N.E.2d at 537.

> This is the **Analysis**. It begins with the transition "here" and a thesis, which references the two most important anchors to the memo's analysis. After the thesis, the core analysis starts with the third anchor—"manner of use"—because it provides the strongest argument. The analysis of the anchor begins with a discussion of the relevant facts of the present case and then compares those facts to an analogous case.

Willis also acted threateningly while wielding the fork. She threatened to take the trophy from her competitor, while poking the air with her fork, unlike the *Luckey* defendant, who never indicated he would strike the witnesses with the starting pistol. *See* 322 N.E.2d at 354. And unlike the starting pistol in *Luckey*, which just made noise, the fork can cause harm because it is designed with sharp, steel points. *See id*. Willis' threatening use of the fork makes this case distinguishable from *Maloney*, where the defendant had concealed nunchakus, and *King*, where the defendant had an ordinary razor, because in those cases, the defendants did not use the items as weapons during the events in question. *See Maloney*, 470 N.E.2d at 211; *King*, 455 N.E.2d at 1327.

The next paragraph continues the core analysis of "manner of use," discussing more relevant facts of the present case and then distinguishing cases.

Second, the large fork's contemplated use makes it a deadly weapon because Willis used it as a bludgeon. The fork is hard and sharp with long steel tines. Like the screwdriver in *Umphries*, the fork—if plunged into a victim's neck—is "capable of inflicting a deadly wound." *See Umphries*, 2003 WL 257410, at *2-3. Also, similar to the metal toy gun in *Hicks* and the wrench-brush combination in *Powers*, the carving fork is nearly 11 inches long and made of sturdy, high-carbon steel, which means it could also be used as a bludgeon. *See Hicks*, 469 N.E.2d at 993; *Powers*, 667 N.E.2d at 32.

The core analysis continues here with a topic sentence that makes an argument based on the second anchor: "contemplated use." Then, the paragraph describes relevant facts of the present case and analogizes to multiple cases.

But Willis could argue that the fork is not a deadly weapon because its design and use here show that it is incapable of inflicting death. First, unlike a gun, which is designed to kill, the fork is designed to hold meat on a cutting board, not to cause harm. *See Hicks*, 469 N.E.2d at 993. The fork, at 5 ounces, is also less dangerous than the wrench in *Powers* and the toy gun in *Hicks* because both of those metal objects are heavy. *Id*.; *see Powers*, 667 N.E.2d at 32. The threat of using the wrench and gun was sufficient to classify them as deadly weapons, but here, even though Willis repeatedly swatted her victim and used it as a bludgeoning device, she left no marks when using it in this way.

This is the counteranalysis. It begins with the transition word "but." Then, it describes the strongest counterargument, which is based on the first anchor: design. Specific facts from the present case are distinguished from specific facts in the cases to give the counterargument legal support.

Nonetheless, Willis stabbed the victim twice with an object that has sharp, metal, 5-inch tines, which inflicted a 1-inch scratch on the victim's neck and shows that the fork can cause great bodily harm. Her actions went further than the defendant's in *Umphries*, who had a screwdriver "capable of inflicting a deadly wound" but did not use it against the victim. *See Umphries*, 2003 WL 257410, at *2-3. Thus, the carving fork likely qualifies as a deadly weapon for aggravated robbery purposes because Willis used it in a manner to inflict harm.

This is the resolution. It shows that the core analysis is stronger than the counteranalysis by refuting the counteranalysis and by drawing a distinction between specific facts and reasoning in the present case and those in a key case.

*The CREAC ends with a **Conclusion**. It states the answer to the legal question and provides a reason.*

Example
Memo 17.2

MEMORANDUM

To: Supervising Attorney
From: Student
Date: July 1, 2018
Re: Analysis of open and notorious possession element under California
         adverse possession law for Despina Blackhurst

QUESTION PRESENTED

Adverse possession claims under California law require the plaintiff to prove open and notorious possession. Despina Blackhurst mistakenly believed that she owned a small parcel of land across an alley from where she lives, she stored equipment in a padlocked shed on the parcel, and she erected "No Trespassing" signs on the parcel, all while the owner was out of the country and unaware of Blackhurst's use. Can Despina Blackhurst establish the open and notorious element?

This **Question Presented** uses the multisentence format and starts with a statement describing the relevant law.

The second sentence describes the legally significant facts—without analysis or inference.

The third sentence presents the specific legal issue as a question.

BRIEF ANSWER

Probably yes. For a use to be open and notorious, the adverse claimant must provide constructive notice of the adverse possession to the owner. Blackhurst's shed and signs provided this constructive notice. Thus, Blackhurst can likely establish that her possession of the small parcel was open and notorious.

This **Brief Answer** gives a direct answer. It also summarizes the applicable law and the strongest argument in support of the Conclusion.

STATEMENT OF FACTS

In June 2011, Despina Blackhurst purchased property in North Lake Tahoe from her uncle. As part of the agreement with her uncle, Blackhurst understood that the property included both a large parcel and a smaller parcel across an alley from the larger parcel. The large parcel contained Blackhurst's two-bedroom home.

The **Facts** section begins with a topic sentence and an opening clause with a date that sets up the chronological story.

On the small parcel, Blackhurst installed a shed that contained snow removal equipment. She used a combination lock to secure the shed. In October 2016, Blackhurst discovered that teenagers were hanging out in the shed on the small parcel. She chased them away and changed the lock's combination. Blackhurst then posted "No Trespassing" signs on the parcel.

Concise descriptions of legally significant facts in short paragraphs tell the story behind the case.

In June 2018, the owner of the property adjacent to the small parcel claimed that, according to county records, he owned the small parcel. He told Blackhurst that he had been living in Norway for the past seven years and had been renting out the property, though he said he could not provide a copy of any lease agreements. Blackhurst said she was unaware of any tenants. Now,

Blackhurst seeks to quiet title by proving that she acquired the parcel through adverse possession.

— The section ends with a summary of the current state of the litigation.

DISCUSSION

Blackhurst can likely establish the open and notorious possession element for an adverse possession claim because using the shed and erecting "No Trespassing" signs on the small parcel provided constructive notice to the owner. In California, adverse possession is defined as follows: "Where it appears that there has been an actual continued occupation of land, under a claim of title, exclusive of any other right, but not founded upon a written instrument, judgment or decree, the land so actually occupied, and no other, is deemed to have been held adversely." Cal. Civ. Proc. Code § 324 (West 2018). Land is "deemed to have been possessed and occupied" only where "it has been protected by a substantial enclosure" and "has been usually cultivated or improved." *Id.* § 325.

— The **Conclusion** states the answer to the precise legal question and provides a reason.

— The **Rule** starts with the highest authority. The second sentence builds on the first by providing a definition of key terms.

To establish adverse possession, a plaintiff must prove (1) actual occupation that is sufficiently "open and notorious" to give the owner reasonable notice; (2) possession "hostile to the owner's title," which includes possession that occurred through mistake; (3) a claim by the possessor that the property is "his own, either under color of title, or claim of right"; (4) "continuous and uninterrupted" possession for five years; and (5) payment by the possessor of "all taxes levied and assessed upon the property." *West v. Evans*, 175 P.2d 219, 220 (Cal. 1946). This memorandum addresses only the open and notorious element for adverse possession.

— This **Rule** paragraph begins with the broadest rule from the case law that interprets the statutes cited above. The sentence quotes selective language and provides the elements in a parallel list.

— This transition explains that the memo will address only one element. A transition like this is necessary only when the reader may be confused about the scope of the memo.

The intent behind the open and notorious element is to give the owner actual or reasonable constructive notice of the adverse use. *Nielsen v. Gibson*, 100 Cal. Rptr. 3d 335, 341 (Cal. Ct. App. 2009). To be open and notorious, an adverse use must provide reasonable notice by being "visible to the true owner and others." *Id.* The use must be open, visible, and notorious to the extent "that it will raise a presumption of notice" of the adverse claim. *Wood v. Davidson*, 145 P.2d 659, 661-62 (Cal. Dist. Ct. App. 1944). When an adverse use is sufficiently open and notorious to raise the presumption of notice, actual notice by the owner is not required. *Nielsen*, 100 Cal. Rptr. 3d at 341-42. An owner, therefore, cannot avoid the legal consequences of an adverse use by ignoring it. *Id.* at 342. For example, an owner was held to have had constructive notice even though he was out of the country during the period of the open and notorious use. *Id.*

— This **Explanation** paragraph provides more specific details about the notice anchor, giving an example from one case. Because the case's facts are comparable to Blackhurst's case, this **Explanation** sets up the **Analysis** to come.

An adverse use is sufficiently open and notorious to provide notice when the adverse claimant has enclosed, maintained, and improved the property. *See, e.g., id.* at 341 (noting that notice is a question of fact that "depends on the particular land and its condition, locality, and appropriate

— This **Explanation** paragraph includes two examples from case law that show how courts have interpreted the "notice" anchor. It also sets up comparisons to Blackhurst's facts in the **Analysis** section.

use"). For example, when adverse claimants fenced, irrigated, improved, and built a go-cart course on the property, the possession was sufficiently open and notorious that it "created a presumption of notice to the world." *Id.* at 342. Similarly, adverse claimants' occupation of a property for 25 years, which included improving and making additions, created "reasonable notice that they claimed the property as their own." *Lobro v. Watson*, 116 Cal. Rptr. 533, 536, 538 (Cal. Ct. App. 1974). The improvements, all made at the claimants' expense, included fencing the lot, replacing the roof, and planting trees and flowers. *Id.*

However, a possession of a vacant lot was not sufficiently open and notorious to provide notice where the land was not improved or regularly cultivated and where evidence was conflicting about the extent that the claimants used the property. *Klein v. Caswell*, 199 P.2d 689, 691-92 (Cal. Dist. Ct. App. 1948). The insufficient "slight use" by the claimant in *Klein* included occasionally visiting the property over a 22-year period for picnics, and at one time, asking a neighbor to keep the lot cleaned up. *Id.* But several neighbors who frequently passed the lot said that it always appeared neglected, the same as other unoccupied, vacant lots in the area. *Id.* Claimants also failed to provide notice where they never improved the property, never put up a fence or barrier, and never kept the owners off the property. *Hacienda Ranch Homes, Inc. v. Superior Court*, 131 Cal. Rptr. 3d 498, 503 (Cal. Ct. App. 2011). The claimants' few attempts to establish open and notorious possession included weeding the property and introducing themselves as the property owners at a meeting—actions that failed to notify the owners "of an unequivocal and hostile claim to their ownership interests." *Id.*

> This **Explanation** paragraph provides two contrasting examples to describe uses that did not provide the required notice. A comparison to these facts will serve as a counterargument.

Blackhurst's possession was open and notorious because her conduct provided reasonable notice to the owner of her adverse possession. In particular, Blackhurst raised the "presumption of notice" by installing and maintaining a shed that she kept locked. *See Wood*, 145 P.2d at 661–62. Further, Blackhurst provided notice by hanging "No Trespassing" signs on the shed after discovering that teenagers were using the parcel without her permission. Like a fence or a go-cart course, Blackhurst's shed and signs were sufficiently visible to provide notice to the owner of her adverse claim. *See Nielsen*, 100 Cal. Rptr. 3d at 342.

> The **Analysis** section begins with a broad thesis statement.

> This **Analysis** paragraph shows the reader how Blackhurst provided notice by giving the facts that best support the notice argument and by making a fact-to-fact comparison to *Nielsen*.

The shed and signs showed the owner that Blackhurst was occupying, maintaining, and improving the parcel. Her actions are comparable to those of the successful claimants in *Lobro*, where installing a fence and planting flowers created "reasonable notice." *See* 116 Cal. Rptr. at 536–37. Because Blackhurst's use of the property was visible to anyone who walked by the parcel, a court will likely presume that the owner had notice of her adverse claim. *See Nielsen*, 100 Cal. Rptr. 3d at 342.

> This **Analysis** paragraph begins with a topic sentence and gives a specific comparison to provide legal support. The last sentence compares the predicted **Conclusion** to the *Nielsen* holding.

In addition, Blackhurst's use of the property was active and not occasional. The use goes far beyond the occasional picnic that was an insufficient use in *Klein* and the occasional weeding and single representation of ownership that was insufficient in *Hacienda Ranch Homes*. *See* 199 P.2d at 691; 131 Cal. Rptr. 3d at 503. Moreover, unlike in *Klein*, where the evidence about the claimants' use was conflicting, the evidence that Blackhurst regularly used the shed and attempted to chase trespassers away is undisputed. *See* 199 P.2d at 691.

— A transition shows that more legal support is being offered. This time, the support comes from distinguishing a case that does not support the Conclusion.

Even so, the owner could argue that Blackhurst's shed falls short of the level of improvement necessary to give notice. Blackhurst made fewer improvements to the property than the claimants in *Lobro*, who replaced the roof, made additions, and installed a fence. *See* 116 Cal. Rptr. at 538. And the owner could argue that Blackhurst failed to keep his tenants off the property, like the failed claimants in *Hacienda Ranch Homes*, who did not keep the owners from the property. *See* 131 Cal. Rptr. 3d at 503. Further, the owner may argue that he did not have actual notice of Blackhurst's adverse use because he was in Norway during the five years of her adverse possession.

— The counteranalysis begins with a topic sentence that summarizes the strongest counterargument. Next, the paragraph distinguishes a key case to provide legal support for the counterargument. The counteranalysis then provides an analogy to a supporting case and a final counterargument about notice.

Still, Blackhurst's actions gave the owner at least the reasonable constructive notice that courts require, and any tenancy on the property is in doubt without proof of a lease agreement. Actual notice also is not required, and an owner cannot defeat an open and notorious use by willfully ignoring it and simply claiming that he was out of the country. *See Nielsen*, 100 Cal. Rptr. 3d at 341. The owner here is like the owner in *Nielsen*, who was in Ireland during the period of adverse possession. *See id.* There, the court rejected the owner's argument that he could not have had notice, holding that "[w]hen an adverse claimant is 'in open possession and the true owner fails to look after his interests and remains in ignorance of the claim, it is his own fault.'" 100 Cal. Rptr. 3d at 342. Similarly, here, if the owner had conducted an inspection of the parcel at any time, he would have seen the shed and signs and had notice of Blackhurst's open and notorious possession.

— The resolution paragraph begins with a topic sentence refuting the counterargument.

— Here, the counterargument is refuted by a comparison to the facts and holding of the Nielsen case.

CONCLUSION

Because Blackhurst installed the shed and signs on the small parcel, she can likely prove the open and notorious possession element for adverse possession.

— The Conclusion states the answer to the precise legal issue and provides a reason.

MEMORANDUM

Example
Memo 17.3

To: Supervising Attorney
From: Student
Date: August 15, 2018
Re: Analysis of Despina Blackhurst's adverse possession claim
        under California law

——This multiple-issue memo includes the analysis of a second element under adverse possession law. As a result, this memo includes two Questions Presented, two Brief Answers, a roadmap paragraph to begin the Discussion section, and two separate CREACs— each addressing a precise legal question.

QUESTIONS PRESENTED

I. Whether under California law, Despina Blackhurst can satisfy the open and notorious element for adverse possession when she mistakenly believed that she owned a small parcel of land across an alley from the larger parcel of land where she lives, she stored equipment in a padlocked shed on the parcel, and she erected "No Trespassing" signs on the parcel while the owner was out of the country and unaware of Blackhurst's use.

II. Whether under California law, Despina Blackhurst can satisfy the continuity of possession element for adverse possession when she used the small parcel to store kayak equipment and access Lake Tahoe, left the small parcel vacant and had a tenant for some months of the summer of 2017, but only visited the parcel five times per year.

——This memo adds a second **Question Presented** to address the second element: continuity of possession. These questions use the "whether" format. The jurisdiction is in the first clause, and the precise legal question is in the second. The third part lists four facts that are parallel and balanced.

BRIEF ANSWERS

I. Probably yes. For a use to be open and notorious, the adverse claimant must provide constructive notice of the adverse possession to the owner. Blackhurst's shed and signs provided this constructive notice. Thus, Blackhurst can likely establish that her possession of the small parcel was open and notorious.

II. Probably yes. For a use to be continuous, the adverse claimant must use the claimed property in an ordinary manner appropriate to the property's character. Blackhurst can likely establish that her possession of the small parcel was continuous because she used the small parcel to store kayak equipment and access Lake Tahoe, which shows that she took advantage of the parcel's design.

——These **Brief Answers** respond to the questions in the order they are presented above. The second answer uses a similar organization to the first. It provides a direct answer and then summarizes the applicable law on the continuity of possession element. Then, the answer references the strongest argument in support of the **Conclusion**.

STATEMENT OF FACTS

In June 2011, Despina Blackhurst purchased property in North Lake Tahoe from her uncle. As part of the agreement with her uncle, Blackhurst understood that the property included both a large parcel and a smaller parcel across an alley from the larger parcel. The large parcel contained Blackhurst's two-bedroom home.

——The **Facts** section uses a chronological organization to tell the story of the case. Note how dates are used throughout the section to keep the order of the story clear to the reader.

The small parcel abutted Lake Tahoe and contained a steeply sloping pathway to the lake's edge. On the small parcel, Blackhurst installed a shed that contained kayak equipment. She used a combination lock to secure the shed. An avid kayaker, Blackhurst typically visited the shed five times per year between April and October to prepare for her kayak trips. She would begin her kayak trips by walking down the steep path to Lake Tahoe and launching her kayak at the lake's edge. In October 2016, Blackhurst discovered that teenagers were hanging out in the shed on the small parcel. She chased them away and changed the lock's combination. Blackhurst then posted "No Trespassing" signs on the parcel.

In 2017, Blackhurst enrolled in a summer study abroad program that started on May 1 and ended on August 31. Blackhurst was able to secure a tenant for the months of June and July. She left the tenant the keys to her home, the combination to the shed, and instructions to return the keys on July 31.

In June 2018, the owner of the property adjacent to the small parcel claimed that, according to county records, he owned the small parcel. He told Blackhurst that he had been living in Norway for the past seven years and had been renting out the property, though he said he could not provide a copy of any lease agreements. Blackhurst said she was unaware of any tenants. Now, Blackhurst seeks to quiet title by proving that she acquired the parcel through adverse possession.

DISCUSSION

Blackhurst will likely prevail on her adverse possession claim. First, she can likely establish the open and notorious possession element for an adverse possession claim because using the shed and erecting "No Trespassing" signs on the small parcel provided constructive notice to the owner. Blackhurst also can likely establish the continuity of possession element for an adverse possession claim because her use of the small parcel to store kayak equipment demonstrates continued possession for the ordinary use of the occupant.

Under the California adverse possession statute, "[w]here it appears that there has been an actual continued occupation of land, under a claim of title, exclusive of any other right, but not founded upon a written instrument, judgment or decree, the land so actually occupied, and no other, is deemed to have been held adversely." Cal. Civ. Proc. Code § 324 (West 2018). Land is "deemed to have been possessed and occupied" only where "it has been protected by a substantial enclosure" and "has been usually cultivated or improved." *Id.* § 325.

> This paragraph provides most of the legally significant facts for the continuous possession element. Note how the facts are presented objectively— so that they do not favor Blackhurst or the owner.

> Each paragraph begins with a topic sentence. This final paragraph ends with a brief summary of the state of the litigation.

> The memo begins with a **Conclusion** on the overall issue. It then provides a Conclusion specific to each CREAC. This framework provides a "roadmap" of the analysis to come, and this section is often called the roadmap.

> The roadmap should provide the broad rules that apply to all the issues. These broad rules establish the legal context for the specific rules in the individual CREACs. The broad rules are not repeated later in the memo. Here, there is a broad **Rule** that applies to both CREACs because the memo analyzes two factors of a five-part test.

To establish adverse possession, a plaintiff must prove (1) actual occupation that is sufficiently "open and notorious" to give the owner reasonable notice; (2) possession "hostile to the owner's title," which includes possession that occurred through mistake; (3) a claim by the possessor that the property is "his own, either under color of title, or claim of right"; (4) "continuous and uninterrupted" possession for five years; and (5) payment by the possessor of "all taxes levied and assessed upon the property." *West v. Evans*, 175 P.2d 219, 220 (Cal. 1946).

*— Note how the **Rule** begins with the broad rule and then provides more narrow rules that logically follow.*

I. Open and notorious possession

*— Headings that summarize the **Conclusion** on each legal issue help guide the reader through the multiple-issue memo.*

Blackhurst can likely establish that her possession of the small parcel was open and notorious because she installed a shed and signs. To be open and notorious, an adverse use must provide reasonable notice by being "visible to the true owner and others." *Nielsen v. Gibson*, 100 Cal. Rptr. 3d 335, 341 (Cal. Ct. App. 2009). The use must be open, visible, and notorious to the extent "that it will raise a presumption of notice" of the adverse claim. *Wood v. Davidson*, 145 P.2d 659, 661–62 (Cal. Dist. Ct. App. 1944). The intent behind the open and notorious element is to give the owner actual or reasonable constructive notice of the adverse use. *Nielsen*, 100 Cal. Rptr. 3d at 341.

*— Note the differences between this memo and the single-issue memo on page 109. The **Conclusion** is worded differently than in the roadmap to avoid repetition, and the **Rule** statement addresses the rule for the precise legal issue, rather than the broad rule for adverse possession, which appears in the roadmap.*

When an adverse use is sufficiently open and notorious to raise the presumption of notice, actual notice by the owner is not required. *Id.* at 341–42. An owner, therefore, cannot avoid the legal consequences of an adverse use by ignoring it. *Id.* at 342. For example, an owner was held to have had constructive notice even though he was out of the country during the period of the open and notorious use. *Id.*

*— This **Explanation** section explains what open and notorious means under California law. The section uses specific facts from case law to first explain what is open and notorious. Then, in the third paragraph, the Explanation illustrates what is not open and notorious.*

An adverse use is sufficiently open and notorious to provide notice when the adverse claimant has enclosed, maintained, and improved the property to determine whether the possession was open and notorious. *See, e.g., id.* at 341 (noting that notice is a question of fact that "depends on the particular land and its condition, locality, and appropriate use"). For example, when adverse claimants fenced, irrigated, improved, and built a go-cart course on the property, the possession was sufficiently open and notorious that it "created a presumption of notice to the world." *Id.* at 342. Similarly, adverse claimants' occupation of a property for 25 years, which included improving and making additions, created "reasonable notice that they claimed the property as their own." *Lobro v. Watson*, 116 Cal. Rptr. 533, 538 (Cal. Ct. App. 1974). The improvements, all made at the claimants' expense, included fencing the lot, replacing the roof, and planting trees and flowers. *Id.*

However, a possession of a vacant lot was not sufficiently open and notorious to provide notice where the land was not improved or regularly cultivated and where evidence was conflicting about the extent that the claimants used the property. *Klein v. Caswell*, 199 P.2d 689, 691–92 (Cal. Dist. Ct. App. 1948). The insufficient "slight use" by the claimants in *Klein* included occasionally visiting the property over a 22-year period for picnics, and at one time, asking a neighbor to keep the lot cleaned up. *Id.* But several neighbors who frequently passed the lot said that it always appeared neglected, the same as other unoccupied, vacant lots in the area. *Id.* Claimants also failed to provide notice where they never improved the property, never put up a fence or barrier, and never kept the owners off the property. *Hacienda Ranch Homes, Inc. v. Superior Court*, 131 Cal. Rptr. 3d 498, 503 (Cal. Ct. App. 2011). The claimants' few attempts to establish open and notorious possession included weeding the property and introducing themselves as the property owners at a meeting—actions that failed to notify the owners "of an unequivocal and hostile claim to their ownership interests." *Id.*

Blackhurst's possession was open and notorious because her conduct provided reasonable notice to the owner of her adverse possession. In particular, Blackhurst raised the "presumption of notice" by installing and maintaining a shed that she kept locked. *See Wood*, 145 P.2d at 661–62. Further, Blackhurst provided notice by hanging "No Trespassing" signs on the shed after discovering that teenagers were using the parcel without her permission. Like a fence or a go-cart course, Blackhurst's shed and signs were sufficiently visible to provide notice to the owner of her adverse claim. *See Nielsen*, 100 Cal. Rptr. 3d at 342.

The shed and signs showed the owner that Blackhurst was occupying, maintaining, and improving the parcel. Her actions are comparable to those of the successful claimants in *Lobro*, where installing a fence and planting flowers created "reasonable notice." *See* 116 Cal. Rptr. at 536–37. Because Blackhurst's use of the property was visible to anyone who walked by the parcel, a court will likely presume that the owner had notice of her adverse claim. *See Nielsen*, 100 Cal. Rptr. 3d at 342.

In addition, Blackhurst's use of the property was active and not occasional. The use goes far beyond the occasional picnic that was an insufficient use in *Klein* and the occasional weeding and single representation of ownership that was insufficient in *Hacienda Ranch Homes*. *See* 199 P.2d at 691; 131 Cal. Rptr. 3d at 503. Moreover, unlike in *Klein*, where the evidence about the claimants' use was conflicting, the evidence that Blackhurst regularly used the shed and attempted to chase trespassers away is undisputed. *See* 199 P.2d at 691.

Even so, the owner could argue that Blackhurst's shed falls short of the level of improvement necessary to give notice. Blackhurst made fewer

The **Analysis** for this issue is the same in the single- and multiple-issue memos. Both begin with a strong thesis statement that summarizes the analysis to come, and both use topic sentences at the start of each paragraph to summarize each major point.

The **Analysis** section provides the core analysis first, then the counteranalysis, and then a resolution to resolve the discrepancies between the two.

improvements to the property than the claimants in *Lobro*, who replaced the roof, made additions, and installed a fence. *See* 116 Cal. Rptr. at 538. And he could argue that Blackhurst failed to keep his tenants off the property, like the failed claimants in *Hacienda Ranch Homes*, who did not keep the owners from the property. *See* 131 Cal. Rptr. 3d at 503. Further, the owner may argue that he did not have actual notice of Blackhurst's adverse use because he was in Norway during the five years of her adverse possession.

Still, Blackhurst's actions gave the owner at least the reasonable constructive notice that courts require, and any tenancy on the property is in doubt without proof of a lease agreement. Actual notice also is not required, and an owner cannot defeat an open and notorious use by willfully ignoring it and simply claiming that he was out of the country. *See Nielsen*, 100 Cal. Rptr. 3d at 341. The owner here is like the owner in *Nielsen*, who was in Ireland during the period of adverse possession. *See id.* There, the court rejected the owner's argument that he could not have had notice, holding that "[w]hen an adverse claimant is 'in open possession and the true owner fails to look after his interests and remains in ignorance of the claim, it is his own fault.'" *Id.* at 342. Similarly, here, if the owner had conducted an inspection of the parcel at any time, he would have seen the shed and signs and had notice of Blackhurst's open and notorious possession.

Thus, because she installed the shed and signs on the small parcel, Blackhurst will likely establish the open and notorious element. — The **Conclusion** provides an answer to the precise legal question and a specific reason in support.

II. Continuous and uninterrupted possession

Because Blackhurst regularly used the small parcel to prepare for her regular kayak outings, she likely will establish continuous possession. — The **Conclusion** here states the answer for the continuity element and provides a reason. To establish adverse possession, an individual must demonstrate continuous and uninterrupted possession for five years. *Cal. Md. Funding, Inc. v. Lowe*, 44 Cal. Rptr. 2d 784, 787 (Cal. Ct. App. 1995). — This **Rule** statement summarizes the rule for the continuity element.

Courts will examine a claimant's intent to determine whether the use amounts to continuous possession. *See Montgomery & Mullen Lumber Co. v. Quimby*, 128 P. 402, 404 (Cal. 1912); *Merrill v. Hooper*, 13 P.2d 786, 787 (Cal. Dist. Ct. App. 1932). If a claimant demonstrates the intent to abandon the property, continuous occupation cannot be found. *Merrill*, 13 P.2d at 787. The claimant's actions in *Merrill*, for example, did not evince "any intention of abandonment" over a period of six years. *Id.* During that time, the claimant rented the property first as a store, then as a cigar factory, and later to tenants whom she was forced to evict. *Id.* Despite the property's vacancy, the court found that because the claimant kept the property locked and advertised for a new tenant, she demonstrated continuous possession. *Id.; see also Quimby*, 128 P.2d at 404 (holding that temporary periods of vacancy between tenancies will not destroy the claimant's continuous possession). — This **Explanation** section illustrates what continuous possession means under California law. The first paragraph explains the anchor of intent, and it uses three cases to provide a comprehensive explanation of the law.

In addition, courts will find continuous use when a claimant uses a property for its "ordinary" use, which "means a use appropriate to the location and character of the property." *Posey v. Bay Point Realty Co.*, 7 P.2d 1020, 1022 (Cal. 1932). If adversely claimed land is suitable only for particular or slight use, a claimant satisfies the requirement for continuous use if he uses the land accordingly. *Id.* In *Posey*, the court found continuous use even though the claimants pastured their cows on the claimed swampland during only part of the year. *Id.* Because high water often made the swampland inaccessible and high salinity made it of poor quality, the use was "ordinary" and sufficiently continuous. *Id.*

— While the first **Explanation** paragraph begins with a topic sentence about the intent anchor, this second paragraph introduces the anchor of ordinary use. Then the specific facts from the *Posey* case explain what equals ordinary use.

Conversely, possession of two residential lots was not sufficiently ordinary or continuous when the claimant made infrequent visits and only three improvements to the property. *Madson v. Cohn*, 10 P.2d 531, 532 (Cal. Dist. Ct. App. 1932). The claimant in *Madson* visited the property four to six times a year and never fenced or leased the property. *Id.* He planted a few bushes and trees, but the plants were later killed by boys who used the lots to play ball. *Id.* The court found that the evidence did not establish continuity of possession sufficient to constitute adverse possession. *Id.*

— The third **Explanation** paragraph adds to the description of the ordinary use anchor by providing a case that explains what does not equal ordinary use. By using cases with opposite holdings, the writer illustrates the parameters of the law.

Here, a court will likely find that Blackhurst's possession of the small parcel was continuous for two reasons. First, Blackhurst made ordinary use of the shed to store her kayak equipment, and that use was appropriate for the property's character. Second, she demonstrated her intent to continuously use the property by renting the large and small parcels when she was out of the country for a brief time.

— This **Analysis** section begins with a thesis paragraph that summarizes the two major arguments — based on the anchors of intent and ordinary use — and it provides specific factual reasons in support of both.

First, Blackhurst used the small parcel in an ordinary manner consistent with its character. In particular, Blackhurst stored kayak equipment in a shed that she installed and used the sloping pathway to bring her equipment to the lake's edge. Blackhurst did not use the land during the winter months, when the frozen lake would prevent kayaking. Blackhurst took advantage of the parcel's ordinary use by using it to access the lake during the summer months, like the claimant in *Posey*, who entered the land to pasture cows only when it was accessible. *See* 7 P.2d at 1022. Her use was sufficiently suited to the land's character to constitute continuous possession. *See id.*

— This paragraph begins with a topic sentence and then details specific facts that support the ordinary use argument. The writer then connects the facts to supporting case law with a substantive, parallel, and specific analogy. The analogy describes the facts of the present case first, before describing the facts of the analogous case.

In addition, Blackhurst's lease of the property during one summer when she was out of the country establishes her intent to continuously occupy the property. More specifically, when Blackhurst left the small parcel vacant from May to August 2017, she provided instructions to her tenant to return the keys to her. *See Quimby*, 128 P. at 404 (holding that continuity of possession does not require "a continuous personal presence on the lot"). Blackhurst's temporary absence fails to show that she intended to abandon the small parcel, much like the claimant in *Merrill*, whose temporary periods of vacancy

— This **Analysis** paragraph follows the same format as the preceding paragraph: It starts with a topic sentence and then provides more specific details in support.

did not show an intent to abandon possession. *See* 13 P.2d at 787. Moreover, Blackhurst's instructions to the tenant to return the keys to the property demonstrate her intent to resume occupancy of the small parcel.

However, the neighboring owner may argue that Blackhurst failed to establish continuous possession because she visited the property only five times per year. The owner could argue that the property can and should be used during the winter months for winter sports, such as skiing. *See Madson*, 10 P.2d at 532 (finding that infrequent visits to two residential lots were not sufficiently ordinary or continuous).

A clear transition marks the start of the counteranalysis. The counteranalysis includes a detailed counterargument using the facts of the present case and a citation to case law as support.

But an adverse claimant does not have to continuously occupy a property to satisfy the continuous possession element. The sloping nature of the property could make the property dangerous in snowy or icy weather, which is comparable to the regularly inaccessible swampland in *Posey*. *See* 7 P.2d at 1022. Thus, Blackhurst's use of the small parcel in the summer for kayaking is "usual and ordinary…according to its particular location and character." *Id.* Blackhurst, therefore, will likely establish continuous possession of the property, despite a brief period of vacancy, due to her ordinary use of the land to store her kayak equipment and access Lake Tahoe.

This paragraph resolves the discrepancy created by the counteranalysis and summarizes the best points in support of the **Conclusion***.*

The **Conclusion** *here focuses specifically on the continuous possession element.*

CONCLUSION

Blackhurst can likely prove the open and notorious possession element for adverse possession because she installed the shed and signs on the small parcel. In addition, because her regular kayaking was an ordinary use of the property, she will likely establish the continuous possession element. Thus, she will likely prevail on her adverse possession claim.

The **Conclusion** *section provides a separate conclusion for each element in dispute. It then provides an answer to the overall question.*

part IV

Writing Tools
for the New
Legal Writer

Introduction to Grammar, Punctuation, and Style

Good lawyers know how to put a sentence together. Their collective reputation as poor writers comes from a simple truth: Too many lawyers too often try to cram too much law, information, and legalese into otherwise proper sentences. The rules of good writing don't vanish because a writer needs to explain a complex set of facts or legal rules. On the contrary, complicated legal doctrine is best explained and understood when presented in plain language. And so, this part of the *Handbook* includes a review of eight basic grammar rules. It also details grammar principles that are particularly important for the new legal writer. In addition, this part includes tips on revising and editing your documents—so that you can transform wordy, legalese-riddled prose into writing that's concise, direct, and more effective.

Grammar Basics

Grammar Basics for the New Legal Writer

1. Sentences
2. Commas
3. Semicolons
4. Colons

5. Modifiers
6. Pronouns
7. Apostrophes
8. Hyphens

---

1. SENTENCES

Sentences—A Brief Review

1. Make the subject match the verb.
2. Avoid run-ons.
3. Fix fragments.

A. Rule 1: Make the Subject Match the Verb

A proper sentence has a subject and a verb that match. Singular subjects, including "each," "neither," "everyone," "corporation," and "defendant," take a singular verb. Plural subjects take a plural verb. That matchup remains true even if many words separate the subject and the verb. In the two examples below, the singular subjects of "opinion" and "court" take singular verbs, despite intervening phrases that contain plural nouns.

> The majority opinion—written by Justice Scalia and joined by Justices Thomas, Ginsburg, Sotomayor, and Kagan—holds that using a drug-sniffing dog on a porch to investigate the contents of a home is a search for Fourth Amendment purposes.

> The court interpreting the statutes is hearing oral arguments today.

While you want to ensure that subjects and verbs match in complex sentences, keep in mind that one principle of good writing is to keep subjects and verbs close together. In the example below, from Justice Kagan's concurrence in *Florida v. Jardines*, note how the main subjects are next to the main verbs.

> For me, a simple analogy clinches this case.... A stranger comes to the front door of your home carrying super-high-powered binoculars. He doesn't knock or say hello. Instead, he stands on the porch and uses the binoculars to peer through your windows, into your home's furthest corners.[1]

B. Rule 2: Avoid Run-Ons

A proper sentence also should contain commas and semicolons as needed to avoid creating a run-on. Fusing two sentences into one without punctuation or with only a comma connecting them creates a run-on. The following examples provide five ways to fix run-ons.

Incorrect

A public figure in a defamation action must prove that a false statement was published by an individual with reckless disregard for the truth, he also must prove that the statement is defamatory. — This run-on fuses two independent clauses together with a comma.

Fix No. 1: Semicolon

A public figure in a defamation action must prove that a false statement was published by an individual with reckless disregard for the truth; he also must prove that the statement is defamatory. — 1. A semicolon can combine two closely related independent clauses.

Fix No. 2: Use a Coordinating Conjunction—and, but, for, or, so, yet

A public figure in a defamation action must prove that a false statement was published by an individual with reckless disregard for the truth, and he must prove that the statement is defamatory. — 2. A coordinating conjunction (and, but, for, or, so, yet) plus a comma can combine the clauses.

Fix No. 3: Use a Conjunctive Adverb,[2] Semicolon, and Comma

A public figure in a defamation action must prove that a false statement was published by an individual with reckless disregard for the truth; furthermore, he must prove that the statement is defamatory. — 3. A semicolon, conjunctive adverb (furthermore, however, therefore, etc.), and a comma can combine the independent clauses.

Fix No. 4: Make Two (or More) Sentences

A public figure in a defamation action must prove that a false statement was published by an individual with reckless disregard for the truth. He also must prove that the statement is defamatory. — 4. Making the two independent clauses into two sentences corrects the run-on.

Fix No. 5: Make One Clause Subordinate

After a public figure in a defamation action proves that a false statement was published by an individual with reckless disregard for the truth, he also must prove that the statement is defamatory. — 5. Make one of the independent clauses into a subordinate clause.

---

1. *Florida v. Jardines*, 569 U.S. 1, 12 (2013) (Kagan, J., concurring).

2. You may use conjunctive adverbs to combine clauses and show their relation. See the chart on page 130 for a list of common conjunctive adverbs.

Depending on how the writer combines the clauses in these examples, the combinations have slightly different meanings. Varying sentence structure allows the writer to emphasize different words and different parts of the sentence. For instance, the writer emphasizes the end of the sentence in the last example and the beginning of the sentence in the first example. Varying sentence length also can make your writing more interesting and less monotonous. Consider using different sentence forms in your writing to emphasize your best points and liven up your prose.

C. Rule 3: Fix Fragments

Finally, a proper sentence should contain a subject and main verb so that it is not a fragment. In the last example, the subordinate clause could not stand alone as a sentence. Similarly, a sentence that incorrectly uses a verb ending in "—ing" (a participle or gerund) or a verb used with "to" (an infinitive) cannot stand alone as a sentence. To fix fragments, make sure that each sentence expresses a complete thought.

Incorrect: Fragment with subordinate clause

After a public figure in a defamation action proved that a false statement was published by an individual with reckless disregard for the truth

Incorrect: Fragment with "—ing" verb

A public figure in a defamation action proving that a false statement was published by an individual with reckless disregard for the truth

Incorrect: Fragment with infinitive

A public figure in a defamation action to prove that a false statement was published by an individual with reckless disregard for the truth

Correct: Main verb

The public figure in a defamation action proved that a false statement was published by an individual with reckless disregard for the truth.

Some writers use fragments purposefully for emphasis. If you choose to copy this technique, make sure your reader will recognize your writing as artful prose—and not a grammar mistake—as Chief Justice Roberts does in this dissent from *Pennsylvania v. Dunlap*:

North Philly, May 4, 2001. Officer Sean Devlin, Narcotics Strike Force, was working the morning shift. Undercover surveillance. The neighborhood? Tough as a three-dollar steak. Devlin knew. Five years on the beat, nine months with the Strike Force. He'd made fifteen, twenty drug busts in the neighborhood. Devlin spotted him: a lone man on the corner. Another approached. Quick exchange of words. Cash handed over; small objects handed back. Each man then quickly on his own way. Devlin knew the guy wasn't buying bus tokens. He radioed a description and Officer

— The fragments (highlighted here) can add emphasis and variety to one's writing.

Stein picked up the buyer. Sure enough: three bags of crack in the guy's pocket. Head downtown and book him. Just another day at the office.[3]

2. COMMAS—FIVE RULES THAT COULD SAVE YOU MILLIONS

Commas create frustration among all writers, but especially for legal writers. A misplaced comma can change the meaning of a sentence and thus, the meaning of a written agreement or opinion. In one contract dispute, a company initially lost $2.13 million dollars[4] because of the second comma in the following statement:

> This agreement shall be effective from the date it is made and shall continue in force for a period of five (5) years from the date it is made, and thereafter for successive five (5) year terms, unless and until terminated by one year prior notice in writing by either party.

Because commas surround the phrase, "and thereafter for successive five (5) year terms," the phrase is nonrestrictive, meaning the clause does not restrict the meaning of the sentence. The sentence can operate without the clause, which means that the initial five-year agreement can be terminated by one year's notice. But without the second comma, the clause about termination would apply only to the successive contracts, creating an initial, firm, five-year deal. This $2 million lesson leads us to the first of five comma rules that will help ensure your prose conveys the intended meaning.

Commas—A Brief Review

1. Use commas to set off nonrestrictive clauses.
2. Use the serial comma.
3. Use commas after the day and year in dates.
4. Use commas to separate elements in locations.
5. Use commas around clauses, phrases, and conjunctive adverbs for clarity.

A. Rule 1: Use Commas to Set Off Nonrestrictive Clauses

Nonrestrictive clauses add nonessential information to a sentence. They typically begin with "which," "when," "who," or "where" and provide information that does not restrict the meaning of the sentence. These phrases or clauses always require commas.

---

3. 555 U.S. 964, 964–65 (2008) (Roberts, C.J., dissenting from denial of cert.).
4. *Rogers Cable Commc'ns Inc. v. Bell Aliant*, Telecom Decision CRTC 2006-45, rev'd, Telecom Decision CRTC 2007-75.

Police took a drug-sniffing dog to Jardines' front porch, where the dog gave a positive alert for narcotics.[5]

Here, police officers came to Joelis Jardines' door with a supersensitive instrument, which they deployed to detect things inside that they could not perceive unassisted.[6]

In addition, I know that odors coming from my building, when they reach these locations, may be strong enough to be detected by a dog.[7]

> These clauses add important information, but their removal would not cause the sentences to lose their basic meaning.

Restrictive clauses, however, restrict the meaning of the sentence. The sentence would lose its meaning if you took a restrictive clause out of it; therefore, no commas should be used. Restrictive clauses often begin with "that" or "who" and have no commas.

Police received an anonymous tip that the defendant was growing marijuana in his home.

Mail carriers and persons delivering packages and flyers are examples of individuals who may lawfully approach a front door without intending to converse.[8]

> These sentences would lose their meaning if you took out the words following "that" and "who."

Determining whether a phrase is restrictive or nonrestrictive can be tricky in some cases. For example, both of the following statements are grammatically correct, but their meanings differ because of the commas.

The team's chocolate Labrador, Franky, alerted its handler to the scent of narcotics.

> The name provides additional, nonessential information.

The team's chocolate Labrador Franky alerted its handler to the scent of narcotics.

> Here, "Franky" identifies the specific dog, which would be necessary if the team has more than one chocolate Labrador.

B. Rule 2: Use the Serial Comma

Lawyers like to make lists: lists of elements in a rule, lists of witnesses, lists of reasons for an outcome. The serial comma—also known as the Oxford comma—clearly identifies each item in a list and helps avoid a potential misreading.

The Maine Legislature recently changed a law about overtime pay after a missing serial comma cost one dairy company $5 million. Dairy truck drivers successfully argued that the phrase "storing, packing for shipment or distribution" in the law referred to a single act because it did not contain the

---

5. Syllabus to *Florida v. Jardines*, 569 U.S. 1 (2013).
6. *Id.* at 12 (Kagan, J., concurring).
7. *Id.* at 25 (Alito, J., dissenting).
8. *Id.* at 16 (Alito, J., dissenting).

serial comma before "or."[9] Here is the tricky provision describing activities exempted from overtime pay—before and after the revision.

The canning, processing, preserving, freezing, drying, marketing, storing, packing for shipment or distribution of:

    (1) Agricultural produce;

    (2) Meat and fish products; and

    (3) Perishable foods.

— Without the serial comma, "packing for shipment or distribution" refers to one act, so drivers who distribute but don't pack aren't exempt from overtime pay.

The canning; processing; preserving; freezing; drying; marketing; storing; packing for shipment; or distributing of:

    (1) Agricultural produce;

    (2) Meat and fish products; and

    (3) Perishable foods.[10]

— With the serial semicolons, packing and distributing are clearly two different acts.

Maine lawmakers made an aggressive correction by using serial semicolons instead of the preferred serial comma. But they were to blame for the initial mistake: The Maine Legislative Drafting Manual incorrectly instructs, "when drafting Maine law or rules, don't use a comma between the penultimate and the last item of a series."[11] Don't make the same $5 million mistake. Always use the serial comma. Note how in the following examples, a missing serial comma would mean that Weaver and Walsh are dogs, not the police officers trained to handle them.

The scent of narcotics was apparent to the drug-sniffing dogs, Weaver and Walsh.

— Without the serial comma, Weaver and Walsh are identified as dogs.

The scent of narcotics was apparent to the drug-sniffing dogs, Weaver, and Walsh.

— With the serial comma, Weaver and Walsh are correctly identified as police officers.

C. Rule 3: Use Commas After the Day and Year in Dates

When listing a specific date in a sentence, always use a comma after the day and the year.

On January 9, 2013, the Court decided *Missouri v. McNeely*.

The attorneys met on April 8, 2018, to discuss the proposed settlement.

— Commas belong after the day and year, even when the date is in the middle of a sentence.

The attorneys met in April 2018 to discuss the proposed settlement.

— But use no commas when only the month and year are included.

---

9. Daniel Victor, *Suit Over Oxford Comma Is Settled, for $5 Million and a Slew of Semicolons*, N.Y. Times, Feb. 10, 2018, at A11.

10. Me. Stat. tit. 26 § 664(3)(F) (2018).

11. Maine Legislative Drafting Manual 113 (Legislative Council, Maine State Legislature 2009), http://maine.gov/legis/ros/manual/Draftman2009.pdf.

D. Rule 4: Use Commas to Separate Elements in Locations

Additionally, commas should follow both elements in a location, including a city and state or a city and country. When listing a full address in a sentence, add a comma where you would separate the mailing address with a line.

The pro bono attorney flew to Guantanamo Bay, Cuba, to meet his client.

> Commas separate the elements in geographic locations, and they set off locations within a sentence.

The Commission issued its decision from Ottawa, Canada, and found that the French version of the contract controlled.

The Oregon Supreme Court heard arguments on March 14, 2013, at 1515 Agate Street, Eugene, Oregon 97403, at the University of Oregon School of Law.

> When listing a mailing address, use commas after the street address, after the city, and after the zip code.

E. Rule 5: Use Commas Around Clauses, Phrases, and Conjunctive Adverbs for Clarity

Clauses, phrases, and conjunctive adverbs at the beginning, middle, and end of sentences often require commas for clarity. First, always use a comma to offset an introductory word or phrase in your sentence. Second, use commas around conjunctive adverbs and other interrupting phrases and clauses in the middle of your sentence. Finally, use a comma to set off a dependent clause at the end of your sentence.

In a decision that drew criticism from veterans groups, Chief Justice Roberts wrote that the First Amendment protects "even hurtful speech on public issues to ensure that we do not stifle public debate."[12]

> A comma follows the introductory clause at the **start** of the sentence.

However, Justice Alito included an emotional appeal in the dissent in *Snyder v. Phelps*, arguing that the church's protest brutalized the family.[13]

> A comma follows the conjunctive adverb "however" and sets off the dependent clause at the **end** of the sentence.

Justice Alito, arguing that the church's protest brutalized the family, included an emotional appeal in the dissent.[14]

> Commas surround a dependent clause in the **middle** of the sentence.

Justice Alito, however, included an emotional appeal in the dissent in *Snyder v. Phelps*, arguing that the church's protest brutalized the family.[15]

> Commas also surround "however" when the conjunctive adverb is in the **middle** of the sentence, and one comma offsets the dependent clause at the **end** of the sentence.

CONJUNCTIVE ADVERBS		
• Accordingly	• Instead	• Similarly
• Consequently	• Moreover	• Still
• Furthermore	• Nevertheless	• Then
• Hence	• Nonetheless	• Therefore
• However	• Otherwise	• Thus

---

12. *See Snyder v. Phelps*, 562 U.S. 443, 461 (2011).
13. *See id.* at 463-75 (Alito, J., dissenting).
14. *See id.*
15. *See id.* at 463.

3. SEMICOLONS

> ### Semicolons—A Brief Review
>
> 1. Use semicolons to separate complex items in a list.
> 2. Use a semicolon to combine two closely related sentences.
> 3. Use a semicolon, a conjunctive adverb, and a comma to combine two related sentences.

Semicolons are useful when combining independent clauses and drafting complex sentences.[16] But because semicolons typically help create longer, more complicated sentences, use them in moderation to keep your writing readable.

A. Rule 1: Use Semicolons to Separate Complex Items in a List

Semicolons can help keep items in a complex list clear. An item in a list is complex if it requires commas. In the next sentence, the rule has five elements and two elements contain commas. Using a comma to separate the items would be confusing. So if you list more than two items and at least one of the items requires a comma, use a semicolon for clarity.

> An adverse possession claim requires the plaintiff to prove that the possession is (1) continuous; (2) hostile or adverse to the interests of the true owner; (3) open and notorious, which provides the true owner with notice of a trespasser; (4) actual, so that the true owner has a cause of action for trespass; and (5) exclusive.

The third and fourth items in the series contain commas; using semicolons to separate all the items in the list creates clarity.

B. Rule 2: Use a Semicolon to Combine Two Closely Related Sentences

Semicolons also can combine two sentences into one (as shown in two examples on page 125. In this example, U.S. Supreme Court Justice Neil Gorsuch combines what could be two stand-alone sentences into one. Follow his lead and use semicolons sparingly—this semicolon was the only one Justice Gorsuch used in his nine-page opinion. And use the semicolon only when combining sentences that are short and have closely related meanings.

> The United States says it may pursue claims for violations of the Compact itself; Colorado says the United States should be permitted to pursue claims only to the extent they arise under the 1906 treaty with Mexico.[17]

The semicolon combines what would otherwise be two short, closely related sentences.

---

16. See page 125 at the start of this chapter for a refresher on using a semicolon and a conjunctive adverb, such as "however," to combine independent clauses into a more complex sentence.

17. *Texas v. New Mexico*, 138 S. Ct. 954, 958 (2018).

C. Rule 3: Use a Semicolon, a Conjunctive Adverb, and a Comma to Combine Two Related Sentences

Using a conjunctive adverb is a more common way to combine two sentences, and it also shows the relation between the two sentences. Familiar conjunctive adverbs include "however," "moreover," "therefore," and others listed in the chart on page 130. In this example, Justice Alito uses the conjunctive adverb "otherwise" to emphasize a consequence. Note that this construction requires a semicolon after the first complete clause and a comma after the conjunctive adverb (and before the second complete clause).

> Only if the jury gave a unanimous yes to the first two questions, and a — The semicolon, when
> unanimous no to the third question, could a death sentence be imposed; followed by a conjunctive
> otherwise, petitioner would receive a sentence of life without parole.[18] adverb and comma, combines
> two sentences into one.

4. COLONS

Colons—A Brief Review

1. Place a colon only after a complete clause.
2. What follows the colon may or may not be a complete clause.

A. Rule 1: Place a Colon Only After a Complete Clause

Colons are useful for setting off lists, explanations, and quotations in legal writing. A colon should not be used before a list that follows an incomplete clause. But colons are required when a complete clause precedes a list or explanation. A colon or a comma may introduce a quotation.

> The court held that only two of the required five adverse possession — A colon is required after an
> elements were met: Possession was continuous, and possession was independent clause that sets up
> exclusive. an explanation. When what
> follows the colon is an indepen-
> dent clause, you may capitalize
> the first letter.

> Chief Justice Roberts wrote the following in conclusion: "Speech is — This colon follows an independent
> powerful. It can stir people to action, move them to tears of both joy clause that sets up a quote. A
> and sorrow, and—as it did here—inflict great pain. On the facts before comma may also be used to offset
> us, we cannot react to that pain by punishing the speaker. As a Nation a short quote.
> we have chosen a different course—to protect even hurtful speech on
> public issues to ensure that we do not stifle public debate."[19]

---

18. *Ayestas v. Davis*, 138 S. Ct. 1080, 1086 (2018).
19. *Snyder*, 562 U.S. at 461.

B. Rule 2: What Follows the Colon May or May Not Be a Complete Clause

What comes after the colon does not need to be a complete clause. For example, a phrase, partial quote, or list of elements could follow the colon. While you may capitalize a complete clause that follows a colon—because it could act as its own sentence—don't capitalize the first word of an incomplete clause, as shown in these examples:

> The court held that only two of the required five adverse possession elements were met: continuous possession and exclusive possession.

— Do not capitalize what follows the colon if it is an incomplete clause.

> To establish adverse possession, a plaintiff must prove the following five elements: (1) continuous possession; (2) hostile possession or possession that is adverse to the interests of the true owner; (3) open and notorious possession, which provides the true owner with notice of a trespasser; (4) actual possession, so that the true owner has a cause of action for trespass; and (5) exclusive possession.

— A colon is required after an independent clause before a list.

5. MODIFIERS

> ### Modifiers—A Brief Review
> 1. Avoid the unclear placement of modifiers.
> 2. Avoid misplaced modifiers.
> 3. Avoid dangling modifiers.

Modifying the wrong word or phrase can make a sentence confusing or incorrect. Just as subjects and verbs should be placed close together, modifiers should be placed next to the word or clause they modify. Modifiers create problems in writing in two ways: their placement makes the sentence's meaning unclear, or they dangle so that the modifier's meaning is unclear.

A. Rule 1: Avoid the Unclear Placement of Modifiers

Note how the meaning changes in the following sentences, depending on where the modifier "only" is placed. The lesson here is to place words like "only," "primarily," "predominantly," "nearly," and "mainly" next to the word or phrase they modify.

Correct
The defendant wanted only to talk to the police.

— This sentence means that the defendant wanted to talk; he did not want to provide a written statement or provide any other type of evidence.

Correct
The defendant wanted to talk only to the police.

— This sentence means that the defendant would talk to the police and no one else.

Incorrect

The defendant only wanted to talk to the police. ——The meaning here is unclear.

B. Rule 2: Avoid Misplaced Modifiers

Placing modifiers gets a bit trickier when a longer clause is involved. The next examples illustrate how to fix misplaced modifying clauses.

Incorrect

The jury weighed the evidence about the defendant and the car contain-——This sentence states that the
ing a large bag of marijuana, which was registered to the defendant's   marijuana, not the car, was
girlfriend.   registered to the defendant's
   girlfriend.

Correct

The jury weighed the evidence about the defendant and the car, which ——This sentence conveys the
was registered to the defendant's girlfriend and contained a large bag of   facts correctly.
marijuana.

C. Rule 3: Avoid Dangling Modifiers

Another problem with modifiers occurs when they are "dangling," or modify-ing a noun that is either unclear or doesn't exist in the sentence. Here are two examples of dangling modifiers and how to fix them—by making the actor in the sentence clear.

Incorrect

Finding the evidence flawed, the conviction was reversed. ——The court is the actor in the
   sentence, but it is missing,
Correct: Add the main subject   leaving the modifier dangling.

Finding the evidence flawed, the court reversed the conviction. ——The introductory clause
   modifies the actor, "court."
Incorrect

Having filed the brief a day late, a motion for extension of time was ——Passive voice allows the actor
required.   to be missing.

Correct: Add the main subject

Having filed the brief a day late, the attorney was required to file a motion ——Adding the actor back into the
for extension of time.   sentence fixes the dangling
   modifier.

6. PRONOUNS

Pronoun errors create ambiguity and imprecision in your writing. The follow-ing four rules will keep the pronouns in your prose clear so that the reader always knows who the "he," "she," "it," and "they" are in a document.

> ### Pronouns—A Brief Review
>
> 1. Make pronouns and antecedents match.
> 2. "It's" is a contraction, not a possessive.
> 3. Pronouns should refer to an existing antecedent.
> 4. "Who" is for subjects; "whom" is for objects.

A. Rule 1: Make Pronouns and Antecedents Match

When a pronoun represents a singular noun or a collective noun, use a singular pronoun[20] (and pair with a matching singular verb). Common collective nouns that should be represented by "it" include court, jury, board, company, majority, committee, family, or team. Similarly, pair plural nouns with a plural pronoun; jurors or corporations pair with "they." And use "who"—not "that"—when clauses refer to people.

Incorrect
The appellate panel erred when they affirmed the defendant's conviction.

> An appellate panel is a collective noun; therefore, the correct pronoun is "it."

Correct
The appellate panel erred when it affirmed the defendant's conviction.

Correct
The appellate judges erred when they affirmed the defendant's conviction.

> If using "it" to refer to a panel of three judges seems awkward, rewrite the sentence.

Incorrect
The appellate judges that affirmed the defendant's conviction agreed to rehear the case en banc.

> Use "who," not "that," when a clause refers to people.

Correct
The appellate judges who affirmed the defendant's conviction agreed to rehear the case en banc.

B. Rule 2: "It's" Is a Contraction, Not a Possessive

The word "it's" means "it is" and should be used only when you want to use an informal contraction. The word "its" is the possessive of "it" and may be used when paired with a singular or collective noun.

Incorrect
The Supreme Court issued it's decision.

> Adding an apostrophe to "it" does not create the possessive form.

Correct
The Supreme Court issued its decision.

> "Its" denotes the possessive correctly here.

C. Rule 3: Pronouns Should Refer to an Existing Antecedent

Avoid using a pronoun when it refers to an ambiguous idea or a nonexisting noun. Pronouns that often are ambiguous when used in legal writing include "it," "this," "that," "such," and "which." A pronoun should always refer clearly

---

20. One exception to this rule is when a person prefers the gender-neutral pronoun "they" instead of "he" or "she." *See* AP Stylebook (2017) ("In stories about people who identify as neither male nor female or ask not to be referred to as *he/she/him/her*: Use the person's name in place of a pronoun, or otherwise reword the sentence, whenever possible. If *they/them/their* use is essential, explain in the text that the person prefers a gender-neutral pronoun. Be sure that the phrasing does not imply more than one person.").

to its antecedent. In the previous sentence, the antecedent for "its" is "pronoun."

Incorrect

Judges become frustrated when attorneys make pronoun errors, so carefully proofread your document to eliminate **them**. — It's unclear whether "them" refers to errors or judges or attorneys.

Correct

Judges become frustrated when attorneys make pronoun errors, so carefully proofread your document to eliminate **all errors**. — Using specific nouns in a sentence can clarify confusing pronouns.

Incorrect

This means that the Court should vacate the conviction.

Correct

This lack of evidence means that the Court should vacate the defendant's conviction. — Even if the writer thinks that the reasons for vacating the conviction were clearly spelled out within the document, "this" is unclear here. "This" and other ambiguous pronouns should always be followed with an explicit noun or phrase, like "lack of evidence" here.

Incorrect

The witness, who testified that she heard Vanya Patel laughing on the other side of the apartment wall around 11 p.m., said that **she** was regularly drunk at night. — It's unclear whether the witness or Patel was drunk.

Correct

The witness, who testified that she heard Vanya Patel laughing on the other side of the apartment wall around 11 p.m., said that **Patel** was regularly drunk at night. — This sentence conveys the correct information.

D. Rule 4: "Who" Is for Subjects; "Whom" Is for Objects

Use the pronoun "who" when referring to the subject of a sentence or the subject of a clause, just as you would use "she" or "he." When referring to the object of a sentence, use "whom," "her," or "him."

Here's a tip to figure out whether to use "who" or "whom": Rework the clause to use either "he" or "him." This reworking is easy because writers don't typically confuse "he" and "him." If the clause would use "he," the pronoun is a subject and "who" is the correct pronoun. If the clause would use "him," the pronoun is an object and "whom" is the correct choice. See how this trick works in the examples below.

Incorrect

The judge sealed the records relating to the juvenile, **whom** was identified only as "TM" in publicly released documents.

Reworking Sentence to Use "He" or "Him"

The judge sealed the records relating to the juvenile; **he** was identified only as "TM" in publicly released documents. — If you rework the sentence, you can see that "who" is the correct pronoun because "he" refers to a subject, not an object.

Correct

The judge sealed the records relating to the juvenile, **who** was identified only as "TM" in publicly released documents.

Incorrect

The newspaper contained allegedly defamatory statements about Zora Jackson, who the union hopes to elect to the vacant County Commission seat.

Reworking Sentence to Use "He" or "Him"

The newspaper contained allegedly defamatory statements about Zora Jackson; the union hopes to elect him to the vacant County Commission seat.

The tip works here too, even though Zora is female. You can see that "whom" is required because it refers to the object of the union's efforts.

Correct

The newspaper contained allegedly defamatory statements about Zora Jackson, whom the union hopes to elect to the vacant County Commission seat.

7. APOSTROPHES

Apostrophes—A Brief Review

1. For singular nouns, add an apostrophe and an "s."
2. For plural nouns, add just the apostrophe.
3. For singular nouns ending in "s," follow rule 1 or 2 consistently.
4. Use contractions conversationally and sparingly.

Apostrophes form possessives and create contractions. These four rules show you how to use apostrophes correctly every time.

A. Rule 1: For Singular Nouns, Add an Apostrophe and an "s"

Incorrect

The defendants testimony led to the courts decision to dismiss the contract dispute case.

— This sentence is missing the apostrophe to form the possessive.

Correct

The defendant's testimony led to the court's decision to dismiss the contract dispute case.

— In this sentence, only one defendant testified.

B. Rule 2: For Plural Nouns, Add Just the Apostrophe

Also Correct

The defendants' testimony led to the court's decision to dismiss the contract dispute case.

— Here, more than one defendant testified.

C. Rule 3: For Singular Nouns Ending in "s," Follow Rule 1 or 2 Consistently

When a singular noun ends in "s," you may follow either option. To form the possessive, add an apostrophe or add an apostrophe and an "s." For example, both Congress' and Congress's are grammatically correct—U.S. Supreme Court justices write the possessive both ways. Just make sure that you are consistent in applying one rule throughout your document.

Justice Alito shows the Court's split view on how to write the possessive of Congress in *Taylor v. United States.*[21] In the same paragraph, he adds an "s" to the possessive for Congress, then quotes an older opinion where Justice John Paul Stevens did the opposite:

> In *Raich*, the Court addressed Congress's authority to regulate the marijuana market. The Court reaffirmed "Congress' power to regulate purely local activities that are part of an economic 'class of activities' that have a substantial effect on interstate commerce."[22]

— Writing either Congress' or Congress's is grammatically correct. Here, it is written both ways because one reference is within a quotation.

Justice Kagan demonstrates how to follow rule no. 1 for singular nouns ending in "s" in the next example. She adds an extra "s" to the possessive of "process," a singular noun. She leaves it off the possessive of "plants" because the word is plural.

> At the outset, EPA determined that regulating plants' emissions of hazardous air pollutants is "appropriate and necessary" given the harm they cause, and explained that it would take costs into account in developing suitable emissions standards.... Indeed, EPA could not have measured costs at the process's initial stage with any accuracy.[23]

— Writing either process' or process's is grammatically correct. Just pick one rule and follow it consistently.

D. Rule 4: Use Contractions Conversationally and Sparingly

Many writers consider contractions too informal for the serious nature of judicial writing. Justice Scalia called contractions "intellectually abominable, but commercially reasonable."[24] But plenty of judges who are respected for their writing prowess inject contractions in their writing, particularly when they are the lone author of an opinion.[25] Justice Kagan explains, "I use contractions in dissents. Only in dissents.... Even in dissents I don't always use

---

21. *Taylor v. United States*, 136 S. Ct. 2074, 2080 (2016).

22. *Id.* (quoting *Gonzales v. Raich*, 545 U.S. 1, 9 (2005)).

23. *Michigan v. E.P.A.*, 135 S. Ct. 2699, 2709–10, 2714–15 (2015) (Kagan, J., dissenting).

24. Alex Carp, *Writing with Antonin Scalia, Grammar Nerd*, New Yorker, July 16, 2012, http://www.newyorker.com/news/news-desk/writing-with-antonin-scalia-grammar-nerd.

25. Even Justice Scalia used contractions on occasion: "And then, in Godfather fashion, the majority makes state legislatures an offer they *can't* refuse: Avoid all the utterly impossible nonsense we have prescribed by simply 'permitting juvenile homicide offenders to be considered for parole.'" *Montgomery v. Louisiana*, 136 S. Ct. 718, 744 (2016) (Scalia, J., dissenting) (emphasis added).

them. But sometimes I just get started, and it seems like I'm writing in a kind of an informal way and I use them."[26]

Justice Kagan avoids contractions in majority opinions "in part because some of my colleagues don't like it, and in part just because when you're writing a majority, you're writing more for the Court. And I try to write it a little bit more formally—still in a way that I hope everybody can understand."[27]

With their questionable acceptability, use contractions sparingly. And use only those you would use in normal conversation. Avoid uncommon contractions, like shan't (shall + not), double contractions she'd've (she + would + have), and archaic constructions, like 'twas (it + was). The following lines show how to use contractions successfully in judicial writing. All are from a single Justice Kagan dissent.

> The concurring opinion similarly, if more vaguely, contends that "tangible object" should refer to "something similar to records or documents"—and shouldn't include colonial farmhouses, crocodiles, or fish.

> To my knowledge, no court has ever read any such provision to exclude things that don't record or preserve data; rather, all courts have adhered to the statutory language's ordinary (i.e., expansive) meaning.

> By contrast, § 1519 wouldn't ordinarily operate in that context because a federal court isn't a "department or agency."

> The plurality doesn't—really, can't—explain why it instead interprets the same words used in two provisions of the same Act addressing the same basic problem to mean fundamentally different things.[28]

8. HYPHENS

Hyphens—A Brief Review

1. Hyphenate phrases with compound adjectives.
2. Hyphenate when ambiguity could result.
3. No hyphen follows words ending in "-ly."

A hyphen combines compound adjectives when they precede a noun. When you can write hyphenated adjectives or nouns as a single word, use the non-hyphenated version. For instance, "re-written" should be "rewritten," "semi-colon" should be "semicolon," "by-laws" become "bylaws," and so on.

---

26. Interview by Bryan A. Garner with Justice Elena Kagan, United States Supreme Court Building, West Conference Room, in Washington, D.C. (July 16, 2015).

27. *Id.*

28. *Yates v. United States*, 135 S. Ct. 1074, 1091–92, 1095–96, 1097 (2015) (Kagan, J., dissenting).

Plenty of compound adjectives, though, cannot be combined into a single word. So "due-process analysis" should be "due-process analysis"—or even due process analysis, without the hyphen, when the meaning of the phrasal adjective is clear. Add a hyphen to compound adjectives like "due process" that collectively modify a noun only when the compound adjective precedes the noun. And use a hyphen to join adjectives when ambiguity could result. One exception is not to hyphenate words ending in "-ly" because typically, their modifying purpose is understood. Use the following three guidelines to choose when and how to hyphenate.

A. Rule 1: Hyphenate Phrases with Compound Adjectives

Finally, in *Johnson v. Glick*, a malicious-and-sadistic-purpose-to-cause-harm factor was not suggested as a necessary condition for liability, but as a factor, among others, that might help show that the use of force was excessive.[29]

— Hyphens show that this long phrase describes "factor."

We consider a legally requisite state of mind. In a case like this one, there are, in a sense, two separate state-of-mind questions.[30]

— Hyphens show the compound adjective for "questions."

B. Rule 2: Hyphenate When Ambiguity Could Result

Officers facing disturbances "are often forced to make split-second judgments—in circumstances that are tense, uncertain, and rapidly evolving."[31]

— With no hyphen, this phrase could mean that "second judgments" are split.

That heuristic makes good sense for considered decisions by the detaining authority but is much weaker in the context of excessive-force claims.[32]

— With no hyphen, this phrase could mean that there is an excessive amount of "force claims."

C. Rule 3: No Hyphen Follows Words Ending in "-ly"

We consider a legally requisite state of mind.[33]

That is because, as we have stated, "liability for negligently inflicted harm is categorically beneath the threshold of constitutional due process."[34]

"Legally requisite" and "negligently inflicted" harm do not require a hyphen for clarity.

---

29. Adapted from *Kingsley v. Hendrickson*, 135 S. Ct. 2466, 2478 (2015).
30. *Kingsley*, 135 S. Ct. at 2472.
31. *Id.* at 2474.
32. *Id.* at 2469, 2472, 2474, 2478.
33. Adapted from *id.* at 2478.
34. *Kingsley*, 135 S. Ct. at 2472.

Grammar Principles for the New Legal Writer

Legal writers face challenges that many other writers do not. Their words are regularly met by doubt, criticism, dissection, and even hostility by judges, supervising attorneys, clients, and opposing counsel. The following four sections provide a review of advanced grammar techniques that the new legal writer should master to write credibly and effectively.

> **Grammar Principles for the New Legal Writer**
>
> 1. Prefer the active voice.
> 2. Use parallel construction.
> 3. Quote with care.
> 4. Use em-dashes and parentheses to shift emphasis.

1. PREFER THE ACTIVE VOICE

The active voice is more direct and therefore preferable to the passive voice. In rare instances, however, a writer may use passive voice to alter the emphasis in a sentence or to deflect attention away from the actor.

Active voice
The jury announced its verdict.   —This statement is more direct.

Passive voice
The verdict was announced by the jury.   —Passive voice puts the actor—the jury—in a wordy prepositional phrase.

Passive voice
The verdict was announced.   —This construction is vague because the actor is unknown.

Learn to identify passive voice by its wordy verb phrase that has two or more words, typically beginning with "was," "were," "has," "has been," "have," or "have been." Then, make the sentence active by adding the subject back to the sentence or swapping the object in the prepositional phrase for the subject. The active voice sentence is likely better.

Although writers should prefer the active voice, some legal writers may choose to use the passive voice when they need to shift the emphasis in a sentence. For instance, consider why the defense team for JK Corp. would prefer the third example below, where the actor is unnamed.

> Active voice
> JK Corp. allegedly spilled millions of gallons of oil into the Gulf of Mexico. — This sentence emphasizes the actor, JK Corp.
>
> Passive voice
> Millions of gallons of oil were spilled into the Gulf of Mexico allegedly by JK Corp. — This construction emphasizes the oil spill and identifies the actor.
>
> Passive voice
> Millions of gallons of oil were spilled into the Gulf of Mexico. — This construction avoids referencing the actor.

2. USE PARALLEL CONSTRUCTION

Parallel phrasing adds elegance and clarity to writing. Parallelism means using a similar grammatical form for elements in a pair or series. Use parallel phrasing each time you list two or more elements, which are typically joined by a conjunction, including "and," "but," "not," "or," "yet," "either," or "neither."

Consider the symmetry in the following famous lines from Abraham Lincoln's Gettysburg Address:

> But, in a larger sense, we cannot dedicate—we cannot consecrate— — These three phrases are parallel because the present tense verbs match.
> we cannot hallow—this ground. The brave men, living and dead, who struggled here, have consecrated it, far above our poor power to add or detract. The world will little note, nor long remember what we say here, — These two verbs are parallel in tense, and the two phrases that follow match almost exactly.
> but it can never forget what they did here.

Lincoln's address uses em-dashes to combine three matching clauses: "we cannot dedicate," "we cannot consecrate," and "we cannot hallow." Each has a subject and a present-tense verb, which makes the series parallel. The fact that each phrase begins with "we cannot" makes the match even more striking. In the last sentence, the phrases around "nor" match—"little note" and "long remember" both have an adverb and present-tense verb. And the phrases at the end, "what we say here" and "what they did here," coordinate as well.

When you identify a pair, list, or series in your writing, make sure that the elements match in parallel construction. When the elements begin with a verb, each element must begin with a verb in the same tense. When the elements begin with a noun, each element must begin with a noun, although the nouns can be singular or plural or include an adjective.

> **Create Parallel Phrasing**
>
> 1. Identify a list, series, or pair of elements, which are typically joined by a conjunction, such as "and," "nor," or "either."
> 2. Make sure all elements—all nouns, all adjectives, all independent clauses, all verbs, etc.,—match.
> 3. Verb tenses must match exactly.

Correct: Parallel list of nouns

The Lucky Dog Food Corp. sued Baxter Brands for misappropriation of the following trade secrets: (1) cheesy dog chow, (2) cheesy dog treats, and (3) Organix Vegetable Mix.

— This phrasing is parallel because it lists three nouns, even though the first element is singular, the second is plural, and the third is a proper noun.

Incorrect

Baxter Brands denied the allegations, arguing that it has no products that are either cheese-flavored or mixed with organic vegetables.

— The elements following "either" do not match.

Correct: Parallel pair of verbs

Baxter Brands denied the allegations, arguing that it has no products that are either flavored with cheese or mixed with organic vegetables.

— The elements beginning with "flavored" and "mixed" match because they are both past-tense verbs.

Incorrect

Under the Illinois burglary statute, is a vacant lot curtilage when it surrounds an abandoned shed, the former owner had abandoned the shed, enclosed by a few bushes, and has been used by neighborhood kids for Chicago-style softball games?

— The elements following "when" do not match.

Correct: Parallel list of independent clauses with matching verbs

Under the Illinois burglary statute, is a vacant lot curtilage when the lot surrounds an abandoned shed, a few bushes enclose the lot, and neighborhood kids use the lot for Chicago-style softball games?

— The elements match because each is an independent clause with a present-tense verb. The second element in the incorrect example was removed because it was repetitive.

3. QUOTE WITH CARE

Careful legal writers make sure that they use quotation marks when using words from an opinion or other source. Generally, you should use quotation marks any time you quote five or more words from a source—or when you want to indicate a single word or phrase that's a legal term of art. Note how "deadly weapon" is quoted throughout the memo on page 105 because the writer's analysis hinges on the interpretation of that term.

Careful legal writers also ensure that each quotation they use is exact. When legal writers modify a quote, they use punctuation to mark the change. A legal writer's credibility depends on quoting sources accurately; the reader may be misled if a writer alters a quote without proper punctuation. The following four rules illustrate how to use quotations and punctuate them correctly.

Quote with Care

1. Use double quotation marks for quotes and single quotation marks for quotes within quotes.
2. Always put commas and periods inside quotation marks.
3. Use brackets, an ellipsis, or both to show a change in a quote.
4. For essential, longer quotes, indent the quote as a text block.

A. Use Double Quotation Marks for Quotes

Quotations should be surrounded by double quotation marks. Single quotation marks denote a quote within a quote.

Incorrect

Chief Justice Roberts wrote, 'Our cases make clear that students do not "shed their constitutional rights to freedom of speech or expression at the schoolhouse gate." — All three quote marks are incorrect here.

Correct

Chief Justice Roberts wrote, "Our cases make clear that students do not 'shed their constitutional rights to freedom of speech or expression at the schoolhouse gate.'"[1] — The quote is surrounded by double quotation marks. Chief Justice Roberts' quote of *Tinker* is surrounded by single quotation marks; hence, the closing quote includes the single and double quotation marks.

B. Always Put Commas and Periods Inside Quotation Marks

Commas and periods always belong inside quotations, no matter their placement in the original quote. Place larger punctuation marks—colons, semicolons, exclamation points, and question marks—inside quotation marks only when they are part of the original quote.

Incorrect

The court noted that "[t]he *way* Frederick was going to fulfill his ambition of appearing on television was by unfurling a pro-drug banner at a school event;" however, Frederick's motive was unclear. — The semicolon is not part of the original text and belongs after the quotation mark.

---

1. *Morse v. Frederick*, 551 U.S. 393, 396 (2007) (quoting *Tinker v. Des Moines Indep. Cmty. Sch. Dist.*, 393 U.S. 503 (1969)).

Correct

The court noted that "[t]he *way* Frederick was going to fulfill his ambition — The semicolon is not part of appearing on television was by unfurling a pro-drug banner at a school of the original text, so it is correctly placed after the event"; however, Frederick's motive was unclear.[2] quotation mark.

Correct

"But that is a description of Frederick's *motive* for displaying the banner;" — The semicolon is in the however, Frederick did not provide any interpretation of the text.[3] original quote, so it is placed inside the quotation marks.

C. Use Brackets, an Ellipsis, or Both to Show a Change to a Quote

Legal writers denote any alteration of a quote with brackets, an ellipsis, or both. The following examples show how to alter the beginning, middle, and end of a quote. Use brackets—not an ellipsis—to show a change at the start of a quote or a change to a word. Use an ellipsis (three spaced periods) to mark an omission in the middle or at the end of a quote. An ellipsis at the end of a quotation should have four spaced periods, with the last marking the end of the sentence.

Original quote

"Our cases make clear that students do not 'shed their constitutional rights to freedom of speech or expression at the schoolhouse gate.'"

Brackets mark a change at the quote's beginning

Chief Justice Roberts wrote, "[o]ur cases make clear that students do not — A bracket—not an 'shed their constitutional rights to freedom of speech or expression at the ellipsis—marks the change in capitalization at the schoolhouse gate.'" beginning of a quote.

Brackets mark a change to a word

Chief Justice Roberts wrote that previous cases "ma[de] clear that stu- — A bracket shows that the dents do not 'shed their constitutional rights to freedom of speech or writer changed the verb tense to "made." expression at the schoolhouse gate.'"

An ellipsis marks an omission in the middle

Chief Justice Roberts wrote, "[o]ur cases make clear that students do not — An ellipsis—consisting of 'shed their constitutional rights . . . at the schoolhouse gate.'" three spaced periods— marks an omission in the middle of a quote.

An ellipsis marks an omission at the end

Chief Justice Roberts wrote, "[o]ur cases make clear that students do not — Here, the ellipsis consists of 'shed their constitutional rights to freedom of speech or expression . . . .'" three spaced periods plus the period to end the sentence. It marks an omission of the end of a quote.

---

2. *Id.* at 402.
3. *Id.*

D. For Essential, Longer Quotes, Indent the Quote as a Text Block

Legal writers should use quotes sparingly. Quotes with multiple brackets and ellipses may appear unreadable, so rewrite these clunky quotations whenever possible. Pages with more quotes than original text appear uninspired. When a page strings together quotations, try rewriting and paraphrasing the lines to make your point more directly. On the rare occasion that you need to use a quote of 50 or more words, set it off without quotation marks, indents on the right and left, and single-spacing.[4] The following example includes a block quotation of 60 words from a statute.

> Florida Statute Section 379.3762 states that individuals must obtain a permit if they wish to own alligators, pythons, or other wildlife that "present a real or potential threat to human safety," but it specifies that some animals may be kept on farms:
>
> > This section shall not apply to the possession, control, care, and maintenance of ostriches, emus, rheas, and bison domesticated and confined for commercial farming purposes, except those kept and maintained on hunting preserves or game farms or primarily for exhibition purposes in zoos, carnivals, circuses, and other such establishments where such species are kept primarily for display to the public.
>
> Fla. Stat. § 379.3762(4) (2018). Thus, the emus kept on Effia Mesah's property are exempt from the wildlife permitting requirements.

— The first sentence explains and introduces the statute.

— A quotation of 50 or more words should look like this block, indented on each side.

— The citation and text that follow a block quotation appear on the next line of regular text.

4. USE EM-DASHES AND PARENTHESES TO SHIFT EMPHASIS

Em-dashes have had a starring role in legal writing since before the time of Abraham Lincoln, who skillfully weaved seven em-dashes within two sentences in the Gettysburg address.

> But, in a larger sense, we cannot dedicate—we cannot consecrate—we cannot hallow—this ground. . . .
>
> It is rather for us to be here dedicated to the great task remaining before us—that from these honored dead we take increased devotion to that cause for which they here gave the last full measure of devotion—that we here highly resolve that these dead shall not have died in vain—that this nation, under God, shall have a new birth of freedom—and that government of the people, by the people, for the people, shall not perish from the earth.

---

4. *Bluebook* Rules B5.2 and 5.1.

Legal writers may set off information within a sentence using three tools: em-dashes, commas, and parentheses. The em-dash calls attention to information—pointing to it with a double-hyphen devoid of spaces. Legal writers also can set off information in a sentence with commas and parentheses—and each demands a varying degree of notice. Em-dashes provide the most emphasis to the information contained within, while parentheses provide the least. Use these tools in moderation and for variation in your writing.

Two em-dashes

The fact that the Air Force chooses to secure a portion of the Base more closely—be it with a fence, a checkpoint, or a painted green line—does not alter the boundaries of the Base or diminish the jurisdiction of the military commander.[5]

> Two em-dashes call attention to the information in the middle of the sentence. As a matter of style, the em-dash has no spaces around it.

The Base commander has also publicly stated that persons who are barred from Vandenberg—for whatever reason—may not come onto the Base to protest.[6]

One em-dash

In a single stroke, the United States gained 365 million acres of land—an area more than twice the size of Texas.[7]

> One em-dash sets off information at the beginning or end of the sentence.

Multiple em-dashes

The first step of *Seagate*—objective recklessness—is reviewed *de novo*; the second—subjective knowledge—for substantial evidence; and the ultimate decision—whether to award enhanced damages—for abuse of discretion.[8]

> Multiple em-dashes can set off a series.

Parentheses: Secondary information

The *Seagate* test aggravates the problem by making dispositive the ability of the infringer to muster a reasonable (even though unsuccessful) defense at the infringement trial.[9]

> Parentheses show the information contained within is of secondary importance.

Will a jury find that the company behaved "recklessly," simply for failing to spend considerable time, effort, and money obtaining expert views about whether some or all of the patents described in the letter apply to its activities (and whether those patents are even valid)?[10]

---

5. *United States v. Apel*, 571 U.S. 359, 370 (2014).

6. *Id.* at 371.

7. *Sturgeon v. Frost*, 136 S. Ct. 1061, 1064 (2016).

8. *Halo Elecs., Inc. v. Pulse Elecs., Inc.*, 136 S. Ct. 1923, 1930 (2016).

9. *Id.* at 1933.

10. *Id.* at 1937 (Breyer, J., concurring).

Parentheses: Adding information from a case

Only Congress may determine a lower federal court's subject-matter jurisdiction." *Kontrick*, 540 U.S. at 452; *Owen Equip. & Erection Co. v. Kroger*, 437 U.S. 365, 370 (1978) ("[I]t is axiomatic that the Federal Rules of Civil Procedure do not create or withdraw federal jurisdiction."). Accordingly, a provision governing the time to appeal in a civil action qualifies as jurisdictional only if Congress sets the time. *See Bowles*, 551 U.S. at 211–12 (noting "the jurisdictional distinction between court-promulgated rules and limits enacted by Congress"); *Sibbach v. Wilson & Co.*, 312 U.S. 1, 10 (1941) (noting "the inability of a court, by rule, to extend or restrict the jurisdiction conferred by a statute").[11]

— Legal writers often use parentheses to provide additional information about a case. Here, the quoted full sentence also requires a period within the parentheses.

— Parentheticals about cases often use a verb ending in -ing, like "holding," "finding," or "noting." Because these last two parentheticals contain clauses, they do not have periods inside the parentheticals.

---

11. *Hamer v. Neighborhood Hous. Servs. of Chicago*, 138 S. Ct. 13, 17 (2017).

Plain Language

Good writing is good writing. Whether writing appears in a legal brief, a novel, or a newspaper, the same principles of good writing apply. Legal writers frequently confront complex subjects, and they should strive to describe and analyze those subjects in plain, simple prose to convey their message most effectively. The following principles should be your guide as you write, rewrite, and revise your documents.

The Handbook's Guiding Principles of Plain Language

1. Make every word count.
   - Cut out the unnecessary, the redundant, and the unhelpful.
2. Use vigorous English.
   - Use forceful, direct, and concise language, avoiding weak and negative wording.
3. Use short words, short sentences, and short paragraphs.

---

1. MAKE EVERY WORD COUNT

Legal writers often don't think through an issue fully until they complete a first draft. The writing process helps them organize their thoughts and analysis, so a first draft might not get to the point as quickly as it should. Thus, legal writers should rewrite and revise until every word in the document counts.

Every word in your document should advance your reader's understanding of your analysis. If a word, phrase, or sentence fails to add to your reader's understanding, cut it. If a word, phrase, or sentence repeats an idea that you have already conveyed, cut it. And if a word, phrase, or sentence fails to help your reader better understand your cause, cut it. By creating a lean document, your writing will be more direct and effective.

A. Cut Out the Unnecessary

First, cut out unnecessary words by focusing on using strong nouns and active verbs. Avoid using too many adjectives and adverbs, which are crutches for a weak writer. Avoid intensifiers, including "clearly," "certainly," and "obviously," unless you have the exceptionally rare case where the issues are clear, certain, or obvious. And avoid qualifiers, such as "really," "very," and "rather," which undermine your point.

> **Weak wording**
> Clearly, Jones was rather enthusiastic about the news that a settlement was reached in the lawsuit.
>
> **Strong wording**
> Jones was enthused because the lawsuit settled.

The revision cuts out the intensifier "clearly" and the qualifier "rather." It also transforms the adjective "enthusiastic" and the noun "settlement" into strong verbs.

Second, cut out phrases that detract from your point because they are timid or serve as mere warm-ups to your main point. These wordy warm-ups often begin with "there is" or the undefined pronoun "it." The following list provides only a sample of the many wordy warm-ups that you should avoid using in legal writing. In most cases, the writer can eliminate the wordy warm-up to create a more direct sentence.

> **Weak wording**
> It is significant to note that the ruling below is inconsistent with this Court's decision in *Stanton*.
>
> **Strong wording**
> The ruling below is inconsistent with this Court's decision in *Stanton*.
>
> **Weak wording**
> There is no evidence showing that Kern Corp. breached the contract.
>
> **Strong wording**
> No evidence shows that Kern Corp. breached the contract.

WORDY WARM-UPS	
• Arguably	• It is to be noted
• As noted above	• It might be said that
• In light of the fact that	• It must be recognized that
• In order to	• It seems
• It could be argued that	• It seems likely that
• It is	• It should also be noted
• It is clear	• It would appear that
• It is crucial to consider	• It would be helpful to consider
• It is important to note that	• The fact that
• It is worth considering	• There are/is/was/were
• It is generally recognized that	• There is little doubt that
• It is interesting to consider	• With regard/respect to

B. Cut Out the Redundant

Because legal writers often use the first draft to think through their analysis, repetition of words, phrases, and ideas is common. As you revise your document, read it aloud to identify needless repetition. Do you have two consecutive paragraphs that explain the same anchor or describe the same argument? If yes, revise your document to make each point only once. In addition, look out for repetitious phrases. Writers sometimes repeat themselves in a single phrase: "First and foremost," "never before," and "past history" use two or three words when one will do. Cutting out unnecessary repetition will make your writing more concise, direct, and effective.

A writer should repeat key legal terms, however, when the repetition is necessary for clarity and consistency. For instance, if a letter to a client details a proposed settlement, a lawyer could confuse the client if she described the settlement in other terms, such as "agreement," "understanding," or "resolution," throughout the letter. Similarly, a writer should describe key aspects of the case in consistent terms. For example, the memo on page 105 refers to the fork as a "deadly weapon" each time—and not a "dangerous instrument" or simply a "weapon" because the term has a precise legal meaning. If referring to a party as "Plaintiff," the writer should use "Plaintiff" for each reference. And when describing an anchor or key fact, the writer should use the same terms to make sure that the reader can easily identify connections throughout the document. Using different words to describe the same term is called "elegant variation"—a tactic that is impractical in legal writing.

Some repetition may enhance a writer's style. The repetition of sounds through alliteration (repeated consonants) or assonance (repeated vowels) can lend elegance. Parallel phrasing also can lend sophistication. But legal writers should use these techniques sparingly. Forcing style can make a writer's prose awkward and ostentatious. Justice Neil Gorsuch drew criticism for overdoing the alliteration in this first sentence of his first U.S. Supreme Court opinion.

> Disruptive dinnertime calls, downright deceit, and more besides drew Congress's eye to the debt collection industry.[1]

Good legal writers focus on conveying their points directly using a style that comes naturally. That's what Justice Alito does in this next example.

> Respondents and other members of their church have strong opinions on certain moral, religious, and political issues, and the First Amendment ensures that they have almost limitless opportunities to express their views. They may write and distribute books, articles, and other texts; they may create and disseminate video and audio recordings; they may circulate petitions; they may speak to individuals and groups in public forums and in any private venue that wishes to accommodate them; they may

Justice Alito's repetition of parallel phrases lends sophistication to this paragraph from a dissent.

---

1. *Henson v. Santander Consumer USA, Inc.*, 137 S. Ct. 1718, 1720 (2016).

picket peacefully in countless locations; they may appear on television and speak on the radio; they may post messages on the Internet and send out e-mails. And they may express their views in terms that are "uninhibited," "vehement," and "caustic." *N.Y. Times Co. v. Sullivan*, 376 U.S. 254, 270 (1964).[2]

C. Cut Out the Unhelpful

Early drafts of a legal document might also be weak because they use placeholders that do not add to a reader's understanding. Placeholders detract from an otherwise effective document because they take up space and do not advance the writer's cause. For instance, the following topic sentences for Explanation paragraphs fail to advance the reader's understanding of the relevant law. Writers should delete unhelpful sentences and replace them with sentences that advance the reader's understanding of the relevant law and analysis.

Weak wording
Michigan courts have decided many adverse possession cases.

— Instead of providing an unhelpful introduction to case law, the writer should summarize an anchor or rule that advances a reader's understanding of the relevant law.

Weak wording
Whether the claimant's possession is open and notorious is a major factor in determining adverse possession.

— This sentence summarizes a relevant anchor without any context.

Strong wording
An individual's possession must be open and notorious to provide notice to the true owner, or the adverse possession claim fails.

— This sentence provides the holding relative to the "open and notorious" anchor to provide context.

2. USE VIGOROUS ENGLISH

Legal writing should be forceful, direct, and concise. Legal writers should avoid weak, negative, and passive wording. They should choose strong nouns and active verbs and keep subjects and verbs close together. Legal writers should also write with authority, avoiding qualifying language. Note the authoritative language that Justice Ginsburg employs in a brief for the ACLU, written 17 years before she joined the Court:

The Oklahoma legislation in question is a curiosity, apparently the only law of its kind left in the nation. Similarly, the ruling below is an anomaly. It is inconsistent with this Court's decision in *Stanton v. Stanton* and out of step with an array of authority in lower courts, federal and state, decisions that have made museum pieces of male/female age of majority differentials.

— Justice Ginsburg demonstrates her authority on the subject through knowledge of the law.

* * *

---

2. *Snyder v. Phelps*, 562 U.S. 443, 463–75 (2011) (Alito, J., dissenting).

The decision below apart, the sole authority for differential treatment of the sexes in relation to alcoholic beverage association is *Goesaert v. Cleary*. Widely criticized in commentary, in square conflict with decisions of this Court in the current decade and with national equal employment opportunity policy, and politely discarded by the nation's lower courts, *Goesaert* is a decision overdue for formal burial. — Justice Ginsburg uses strong language to urge the court to overturn *Goesaert*.

* * *

Just as drinking preferences and proclivities associated with a particular ethnic group or social class would be perceived as an unfair and insubstantial basis for a beverage sale or service prohibition directed to that group or class, so a gender-based classification should be recognized as an inappropriate, invidious means to the legislative end of rational regulation in the public interest.[3] — Justice Ginsburg continues her constitutional attack on the Oklahoma statute.

One way to energize your prose is to choose positive wording and avoid grouping multiple negative words together. Any time you use the word "not" with an adjective, consider that the English language probably provides one word for you to use instead—and that word might be more precise.

Negative wording	→	Positive wording
Not current	→	Outdated or obsolete
Not correct	→	Incorrect
Not on time	→	Late
Not precise	→	Imprecise
Not significant	→	Insignificant

In addition, using more than one negative in a sentence confuses meaning. Consider the following revision from a negative to a positive statement:

Negative statement
The contract stated, however, that the provision would not become null and void, unless one party provides notice that the other party has not acted reasonably.

Positive statement
The contract stated that the provision is void when one party provides notice that the other party acted unreasonably.

Legal writers also can energize their prose by making sure they do not turn active verbs into nouns called "nominalizations." Nominalizations not only add unnecessary words to your document, but they also make your writing less direct by burying the action in a sentence. The list on the next page shows how to transform some common nominalizations into active verbs. Note that nominalizations often end in "—ing," "—ion," or "—ment."

---

3. Brief for ACLU as Amici Curiae Supporting Appellants, *Craig v. Boren*, 429 U.S. 190 (1976) (No. 75-628), 1976 WL 181333 at *10-11, 24.

Nominalization	→	Active verb
Advancement	→	Advance
Agreement	→	Agree
Assumption	→	Assume
Commencement	→	Commence (or begin, start)
Consideration	→	Consider
Decision	→	Decide
Dependence	→	Depend
Determination	→	Determine
Emphasis	→	Emphasize
Expansion	→	Expand
Failure	→	Fail
Filed a motion	→	Moved
Improvement	→	Improve
Investigation	→	Investigate
Modification	→	Modify
Settlement	→	Settle
Violation	→	Violate

Statement with nominalizations

The parties' contract contained provisions requiring good-faith dealings and allowing the wronged party to effect a termination upon the violation of the good-faith provision.

Revised statement

The parties' contract provided that the parties must deal in good faith or the wronged party may terminate the agreement.

3. USE SHORT WORDS, SHORT SENTENCES, AND SHORT PARAGRAPHS

No matter how complicated the topic or dense the issue, lawyers convey their point best when they write in plain, simple prose. Start by using simple words. Consider this timeless advice from *The Elements of Style* to be a guiding principle: "Avoid fancy words. Avoid the elaborate, the pretentious, the coy, and the cute. Do not be tempted by a twenty-dollar word when there is a ten-center handy, ready and able."[4] The ten-centers will endear you to busy readers more than the vague, obscure, and foreign.

Big words abound in the law, and using them may be required on occasion. But make sure that each word you choose is the best word to convey your meaning—not the most impressive choice out of a thesaurus search. A "good test," said Justice Scalia, is "if you used the word at a cocktail party, would

---

4. William Strunk, Jr., & E.B. White, *The Elements of Style*, 76-77 (4th ed. 2000).

people look at you funny? You talk about *the instant case* or *the instant problem*. That's ridiculous. It's legalese. *This case* would do very well."[5]

The same principle holds true for foreign words. Translate Latin phrases for clarity—so inter alia becomes "among others," sui generis becomes "one of a kind" or "unique," and so on. Reserve Latin and legal jargon for the rare legal term of art, including de novo and mens rea. Additionally, choose precise replacements for clichés, which, by definition, have lost their original meaning. Instead of "slippery slope" or "tip of the iceberg," write what you mean.

Judges have become increasingly impatient with wordy, legalese-ridden filings. U.S. District Judge Steven D. Merryday, for example, denied one party's request to increase the page limit for a motion and instead edited the opening paragraph from 168 words to a lean 42 words.[6] Judge Merryday chastised the party's lawyer in an exaggeratingly wordy rebuke: "A review of the proposed twenty-nine-page motion's commencement confirms that a modicum of informed editorial revision easily reduces the motion to twenty-five pages without a reduction in substance."[7] Judge Merryday, no doubt, knew he could trim more than half the words from his own sentence without a loss of meaning.[8]

Lawyers do not safeguard an exalted profession by using words that only other lawyers can understand; instead, they isolate themselves from clients, juries, and the public. Chief Justice Roberts, who writes in an approachable style, says that he admires Justice Robert H. Jackson's writing for its plain style:

> You read one of his opinions, and it makes an impression on you—not just the law, but the felicity of expression and the breadth of analogy and reference. And at the same time, it has a very plainspoken approach to it. You don't have to be a lawyer to read one of Justice Jackson's opinions and understand exactly what he's saying. And that's very valuable.[9]

In addition to short words, good legal writers know the value of a short sentence. Concise, punchy sentences add interest to your prose. They emphasize your point. Although compound sentences are common in legal writing, declarative statements express meaning most directly. While the average sentence should be about 20 words,[10] varying sentence length is a hallmark of good legal writing.

---

5. Bryan A. Garner, ed., *The Scribes Journal of Legal Writing*, "Interviews with Supreme Court Justices," 58 (2010), available at http://legaltimes.typepad.com/files/garner-transcripts-1.pdf.

6. Joseph Kimble, *Michigan Bar Journal*, "A Federal Judge Takes On Legalese," 1 (Jan. 2013), available at http://www.michbar.org/journal/pdf/pdf4article2139.pdf.

7. *Belli v. Hedden Enters.*, No. 8:12-cv-01001 (M.D. Fla., filed Aug. 7, 2012).

8. Here's one way to reduce Judge Merryday's sentence from 28 to 13 words: "Informed editing easily reduces the 29-page motion to 25 without reducing its substance."

9. Bryan A. Garner, ed., *The Scribes Journal of Legal Writing*, "Interviews with Supreme Court Justices," 9 (2010), available at http://legaltimes.typepad.com/files/garner-transcripts-1.pdf.

10. *See, e.g.*, Bryan A. Garner, *LawProse Lesson #269: Average Sentence Length*, (June 19, 2018, 4:25 PM), http://www.lawprose.org/lawprose-lesson-269-average-sentence-length/.

Good legal writers also know the value of short paragraphs. No reader wants to encounter a wall of text upon turning the page. Help maintain your reader's interest by breaking long blocks of text into shorter paragraphs. Keep in mind that every paragraph should have a clear focus, preferably identified in a topic sentence or thesis statement. In addition, help your reader understand the connection between paragraphs by using transitions, such as "first," "second," and "third" or "and," "also," "but," "yet," and "still." Consider Justice Clarence Thomas' advice: "the genius is having a ten-dollar idea in a five-cent sentence, not having a five-cent idea in a ten-dollar sentence."[11] Note how Justice Alito ends the following paragraph with a three-word zinger.

> Although the elements of the IIED tort are difficult to meet, respondents long ago abandoned any effort to show that those tough standards were not satisfied here. On appeal, they chose not to contest the sufficiency of the evidence. They did not dispute that Mr. Snyder suffered "'wounds that are truly severe and incapable of healing themselves.'" Nor did they dispute that their speech was "'so outrageous in character, and so extreme in degree, as to go beyond all possible bounds of decency, and to be regarded as atrocious, and utterly intolerable in a civilized community.'" Instead, they maintained that the First Amendment gave them a license to engage in such conduct. They are wrong.[12]

— Justice Alito ends the paragraph with a zinger.

---

11. Bryan A. Garner, ed., *The Scribes Journal of Legal Writing*, "Interviews with Supreme Court Justices," 100 (2010), available at http://legaltimes.typepad.com/files/garner-transcripts-1.pdf.
12. *Snyder*, 562 U.S. at 464-65 (Alito, J., dissenting) (citations omitted).

Confused, Misused, and Misspelled Words

Legal writers strive to convey their meaning with precision. For that reason, the following list of commonly confused, misused, and misspelled words may be helpful in guiding you to choose the precise word you need. Additionally, consider consulting a standard dictionary, a legal dictionary, a legal style manual—or all three—to ensure that the word you choose has the precise meaning you intend.

Sources may vary in their definitions. For instance, "since" is typically defined as referring to a temporal relationship. For that reason, some writers always choose "because" to denote a causal relationship. Even U.S. Supreme Court justices are split on how to use this word, with some using "since" and "because" interchangeably and others using the terms only according to their traditional meanings.[1] Some authorities state that "since" may express a causal relationship but one that is milder than a relationship described with "because."[2] This subtle distinction shows why legal writers should make precise choices for every word. Because nuance is critical in legal writing, referring to dictionaries and related authorities when choosing the precise word you want will be helpful.

---

1. Jill Barton, *Supreme Court Splits on Grammar and Writing Styles*, 17 Scribes J. Legal Writing 33 (2016-17).

2. *See, e.g., Garner's Usage Tip of the Day: since*, http://www.lawprose.org/blog/?p=602.

Commonly Confused, Misused, and Misspelled Words

Adverse / Averse Unfavorable / Opposed	Council / Counsel An assembly / To advise
Affect / Effect *Verb / Noun*	Fewer / Less *Use with multiple items / Use with single item*
Allude / Elude Refer indirectly / Escape	Imply / Infer Suggest / Deduce
Among / Between *Use with three things / Use with two*	Its / It's *Possessive / Contraction*
Assure / Ensure / Insure Make promises / Make certain / Indemnify	Prescribe / Proscribe Dictate / Prohibit
Because / Since *Generally denotes a causal relationship /* *denotes a temporal relationship*	Principal / Principle Primary (*adj.*) / A truth (*noun*)
Can / May Expresses ability / Expresses permission	Their / There / They're *Possessive / Used to show existence /* *Contraction*
Complement / Compliment Something that completes / To praise	Tortious / Tortuous / Torturous Relating to a tort / Twisting and turning / Relating to torture
Compose / Comprise The parts compose the whole / The whole comprises the parts	Trail / Trial A common misspelling / A court proceeding
Continual / Continuous Frequently recurring / Unceasing	Your / You're *Possessive / Contraction*

Writing Style

Before finishing your legal document, make sure that you use a consistent style throughout. Review your use of capitalization, first person, fonts, numbers, and references to parties and people.

Capitalization

☑ Capitalize "court" only when referring to the U.S. Supreme Court and the court where you file your document. If you file a brief in the U.S. Court of Appeals for the First Circuit, refer to "this Court" for opinions issued by the First Circuit.

☑ Capitalize "Plaintiff" and "Defendant" only when referring to the parties in your case. Refer to the parties using the article "the" to make your prose less stilted.

☑ Capitalize proper nouns; avoid needless capitalization of other terms.

First Person

☑ Avoid using the first person ("I," "we," "our") in any formal legal document (e.g., memoranda, appellate briefs, and motions to dismiss, not letters and emails).

☑ Judges may use the first person; appellate courts often use "we" in their opinions.

☑ When speaking, avoid using first person. Instead of "I believe the evidence shows," state "the evidence shows," which is more direct.

Fonts

☑ Be consistent in using bold, italicized, and underlined fonts for headings and citations.

☑ Avoid using bold, italicized, or underlined fonts for emphasis—use strong words instead.

Numbers

☑ Spell out numbers zero to ten or when the number begins a sentence.

☑ Use numerals for money, percentages, and measurements (e.g., $7 million, 6%, and 10 feet).

☑ Do not waste space by repeating numbers—"$2 million" should not be written as $2 million ($2,000,000).

☑ Write times in this style: 9 p.m. or 10:30 a.m.

References to Parties and People

☑ If using courtesy titles to refer to a party or person, use the full name on first reference and the courtesy title with the surname for the second. So, for example, list "Marjory Callahan" on the first reference and "Ms. Callahan" for every subsequent reference. Using only surnames for the second and subsequent references is also proper.

☑ Use parentheses to indicate an abbreviation or acronym only when shortening a name to an abbreviation or acronym that is not obvious. James Binkler ("Binkler") wastes space. But Maryland Center for Strategic Planning ("MCSP") would be helpful for readers unfamiliar with the acronym.

As with any skill, writing takes practice. Drafting an effective legal document requires sound analytical thinking, organization, rewriting, and revision. To continue improving your writing skills, practice writing a variety of documents and practice editing your writing and the writing of others. Also, read examples of good writing—from law or literature. And read about good writing. The following list includes some of our favorite books on good writing.

- Bryan A. Garner, *The Elements of Legal Style* (2d ed., Oxford Univ. Press 2002).
- Anne Lamott, *Bird by Bird* (Anchor 1995).
- William Strunk, Jr., & E.B. White, *The Elements of Style* (4th ed., Pearson 2000).
- John R. Trimble, *Writing with Style* (Prentice Hall 1975).
- Richard C. Wydick, *Plain English for Lawyers* (5th ed., Carolina Acad. Press 2005).

part V

Persuasive Writing

Constructing CREAC in Persuasive Documents

A lawyer's job is to persuade. When a client comes to a lawyer with a problem, the first step is to analyze the problem and predict the most likely outcome. Then, the fun part begins. A lawyer needs to plan a winning strategy for solving the client's problem. That strategy often includes drafting persuasive documents and arguing in court. The lawyer hopes that these written and oral arguments will convince the court that the client should prevail.

These next two parts of the *Handbook* introduce you to the types of persuasive documents that lawyers write, explaining step-by-step how to write a trial motion and an appellate brief. In addition, Chapter 38 in Part VII guides you as you prepare for your first oral argument—and the many arguments that come after it.

In your legal career, you may regularly draft various types of persuasive documents. To initiate a lawsuit, a lawyer files a complaint, which is called a petition in some state courts. Opposing counsel may file an answer or motion in response to the complaint, including a motion to dismiss. During discovery, either party may file a motion to compel or motion for protective order. Before trial, one or both of the parties may file a motion for summary judgment or a motion in limine. In criminal cases, the defense may file a motion to suppress evidence. During and after trial, a party may file a motion for a directed verdict or a new trial. Any time a party files a motion, the party opposing the motion may file a response, and the party filing the motion typically gets the final word by filing a reply to the response.

The party that loses in the trial court may appeal and file an appellate brief, and the opposing party files a brief in response. A party that loses in a federal appellate court or state supreme court and wants to appeal to the U.S. Supreme Court will file a Petition for Writ of Certiorari, and the opposing party will file a Brief in Opposition. If the Court grants certiorari, both the petitioner and respondent will file extensive briefs on the merits of the case.

This far-from-exhaustive list of persuasive documents might seem overwhelming. But rest assured that for each of these documents, you will use many of the techniques, including the CREAC organization, that you already know. You will also use new persuasive techniques to make the best case you can for your client.

Persuasive documents follow the same general CREAC framework as objective documents, even though you write them with a different purpose in mind. The major difference is that for each CREAC part, the writer attempts to advance the client's case and achieve a particular outcome, rather than predict the most likely result.

Writing a Persuasive Conclusion

Every persuasive document will contain an Argument section that is logically organized according to the CREAC framework. And so the Argument section always begins with a Conclusion, which is an early opportunity to persuade the court to grant the relief that you seek. The Conclusion should ask the court for a particular outcome and provide a reason. Many writers incorporate references to legally significant facts and the controlling law when giving the reason in the Conclusion.

> **Writing a Persuasive Conclusion**
>
> 1. Identify the requested relief and the issue.
> 2. State your Conclusion and give a reason.
> 3. Develop a theme.
> 4. Draft your point headings.

1. STEP ONE: IDENTIFY THE REQUESTED RELIEF AND THE ISSUE

When tackling a new persuasive writing assignment, identify the relief you are seeking as a preliminary step. For trial court documents, such as a motion to dismiss or motion for summary judgment, the writer will ask the court to grant or deny the motion. For appellate filings, the writer will ask the court to reverse or affirm the lower court's decision. A typical Conclusion in a persuasive trial court document could start like this: "The Court should grant the Motion to Dismiss because _____." Similarly, the Argument section of an appellate brief could begin: "The Court should affirm the decision below because _____."

Next, identify the legal issue or issues. Each major legal issue should have its own CREAC, so try to determine whether your document should be organized around one issue or multiple issues. A simple motion to dismiss might turn on a single issue, while a more complicated motion for summary judgment or appellate brief would likely address multiple distinct issues—and thus have multiple CREACs.

Take care to frame your issue in specific legal terms, which will require an understanding of the relevant facts and underlying law. For instance, suppose your client asks you whether he has to honor an agreement to sell his classic Volkswagen Beetle to a neighbor. Your client put a "For Sale" sign on the car with a very low price to play a practical joke on the neighbor, but the neighbor said he accepted the offer and has sued for specific performance of the contract.

Once you gather facts about the case and research the law, you may determine that the precise legal issue is whether the client made a binding offer to sell the car. Because the case turns on whether an offer was made, you should frame your Conclusion around this specific issue—rather than the larger issue of the contract's validity. If the neighbor's acceptance of the offer is also in dispute, that could be an issue for a second CREAC. An introductory roadmap paragraph addressing the validity of the contract could introduce the two issues in the Argument section of your persuasive document.

2. STEP TWO: STATE YOUR CONCLUSION AND GIVE A REASON

Every Argument section should begin with a Conclusion. Simple issues can be summarized within a single Conclusion sentence, while more complicated issues might deserve a full paragraph or more. The first step in developing your Conclusion is to identify your issue. A persuasive Conclusion should do more than summarize what the case is about. It should also frame the issue in a way that favors the writer's position and provide a convincing reason in support.

For a simple issue, the persuasive Conclusion can summarize the issue, the requested relief, and a reason in support in a single sentence. The reason in support should typically reference key facts, the anchor or rule that justifies the relief that you seek, or both.

Suppose your supervising attorney suggests filing a motion to dismiss in the example above regarding the VW Beetle. You could draft your Conclusion using the following steps:

- **Relief Sought:** Grant the Motion to Dismiss the complaint for specific performance
- **Issue:** Whether the client made a valid offer to sell his car
- **Conclusion:** The Court should grant Defendant's Motion to Dismiss because Defendant never made a binding offer to sell his car and the contract is therefore unenforceable.

In addition to stating the relief sought, Conclusions often reference the controlling law, legally significant facts, or both when providing a reason. Consider the following examples:

> Jackson's Motion to Dismiss should be granted because the Complaint does not contain sufficient factual allegations to state a claim that is plausible on its face for any of the asserted causes of action.

— This Conclusion references the relief sought and a procedural rule in support.

> Tom Chapman's burglary conviction should be upheld because the picket fence enclosing most of the victim's compound qualifies the yard as curtilage.

— This Conclusion references the relief sought and specific facts relating to an applicable anchor in support.

> The Court should grant the Tribune's Motion for More Definite Statement because the Complaint fails to state the defamation claim with the required specificity and makes no reference to any false statements allegedly made by the Tribune.

— This Conclusion references the relief sought as well as a rule and facts in support.

More complicated issues merit a more extensive Conclusion. Some Conclusions use a paragraph or more to introduce the reader to the issues, the legally significant facts, the underlying law, and the arguments to come. Chief Justice Roberts' brief, filed in 2002 before he joined the Court, in *Godfrey v. John Doe I* includes an introduction that begins with this type of Conclusion paragraph.

> The Alaska Sex Offender Registration Act ("ASORA") was enacted to protect the public and to assist law enforcement in investigating future crimes. It requires state law enforcement entities to gather truthful information about sex offenders and to make certain of that information available to the public. The State has chosen to make such information available on the Internet. Like all other courts to have considered sex offender registration laws, the Ninth Circuit concluded that the legislature acted with non-punitive intent when it passed the ASORA. The court of appeals erroneously departed from the overwhelming majority of courts, however, in holding that the ASORA was nonetheless so punitive in effect that it violated the Ex Post Facto Clause.[1]

— This paragraph-long Conclusion begins by introducing the relevant law.

— Then, it summarizes the arguments to come using the significant facts and underlying law.

— Last, it refers to the relief sought.

3. STEP THREE: DEVELOP A THEME

A theme in a persuasive document allows you to connect your most persuasive arguments to each other and to the outcome that you seek. An effective theme tells the reader what the case is about from your client's point of view.

The following example starts the Argument section of the Respondent's brief in *Florida v. Jardines*. In that case, the Respondent argued to the Supreme

---

1. Brief for Petitioners at 2, *Godfrey v. John Doe I*, 536 U.S. 92 (2002) (No. 01-729), 2002 WL 1275055.

Court that police violated the Fourth Amendment when they took a trained drug-detection dog to the door of a suspected marijuana grow house. The Argument section starts by introducing the reader to the theme developed throughout the brief. The theme describes the case in a memorable way. In particular, the theme presents the dog sniff as a threat to privacy that undermines the core of the Fourth Amendment's protections.

> The issue in this case goes to the very heart of the rights secured to an individual by the Fourth Amendment. A dog sniff at the front door of a home by a narcotics detection dog is a Fourth Amendment search requiring a warrant based upon probable cause for two reasons. First, a homeowner's reasonable expectation of privacy is violated where a police officer uses a narcotics detection dog to reveal any details within the interior of a home that could not be discovered by the officer's ordinary powers of perception without a physical intrusion into the home. Second, and aside from the officer's use of a narcotics detection dog to reveal details inside the home, the actions of a police officer in taking a narcotics dog to the front door of a home also constitute a Fourth Amendment search. This is so because the officer's entry into the curtilage of the home with a narcotics detection dog is a common law trespass upon a constitutionally protected area in order to conduct a search for evidence and also because that entry violates the homeowner's reasonable expectation of privacy.[2]

— The first sentence establishes the theme using vivid language to show why the case is important. Then, the paragraph states the Respondent's broad Conclusion and summarizes the party's strongest points as a roadmap of the arguments to come.

While the theme developed by the Respondent in *Jardines* connects the case to ideals enshrined in the Constitution, in many cases the appropriate theme might seem more mundane, but it still can be meaningful. For example, in *Masterpiece Cakeshop v. Colorado Civil Rights Commission*, the Respondents presented a theme based on the case's simplicity. That case was about whether a baker's refusal on religious grounds to bake a cake for a gay wedding was protected by the First Amendment or could be required under a state public accommodations law. The Respondents were the gay couple who had been refused, and their theme presented the issue in the case as an easy one:

> This is a routine application of a standard public accommodation law. Like virtually all public accommodation laws, Colorado's Anti-Discrimination Act applies to businesses that are open to the public. It regulates their sales by prohibiting them from refusing to serve a customer based on certain personal characteristics—specifically, disability, race, creed, color, sex, sexual orientation, marital status, national origin, or ancestry. Colo. Rev. Stat. § 24-34-601(1), (2). Its prohibition on discrimination in sales is entirely indifferent to whether the product being sold is artistic or expressive; it applies equally to sales of coffee cups or jewelry, to admissions to hotels or theaters, and to services provided by gas stations or

— The first sentence is short and establishes the theme using plain language. The rest of the paragraph embellishes the theme with supporting details.

---

2. Brief for Respondent at 14-15, *Florida v. Jardines*, 569 U.S. 1 (2013) (No. 11-564), 2012 WL 2486026.

sign painters. The Anti-Discrimination Act is also indifferent to any message the business seeks to communicate—or not communicate—by refusing service to customers on the prohibited grounds. If a business denies service to a customer because she is Catholic, or African American, or gay, it does not matter whether the refusal was motivated by a religious belief, a desire to express a particular message, or bare animus.[3]

As you begin drafting your Conclusion and the rest of the CREAC, consider how you can develop and incorporate a compelling theme. A well-developed theme will keep your writing consistent and focused, and it will make your arguments more persuasive.

4. STEP FOUR: DRAFT YOUR POINT HEADINGS

Most persuasive documents also highlight a version of your Conclusion in headings and subheadings. These statements—called point headings—are single sentences that are often bolded, underlined, or capitalized to stand out on the page. A simple motion might have just one point heading at the start, while a more complicated motion or appellate brief will have multiple point headings and subheadings throughout the document.

Point headings should serve as an outline of the arguments in your document. And they can also be used to mark each part of the CREAC analysis. For a more complex CREAC, you can have separate point headings for the Rule, Explanation, and Analysis. Longer trial court motions and all appellate briefs list each point heading and subheading in a table of contents, so a reader can easily scan the major points. Point headings break up the argument into smaller sections that are easier for the reader to understand. In many persuasive documents, there is a point heading every two to three pages.

Like a Conclusion, each point heading can identify the relief you seek, the anchor or rule that justifies that relief, and key facts. But your point headings must be readable. In general, they should not take up more than three or four lines on the page. And often, the most persuasive headings are those that are simple and short. So you might not be able to fit in a reference to the relief you seek, the anchor or rule that justifies that relief, *and* key facts. Instead, try to maintain a balance between providing a comprehensive summary of your argument and presenting a statement that is readable.

Keeping your point headings at a readable length will also make them more persuasive. Short, punchy sentences are powerful. Readers who encounter overly complex point headings tend to skip over them. For persuasive documents, you want to take advantage of every opportunity you have to make your best case, and point headings provide an excellent platform to do so.

---

3. Brief for Respondents at 13-14, *Masterpiece Cakeshop, Ltd. v. Colo. Civil Rights Comm'n*, No. 16-111 (Oct. 23, 2017), 2017 WL 4838415.

The example below includes the point headings and subheadings in the State's brief in *Florida v. Jardines*, the Fourth Amendment case regarding the dog sniff. Note that each heading is a single sentence that is authoritative, direct, and concise. Together, the headings provide an outline of the brief's argument.

Argument

I. A Dog Sniff at the Base of a House's Front Door Is Not a Fourth Amendment Search Requiring Probable Cause. — This point heading emphasizes the controlling law and key facts.

II. A Dog Sniff Does Not Become an Unlawful Fourth Amendment Search Just Because It Occurs Outside a House. — This point heading reinforces the theme—the noninvasive nature of a dog sniff.

    A. The Sniff of a Detector Dog Outside Along the Ordinary Path to the Front Door Did Not Violate the Sanctity of Jardines' Grow House. — This subheading emphasizes key, compelling facts.

    B. *Kyllo*'s Prohibition on the Use of Imaging Devices Does Not Apply to Dog Sniffs. — This subheading distinguishes a crucial case.

    C. This Case Involves a Century-Old Law Enforcement Technique that Will Not Lead to Dragnet-Style Sweeps.[4] — This subheading refutes one of the Respondent's arguments and offers an alternate view of the search.

Checklist for your persuasive Conclusion
Does my persuasive Conclusion...

☑ Identify the requested relief and the legal issue?
☑ Provide a reason for my Conclusion?
☑ Work with a theme that provides a memorable description of what the case is about?

---

4. Brief for Petitioner at 13-16, *Florida v. Jardines*, 569 U.S. 1 (2013) (No. 11-564), 2012 WL 1594294.

Writing a Persuasive Rule Section

As with objective documents, the Rule section in persuasive documents provides the controlling law, beginning with the broadest and most important rule. But when your document is persuasive, you need to consider how you can frame the rule in a favorable way. Try to frame the rules and choose wording that is persuasive, but take care not to overreach—any misstatement of the law will hurt your credibility and your case.

> **Writing a Persuasive Rule Section**
> 1. Organize rules from general to specific.
> 2. Quote only key language.
> 3. Check your citations.

1. STEP ONE: ORGANIZE RULES FROM GENERAL TO SPECIFIC

The Rule section should start with the broadest applicable rule. Consider the hierarchy of authority: Constitutions carry more weight than statutes, which carry more weight than case law, and so on. Make sure to use only primary authorities that are binding in your jurisdiction. If you have the rare case of first impression, where there is no binding authority in your jurisdiction, choose persuasive authorities from other jurisdictions that favor your position.

A. Start with Constitutions and Statutes

When the legal question is governed by a constitutional provision, the language of the provision would be the broadest rule and should appear first in the Rule section, followed by rules from case law that interpret it. Legal questions governed by statutes should use a similar approach—providing the broadest statute first, then more specific, definitional statutes if applicable, and then rules from case law interpreting the statutory language. If you have a constitutional or statutory provision as your main rule, you can use additional, narrower rules from case law in your Rule section to focus your reader's attention on the specific issues in your case. You want to present the rules in a logical way so that a reader unfamiliar with the area of law would easily understand the legal context.

In *Florida v. Jardines*, the case about the dog sniff outside a home, the starting point is easy to identify: The Fourth Amendment applies and is the broadest applicable rule. The brief for the Respondent begins with this rule and then uses two cases to demonstrate a favorable interpretation of the rule and focus the reader's attention on the theme of protecting individuals' privacy inside their homes.

> The Fourth Amendment to the United States Constitution guarantees that "[t]he right of the people to be secure in their persons, houses, papers, and effects, against unreasonable searches and seizures, shall not be violated, and no Warrants shall issue, but upon probable cause, . . . and particularly describing the place to be searched, and the persons or things to be seized." U.S. Const. amend. IV. "'At the very core' of the Fourth Amendment 'stands the right of a man to retreat into his own home and there be free from unreasonable governmental intrusion.'" *Kyllo v. United States*, 33 U.S. 27, 31 (2001) (quoting *Silverman v. United States*, 365 U.S. 505, 511 (1961)). The Fourth Amendment draws "a firm line at the entrance to the house." *Payton v. New York*, 445 U.S. 573, 589 (1980). The line drawn at the entrance to the house "must be not only firm but also bright—which requires clear specification of those methods of surveillance that require a warrant." *Kyllo*, 533 U.S. at 40. "With few exceptions, the question whether a warrantless search of a home is reasonable and hence constitutional must be answered no." *Id.* at 31.[1]

Margin annotations:

— For the rule, the writer quotes key language from the amendment.

— This favorable language from a controlling case references the major theme of the case.

— *Payton* introduces a convincing rule.

— The Rule section ends with a statement of the rule that the Respondent wants the Court to adopt.

In developing your Rule section, keep in mind that attorneys have an obligation of candor to the court, and they cannot omit an unfavorable case simply because it does not help their client's position. Although you must present the holdings and facts of unfavorable cases accurately, you can—and should—try to describe unfavorable cases in a way that will allow you to distinguish them later in your argument.

B. Outline Your Case Law

If no constitutional or statutory provision applies, your Rule section will begin with case law. To identify the broadest, most general rule, review your cases to see how the courts present the rules relevant to your issue. Courts

---

1. Brief for Respondent at 16, *Florida v. Jardines*, 569 U.S. 1 (2013) (No. 11-564), 2012 WL 2486026.

usually start with the broadest rule, so your Rule section could use the same starting point.

The organization from broad to narrow rules is logical. You may recall from Chapter 9 that rules fit into at least five categories:

1. Rule with key terms that need to be defined
2. Legal test with elements
3. Factors test
4. Balancing test
5. Rule with exceptions

For each type of rule, the reader needs to understand the broad legal context to understand the law surrounding your narrow issue. The rule with key terms that need to be defined, for instance, should start with a rule statement that includes key terms and then define those key terms.

Suppose, for example, that you are defending an intentional infliction of emotional distress claim. The rule for intentional infliction of emotional distress is a legal test with elements, and only one element is in dispute in your case. The reader might be confused if you start by providing a rule relating to only one element. Instead, you should start with the broad rule listing all the elements and then provide the more specific rule that relates to your issue. This organization allows the reader to understand and identify the broad legal context for your issue.

As you develop your Rule section, try to frame each part of the rule in a favorable way. If one of your binding cases uses language that favors your position, you may want to quote that language in your Rule section. Consider that every word and every sentence in your document gives you an opportunity to persuade your reader that your Conclusion is correct.

The following example could start the Argument section of a motion to dismiss the intentional infliction of emotional distress claim.

> The Court should dismiss Plaintiff's claim for intentional infliction of emotional distress because Widelene Jean did not act outrageously when she asked Plaintiff to leave the store after he removed all of his clothes. — Conclusion
>
> The tort of intentional infliction of emotional distress requires a plaintiff to prove (1) extreme and outrageous conduct; (2) intent to cause, or disregard of a substantial probability of causing, severe emotional distress; (3) a causal connection between the conduct and the injury; and (4) severe emotional distress. *Howell v. N.Y. Post Co.*, 612 N.E.2d 699, 702 (N.Y. 1993). — The first rule lists the four elements for the tort in a way that emphasizes the Plaintiff's burden of proof.
>
> Outrageous conduct is "conduct exceeding all bounds usually tolerated by decent society." *Id.* — The second rule statement defines the narrower rule for the element at issue.
>
> Proof of this element "serves the dual function of filtering out petty and trivial complaints that do not belong in court and assuring that plaintiff's claim of severe emotional distress is genuine." *Id.* (noting that "of the intentional infliction of emotional distress claims considered by this Court, every one has failed because the alleged conduct was not sufficiently outrageous"). — The writer then chooses favorable language from the case to introduce the Plaintiff's high burden of proof, which allows the writer to begin to develop the theme.

While the example on the previous page from the Defendant's Motion to Dismiss presents language that is favorable to the Defendant's position from controlling case law, the Plaintiff would do the opposite in the Response to the Motion to Dismiss:

> The Court should deny Defendant's Motion to Dismiss because the — Conclusion
> Complaint states a plausible claim that the Defendant acted outrageously
> when she publicly humiliated the 92-year-old Plaintiff who was suffering
> from dementia. The tort of intentional infliction of emotional distress has — The first rule lists the four
> four elements: (1) extreme and outrageous conduct; (2) intent to cause, elements in a straightforward
> or disregard of a substantial probability of causing, severe emotional way, deemphasizing Plaintiff's
> distress; (3) a causal connection between the conduct and the injury; and burden.
> (4) severe emotional distress. *Howell v. N.Y. Post Co.*, 612 N.E.2d 699, 702
> (N.Y. 1993). The tort "imposes liability based on after-the-fact judgments — The second rule emphasizes
> about the actor's behavior" and "is as limitless as the human capacity for language that is favorable for
> cruelty." *Id.* the Plaintiff.

2. STEP TWO: QUOTE ONLY KEY LANGUAGE

Choosing your words carefully is particularly important when writing persuasive documents because every word gives you an opportunity to advance your client's case. The rules should be written in present tense because these are the rules that will govern your case. In the previous examples, each writer used present tense and chose to quote short but key phrases from controlling case law that favor the client's position. Each writer also chose to paraphrase statements that were not particularly eloquent or helpful. In the same way, you should quote only the most helpful language from court opinions.

In many cases, you can choose to paraphrase the wording in a court opinion to make it more persuasive. You can change some rules from positive statements to negative statements, for instance, to favor your client's position.

Consider the examples below. Note how the first statement favors the plaintiff by emphasizing when the manufacturer is liable. The second statement also states the rule accurately, but the writer emphasizes when the manufacturer is *not* liable by changing the rule statement from a positive to a negative one. Both statements are effective and include no quotations.

Plaintiff's rule statement: Positive statement
A manufacturer will be held strictly liable for failure to warn when the danger involved is foreseeable. *Zaza v. Marquess & Nell, Inc.*, 675 A.2d 620, 632 (N.J. 1996).

Defendant's rule statement: Negative statement
A manufacturer of a component part cannot be held strictly liable for failure to warn unless the danger involved is foreseeable. *Zaza v. Marquess & Nell, Inc.*, 675 A.2d 620, 632 (N.J. 1996).

The key to paraphrasing case law is to maintain accuracy while thinking about how to make every word and statement more persuasive for your client.

Although paraphrasing language from case law can help your case, the same practice does not apply when using constitutions and statutes. In general, you should quote the precise language from constitutions and statutes. Unlike rules, holdings, and facts from case law, which are often paraphrased by one court to the next, the precise wording in constitutions and statutes is important. Many legal issues you will analyze in law school and your legal career will relate to interpreting this precise wording. The Rule section closing out the next example, from the respondent's brief in *Trinity Lutheran Church of Columbia, Inc. v. Comer*, quotes key language from the First Amendment, then paraphrases a short rule from case law.[2]

ARGUMENT

I. The State's decision not to subsidize Trinity Lutheran does not violate the Free Exercise Clause of the First Amendment. — The point heading succinctly states the State's position.

Trinity Lutheran contends that the State has violated the Free Exercise Clause by categorically declaring religious organizations ineligible to compete for a playground-resurfacing subsidy. But Trinity Lutheran's argument misinterprets the Free Exercise Clause, ignoring its text, history, and this Court's precedent. The Free Exercise Clause, by its plain language, prevents the government from "prohibiting" the free exercise of religion. It does not guarantee churches opportunities for public financing, nor does it require that the government act with strict neutrality toward religious and nonreligious interests. The challenged policy places no meaningful restraint on Trinity Lutheran's ability to freely exercise its religion. For that reason, Trinity Lutheran's free exercise claim was properly dismissed. — This first paragraph is the Conclusion. It uses key language from the First Amendment's free exercise clause in support.

A. The Free Exercise Clause forbids only government action that "prohibits" the free exercise of religion; it does not require that government subsidize churches. — A point heading introduces the Rule section and quotes the most important word: "prohibits."

The Free Exercise Clause of the First Amendment states that "Congress shall make no law respecting an establishment of religion, or *prohibiting the free exercise thereof....*" U.S. Const. amend. I (emphasis added). It has been incorporated into the Fourteenth Amendment and is thus applicable to the states. *E.g., Emp't Div., Dep't. of Human Res. of Or. v. Smith*, 494 U.S. 872, 876–77 (1990).[3] — The Rule section then quotes the key part of the amendment. — It includes a brief, paraphrased statement from case law, describing why the rule is applicable here. The rule is in present tense.

---

2. *Trinity Lutheran Church of Columbia, Inc. v. Comer*, 137 S. Ct. 2012 (2017).

3. Brief for Respondent at 5-6, *Trinity Lutheran Church of Columbia, Inc. v. Comer*, 137 S. Ct. 2012 (2017) (No. 15-577), 2016 WL 3548944.

3. STEP THREE: CHECK YOUR CITATIONS

Finally, make sure that you have a citation for every rule in your Rule section. In general, every sentence in the Rule and Explanation sections of your CREAC will have a citation. Make sure too that every citation is in proper citation form and that you follow local citation rules when they apply.[4] Incomplete or incorrect citations could prevent the reader from finding the authorities cited in your Rule section, and they weaken the credibility of your persuasive document.

> ### Checklist for your persuasive Rule section
> ### Does my persuasive Rule section...
> ☑ Organize the rules from general to specific with attention to the hierarchy of authority?
> ☑ Frame the rule persuasively?
> ☑ Quote key language?
> ☑ Use present tense?
> ☑ Correctly cite authority for every sentence?

---

4. Refer to Chapter 43 for detailed instructions on following proper *Bluebook* form.

Writing a Persuasive Explanation Section

A persuasive Explanation has a similar structure to an objective Explanation, but a persuasive Explanation has a different purpose and audience. Unlike an objective Explanation, which is a balanced demonstration of how a rule has been interpreted to justify your prediction, a persuasive Explanation advocates for an interpretation of the law that will result in the court granting your requested relief. Your task is to explain the law so the court interprets it to support your position, rather than your opponent's. If you are writing a motion asking the court to dismiss your opponent's claim, for example, you need to convince the court that the law favors your request.

Writing a Persuasive Explanation Section

1. Categorize the cases.
2. Identify the anchors and synthesize multiple cases.
3. Use cases to emphasize the persuasive anchors.

---

1. STEP ONE: CATEGORIZE THE CASES

To write a persuasive Explanation, you first need to master the universe of relevant cases that interpret and apply your rule. Once you have researched and identified the relevant cases,[1] you need to separate those cases that have a favorable outcome for your case from those that do not. A case with a favorable outcome is one where the court (1) interprets the rule in the way that you are asking the court to interpret the rule in your case and (2) holds for the party that was in the same position as your client. A case with an unfavorable outcome is one that (1) supports your opponent's interpretation of the rule and (2) holds for the party in your opponent's position.

---

1. Refer to Chapters 39–42 for detailed instructions on finding relevant authorities.

In your Analysis section, you will analogize to those cases with a favorable outcome and distinguish those with an unfavorable outcome. So your Explanation should use the cases to describe the law in a way that sets up these analogies and distinctions.

For instance, if you were writing a defendant's motion to dismiss for lack of personal jurisdiction, you would want to use cases in the Explanation where the courts held that there was no personal jurisdiction over the defendant—because that is the holding you want the court to reach in your case. Cases that describe in detail why jurisdiction was lacking would be helpful because they would offer facts and reasoning that you could use for analogizing in your Analysis section.

But you may also want to use unfavorable cases in your Explanation for two reasons. First, if a case has an unfavorable outcome but it is easily distinguishable, describing the specific facts that are distinguishable can help illustrate the law and advance your position. Keep in mind that because unfavorable cases have an outcome that is contrary to your position, they can undermine your persuasive interpretation of the rule and your request for relief. But when the specific facts contrast starkly with your own, you can use these specific facts to illustrate the law in a persuasive way in your Explanation. And that helps set up a strong distinction in your Analysis section.

Second, because you have an obligation of candor to the court, you cannot ignore unfavorable authority that is binding in your jurisdiction. Thus, even if the facts are not easily distinguishable, you may need to cite unfavorable cases. Your task in doing so is to cite only those unfavorable cases that are legally binding and so factually and legally similar to your own case that it would be unethical to omit them. And then you should try to cite those cases in a way that minimizes their impact in relation to the favorable cases in your Explanation.

2. STEP TWO: IDENTIFY THE ANCHORS AND SYNTHESIZE MULTIPLE CASES

A persuasive Explanation should be organized around anchors that are drawn from multiple cases and that explain how the rule has been interpreted and applied. The anchors are the grounds for a court's decision, whether those reasons are stated explicitly or implicitly. To identify the anchors in multiple cases, you must read each case closely and determine what the outcome in each case depends upon. Then, you can synthesize these determinative issues—or anchors—across cases. Organizing your Explanation around these anchors allows you to describe what matters in the law as a whole and advance your position, rather than just describing each case one by one.

A single case will rarely be sufficient to identify the anchors that explain a rule because different courts often consider different anchors based on the facts of the cases before them. Thus, you will need multiple cases to find and describe all the relevant anchors that courts have used to understand and apply the rule. Your Explanation should be a combination or synthesis of the anchors from all the relevant cases.

Although your presentation of the anchors should be persuasive, your selection of the anchors cannot be misleading. If you do not acknowledge all the relevant anchors, your persuasive document will lack credibility with the court because you will be misrepresenting the applicable law. You do not want to ignore or omit relevant anchors just because they do not serve your persuasive arguments.

For instance, in a motion to dismiss a burglary charge because the defendant was not within the curtilage of the home, the cases establish the following anchors to define curtilage:

1. whether the area has an enclosure;
2. whether the enclosure has openings for entering and exiting the property; and
3. whether the enclosure is irregular, like sparse shrubs, or fortifying, like a privacy fence.

If the facts of your case involve a yard that was completely surrounded by low, uneven shrubs, Anchor No. 1 would not be persuasive, Anchor No. 2 would be neutral, and Anchor No. 3 would support your argument that the charge should be dismissed.

To fully explain the law, you need to describe all relevant anchors. In the burglary example, Anchor No. 1 is relevant because the yard in your case is enclosed. Thus, you need to mention Anchor No. 1 in your Explanation. In contrast, Anchor No. 2 does not apply to your case because there was no opening for entry or exit. It is appropriate to either omit Anchor No. 2 or mention it only briefly. Last, you would obviously want to discuss and emphasize Anchor No. 3 in your Explanation because it is the anchor that supports your request for relief.

You might be inclined to discuss only Anchor No. 3 because it is the only anchor that will help you argue that the yard was not curtilage. But doing so would provide the court with an incomplete explanation of the rule, which hurts the credibility of your document. And your opponent would almost certainly make arguments based on Anchor No. 1. By omitting it, you would be forfeiting your opportunity to rebut those arguments. Your persuasive Explanation must balance your ethical obligations of candor to the court and zealous advocacy of your client's position.

3. STEP THREE: USE CASES TO EMPHASIZE THE PERSUASIVE ANCHORS

Once you identify the anchors that you will use to explain the rule, you can organize your anchor paragraphs to emphasize the anchors and cases that are persuasive for your side. An anchor or case is persuasive when it supports your interpretation of the rule and has a favorable outcome that is analogous to your case or an unfavorable outcome that is distinguishable from your case. Although you are not going to analogize or distinguish your case in this section,[2] your persuasive Explanation should set up and support the arguments that you will make later in your document.

A. Start with Persuasive Topic Sentences

Like in an objective Explanation, each persuasive Explanation paragraph must begin with a topic sentence. In a persuasive Explanation, the topic sentences should introduce or summarize the anchors in the most persuasive way for your client. The topic sentences should persuasively guide the court through your Explanation and advance your reader's understanding of the law.

The topic sentences should be broad, persuasive statements about the anchors. The sentences that follow should provide more specific details and reasoning to illustrate the broad statements. The organization is comparable to an upside-down triangle—the broad statements are at the top giving the big picture and the more specific details follow. Sentences that describe legal principles are written in present tense because those principles can be applied to your case in the present. Sentences that describe the holdings of cases are written in past tense because those cases have already been decided.

For instance, in the motion to dismiss a burglary charge because the defendant was not within the curtilage, your topic sentence on Anchor No. 3 (regarding whether the enclosure is irregular, like sparse shrubs, or fortifying, like a privacy fence) would persuasively summarize the anchor. You can do this by explaining how the law supports the outcome you want—in this case, a decision that the area was not curtilage. Then, the paragraph would provide specific details to illustrate the anchor, including any facts, holdings, reasoning, or language from relevant cases. Although your Explanation should not mention any of the facts of your case, you would want to keep in mind that in your case, the yard was completely surrounded by low, uneven shrubs, so that you can set up the arguments to come.

The following is a persuasive Explanation paragraph for Anchor No. 3:

This topic sentence persuasively summarizes Anchor No. 3 by describing what is "not" curtilage. It states a general legal principle, so it is in the present tense.

An area is not curtilage unless it has a fortifying enclosure that erects a barrier to entry. *Martinez v. State*, 700 So. 2d 142, 144 (Fla. Dist. Ct. App. 1997). An irregular enclosure will not qualify as curtilage to support a burglary charge. *Hamilton v. State*, 660 So. 2d 1038, 1046 (Fla. 1995). For example, an unfenced area that was bordered only by "several unevenly

The next sentence provides a more specific description of the anchor by describing what curtilage does not include. It also states a general principle, so it is in present tense.

The third sentence uses details from a case to illustrate what is not curtilage. It describes the holding of a case, so it is in past tense.

---

2. Analogizing and distinguishing your case occurs in the Analysis section.

spaced trees" did not have a sufficient enclosure to be curtilage. *Id*. But a yard with a chain link fence around it, with an opening for the driveway, was curtilage. *Dubose v. State*, 210 So. 3d 641, 653–54 (Fla. 2017).

> The last sentence provides a counterexample, setting up a distinction for the Analysis section. It is also in past tense.

This Explanation paragraph is effective because it starts with a broad topic sentence and narrows to describe the favorable facts, holding, and outcome of a relevant case using key, quoted language. It also combines details from multiple cases to persuasively explain Anchor No. 3.

B. Organize to Account for the Primacy and Recency Effects

For a persuasive Explanation to be an accurate description of a rule, you may need to discuss anchors that are not persuasive for your side. You can minimize the unfavorable impact of these anchors by situating them between the anchors that are most helpful. Readers best remember and pay the most attention to information that they encounter first (primacy effect) and last (recency effect). Thus, your Explanation section and each of the paragraphs in that section should begin and end with persuasive information with the less persuasive information sandwiched in the middle.

Here is an example of a persuasive Explanation that is organized to emphasize favorable Anchor No. 3 (whether the enclosure is irregular or fortifying). The example de-emphasizes Anchor No. 1 (whether the area has an enclosure) by sandwiching it after a persuasive topic sentence broad enough to cover both anchors and before the persuasive details about Anchor No. 3.

> This Conclusion begins the CREAC and states that the burglary charge should be dismissed.

Chapman's burglary charge should be dismissed because he was not within the curtilage of the Perry compound. A burglary charge requires "entering or remaining in a dwelling, a structure, or a conveyance with the intent to commit an offense therein...." Fla. Stat. § 810.02(b)(1) (2018). A "dwelling" includes only "a building or conveyance...which has a roof over it and is designed to be occupied by people lodging therein at night, together with the curtilage thereof." Fla. Stat. § 810.011(2) (2018).

> This Rule section persuasively describes the two relevant Florida burglary statutes to set up the argument that the burglary charge should be dismissed.

> This topic sentence acknowledges Anchor No. 1 and persuasively summarizes Anchor No. 3.

An area surrounding a residence is not curtilage unless it has a fortifying enclosure that erects a barrier to entry. *Martinez v. State*, 700 So. 2d 142, 144 (Fla. Dist. Ct. App. 1997). The requirement that curtilage involve "some form of an enclosure" avoids "unreasonable, harsh, or absurd consequences," such as convicting a person of burglary after he innocently wanders into an open yard "in broad daylight, without the

> This sentence describes Anchor No. 1 and hides it in the middle of a paragraph that is in the middle of the Explanation. The sentence ends with a persuasive detail.

homeowner's consent, with the intent to take a piece of fruit from a tree." *Hamilton v. State*, 660 So. 2d 1038, 1045 (Fla. 1995). An irregular enclosure will not support a burglary charge. *Id*. at 1046. For example, an unfenced area that was bordered only by "several unevenly spaced trees" did not have a sufficient enclosure to support a burglary conviction. *Id*.

— This sentence provides a more specific, persuasive explanation of Anchor No. 3 by describing what does not satisfy the anchor.

— This sentence describes the facts, holding, and language of a favorable case to explain Anchor No. 3.

The Explanation paragraphs from the Petitioners' brief in the 2007 U.S. Supreme Court case *Morse v. Frederick* demonstrate how to write an effective persuasive Explanation by emphasizing the persuasive anchors from multiple cases. The Petitioners successfully argued that a public school had the right to prohibit students at a school-sponsored, off-campus event from displaying a banner that read "Bong Hits 4 Jesus":

This topic sentence broadly and persuasively describes Anchor No. 1— the important role of public education in America—setting up the more specific explanation relating to the permissibility of regulating the rights of public school students.

Throughout the fifty States (and the District of Columbia), public education serves what this Court long ago described as "a principal instrument in awakening the child to cultural values." *Brown v. Bd. of Educ.*, 347 U.S. 483, 493 (1954). Through government-operated educational institutions, large and small, the vast majority of young Americans are prepared "for later professional training" and for "adjust[ing] normally to [their] environment." *Kuhlmeier*, 484 U.S. at 272 (quoting *Brown*, 347 U.S. at 493). Those who serve as teachers and administrators in this challenging environment are tasked with a weighty and delicate responsibility. In prescribing and controlling student conduct, public educators are inexorably required to balance students' constitutionally guaranteed liberties with the bedrock duty to educate young minds, including fashioning "the boundaries of socially appropriate behavior." *Bethel Sch. Dist. No. 403 v. Fraser*, 478 U.S. 675, 681 (1986). Pursuit of these goals inevitably requires authorities to regulate speech, symbolic and otherwise, in a manner impermissible outside the school setting. *Id*. at 682; *accord Bd. of Educ. v. Earls*, 536 U.S. 822 (2002) (upholding high school's random suspicionless drug testing policy); *Vernonia Sch. Dist. 47J v. Acton*, 515 U.S. 646 (1995) (permitting random drug testing of high school student athletes).

— These sentences are a detailed explanation of why public schools need to regulate students' rights, and they quote favorable language from relevant cases.

— This sentence is a detailed explanation of why public schools must specifically regulate students' free speech rights.

— These parentheticals briefly summarize the favorable outcomes of cases that support Anchor No. 1.

In the First Amendment context, this Court has long emphasized that the rights of students in the public schools "are not automatically coextensive with the rights of adults in other settings." *Fraser*, 478 U.S. at 682 (citing *New Jersey v. T.L.O.*, 469 U.S. 325, 340-42 (1985)). Thus, while students do not "shed their constitutional rights to freedom of speech or expression at the schoolhouse gate," students' rights must be "applied in light

— This topic sentence introduces Anchor No. 2—that students' free speech rights in public schools are limited— which prepares the reader for an explanation of what justifies such limits.

of the *special characteristics* of the school environment." *Tinker v. Des Moines Indep. Cmty. Sch. Dist.*, 393 U.S. 503, 506 (1969). The "uninhibited, robust, and wide-open" free speech in adult discourse, as ordained in *New York Times Co. v. Sullivan*, 376 U.S. 254, 270 (1964), is manifestly different from the latitude accorded to schoolchildren in a "custodial and tutelary" environment. *Vernonia*, 515 U.S. at 655. — These sentences describe unpersuasive Anchor No. 3—that students retain a right to free speech at school—which has been sandwiched between details regarding persuasive Anchor No. 2.

As this Court has acknowledged on numerous occasions, the resolution of conflicts arising in the daily operation of school systems "is primarily the responsibility of parents, teachers, and state and local school officials, and not of federal judges." *Kuhlmeier*, 484 U.S. at 273. Only when a decision to censor student expression has no valid educational purpose is the First Amendment so "directly and sharply implicate[d]" as to require judicial intervention to protect students' constitutional rights. *Id.* (quoting *Epperson v. Arkansas*, 393 U.S. 97, 104 (1968)). Thus, in discerning the proper doctrinal limitations upon the baseline liberty guaranteed by the Free Speech Clause, a guiding principle unifying this Court's teachings is that "[a] school need not tolerate student speech that is inconsistent with its 'basic educational mission.'" *Id.* at 266 (citing *Fraser*, 478 U.S. at 685).[3] — This topic sentence introduces and summarizes Anchor No. 4—that students' free speech rights should be decided by schools, not federal judges.

— The sentences in this paragraph quote favorable language from relevant cases to include specific details about public schools' broad authority to regulate students' free speech rights.

C. Use Signals and Parentheticals to Add Support

Because a persuasive Explanation needs to convince the court that your interpretation of the rule is correct, it should demonstrate that there is extensive support in the case law for your interpretation. You show this support through citations to multiple cases. You can easily add case support to your persuasive Explanation by using signals and parentheticals.

Signals are shorthand to tell the court how the cited cases relate to your proposition.[4] By using signals, you can efficiently include favorable cases and quietly acknowledge unfavorable cases. The most commonly used persuasive signals are *see*, *see also*, and *see, e.g.*

Explanatory parentheticals are an efficient way to include the facts, holdings, reasoning, and language of cases that explain your anchors. By adding citations with explanatory parentheticals, you show the court that your interpretation of the rule is credible and well supported.

The following is an Explanation paragraph for the motion to dismiss the burglary charge that is similar to the one on pages 181-82 but with signals and parentheticals added for support:

---

3. Brief for Petitioner at 17–19, *Morse v. Frederick*, 551 U.S. 393 (2007) (No. 06-278), 2007 WL 118979.

4. Refer to sections 3.E. and 3.G. in Chapter 43 for detailed instructions on how to incorporate signals and parentheticals into your document.

An area surrounding a residence is not curtilage unless it has a fortifying enclosure that erects a barrier to entry. *Martinez v. State*, 700 So. 2d 142, 144 (Fla. Dist. Ct. App. 1997) ("Under the common law, merely identifying the boundaries of a property, as opposed to erecting a barrier to entry to the extended residence of the curtilage, falls short of bringing unattached structures within the curtilage of the home."). The requirement that curtilage involve "some form of an enclosure" avoids "unreasonable, harsh, or absurd consequences," such as convicting a person of burglary after he innocently wanders into an open yard "in broad daylight, without the homeowner's consent, with the intent to take a piece of fruit from a tree." *Hamilton v. State*, 660 So. 2d 1038, 1045 (Fla. 1995); *see also* *J.L. v. State*, 57 So. 3d 924, 926 (Fla. Dist. Ct. App. 2011) (holding that stealing a go-cart, a four-wheeler, and a skateboard from an unenclosed yard was similar to removing a piece of fruit). An irregular enclosure will not support a burglary charge. *Hamilton*, 660 So. 2d at 1046; *cf. Baker v. State*, 636 So. 2d 1342, 1343–44 (Fla. Dist. Ct. App. 1994) (holding that a yard separated from the neighbor's house by a 6-foot privacy fence and secluded by shrubs was curtilage). For example, an unfenced area that was bordered only by "several unevenly spaced trees" did not have a sufficient enclosure to support a burglary conviction. *Id.*

> — This parenthetical includes quoted language that supports the persuasive anchor introduced in the topic sentence.

> — This citation with a signal and parenthetical describes a favorable outcome to add support to the detailed explanation of the anchor.

> — This citation with a signal and parenthetical describes a distinguishable, unfavorable outcome to further explain the anchor.

D. Illustrate Seminal or Unavoidable Cases

i. Determine Whether a Single-Case Illustration Is Appropriate

An Explanation section is usually made up of paragraphs that are organized around anchors and that synthesize and use multiple cases to persuasively explain the law. In some persuasive documents, however, you will need to include an illustration in your Explanation that focuses on a single case and isolates the relevant anchors, holding, facts, background, and reasoning of that case.

Not every persuasive Explanation section will need a single-case illustration. A single-case illustration is necessary only when there is a seminal or unavoidable case that governs your rule. For example, when the highest court in your jurisdiction or the court that will decide your case has issued a single decision on your issue or issued a decision very recently, that case is likely seminal or unavoidable. You should include an illustration of a seminal or unavoidable case in your persuasive Explanation, even if that case has an unfavorable outcome, keeping in mind that you will need to distinguish the case in your Analysis. To determine whether your issue is controlled by a seminal or unavoidable case, ask the following questions:

- Does the case dominate the field of this legal issue due to its weight of authority or recency?
- Would the typical legal reader expect an in-depth discussion of this case?
- Would the absence of a case illustration give my opponent a strong argument that I am ignoring negative authority?

• Would the absence of a case illustration hurt the credibility of my document?

If you answer yes to any of these questions, you have a seminal or unavoidable case that will require an illustration, even if it has an unfavorable outcome.

ii. Present the Seminal or Unavoidable Case Persuasively

When your rule is governed by a seminal or unavoidable case, you need to write a persuasive case illustration in your Explanation. Because a seminal or unavoidable case is sure to be familiar to both the court and your opponent, you should be scrupulously accurate. If the seminal or unavoidable case has a negative outcome, you should acknowledge it, rather than ignore it.

Then, the illustration should describe the relevant facts, holding, background, reasoning, and language of the case in the best possible light for your side. In particular, you should identify persuasive anchors in the seminal or unavoidable case. These anchors can be facts that make the case analogous or distinguishable from your case, bases for the court's decision that apply in your case, or language that is persuasive for your side. Your illustration should focus on these persuasive anchors.

In *Morse v. Frederick*, the Petitioners had to illustrate the seminal case *Tinker v. Des Moines Independent Community School District*,[5] which defined students' First Amendment rights and set forth the standard for determining when a school's disciplinary actions are unconstitutional. In *Tinker*, the Supreme Court held that the school had violated the students' right to free speech. Thus, for the *Morse* Petitioners, who were the principal and school district, *Tinker* was a seminal case with an unfavorable outcome. The Petitioners' brief includes an illustration that acknowledges the unfavorable outcome in *Tinker* but also establishes the bases on which the Petitioners persuasively argued that the case was distinguishable.

Here is the illustration of *Tinker* from the Petitioners' brief:

> The illustration begins by acknowledging that *Tinker* is a seminal case with an unfavorable outcome. It then describes key facts that impacted the Court's holding.

The framework for student speech doctrine begins with *Tinker*. 393 U.S. 503 (1969). In that landmark case, the Court upheld the free speech rights of three students to wear anti-war armbands during the school day as a silent, passive political protest. 393 U.S. at 514. The Court reasoned that wearing black armbands, a traditional sign of mourning, was expressive conduct akin to pure speech, which is entitled to comprehensive protection. *Id.* at 505-06. At the same time, the *Tinker* majority recognized the unique characteristics of a public school and the unavoidable reality that administrators and teachers may suppress student speech, whether in class or out of it, that "intrudes upon the work of the schools or the

> Many of these facts distinguish *Tinker* from *Morse*.

> This sentence describes an aspect of the *Tinker* opinion that is persuasive for Petitioners.

---

5. 393 U.S. 503 (1969).

rights of other students." *Id.* at 508. In the record before it, however, the Court could discern no evidence that the passive wearing of 2-inch arm-bands disrupted school operations. *Id.*

— This sentence describes the Court's holding. Again, this sentence focuses on a fact that distinguishes *Tinker* from *Morse.*

The *Tinker* Court had no occasion to spell out in detail the extent or nature of "disruption" necessary to trigger a school's authority to curtail student speech. *Id.* The Court described the requisite disruption as "interference, actual or nascent, with the schools' work," which is something more than "undifferentiated fear or apprehension of disturbance." *Id.* Under this standard, if a school administrator reasonably perceives (or forecasts) that a student's expressive conduct is presently interfering (or would eventually interfere) with the school's work, then the administrator is warranted in suppressing the particular expression (or expressive conduct). *Id.* Student speech rising to this level of disruption may occur "in class or out of it" and may "stem[] from time, place, or type of behavior." *Id.* at 513. The Court provided further guidance by distinguishing John Tinker's silent, passive conduct from the disciplinary problems posed by "aggressive, disruptive action or even group demonstrations." *Id.* at 507-08. The *Tinker* Court thus foreshadowed its willingness to approve school intervention when speech is accompanied by antisocial conduct. *See id.*

— This paragraph persuasively describes anchors in *Tinker* that favor Petitioners. Petitioners use this illustration paragraph to show the Court that *Tinker* supports their position in *Morse.* Petitioners quote the Court's language and use details from *Tinker* to establish the same persuasive anchors that Petitioners explained in their anchor paragraphs.

Justice Black dissented. *Id.* at 517 (Black, J., dissenting). He lamented that the broad sweep of the majority decision invited students to "use the schools at their whim as a platform" and that courts, rather than schools, "will allocate to themselves the function of deciding how the pupils' school day will be spent." *Id.* Although his opinion failed to carry the day, Justice Black's plain-spoken words continue to echo through the body of student speech law.[6]

— This paragraph describes a dissent in *Tinker* that supports Petitioners' argument.

iii. Avoid Serial Case Briefing

If you do not have a seminal or unavoidable case, you should probably not include single-case illustration paragraphs in your Explanation. In early drafts, many students try to write an Explanation that is a series of case illustrations or case briefs. But these series of case briefs typically explain too much about each case and lack the organization that can help advance your position. A series of case briefs also deprives you of an opportunity to use the Explanation to convince the court to interpret the rule favorably for your side based on your anchors.

If there are three relevant cases and you simply write a paragraph summarizing each case, you have not synthesized the persuasive anchors that will convince the court that you should prevail. Serial case briefs just report the facts, holdings, and outcomes of the cases without persuading the court that

---

6. Brief for Petitioner at 20–21, *Morse v. Frederick*, 551 U.S. 393 (2007) (No. 06-278), 2007 WL 118979.

your interpretation of the law is correct. Even when the cases do have positive outcomes, writing case illustrations, rather than synthesizing the persuasive anchors that the cases share, will make your Explanation less persuasive and effective. So if the first or second draft of your Explanation section has one case per paragraph, rethink your approach and organization according to the guidance offered throughout this chapter. In this way, you can advance your position and the reader's understanding of the law with every sentence.

Checklist for your persuasive Explanation section
Does my persuasive Explanation section...

☑ Explain the rules to the reader by identifying the anchors that were the grounds for the courts' decisions in relevant cases?

☑ Use a persuasive organization that employs the primacy and recency effects to minimize the impact of unfavorable anchors or cases?

☑ Illustrate each anchor using several cases, emphasizing the cases with favorable outcomes or the distinguishable aspects of cases with unfavorable outcomes?

☑ Use present tense for legal principles and past tense for the holding of past cases?

☑ Add support through signals and parentheticals?

☑ Illustrate any seminal or unavoidable cases as persuasively as possible?

☑ Avoid serial case briefing, which provides too much detail about each individual case and doesn't show the reader how the law helps you win?

☑ Cite authority after every sentence?

Writing a Persuasive Analysis Section

The Analysis section in a persuasive CREAC details the legal arguments that support your Conclusion. In this section, you will apply the law to your facts and draw case analogies and distinctions to show your reader why your arguments are sound and why the court should grant the relief you seek. The key to a strong Analysis section is to make arguments based on the anchors you identified in the Explanation section. Because the anchors will be the basis for the court's decision, you need to show the court how your facts fit with the anchors to prove your Conclusion. The effectiveness of your persuasive Analysis will depend on the factual and legal support you provide for the arguments you make based on the anchors.

Unlike the Analysis section in objective documents, a persuasive Analysis section has no counteranalysis. That's your opposing counsel's job. Instead, you will provide the strongest arguments that support your Conclusion, refute any arguments that opposing counsel has made, and preemptively refute any potential counterarguments or weaknesses in your position.

A persuasive Analysis should be written in an authoritative style. An objective Analysis might begin with a thesis statement that states: "A court will likely find that _____." But a persuasive Analysis section should use more convincing language—without any hedging. For instance, the following thesis statement could begin the Analysis section of an argument relating to the contract dispute:

> Defendant did not make a binding offer to sell his car because he had no intent to sell his revered Volkswagen Beetle when he jokingly placed a "For Sale" sign on it.

Make sure that each sentence you write in the Analysis section shows that you have no doubts about your position. After all, if your writing style is less than convincing, the court likely won't be persuaded by your arguments.

> **Writing a Persuasive Analysis Section**
> 1. Start off strong: Organize and outline your Analysis.
> 2. Start with a broad thesis that incorporates your theme.
> 3. Use topic sentences to organize your Analysis, and start with your best argument.
> 4. Provide factual support for each argument by recruiting relevant facts.
> 5. Provide legal support for each argument by analogizing and distinguishing relevant cases.
> 6. Affirmatively refute counterarguments.

1. STEP ONE: START OFF STRONG: ORGANIZE AND OUTLINE YOUR ANALYSIS

The purpose of the Analysis section is to advocate for your client's position in the most compelling and credible way you can. Authoritative language and specific arguments based on the anchors and the facts of your case are essential. In addition, the arguments within a persuasive Analysis section should be organized and presented in a persuasive way.

The arguments should be logically organized to help the court follow the substance of your Analysis. If you have a threshold argument, that will need to come first. When organizing your arguments, remember the primacy and recency effects—readers pay the most attention to information that they encounter first and last. For this reason, you should begin your Analysis with your best point. You may want to bury weaker points in the middle of the Analysis or organize your Analysis with the arguments in descending order, from strongest to weakest.

To identify your best point and rank your other arguments, you will need to create a clear outline. Review the anchors you identified for the Explanation section and review your facts. Then, combine the anchors and facts into arguments that show why your client should prevail. Make a list of these arguments. These arguments will need to have two types of support, both of which are critical:

1. factual support from the facts of your own case and
2. legal support through comparisons to other cases.

So for each argument, identify the relevant facts from your case and the cases from the Explanation section that you can analogize or distinguish. Then, rank your arguments according to their strength. Think critically about your arguments and evaluate them as a judge or opposing counsel might. The first point should be virtually unassailable, allowing you to capture the reader's attention and build up momentum before you deliver your other points.

An outline of the analysis in an appellate brief arguing that the burglary conviction on the curtilage issue should be reversed could look like the following example. Note that for each argument, the writer includes a summary of the topic sentence and both factual and legal support.

Argument 1: The area surrounding the compound isn't fully enclosed.
- Facts: The back of the property is completely unbounded; it has no fence or natural border; the back of the property makes up a large percentage of the square footage of the property.
- Cases: *State v. Caiozzo* (property was partially enclosed); *State v. Melvin* (property was partially enclosed with the largest section unbounded); *State v. Lepkin* (property was completely enclosed on all sides).

Argument 2: The only enclosure is more decorative than functional.
- Facts: The front of the property is surrounded by sporadic, low hedges and a short piece of ornamental fencing; the hedges and fence are both less than 3-feet high; they aren't impenetrable; the fence ends with an unlocked gate.
- Cases: *State v. Melvin* (court considered the purpose of the partial enclosure); *State v. Orr* (enclosure was unlocked and not impenetrable).

Argument 3: There are significant gaps in the property's perimeter.
- Facts: There are three openings in the compound's perimeter that allow any person or vehicle to access the property at any point; the openings are each at least 5-feet wide; one of the openings is paved as a driveway.
- Cases: *State v. Caiozzo* (five gaps); *State v. Melvin* (paved driveway); *State v. Bassett* (court compared total length of perimeter to size of the gaps).

2. STEP TWO: START WITH A BROAD THESIS THAT INCORPORATES YOUR THEME

A thesis statement at the start of the Analysis section provides the reader with an overview of your best arguments. A thesis also reminds the reader of the relief you seek and aims to sway the reader to agree with your position. For shorter Analysis sections that analyze only one or two anchors, a single thesis sentence could suffice as an introduction. But for more complex Analysis sections, a thesis paragraph will keep your reader focused on your major points.

Including each argument in the order it will be discussed in the thesis sentence or paragraph serves as a helpful roadmap for the reader. The following examples relating to curtilage demonstrate a short and long version of a thesis. The first thesis example summarizes arguments in a single sentence relating to two anchors: the type of enclosure and the extent of the enclosure.

The second example draws out the summary in a paragraph and analyzes a third anchor: gaps in the enclosure.

> Defendant's burglary conviction should be affirmed because the picket fence and hedgerow enclosing most of the victim's yard are more than adequate to qualify the area around the home as curtilage.

— A single-sentence thesis can begin a shorter Analysis section. The rest of the paragraph will describe the best argument.

> Mr. Chapman's conviction should be reversed because the Perry compound does not qualify as curtilage for three reasons. First, only the front area is enclosed; the back is unbounded. Second, the front is bordered only by a short, decorative fence and a line of low, uneven shrubs. Last, the area has three extensive gaps allowing any person or vehicle to easily enter or exit the area.

— A longer thesis paragraph summarizes the arguments for a more in-depth Analysis section.

In these examples, the State and defense counsel emphasize the arguments most helpful to their respective positions. By doing so, they also present the major themes of their arguments. In the first example, the State emphasizes the sufficiency of the enclosure around an individual's home. The State's choice of words, such as "burglary," "picket fence," "hedgerow," "victim," "yard," and "home," help illustrate the crime for the reader. The language focuses the reader on the theme that the defendant encroached upon the clear border to an individual's home.

In the second example, the thesis statement supporting the defendant presents an entirely different theme—that the large compound at issue has an inadequate and ineffective enclosure. The second thesis also humanizes the defendant by using his name, and the paragraph avoids mentioning the term "victim." Additionally, instead of referencing a home with a picket fence, the writer uses impersonal references to the "Perry compound" and "area," which paint a different picture than that of a home with a picket fence and neat row of hedges. Finally, the thesis paragraph emphasizes the gaps in the enclosure and the difference between the enclosures in the front and back yards, analyzing an anchor that the State chose to leave out. All these details help illustrate the theme that the enclosure around an impersonal compound is inadequate.

Your theme will likely emerge as you outline your Analysis section. To identify a theme or themes for your argument, review the outline of your anchors and the facts you want to emphasize in your arguments. Consider how your arguments interconnect and how they might relate to policy considerations. For instance, the State's thesis in the curtilage example touches upon the policy concern that individuals have certain privacy guarantees inside their homes' borders.

Your theme is the thread that connects the anchors and facts to your Conclusion, and that thread should be a constant throughout your document. Incorporating a theme—not just in the thesis for the Analysis section but in your Argument section as a whole—will make your document cohesive, logical, and more compelling. A strong theme will guide the court through your document and give the court a reason to rule in your favor.

To check whether you have successfully incorporated your theme through-out your document, try this self-editing test after completing your first draft: Read every paragraph independently and ask yourself, "Does this paragraph incorporate my theme and support my Conclusion?" If the answer is "no," revise or delete it, and try again.

Note how in the next example, the writers summarize three major arguments and advance the theme that privacy rights under the Fourth Amendment extend to individuals when they are in cars. The principal writer was a law student, who filed her brief in the United States Court of Appeals for the Third Circuit in 2017.

> Looking at the Court's jurisprudence, three reasons support the conclu-sion that an unauthorized driver has a reasonable expectation of privacy in a rental vehicle. First, the Court has long established that legal property rights are not a prerequisite for asserting Fourth Amendment protection. Rather, an individual may have the capacity to assert Fourth Amendment protection if the individual has an "interest that is recognized and per-mitted by society." An unauthorized driver has such interest because the driver is like an overnight guest in that the driver possesses the vehicle, has some measure of control over it, has the ability to exclude others except for the rental company and the authorized renter, and the unauthorized driver shares in the expectation of privacy of the authorized renter. Second, automobiles are vital to society. Third, the Court has recognized that an individual does not shed his or her constitutional right to privacy merely because the individual steps into an automobile.[1]

— With a clear organization, this thesis paragraph emphasizes policy concerns and constitutional guarantees to develop its theme.

3. STEP THREE: USE TOPIC SENTENCES TO ORGANIZE YOUR ANALYSIS, AND START WITH YOUR BEST ARGUMENT

Now that you have an outline of your arguments, a thesis to begin your Analysis section, and a convincing theme, you can begin drafting the indi-vidual argument paragraphs within the Analysis. Consider the paragraph structure of your Analysis section. Devoting one paragraph to each major point or anchor you plan to analyze is a logical organization. Or if one point or anchor deserves extensive analysis, you might devote two or more para-graphs to it. If two or three minor points or anchors are related, you could combine the analysis of them in a single paragraph.

Whether you have one argument or multiple arguments in a paragraph, each paragraph should have a topic sentence that persuasively introduces the reader to the topic of the paragraph or summarizes the paragraph's main

---

1. Brief for Lindsey N. Ursua, et al. as Amici Curiae Supporting Petitioner at 2, *United States v. Byrd*, 679 F. App'x 146 (3d Cir. 2017) (No. 16-1371), 2017 WL 5591727.

point. Topic sentences help your document maintain a logical and compelling structure. They also serve as mini conclusions that combine to provide convincing support for your thesis and Conclusion.

The following thesis from the curtilage example introduces arguments analyzing three relevant anchors:

> Mr. Chapman's conviction should be reversed because the Perry compound does not qualify as curtilage for three reasons. First, only the front area is enclosed; the back is unbounded. Second, the front is bordered only by a short, decorative fence and a line of low, uneven shrubs. Last, the area has three extensive gaps allowing any person or vehicle to easily enter or exit the area.

As a next step, you would write a topic sentence summarizing each major argument you want to make. Each topic sentence would begin a new paragraph:

> First, the area surrounding the compound cannot be considered curtilage because the enclosure is intermittent in the front and nonexistent in the back.

> Second, the compound is ringed by only sporadic hedges and a short piece of ornamental fencing, which fail to provide the type of enclosure that would allow the yard to be designated curtilage.

> Finally, multiple wide-open gaps in the compound's perimeter allow any person or vehicle to access the property at any point, further demonstrating the lack of definition in the property's border.

These topic sentences are a first step in showing your reader how the analysis of the anchors supports your Conclusion. These topic sentences will be followed by factual support from the facts of your case and legal support from analogies and distinctions to relevant cases. Note that the topic sentences do not reference or depend on one specific case. Instead, the topic sentences broadly summarize how the analysis of the anchor according to the facts supports the Conclusion.

4. STEP FOUR: PROVIDE FACTUAL SUPPORT FOR EACH ARGUMENT BY RECRUITING RELEVANT FACTS

Each argument needs two types of support: (1) factual support from the facts of your own case and (2) legal support through comparisons to other cases. A successful Analysis section will recruit all the relevant facts from the record to gather support for your Conclusion. A successful Analysis also will show how these facts connect to the law. Simply restating the facts is not enough—because facts alone do not create a legal argument. By describing how the facts fit with the law, you can provide credible support for each argument.

This factual support is in many ways the heart of your Analysis. Detailed factual support connects the dots for the court. The factual support that you include for each argument should be tied to the anchor that is the basis for that argument and should correspond to the facts of the cases you will use for legal support. By persuasively presenting the facts of your case that are relevant to each argument, you show the court how the anchors apply to your case and support your Conclusion.

The factual support for your arguments needs to be thorough and persuasive. Find every relevant fact in your record that relates to the argument. Read and reread your factual documents to make sure that no fact has been overlooked. And then present those facts with style. Use writing tools like parallel construction, short sentences, and transitions to highlight for the court how the facts support your arguments.

The following example provides detailed factual support for the argument it makes in its first two sentences: that a Defendant's Sixth Amendment rights were violated when his attorney admitted the Defendant's guilt to the jury over the Defendant's objection. The paragraph presents the facts persuasively and connects them with transitions like "and," "for example," and "however." It also shows how the facts fit with the law by citing a case and incorporating key legal language, like "the right to choose whether to remain silent."

> A defendant also has the right to choose whether to remain silent or to testify in his defense—a decision to be made "in the unfettered exercise of his own will." *Brooks*, 406 U.S. at 610. That choice was rendered self-destructive for McCoy. Because of English's conduct, McCoy had no way to present his defense but to testify himself, and to do so under the pall of an admission of guilt by his attorney. And when McCoy did testify, English used his own examination to impeach his own client's testimony in ways the prosecution did not do and could not have done. He introduced inculpatory facts and adversely mischaracterized the evidence through his own questioning of his client. For example, English confronted McCoy with the assertion that the prosecution had evidence of phone records showing that a phone number linked to McCoy made calls in Louisiana during the time McCoy claimed to be in Houston. The prosecution, however, had introduced no such evidence. And English confronted McCoy with the claim that the person shown in footage fleeing the crime scene was McCoy, even though no prosecution witness had identified him.[2]

In the next example, the Respondents argued that there was a dispute of fact regarding whether the police had received an anonymous tip about a party in a vacant house. The paragraph uses parallel construction and numerous details to provide factual support for an argument about the lack of factual support in the record to support the existence of an anonymous tip.

---

2. Corrected Brief of Petitioner at 46, *McCoy v. Louisiana*, 138 S. Ct. 1500 (2018) (No. 16-8255), 2017 WL 6885223.

First, Petitioners claim someone received a tip about the house. That evidence should be disregarded on Petitioners' motion, however, because there are multiple reasons to doubt the tip was ever given or received. The only evidence about the tip comes from people without personal knowledge of it. No one described personally receiving the tip, nor the circumstances in which the tip was received. And no documentary evidence corroborates that the tip was ever given. There is no transcript of a call to the police, no letter from a concerned citizen, no police report contemporaneously documenting the tip by the person who supposedly received it. While Respondents cannot offer affirmative evidence disproving the tip—because evidence as to the tip is necessarily in the possession of Petitioners alone—they have identified a number of reasons that they should be permitted to cross-examine Petitioners about the tip at trial. There is thus a genuine dispute about whether the alleged tip was ever actually given to the police.[3]

5. STEP FIVE: PROVIDE LEGAL SUPPORT FOR EACH ARGUMENT BY ANALOGIZING AND DISTINGUISHING RELEVANT CASES

In addition to factual support, each of your arguments needs legal support. To provide this legal support, you need to show the reader how the analysis of an anchor in relevant cases supports your analysis of the anchor with your facts. You can do this by drawing analogies and distinctions between your case and the cases you described in your Explanation. Each analogy and distinction should be substantive, parallel, and specific. Consider that the more support you provide in each Analysis paragraph—that is, the more analogies and distinctions you have—the stronger your Analysis section will be.

A. Draw Analogies to Make Affirmative Arguments

Start by drawing analogies to cases with favorable outcomes—those cases that interpreted the rule in the way that you want the rule interpreted. Analogies create affirmative arguments, which can be more persuasive than defensive arguments. For each anchor you plan to analyze, determine which cases you can use to draw analogies to support your argument. The comparisons to your case might strike you as obvious. As a result, new legal writers often are tempted to write conclusory or poorly constructed analogies, such as the following:

Like *Jones v. Bradwick*, the offer here is not valid.

---

3. Brief for Respondents at 27, *D.C. v. Wesby*, 138 S. Ct. 577 (2018) (No. 15-1485) (citations omitted), 2017 WL 2983406.

This statement is ineffective because it does nothing to advance the writer's argument. Opposing counsel could easily refute this statement with the following:

> Unlike *Jones v. Bradwick*, the offer here is valid.

The strongest analogies show the reader how and why the cases are comparable. They are not conclusory like the two previous, poorly written examples. Instead, effective analogies are substantive, parallel, and specific. This means that each analogy should be connected to an anchor, compare like with like, and use detailed comparisons.

i. Substantive Analogies

Analogies are substantive when they connect your facts with the relevant law. The topic sentences for your Analysis section should identify one of your major arguments and a relevant anchor. When drawing analogies to provide legal support for your argument, make sure that each analogy is connected to the relevant anchor. Keep in mind that cases may address multiple issues or include interesting but irrelevant details. A good outline and a focused topic sentence will help you keep your argument on track.

ii. Parallel Analogies

Analogies are parallel when they compare like with like. The conclusory analogies in the two previous examples make a strategic mistake because they require the reader to figure out how the two cases are related. In addition, the statements make a grammatical error by comparing a case, *Jones v. Bradwick*, to the offer, which is not a parallel construction. A parallel analogy will compare the same types of information from your case and the cases you are using for analogies. Drawing a parallel analogy means you will compare facts to facts, reasoning to reasoning, and holding to holding.

TYPES OF PARALLEL ANALOGIES

- **Fact to fact:** The irregular border around the Perry compound, because it is made up of sporadic shrubs, is less continuous than the fence in *Martinez*, which also was inadequate because it only traced the north and east edges of the property.
- **Reasoning to reasoning:** Mr. Chapman's actions are exactly what the Legislature wanted to protect. Mr. Chapman innocently wandered into the Perry compound because it was open and unbounded. As the court in *J.L.* stated, the Legislature did not intend to apply the burglary statute to an individual who entered an open yard intending to pick a piece of fruit from a tree. And thus, the burglary statute should not apply to Chapman who, like the fruit picker, acted innocently and did not cross over a fenced border.

- **Holding to holding:** Sporadic fencing and landscaping do not create a sufficient enclosure to support a burglary conviction, just as in *Hamilton*, where "several unevenly spaced trees" were not enough of an enclosure, so the defendant's conviction was reversed.

Some cases could be so helpful to your position that you can compare their facts, reasoning, and specific holdings to your case. Those cases will provide the strongest support for your Conclusion. But keep in mind that you can and should use multiple cases to support each argument. Thus, in a single Analysis paragraph, you might have comparisons to the facts, reasoning, and holding of one case, a comparison to the facts of a second case, and a comparison to the holding of a third case. More legal support means a more solid and credible argument. A single case rarely can provide enough support for an argument, so try to use multiple cases to support each point throughout your Analysis.

iii. Specific Analogies

The third step in making sure your analogy is not conclusory is to make it specific. To find specific, relevant details to use in your analogies, read and reread your cases. Pull out any detail that you can use to show your reader how and why a case is comparable to yours. More specific analogies produce more effective arguments.

- **Lacks specificity:** Like the claimant's possession in *Klein*, Karr's possession of the property was not sufficiently open and notorious.
- **Some improvement:** Karr, like the claimant in *Klein* who only occasionally visited the vacant lot, rarely paid visits to the cabin.
- **Very specific:** Karr camped on the property only seven times in six years and left the cabin in disrepair—much like the claimant in *Klein*, who never occupied the lot except for the occasional picnic and left the landscaping unkempt.

The last example is effective because it uses a comparison of specific details to show the reader how and why the *Klein* case is like Karr's. It also puts the facts of Karr's case first—ahead of the comparable facts from the case law—to focus the court on the argument about Karr's case.

Some cases will be so helpful to your position that you will want to devote an entire paragraph or more to developing a detailed comparison. Just keep in mind that the Analysis should focus on putting forth your argument and referencing cases for support, not on repeating the Explanation. And your ultimate goal is to focus the court on the arguments that support your Conclusion. The comparisons to the cases are not your arguments; they are the legal support for your arguments.

The next example uses four cases and a short paragraph to put forth one of the major arguments in the petitioner's brief in *Hollingsworth v. Perry*, one of the cases that legalized same-sex marriage in California. The specific argument here states that proponents of a statewide ballot initiative to eliminate that marriage right do not have standing.

> Further, this Court has already determined that status as an initiative proponent is insufficient to confer Article III standing. *See Don't Bankrupt Wash. Comm. v. Cont'l Ill. Nat'l Bank & Trust Co. of Chi.*, 460 U.S. 1077 (1983); *Arizonans*, 520 U.S. at 66 (expressing "grave doubts" whether initiative proponents have standing to defend an initiative on appeal). And Proponents, who are not public officials, do not have a close relationship with the State like the state legislators did in *Karcher v. May*, 484 U.S. 72, 81–82 (1987). Because Proponents themselves will suffer no judicially cognizable injury if gay men and lesbians are permitted to marry, they have no standing to appeal. *See Diamond v. Charles*, 476 U.S. 54, 68–69 (1986).[4]

iv. Parenthetical Support

In addition, you can use signals and parentheticals to add specific legal support to your arguments. The most common signals in a persuasive Analysis section are *see, see also*, and *see, e.g.*[5] Signals with parentheticals can effectively and concisely show the court that relevant cases have comparable facts, reasoning, and holdings. When constructing a parenthetical, keep in mind that it should also be substantive, parallel, and specific.

ANALOGIES WITH PARENTHETICAL SUPPORT

- Karr's possession of the property was not open and notorious because he camped on the property only seven times in six years and left the cabin in disrepair. *See Klein*, 199 P.2d at 691–92 (holding that possession was not open and notorious where the claimant occasionally picnicked on a vacant lot and left the landscaping unkempt).
- Blackhurst installed a shed and "No Trespassing" signs on her land, which shows she was occupying, maintaining, and improving the land enough to provide notice to the owner. *See Nielsen*, 100 Cal. Rptr. 3d at 341; *see also Lobro*, 116 Cal. Rptr. at 536–38 (finding that the adverse claimants' occupation of the property for twenty-five years, which included improving and making additions, constituted "reasonable notice that they claimed the property as their own").
- Mr. Chapman innocently wandered into the Perry compound because it was open and unbounded, and he had no intent to enter a private yard. *See, e.g., J.L.*, 57 So. 3d at 926 ("[T]he Legislature did not intend the burglary statute to be applied to an individual who, without the homeowner's consent, enters an open yard with the intent to take a piece of fruit from a tree located in the yard.").

---

4. Brief for Respondents at 17, *Hollingsworth v. Perry*, 570 U.S. 693 (2013) (No. 12-144), 2013 WL 648742.

5. Refer to sections 3.E. and 3.G. in Chapter 43 for instructions on how to incorporate signals and parentheticals into your document.

These parentheticals provide specific and substantive information to support the writer's argument. The information in each parenthetical also is relevant to the anchor referenced in the statement preceding it. The first two examples address whether the property was properly maintained; the third addresses legislative intent.

B. Distinguish Unfavorable Cases

You can provide additional support for each argument you make in the Analysis section by drawing distinctions. If you identified binding cases that have an unfavorable outcome in your Explanation, then you should consider distinguishing those cases in your Analysis. You should draw case distinctions in your persuasive Analysis when (1) the distinction is obvious and strengthens your argument or (2) the case is recent, mandatory authority and your opponent will likely use the case as support. For some legal issues, the majority of cases will have unfavorable outcomes. Distinctions will then make up much of the legal support for your arguments. A well-crafted distinction can have as much persuasive force as an analogy.

To make case distinctions effective, they also should be substantive, parallel, and specific. The following examples show distinctions that are substantive, parallel, and specific. The first provides an effective distinction with a parenthetical for added legal support. The second example uses specific facts to support the argument that a checkpoint set up to get information from passing motorists about a fatal hit-and-run accident was constitutional.

DISTINCTIONS THAT ARE SUBSTANTIVE, PARALLEL, AND SPECIFIC

- The hedgerow and fencing that enclose most of the Perry compound are far more extensive than the unevenly spaced trees that were found to be inadequate in *Hamilton*. *See* 660 So. 2d at 1046 (noting that the evidence was undisputed that the victim's yard was not enclosed in any other manner).
- The informative checkpoint in this case is no threat to the Fourth Amendment. Unlike the drug checkpoint in *Edmond*, it carries its own limits. *See Indianapolis v. Edmond*, 531 U.S. 32 (2000). This checkpoint is limited to one automotive crime, tying it closely to the roads. The officers conducting the checkpoint also had little discretion in setting its time and place. Since the checkpoint's rationale extends only to a relatively small number of serious automotive offenses, there is no threat of its rationale spreading through the Fourth Amendment like the drug checkpoint in *Edmond*.[6]

---

6. Brief of Amicus Curiae Supporting of Petitioner at 4, *Illinois v. Lidster*, 540 U.S. 419 (2004) (No. 02-1060), 2003 WL 21648786.

C. Draw Analogies and Distinctions for Each Anchor

Once you have drafted the relevant analogies and distinctions for your analysis of the first anchor, repeat the process for each anchor you plan to analyze. Consider using a transition to guide your reader to each of the points you identified in your thesis. Transitions like "first," "second," and "third," "finally," "similarly," "in addition," "furthermore," and "moreover" build momentum from one argument to the next and make your analysis more confident and persuasive.

Also, make sure you use topic sentences to keep your reader focused on the specific anchor you are analyzing. This method of providing specific and substantive case analogies and distinctions—without hyperbole or inflation—will reveal the merits of your case and allow you to present a compelling and credible argument that the relief you seek is warranted.

6. STEP SIX: AFFIRMATIVELY REFUTE COUNTERARGUMENTS

Within your Analysis section, you will need to decide how to strategically confront and rebut counterarguments. If your argument is unassailable and every case on point supports your position, you probably would not be litigating the matter. Every case has certain weak points. And every good lawyer has to be aware of those weak points and determine how and when to refute them.

First, try to identify the major weaknesses in your position. Consider what your opponent is likely to argue based on the facts and applicable case law. And consider what arguments a judge will likely find relevant upon reviewing the legal documents and applicable law. Your job is to identify the obvious weaknesses in your position so you can confront them and move the argument along to your stronger points.

Second, consider that your rebuttal does not need to be comprehensive and address every potential counterargument that your opponent may raise. If your analysis reveals a counterargument that is obscure, addressing it might disclose an otherwise unknown argument. Lawyers have to strike a careful balance when preemptively refuting an opponent's argument.

After you identify which counterarguments you need to refute, think about how you can present your rebuttal in a way that is not defensive. Also, make sure you do not make your opponent's argument by restating it, especially at the start of the paragraph—the place you should use to emphasize your best points.

For example, suppose you represent the defendant in a lawsuit for intentional infliction of emotional distress and plan to file a motion to dismiss. The only element at issue is whether your client's conduct was outrageous when she asked the plaintiff to leave her store after he took off all of his clothes.

From the plaintiff's complaint, you are aware that the plaintiff is 92 years old and suffers from dementia. And from your research, you are aware of a major weakness in your position—that the law in this area generally favors vulnerable plaintiffs, including the elderly and those with mental illness.

As a result, you need to preemptively refute the argument that the plaintiff is vulnerable. Consider how you can affirmatively address the vulnerable-plaintiff counterargument with the facts, applicable law, or both. And consider how you can present an affirmative argument and not restate the plaintiff's argument. Start your rebuttal by focusing your topic sentence on your argument, rather than your opponent's argument.

- **Weak rebuttal:** Opposing counsel may argue that the plaintiff is vulnerable because he is 92 years old and suffers from dementia, but the plaintiff regularly takes cycling trips.
- **Strong rebuttal with factual support:** The plaintiff is an active, independent 92-year-old, who traveled alone to Texas six days before the incident and completed a 50-kilometer bicycling race.
- **Strong rebuttal with legal and factual support:** Intentional infliction of emotional distress claims have failed in New York courts even where the plaintiff is a patient at a psychiatric facility, and here, the plaintiff is an active, independent 92-year-old, who traveled alone to Texas six days before the incident and completed a 50-kilometer bicycling race. *See Howell v. N.Y. Post Co.*, 612 N.E.2d 699, 702 (N.Y. 1993) (noting that "of the intentional infliction of emotional distress claims considered by this Court, every one has failed because the alleged conduct was not sufficiently outrageous").

The first example is weak because it restates the opponent's argument, which puts the writer on the defensive. To refute an argument effectively, you need to use the facts or law in a way to gain the advantage. Also, consider how you can strategically place your rebuttal within your Analysis section. Taking into account the primacy and recency effects, the best location for a rebuttal is often buried in the middle of the stronger arguments within your Analysis section.

In the next example, the Petitioners tackle their opponent's argument first by characterizing it as flawed and then by offering two points in support of same-sex marriage in California.

In the absence of any factually supported belief that marriage equality would have negative effects on society, Proponents have nothing but a *theory*—unsupported by empirical evidence or other facts—that marriage equality *might* have negative effects. *See* Prop. Br. 55 ("[T]he ultimate outcome of redefining marriage cannot yet be foreseen with confidence from our current vantage point."). The question is whether that theory constitutes a basis for perpetuating inequality. For at least two reasons, it does not.

First, Proponents' unsubstantiated fear that negative externalities might flow from marriage equality fails to come to grips with the fact that, before Proposition 8 was enacted, some 18,000 same-sex couples were married in California, and those marriages remain valid and recognized today. *See Strauss*, 207 P.3d at 121-22. Even beyond that, California has among the most robust legal protections for same-sex couples in the Nation, providing them with all the rights, incidents, and benefits of marriage under state law, save the designation of their relationships as "marriages." *Marriage Cases*, 183 P.3d at 434-35....

Second, and perhaps more importantly, if Proponents are correct that an unsubstantiated fear of negative externalities of *equality* is sufficient to justify *inequality*, then discrimination is self-justifying. *See Cleburne*, 473 U.S. at 448 ("mere negative attitudes, or fear, unsubstantiated by factors which are properly cognizable...are not permissible bases for" differential treatment). And the more valued the institution from which a class is excluded—which is to say, the more injurious the inequality—then the stronger the self-justification for the inequality becomes. On this view, in *Moreno*, the mere articulation of a *fear* that unrelated persons living in a single household might be fraudsters would have been sufficient to dispose of the equal protection attack on the statute excluding them from Food Stamps benefits. *But see* 413 U.S. at 535-37. And in *Romer*, the actually stated fear that gay men and lesbians might flood legislatures and city councils with demands for antidiscrimination laws would have been sufficient to sustain Colorado's Amendment 2. *But see* 517 U.S. at 635.

It cannot be the law that public concern about equal treatment itself can justify a denial of equal treatment. *See Brown v. Bd. of Educ.*, 349 U.S. 294, 300 (1955) ("[I]t should go without saying that the vitality of these constitutional principles cannot be allowed to yield simply because of disagreement with them.").[7]

---

7. Brief for Respondents at 46-48, *Hollingsworth v. Perry*, 570 U.S. 693 (2013) (No. 12-144), 2013 WL 648742.

Checklist for your persuasive Analysis section
Does my persuasive Analysis section...

☑ Use an easy-to-follow organization, beginning with a thesis statement or thesis paragraph that summarizes the major points?

☑ Use a transition like "here" at the beginning of the thesis statement to signal the start of the Analysis section?

☑ Organize each argument point strategically—with the strongest argument first?

☑ Organize each point into paragraphs (keeping in mind that complex arguments might deserve multiple paragraphs, while simpler points can be combined into one paragraph)?

☑ Start each paragraph with a topic sentence that summarizes its main point?

☑ For each argument, recruit all of the relevant facts in the record for factual support and present those facts persuasively?

☑ For each argument and in each paragraph, detail specific, substantive, and parallel analogies and distinctions to describe the support for the argument?

☑ Discuss the present case before the comparable cases to make the Analysis paragraphs focused on the present case and distinct from the Explanation paragraphs?

☑ Refute any major, potential counterargument(s) affirmatively with specific, substantive, and parallel analogies and distinctions?

☑ Use consistent terms and verb tenses?

☑ Use plain language?[8]

☑ Provide convincing support for my Conclusion overall?

---

8. See Chapter 21 for more guidance.

Writing a Persuasive Conclusion

A Conclusion in a persuasive document gives you an opportunity to make your client's case and to put forth your strongest reason or reasons. To keep the court focused on the outcome you seek, start and end each CREAC with a Conclusion.

The ending Conclusion in your CREAC should not be exactly the same as the opening Conclusion. Restating the exact same sentence could make your document seem monotonous, and obvious cutting and pasting of the same language may irritate the court. Even a small variation in wording can help maintain the court's interest.

When you rephrase your Conclusion, try to incorporate the theme you have developed throughout your document. Also, make sure to provide a specific reason in support—whether the reason is factually based, legally based, or both. The following Conclusions could begin and end an Argument section in the contract dispute case.

Opening Conclusion

The Court should grant Defendant's Motion to Dismiss because he never made a binding offer to sell his car and the contract is therefore unenforceable.

Ending Conclusion

Defendant did not make a binding offer to sell his revered Volkswagen Beetle when he jokingly put a sign on it that read: "The World Ends Tomorrow. Must Sell Today. $150 obo." Therefore, the Court should grant Defendant's Motion to Dismiss.

Both Conclusions persuade the court to find for the defendant and provide specific reasons in support. Keep in mind that the Conclusion statements give you the first—and last—opportunity to convince the court to grant the relief you seek. Take advantage of this opportunity by putting forth your best reason.

The next examples begin and end a major argument in the respondent's brief in *Masterpiece Cakeshop, Ltd., v. Colorado Civil Rights Commission*, which examined whether Colorado's Anti-Discrimination Act forbids businesses from denying service because of a customer's sexual orientation. The Colorado Civil Rights Commission argued that the First Amendment did not grant a retail bakery, owned by Jack C. Phillips, the right to refuse to sell a wedding cake of any kind to any same-sex couple.

Opening Conclusion

This Court has never questioned a State's authority to apply a public accommodations law to a business's sale of goods and services. Only in two non-commercial settings—when public accommodations laws were applied either to edit the messages of a private parade or to alter a private organization's membership decisions—did the Court sustain First Amendment challenges to such laws. Phillips seeks a far broader, and indeed unprecedented, exemption for his bakery. Although he has repeatedly conceded that his business is a public accommodation, he claims that he has the right to deny service to customers with protected characteristics because the products he wishes to withhold can be characterized as "creative" or "expressive." This logic finds no support in the First Amendment. A business's decision of whom to serve is not "speech," and discrimination has never been granted constitutional protection.

Closing Conclusion

A business may refuse service for many reasons, including the specific design of a requested product. But it may not refuse service based on a customer's identity. The three bakeries targeted by this customer would have refused to sell a cake with an anti-gay inscription to anyone—a Jewish person, a customer of a different race, or a heterosexual couple. Phillips likewise has the right to decline an order for a cake with an "anti-family," "hateful," "or "vulgar" message, a right he claims to have exercised in the past. Pet. Br. at 9. What Phillips may not do is make a cake of a particular design for anyone but same-sex couples (or African-Americans, Muslims, or women). If applying a public accommodations law in this unremarkable way amounts to viewpoint discrimination, no public accommodations law would be immune from constitutional challenge, and this Court's history of upholding them under the First Amendment would require reexamination.[1]

Checklist for your persuasive Conclusion
Does my persuasive Conclusion...

☑ Differ stylistically from my opening Conclusion?
☑ Identify the requested relief and the legal issue?
☑ Provide a reason for my Conclusion?
☑ Work with a theme that provides a memorable description of what the case is about?

---

1. Brief for Respondent at 19, 48-49, *Masterpiece Cakeshop, Ltd., v. Colo. Civil Rights Comm'n*, 137 S. Ct. 2290 (2018) (No. 16-111), 2017 WL 4838416.

Putting Persuasive Documents Together

Introduction to Persuasive Documents

Lawyers write persuasive documents to advocate for their clients. Throughout your law school and legal career, you may write persuasive documents, including trial court motions and appellate briefs, that ask a court to resolve an issue in your client's favor. These persuasive documents are read by the judge or judges presiding over your case, opposing counsel, and possibly the clients on both sides. This part of the *Handbook* provides directions for how to incorporate a persuasive CREAC into formal documents that could be filed with a court.

An effective persuasive document presents a cohesive and zealous argument supporting the relief it requests, while also satisfying the lawyer's ethical obligation to be candid and truthful about the facts and law. It also establishes the author's credibility through scrupulous proofreading and adherence to the rules governing format, substance, and timeliness.

Trial Court Documents

Trial court documents are one form of persuasive legal writing. The most common form of trial court document is a motion, which is a written request to the court. During the trial court phase of a case, lawyers may prepare and respond to several motions. Motions can be narrow, for example, asking the court to enter an order requiring a party to make a witness available for deposition, or broad, asking the court to decide the issues in the case as a matter of law.

Motion formats vary widely from jurisdiction to jurisdiction. Filings often consist of two parts. First, the "notice of motion" contains legally operative language describing the requested relief and information regarding when the court will hear the motion. Second, the "memorandum of law" or "memorandum of points and authorities" includes the persuasive arguments for why the motion should be granted. In some courts, these documents are combined into a single document, while in other courts they are filed separately. Either way, together they compose the "motion."

Once a motion has been filed, the opposing party must prepare a response (also called an opposition), and then the moving party may be allowed to file a reply. The response and reply use a format that is similar to the format for the memorandum of law in support of the motion.

This chapter provides general instructions for preparing a trial court memorandum of law, but you should always follow any jurisdiction-specific rules that govern the document you are preparing.

Writing a Trial Court Memorandum of Law

1. Create a template for your document.
2. Prepare a persuasive Facts or Background section.
3. Prepare a Legal Standard section if necessary.
4. Add persuasive roadmaps and subheadings to guide the court.
5. Write a compelling Introduction.
6. Scrutinize and revise.

---

1. STEP ONE: CREATE A TEMPLATE FOR YOUR DOCUMENT

The format of a trial court memorandum of law is determined by the rules of civil procedure and local rules of the court where the document will be filed. The court can reject any document that does not comply with the rules, so you must follow them closely. Most trial court memoranda of law have some variation of the following format:

Trial Court Memorandum of Law

1. Caption
2. Introduction
3. Facts or Background section
4. Legal Standard
5. Argument with CREAC for each issue and point headings
6. Conclusion section
7. Signature block

Put your trial court memorandum of law together by creating a template for your document, beginning with the caption. Follow the rules regarding the required font type, size, and spacing, and take note of any page or word limits. In addition, check the rules for deadlines to ensure that your document is timely filed.

A. Create the Caption

The caption appears at the beginning of a trial court memorandum of law and usually contains the following pieces of information: (1) the court, (2) the name of the case, (3) the docket number, and (4) the title of the document. In

**UNITED STATES DISTRICT COURT
FOR THE SOUTHERN DISTRICT OF FLORIDA
MIAMI DIVISION
CASE NO. 06-21265-CIV-JORDAN**

LEAGUE OF WOMEN VOTERS OF FLORIDA, PEOPLE
ACTING FOR COMMUNITY TOGETHER (PACT), *et al.*

    Plaintiffs,

      v.

SUE M. COBB, individually and in her official capacity as
Secretary of State for the State of Florida, and DAWN
ROBERTS, individually and in her official capacity as
Director of the Division of Elections,

    Defendants.

**DEFENDANTS' MOTION TO DISMISS
AND MEMORANDUM OF LAW IN SUPPORT THEREOF**

Figure 31.1

some courts, the caption will also include the name and contact information for the lawyers representing the party filing the document.

Court rules differ regarding the spacing, orientation, and organization of the information in the caption. Court websites often provide a template for a properly formatted caption. Figure 31.1 (on the previous page) shows an example of a caption for a memorandum of law filed in the federal District Court for the Southern District of Florida.

B. Add Headings for Each Section

Next, add headings for each additional section of your memorandum of law: (1) Introduction, (2) Background or Facts, (3) Legal Standard, (4) Argument, and (5) Conclusion. Put into place the Argument section with the persuasive CREAC(s) and point headings that you have already prepared. (See Part V for a review.) Now, you can create and fill in the missing pieces. You don't have to prepare the sections of the document in order. You may want to start with the Conclusion section, which is easy and formulaic, and end with the Introduction, which is challenging because it needs to summarize the cohesive document.

C. Insert the Conclusion Section and Signature Block

A trial court memorandum of law usually ends with a Conclusion section and signature block. The Conclusion section states in a single sentence, using customary language, what the document has asked the court to do, and the signature block provides a place for the attorney submitting the document to sign her name. The typical language for a Conclusion is as follows:

"For these reasons, _____[party]_____ requests that the Court _____[relief]_____."

CONCLUSION

For the foregoing reasons, the Court should deny Defendant's Motion to Dismiss Plaintiff's Complaint.

Dated: November 11, 2018

Respectfully submitted,

/s/ Levon I. Cavin
Levon I. Cavin (Fla. Bar No. 11111)
1400 Prudence Blvd.
Suite 13
Miami, FL 33133
(305) 288-1111
(305) 288-2222 (fax)
levonicavin@cavinlaw.com

Figure 31.2

By signing the filing, the attorney represents to the court that the document has legal and evidentiary support and that it is filed for a proper purpose.[1] Many documents are now filed electronically and have an electronic signature, rather than a handwritten signature. An electronic signature is the author's name, preceded by "/s/." Check the local rules and then insert a properly formatted signature block.

Figure 31.2 (on the previous page) shows an example of a Conclusion section with the Conclusion section heading and signature block for a memorandum of law for the District Court for the Southern District of Florida.

2. STEP TWO: PREPARE A PERSUASIVE FACTS OR BACKGROUND SECTION

In a trial court memorandum of law, the Facts or Background section must tell a story from your client's point of view that supports the relief you request. The title of this section depends on the court where you will submit your document. This section may be titled "Background," "Factual Background," or "Statement of Facts," depending on the court and type of document. Because trial courts are the triers of facts, the facts are often in dispute at this point in a case. Accordingly, the type of facts you include and how you present them can be critical to your document's effectiveness.

The factual story needs to (1) describe the facts that are legally significant to the issue in the memorandum of law, (2) provide any necessary background information and the procedural context underlying the memorandum of law, and (3) advance a theme that helps your client's position.

The Three Types of Facts in a Persuasive Facts or Background Section

1. Legally significant facts relevant to the issue in the memorandum of law
2. Procedural facts that provide necessary background and context
3. Emotional facts that serve your persuasive theme

The Facts section in a trial court memorandum of law should present the facts persuasively. The Facts section should not be objective, like the Facts section in an office memo. The court should be inclined to decide the issue in your client's favor based on the Facts section alone. This does not mean, however, that you can misrepresent or ignore contrary facts that weigh against your arguments. Avoiding contrary facts will hurt your credibility with the

---

1. *See* Fed. R. Civ. P. 11(b).

court, and when your opponent points out the facts you have omitted, under-mine your arguments. Instead of ignoring contrary facts, you should use legal writing techniques to portray the facts accurately and persuasively.

A. Categorize the Legally Significant Facts

The Facts section should describe all the facts that are legally significant to the issue in your memorandum of law. To identify the legally significant facts, review the anchors from your applicable authorities. Then, review the facts of your case and note every fact that is connected to an anchor. Make a list of these legally significant facts; they will form the basis of your Facts sec-tion. Check this list against the facts you used to make the outline of your arguments in the Analysis. This process should allow you to capture every relevant fact.

You need to identify all the facts that are relevant to the anchors—even those that weigh against your arguments. Do not omit contrary facts. Any fact included in the Analysis section of your CREAC must be included in your Facts section. If you identified a legally significant fact that you have not included in your Analysis, you may have missed an important argument. Once you have your list, you should categorize the helpful facts that you want to highlight and the contrary facts that you want to minimize.

B. Provide Procedural Context

Trial court documents are governed by rules of procedure. You should in-clude facts that establish that your request to the court is procedurally proper. Moreover, you must describe the facts in procedurally appropriate terms.

For example, a motion to dismiss under Federal Rule of Civil Procedure 12(b)(6) should include procedural facts that show you have not yet filed a responsive pleading, which is required by the rule.[2] Moreover, you would limit the facts in the motion to the allegations in the complaint—because those are the only "facts" of record at that stage of the case. Thus, you would describe the facts as allegations, not evidence. You would also use the title "Background" or "Factual Background" so that it doesn't appear that you are putting forth allegations as facts. Indeed, if you are the defendant's attorney hoping to win a motion to dismiss, you would not want to concede that any of the allega-tions in the plaintiff's complaint are facts. Conversely, in a memorandum of law in support of a motion for summary judgment, you would establish that the facts you were relying upon were "undisputed," which is required by most summary judgment standards.[3] In a summary judgment motion, the allega-

---

2. *See* Fed. R. Civ. P. 12(b) ("A motion asserting any of these defenses must be made before pleading if a responsive pleading is allowed.").

3. *See* Fed. R. Civ. P. 56(a) ("The court shall grant summary judgment if the movant shows that there is no genuine dispute as to any material fact and the movant is entitled to judgment as a matter of law.").

tions in the complaint are largely irrelevant because the motion depends on the evidence established by the depositions, affidavits, documents, and discovery responses.

C. Advance Your Theme Through Emotional Facts

Your theme is a comprehensive argument for why your client should prevail, not just on the issue in the memorandum of law, but in the entire case. Because a memorandum of law provides an opportunity to advocate for your client's position, you should include emotional facts in your Facts section that are at the heart of the dispute between the parties and advance your theme.

If facts that are not directly relevant to your legal issue could make the court sympathetic to your client, you should consider working those facts into your Facts section. For example, imagine that you represent the plaintiff in a products liability case and the defendant has moved to dismiss. Even if facts regarding how severely your client was injured do not impact whether the case should be dismissed, you would want to include those facts to give the court your client's perspective.

This technique requires subtlety. The court will not want to waste its time reading irrelevant facts. Thus, you should include only the most persuasive emotional facts to develop your theme and to help the court understand the case from your client's point of view.

D. Tell a Persuasive Story

After you identify the legally significant, procedural, and emotional facts that will make up your Facts section, you should weave them into a persuasive story. Although the Facts section in a plaintiff's document will likely include many, if not all, of the same facts as the defendant's document, the plaintiff and defendant should organize and characterize those facts very differently.

Your Facts section should be organized logically and use topic sentences and transitions between short paragraphs. But to make the section a persuasive story, you need to highlight the positive facts and minimize the negative facts. One of the best ways to do this is by taking into account the primacy and recency effects.[4] Readers pay more attention to information at the beginning and the end of a section of text; thus, where possible, you should begin and end your Facts section, and each paragraph within your Facts section, with helpful facts. You can minimize contrary facts by burying them in the middle of the Facts section and in the middle of paragraphs.

Another way to highlight positive facts and minimize negative facts is through word choice. For example, using party designations like "Plaintiff" and "Defendant" has a different impact than using the parties' names. Simi-

---

4. These techniques are also discussed in Chapters 27 and 28.

larly, describing something as an "event" has a different connotation than "accident." Choose every word you use in your Facts section to present the facts as persuasively as possible for your side.

E. Use Subheadings to Guide the Reader Through Long, Complicated Facts

Some motions will be fact intensive. When writing a Facts section that is long and complicated, it can be helpful to break up the Facts with subheadings. Subheadings put the factual information into "chunks" that will be easier for the court to understand and remember. Factual subheadings don't need to be complete sentences like headings in the Analysis. Instead, they can be short phrases that organize the factual story persuasively. These subheadings can be numbered or can just use bold type or underlining to make them stand out to the reader.

In the case *Hawaii v. Trump*, the State of Hawaii challenged the third executive order limiting immigration to the United States from certain countries. Early in the case, Hawaii filed a Motion for Temporary Restraining Order with a memorandum in support. The Factual Background section in the memorandum includes the following subheadings:

FACTUAL BACKGROUND

A. The First and Second Executive Orders
B. The Third Executive Order
C. The Effects of EO-3 on Plaintiffs
　　1. The State of Hawaii
　　2. The Individual Plaintiffs
　　3. The Muslim Association of Hawaii[5]

The Government filed a memorandum in opposition to the motion for restraining order. The Background in that memorandum included the following subheadings.

BACKGROUND

I. LEGAL FRAMEWORK
II. EXECUTIVE ORDER NO. 13,780
III. THE PRESIDENT'S PROCLAMATION
　　A. DHS's Worldwide Review and Recommendations
　　B. The President's Findings and Suspensions Of Entry[6]

---

5. Memorandum in Support of Plaintiff's Motion for Restraining Order at i, *Hawaii v. Trump*, 265 F. Supp. 3d 1140 (D. Haw. 2017) (1:17-cv-00050-DKW-KSC), 2017 WL 6547034.

6. Defendants' Memorandum in Opposition to Plaintiffs' Motion for Temporary Restraining Order at i, *Hawaii v. Trump*, 265 F. Supp. 3d 1140 (D. Haw. 2017) (1:17-cv-00050-DKW-KSC), 2017 WL 6547036.

Both examples use subheadings to break up the extensive facts into chunks. And they do so using concepts that help the court see their perspective: the challengers of the travel ban have headings about the effects of the third executive order, while the Government has headings about the process that preceded it.

F. Include Citations to Litigation Documents

Because the Facts section of your memorandum of law advances your client's view of the facts, you need to support the facts with citations to litigation documents. Citations to litigation documents show that you have evidentiary support for your factual assertions, in the same way that citations to cases and statutes show that you have legal support for your arguments. Remember that opposing counsel will file a document telling the story from your opponent's point of view. For the court to evaluate each party's view of the facts, it needs to be able to verify the facts in the underlying factual documents.

Every sentence in your Facts section should be followed by a citation to the litigation document that establishes the facts described in that sentence. The citation format for litigation documents is described in the *Bluebook*. But in practice, the citation format for litigation documents varies widely by jurisdiction and practitioner. These citations typically are enclosed in parentheses and include (1) the abbreviated name of the document and (2) a pinpoint citation to where the fact appears in the document. Litigation document citations should be as specific as possible to make it easy for the court to verify the facts you describe in the record. Your citation should include the specific page and where possible, the specific paragraph or line number.

For example, in a memorandum of law in support of a motion to dismiss, you would need to cite the complaint, which is usually the only litigation document at that stage of the case. Here is a portion of a Facts section that includes citations to the complaint.

> Plaintiff admits that the box her helmet came in contains numerous warnings. (Compl. ¶ 23.) Among these warnings is the following language, "[i]f not fastened correctly, helmet chinstrap can come unbuckled." (Compl. ¶ 24.) The Plaintiff alleges that the helmet came unbuckled during her accident because the chinstrap was pulled too tight and therefore, not fastened correctly. (Compl. ¶¶ 3-7.)

With citations to litigation documents, your goal is to be precise and economical. Notice that because the entire citation is in parentheses, the period at the end of the citation is also within the parentheses. You can use *id.* for litigation document citations, as long as the reader will understand what source the *id.* refers to and it will save significant space. The example above could use *id.* as follows:

> Plaintiff admits that the box her helmet came in contains numerous warnings. (Compl. ¶ 23.) Among these warnings is the following language,

"[i]f not fastened correctly, helmet chinstrap can come unbuckled." (*Id.* ¶ 24.) Plaintiff alleges that the helmet came unbuckled during her accident because the chinstrap was pulled too tight and therefore, not fastened correctly. (*Id.* ¶¶ 3-7.)

For motions filed during and after discovery, you need to cite to litigation documents, such as depositions, declarations, and affidavits. Here is an example of a paragraph from a Facts section followed by citations to a declaration; the first citation includes the page and line numbers of a deposition attached to the declaration as an exhibit.

Plaintiff admitted that she saw the warnings on the helmet box and read them while she was in the store. (Jones Decl. Ex. A at 45:6-46:18.) The warnings are printed in large, bright red type. (Jones Decl. Ex. E at 2.) The warnings on Happy Helmet boxes are the same size and type as the warnings on boxes from the three other major bicycle helmet manufacturers. (Jones Decl. Exs. B, C, and D.)

G. Omit Arguments

Do not let legal arguments infiltrate your Facts section. If you present the facts persuasively, they may sound similar to your arguments. But you will connect your facts to the law in the Analysis section to create your legal arguments. Your Facts section should include only facts.

For example, in a products liability case where you represent a plaintiff who claims that her bike helmet was defective, the following facts would be persuasive:

- Plaintiff was wearing a helmet manufactured by Defendant when she was in a bike accident.
- The chinstrap of the helmet unbuckled during the crash.
- There are no warnings affixed to the helmet regarding how to properly buckle the chinstrap.

In contrast, the following statements consist of legal arguments that would not be appropriate in the Facts section because they connect facts and law:

- The risk of the chinstrap unbuckling was an inherent danger, and Defendant had a duty to warn consumers of dangers inherent in the bicycle helmet.
- Defendant was negligent in failing to warn that the chinstrap would come undone during a crash if it were buckled too tightly.

Finally, to make your document cohesive, the last sentence of the Facts section can be a transition that sets up the arguments to come. Often, the best way to conclude your persuasive Facts section is with a sentence stating the relief you are requesting.

The following are examples of Facts sections for and against a motion to dismiss.

Facts Section in Motion to Dismiss

This Facts section begins with a sentence that establishes when the Complaint was filed and uses persuasive party designations.

On April 11, 2018, Plaintiff filed a Complaint alleging that Happy Helmets is legally obligated to include a warning label on its bicycle helmets explaining that the chinstrap could come unbuckled if fastened too tightly. (Compl. ¶ 3.) Plaintiff claims that she was injured when she hit a pothole while riding her bicycle, which caused her to lose control and flip over the handlebars. (*Id.* ¶ 6.) As this occurred, Plaintiff alleges that the chinstrap of her helmet came unbuckled, causing the helmet to fall off. (*Id.* ¶ 5.) Plaintiff claims that if the helmet had stayed on, she would not have been injured. (*Id.* ¶ 2.) Plaintiff does not allege that the helmet in any way caused the accident.

To minimize the facts regarding plaintiff's injury, they are placed in the middle of the paragraph and characterized as allegations.

The first paragraph ends with a persuasive fact for Defendant.

Plaintiff admits that the box her helmet came in contains numerous warnings. (*Id.* ¶ 23.) Among these warnings is the following language, "[i]f not fastened correctly, helmet chinstrap can come unbuckled." (*Id.* ¶ 24.) Plaintiff alleges that the helmet came unbuckled during her accident because the chinstrap was pulled too tight and therefore, not fastened correctly. (*Id.* ¶ ¶ 3-7.) Because Plaintiff admits that Happy Helmets warned of the risk of the chinstrap coming unbuckled, the Court should grant Happy Helmets' Motion and dismiss Plaintiff's Complaint.

The second paragraph begins with another persuasive fact for Defendant.

The last sentence is a transition to the Argument.

Facts Section in Opposition to Motion to Dismiss

This Facts section begins with persuasive facts for Plaintiff and uses vivid language.

On November 11, 2017, Augustine Hemingway was severely injured when her bicycle helmet failed to protect her during a crash. (Compl. ¶ 5.) Ms. Hemingway was thrown over the handlebars of her bicycle after hitting a pothole. (*Id.* ¶ 6.) Her helmet flew off during the crash, and she suffered a severe concussion and numerous cuts and scrapes on her head and face. (*Id.* ¶ 5.) If her helmet had not come off, these injuries would not have occurred. (*Id.* ¶ 2.)

Notice that in this Facts section the helmet "flew off," while in the prior one it "fell off."

This paragraph includes persuasive facts for Plaintiff and does not describe them as allegations.

There are no warnings on the helmet or chinstrap. (*Id.* ¶ 3.) Moreover, there is no warning that users must take care not to make the chinstrap too tight because it can cause the chinstrap to come unbuckled during a crash. (*Id.*) A warning on the box, which Ms. Hemingway discarded soon after purchasing the helmet and long before the accident, states only, "[i]f not fastened correctly, helmet chinstrap can come unbuckled." (*Id.* ¶ ¶ 23-25.) Because Defendant did not adequately warn of the danger that resulted in severe injury to Ms. Hemingway, the Court should deny Defendant's Motion to Dismiss.

This paragraph begins with a persuasive fact for Plaintiff.

To minimize the fact regarding the warning on the box, this sentence uses the word "only."

The last sentence is a transition to the Argument.

3. STEP THREE: PREPARE A LEGAL STANDARD SECTION IF NECESSARY

In addition to the substantive legal issues in your memorandum of law, the court's decision may depend on the legal or procedural standard governing that type of motion. Certain motions have burdens or presumptions that can impact the outcome. When preparing a motion with a special legal standard, it is helpful to set out that standard—persuasively—in a separate Legal Standard section before the Argument. This Legal Standard section states only the procedural standard, not the rule that governs the substantive legal issue, which appears in the Rule section of your CREAC. That procedural standard overlays the specific legal question in a given motion. Through word choice, organization, and case selection, you should present this Legal Standard as persuasively as you can.

For example, in a Rule 12(b)(6) motion to dismiss, the moving party would want to emphasize that the court is required to take only factual allegations—not legal conclusions—as true, while the nonmoving party would emphasize that the court must view the allegations in the light most favorable to the nonmoving party. The parties will present the same legal standard, but each side should tailor it to make it persuasive. And each party will cite legal support for the standard. So if possible, the Legal Standard should use at least one case with a favorable outcome and note it in a parenthetical.

The following examples show how persuasive Legal Standard sections can differ:

Legal Standard for Motion to Dismiss Under Rule 12(b)(6)

A motion to dismiss pursuant to Fed. R. Civ. P. 12(b)(6) is appropriate where, as here, the pleadings fail to state a claim upon which relief can be granted. The Court should dismiss the Complaint when, taking the Complaint's well-pleaded allegations as true and drawing reasonable inferences in Plaintiffs' favor, it concludes that Plaintiffs have failed to state a claim that would entitle them to relief. *S. Cherry St., LLC v. Hennessee Group LLC*, 573 F.3d 98, 103-04 (2d Cir. 2009). The Court should not accept the Complaint's legal conclusions as true. *Harris v. Mills*, 572 F.3d 66, 72 (2d Cir. 2009) (affirming grant of motion to dismiss).

Legal Standard for Opposition to Motion to Dismiss Under Rule 12(b)(6)

A complaint should be dismissed under Fed. R. Civ. P. 12(b)(6) only if "it appears beyond doubt" that Plaintiffs can prove no set of facts that would entitle them to relief. *Goldman v. Belden*, 754 F.2d 1059, 1065 (2d Cir. 1985). In reviewing a motion to dismiss under 12(b)(6), the Court is required to accept Plaintiffs' allegations as true, draw all reasonable inferences in Plaintiffs' favor, and view the allegations in the light most favorable to Plaintiffs. *Chambers v. Time Warner, Inc.*, 282 F.3d 147, 153 (2d Cir. 2002) (reversing grant of motion to dismiss).

Compare how the same rule is stated differently, persuasively, and accurately for each side. The standard sections use persuasive language from favorable cases to support each side's position.

Motions to dismiss and motions for summary judgment are common motions with special procedural standards that make a Legal Standard section helpful. But for every type of memorandum of law that you prepare, research the procedural standard and include a section like this if it will help the court.

4. STEP FOUR: ADD PERSUASIVE ROADMAPS AND SUBHEADINGS TO GUIDE THE COURT

The purpose of your memorandum of law is to persuade the court. To do this, your document must be clear and cohesive. Thus, you should review your Argument section and point headings and then insert roadmaps, transitions, and headings where they will be useful to the court.

A. Draft Persuasive Roadmaps for Complex Arguments

If your trial court memorandum of law involves more than one issue or a complex issue with multiple subissues, you should draft at least one persuasive roadmap to introduce your arguments on each issue and to show how the issues relate. If you are writing more than one CREAC, then you need a roadmap to show how those CREACs relate. A persuasive roadmap sets up the structure of the argument that follows and provides crucial guidance for the court.

The roadmap begins with your Conclusion on the broadest issue. Then, it typically states your Conclusion on each subissue in the order that you will discuss the subissues. If your memorandum of law includes multiple complex issues, you should insert a persuasive roadmap for each main issue.

For example, if you have multiple CREACs with a point heading for each, put the roadmap before the first point heading to introduce the issues that follow. Or for a document with one major point heading with multiple subissues, like the example below, put the roadmap after the main point heading to introduce the subissues that follow. The following is an example of a roadmap paragraph for a memorandum of law in opposition to a motion to dismiss.

I. The Court Should Not Dismiss Hemingway's Claim for Negligent Failure to Warn.

The Court should deny Defendant's Motion to Dismiss. Hemingway's Complaint includes sufficient allegations that the risk of the chinstrap unbuckling was an inherent danger that triggered Defendant's obligation to warn. Further, Hemingway has demonstrated that Defendant did not include any warnings on the helmet or chinstrap that warned of this inherent danger. Last, Defendant will not be able to prove that the small warning that appeared on the helmet box was sufficient as a matter of law.

This is a roadmap paragraph for the complex issue of negligent failure to warn. This issue has three subissues. The roadmap paragraph begins with the Conclusion on the main issue.

Then, the roadmap states the Conclusions for the three subissues in the order those issues are discussed.

Note that the language in the roadmap and the subheadings is similar, but not identical.

A. Hemingway Has Sufficiently Alleged That Defendant Was Obligated to Warn of the Inherent Danger of the Chinstrap Unbuckling.

[CREAC]

B. Defendant Failed to Affix Any Warnings to the Helmet or Chinstrap Regarding the Risk of Unbuckling.

[CREAC]

C. The Small Warning on the Box Was Not Sufficient as a Matter of Law.

[CREAC]

As you can see from this example, the sentences in the roadmap track the point headings for the subissues. Make sure, however, that the roadmap sentences and the point headings are not identical to avoid monotony.

The best roadmaps provide an easy-to-follow overview of what's to come for the court. The following example is an excerpt from a memorandum in support of summary judgment. The technology corporation Intel sought summary judgment on all six of the plaintiff's claims, and the memorandum includes a roadmap for each, including this one for the fourth claim.

> Plaintiff's fourth claim, for invasion of privacy/false light, fails for five independent reasons. Plaintiff contends that Intel's automated job history line "falsely disseminated" information regarding his dates of employment at Intel. First, Plaintiff cannot establish the required element of "publicity," because, according to Plaintiff, Intel provided this information only to one person. Second, Plaintiff cannot establish that he was placed in "false" light, because Intel's job reference line accurately reflected the fact that Plaintiff was last hired by Intel in 2000. Third, Plaintiff cannot establish that the information provided on the job history line was offensive to a reasonable person. It was Plaintiff, not Intel, who provided an incorrect employment duration on his résumé, resulting in a discrepancy with Intel's accurate information. Thus, it would not have been Intel's accurate information, but rather Plaintiff's misrepresentation, that caused any inference of dishonesty that would be offensive. Fourth, Plaintiff cannot establish that Intel had knowledge or acted in reckless disregard of the alleged falsity of the information on the job history line. Fifth, Plaintiff cannot establish any damages as a result of Intel's alleged conduct.[7]

B. Insert Persuasive Subheadings

Point headings help make a trial court memorandum of law persuasive because they present concise, readable arguments that stand out from the rest of the text. Point headings grab the court's attention and provide the court

---

7. Defendant Intel's Memorandum in Support of Motion for Summary Judgment at 1, *Bhattacharyaa v. Intel*, No. 3:09-CV-06323 (D. Or. 2010), 2010 WL 11425405.

with a break. From reading Chapter 25, you should already have point headings that outline your Argument. Now, look through your Argument to see whether there are any stretches of two or more pages of text where no headings or subheadings appear. If so, consider inserting additional subheadings. You may want to include subheadings to break up a long Analysis section or to separate the Rule, Explanation, and Analysis sections.

You can add as many layers of subheadings as you think are necessary to guide and persuade the court. The subheadings should follow an alphanumeric outline format that toggles between numbers and letters. There must be at least two headings at each level of your outline. For example, if you added subheading A.1. below, you would also have to add subheading A.2.

A. Hemingway Has Sufficiently Alleged That Defendant Was Obligated to Warn of the Inherent Danger of the Chinstrap Unbuckling.
   1. Defendant was aware that the chinstrap could unbuckle if fastened too tightly.
   2. Hemingway could have loosened the chinstrap if the helmet contained an adequate warning.

Similarly, if you added subheading a. under A.2., you would also need to add subheading b.:

   2. Hemingway could have loosened the chinstrap if the helmet contained an adequate warning.
      a. Hemingway has alleged that she read and followed the other warnings printed on the helmet box.
      b. Other helmet manufacturers include warnings on their chinstraps.

Like point headings, every subheading is a complete sentence that states a persuasive argument for your side and ends with a period. When taken together, the point headings and subheadings create a persuasive outline of your Argument.

5. STEP FIVE: WRITE A COMPELLING INTRODUCTION

The court will likely read the Introduction in your memorandum of law first. You can think of the Introduction as your opening statement. It tells the court what you are going to prove in the memorandum of law that follows. The Introduction should be concise and compelling. It should grab the court's attention and explain why your position is correct.

Try writing the Introduction last, after you have prepared the Argument and Facts sections. At that point, you are familiar with the anchors, your best arguments, and how to present them effectively. You also know the facts that are helpful and persuasive for your side. Moreover, you are comfortable with your theme and will be able to weave it through the Introduction.

An Introduction is typically only a paragraph or two. It should follow the general organization of your Argument—meaning that you present the points in the same order that you argue them. It does not need to cite factual documents or legal authorities. The following are Introductions that would work for the memoranda of law for and against the motion to dismiss involving the bicycle helmet.

Introduction for Memorandum of Law in Support of Motion to Dismiss

The Court should dismiss Plaintiff's Complaint for negligent failure to warn. Plaintiff admits that she saw the numerous warnings on the Happy Helmets box. Plaintiff admits that she read those warnings when she bought the helmet. And Plaintiff admits that there was a warning that stated that the chinstrap could come unbuckled if not fastened correctly. That warning is legally adequate. For all these reasons, Plaintiff's Complaint fails to state a claim as a matter of law and should be dismissed.

Introduction for Memorandum of Law in Opposition to Motion to Dismiss

The Court should deny Defendant's Motion to Dismiss because Augustine Hemingway has stated a viable claim for negligent failure to warn based on Happy Helmets' legally inadequate warnings. Happy Helmets is aware that if the chinstrap on one of its helmets is buckled too tightly, it can come undone during an accident. Yet, there is no warning on the helmet or chinstrap telling consumers not to buckle the chinstrap tightly. Indeed, even a consumer, like Augustine Hemingway, who reads all of the warnings on the box will have no idea that tightly buckling the chinstrap creates a risk that the helmet will fail so that it will provide no protection in the event of a bicycle crash. This failure is a risk, inherent in the helmet, that gives rise to a duty to warn. Because Defendant failed to adequately warn of this risk, its Motion to Dismiss should be denied.

6. STEP SIX: SCRUTINIZE AND REVISE

A trial court memorandum of law will be scrutinized by the court and opposing counsel. Use the following checklist to ensure that your document will hold up under this intense scrutiny.

Trial Court Memorandum of Law

☑ Does the caption follow the formatting rules that govern your document?

☑ Read the Introduction. Does it present a persuasive synthesis of your theme and Argument?

☑ Read the Facts section. Does it include all legally significant, procedural, and emotional facts that are relevant to the issue in the memorandum of law and support your theme?

☑ Does the Facts section include legally relevant contrary facts?

☑ Does the Facts section omit legal arguments?

☑ Does the Facts section tell a persuasive story from your client's point of view?

☑ Does the Facts section include a specific citation to a factual document for every fact or allegation that it includes?

☑ Read the point headings. Is every point heading a persuasive sentence?

☑ Do the point headings provide an outline of the points of your Argument?

☑ Does a point heading appear at least every two pages or so?

☑ Are there at least two point headings at every outline level?

☑ Read the Argument. Does every complex issue begin with a persuasive roadmap that introduces the subissues that follow?

☑ Does the document end with a separate Conclusion section that uses the customary language for your jurisdiction and a properly formatted signature block?

The examples on the next pages show a trial court memorandum of law for a Motion to Dismiss and a Motion for Summary Judgment.

Example
Motion 31.1

UNITED STATES DISTRICT COURT
FOR THE SOUTHERN DISTRICT OF FLORIDA
CASE NO.: 17-3467-Civ-TUDOR/PHELIPPE

Kieran G. Mahoney

    Plaintiff,

      v.

Gold Coast Herald Tribune

    Defendant.

— The caption is properly formatted according to court rules.

DEFENDANT HERALD TRIBUNE'S MEMORANDUM OF LAW IN SUPPORT OF THE MOTION TO DISMISS PLAINTIFF'S COMPLAINT

Despite having courted publicity relentlessly to promote herself and the show, reality star Kieran G. Mahoney is attempting to use a defamation claim to chill the Herald Tribune's ability to comment and opine on her life. The Herald Tribune moves to dismiss Mahoney's Complaint for three reasons. First, the challenged statements were not defamatory as a matter of law but were instead "rhetorical hyperbole," which means they are protected as pure opinion and cannot be the basis for a defamation claim. Second, a gossip column is understood to convey hyperbole. And finally, the context and language of the statements convey that they are not meant to be taken literally. Thus, this Court should grant the motion to dismiss Mahoney's Complaint.

— The **Introduction** grabs the court's attention, advances the party's theme, and summarizes the arguments in the order they are made in the **Argument** section. It doesn't include citations to factual documents or legal authorities.

BACKGROUND

Kieran G. Mahoney is a former "reality television star" who was a cast member of the popular reality television program "The Real Wives of Dade County." (Compl. ¶ 3.) "The Real Wives of Dade County" follows the lives of six women living in South Florida. (Compl. ¶ 2.) The show depicts the women's daily activities and interactions. (*Id.*)

From April 2015 to May 2017, Mahoney appeared regularly on the program, which airs on the Brave Television Network. (Compl. ¶ 3.) In addition to appearing on episodes of "Real Wives," Mahoney appeared at various media events to promote the program, and she frequently was the subject of media coverage that included discussion on radio and television talk shows and articles posted online and printed in newspapers and magazines. (Compl. ¶ 12.)

— The **Background** section weaves legally significant, procedural, and emotional facts into a persuasive story that advances the party's theme. It doesn't include any legal arguments.

— The facts are organized persuasively to highlight the helpful facts that will serve the arguments that appear later in the memorandum.

— Every sentence is followed by a citation to a litigation document. Because this is a motion to dismiss, all of the facts are allegations from the Complaint.

On March 3, 2017, the Gold Coast Herald Tribune ran an item in its "Loose Lips" column about Mahoney. (Compl. ¶ 4.) Loose Lips is a celebrity gossip column that is written by Julie Lipkin. (Compl. ¶ 5.) Loose Lips often discusses reality television stars. (Compl. ¶ 6.) The column's tagline is "Entertainment News with a View." (Compl. ¶ 7, Exs. A, B.) The column appears on the paper's website under the "Entertainment" tab and on the comics page of the print version, next to the horoscopes, comic strips, and Daily Jumble. (*Id.*) The March 3 column stated as follows:

> Mahoney a Charlatan in Chanel?
> A source close to Real Wives diva Kieran Mahoney says Mahoney is about to file for bankruptcy and is about to be investigated for tax fraud. Despite this, the bankrupt basket case has been all over town pretending she can still handle the Miami lifestyle.

(*Id.*) Mahoney's Complaint alleges that, contrary to the information in the column, Mahoney did not file for bankruptcy and was never investigated by the IRS. (Compl. ¶ 10.) The Complaint alleges that the source of the information was likely a disgruntled former employee of Mahoney. (Compl. ¶ 11.)

On April 3, 2017, the Brave Network released a statement revealing its decision not to extend Mahoney's contract to appear on "Real Wives" for the next season. (Compl. ¶ 22.) The statement explained that "poor viewer response," a decline in the ratings, and a desire to bring "fresh faces" to the cast were the reasons for its decision to not include Mahoney in the next season. (Compl. ¶ 23.) Mahoney alleges that her contract was not renewed because of the information in the Loose Lips column about her financial problems, despite the language in the Brave Network's statement to the contrary. (Compl. ¶ 25.)

A month after Brave's decision, Mahoney brought this action against the Herald Tribune alleging that the column was defamatory. (Compl. ¶ 1.) In particular, Mahoney alleged that the statements that she is a "charlatan" and a "bankrupt basket case" and that she "is about to file for bankruptcy and is about to be investigated for tax fraud" were defamatory. (Compl. ¶ 14.) Because Mahoney fails to state a claim upon which relief can be granted, her Complaint should be dismissed.

— The facts are characterized persuasively for Defendant. For example, it refers to "Loose Lips" as a column, rather than an article.

— Negative facts are minimized by being placed in a less conspicuous place and described as allegations.

— The facts include details like dates and quoted language, where relevant.

— The Facts section avoids legal argument, pointing out instead where Plaintiff's case lacks facts in support.

— The facts refer to Plaintiff as "Mahoney" to avoid humanizing her for the court.

— All facts relevant to the issue in the memorandum of law are included in the **Background** section.

— The Background section concludes with a transition to the **Argument**.

2

LEGAL STANDARD

A complaint should be dismissed under Federal Rule of Civil Procedure 12(b)(6) unless the plaintiff can present enough facts to state a claim for relief that is "plausible on its face." *Five for Entertainment S.A. v. Rodriguez*, 877 F. Supp. 2d 1321, 1326 (S.D. Fla. 2012) (granting motion to dismiss on defamation claim) (citing *Ashcroft v. Iqbal*, 566 U.S. 662 (2009)). A complaint can survive a 12(b)(6) motion to dismiss only "if it contains factual allegations that are 'enough to raise a right to relief above the speculative level, on the assumption that all the [factual] allegations in the complaint are true.'" *Id.* (citing *Bell Atl. Corp. v. Twombly*, 550 U.S. 544 (2007)).

— The **Legal Standard** section describes the procedural standard for a motion to dismiss under Fed. R. Civ. P. 12(b)(6). This standard is stated persuasively, using words like "unless" and "only" to make it appear easy for a motion to dismiss to succeed. Authorities from this court and higher courts are cited for support, including a case that resulted in the outcome requested in the memorandum of law, which is noted in a parenthetical.

ARGUMENT

I. The Complaint Should Be Dismissed Because The Statements Were Rhetorical Hyperbole.

— This point heading is a concise, persuasive sentence that states the **Conclusion** on the precise issue.

The Court should dismiss the Complaint because the challenged statements were not defamatory but instead were rhetorical hyperbole. Under Florida law, a plaintiff cannot succeed on a defamation claim unless she establishes the following five elements: (1) the statement was published; (2) the statement was false; (3) the statement was defamatory; (4) the defendant acted with actual malice, meaning knowledge or reckless disregard of the falsity on a matter concerning a public figure; and (5) the plaintiff suffered actual damages. *Jews for Jesus, Inc. v. Rapp*, 997 So. 2d 1098, 1106 (Fla. 2008). The question of whether the statement was defamatory or "whether the complained of words are actionable expressions of fact or non-actionable expressions of pure opinion/rhetorical hyperbole" is for the Court to decide as a matter of law. *Fortson v. Colangelo*, 434 F. Supp. 2d 1369, 1379 (S.D. Fla. 2006); *From v. Tallahassee Democrat, Inc.*, 400 So. 2d 52, 56 (Fla. Dist. Ct. App. 1981).

— The CREAC begins with a **Conclusion** and includes a specific reason in support.

— The **Rule** section begins with the most general rule, which defines the defamation rule. All rules are stated as persuasively as possible.

— The **Rule** section then narrows the court's focus to element 2—and the more specific issue of whether the statement was opinion or rhetorical hyperbole.

A. Defamation Cannot Be Premised On A Statement Of Pure Opinion Or Rhetorical Hyperbole That Discloses The Factual Basis For The Statement.

Statements of pure opinion cannot be defamatory. *Fortson*, 434 F. Supp. 2d at 1379. A statement is pure opinion, rather than a mixed expression of opinion, when the facts that form the basis for the opinion are stated in the publication or available to the public. *From*, 400 So. 2d at 57 (citing Restatement (Second) of Torts § 566); *see also Hay v. Indep.*

— This topic sentence begins the **Explanation** and persuasively explains the broadest part of the relevant law.

Newspapers, Inc., 450 So. 2d 293, 295 (Fla. Dist. Ct. App. 1984) ("Mixed opinion is based upon facts regarding a person or his conduct that are neither stated in the publication nor assumed to exist by a party exposed to the communication.... Pure opinion is protected under the First Amendment, but mixed opinion is not.").

— This paragraph begins to set up the first major argument in the **Analysis**: that the statements were pure opinion.

Pure opinion sometimes takes the form of "rhetorical hyperbole." *Fortson*, 434 F. Supp. 2d at 1378. The Supreme Court has described rhetorical hyperbole as "imaginative expression" and "loose, figurative, or hyperbolic language." *Horsley v. Rivera*, 292 F.3d 695, 701 (11th Cir. 2002) (citing *Hustler Magazine v. Falwell*, 485 U.S. 46, 50, 53-55 (1987)). When a writer states an opinion using this kind of language, the statement "cannot reasonably be interpreted as stating actual facts" about the subject. *Milkovich v. Lorain Journal Co.*, 497 U.S. 1, 20 (1990) (quoting *Colodny v. Iverson, Yoakum, Papiano & Hatch*, 936 F. Supp. 917, 924 (M.D. Fla. 1996)).

— The second **Explanation** paragraph continues to advance the court's understanding of the law relating to the key issue: rhetorical hyperbole.

A statement is rhetorical hyperbole when its medium, context, and language show it is opinion. *Colodny*, 936 F. Supp. at 923. A statement that appears in an opinion piece or column, rather than a news article, is rhetorical hyperbole because the medium communicates that the statement is an opinion. *Id.* at 924 (holding that the context of a letter published in a "Commentary" section of a newspaper like a letter to the editor "unambiguously reveals that it is an opinion"); *see also Hay*, 450 So. 2d at 295 (holding that a statement published as a letter to the editor in a section of the newspaper titled "The Forum, Opinion," was pure opinion).

— The topic sentence for the third **Explanation** paragraph provides a further description of how a court decides that a statement is rhetorical hyperbole.

For example, statements in a sports column were rhetorical hyperbole when they appeared in "a medium that fosters debate ... and that routinely uses figurative or hyperbolic language." *Fortson*, 434 F. Supp. 2d at 1381. Those statements in *Fortson* were about an NBA basketball player and in a column called "Hoop du Jour," which "held itself out as containing subjective content" and was a vehicle for the writer's "thoughts and opinions on the NBA." *Id.* Accordingly, "a reasonable reader is more likely to regard its content as opinion and/or rhetorical hyperbole." *Id.*

— The next paragraph provides additional examples to illustrate the meaning of rhetorical hyperbole. It focuses on the medium, which sets up the second major point in the **Analysis** section. These specific illustrations help set up substantive and specific analogies in the **Analysis** section.

Further, a statement is rhetorical hyperbole when the language and context establish that the writer is stating an opinion, not a fact, or speaking figuratively, rather than literally. *See Horsley v. Feldt,* 304 F.3d 1125, 1132 (11th Cir. 2002) (holding that the "context" and "flavor" of the challenged statements made them rhetorical hyperbole). For example, the

— These last two **Explanation** paragraphs add to the court's understanding of rhetorical hyperbole. Both paragraphs detail additional examples from cases to persuasively describe how a court has interpreted the law in a favorable way.

4

circumstances of a television interview by talk show host Geraldo Rivera "instill upon a reasonable viewer the impression that the parties were exchanging dialogue at a non-literal level." *Rivera*, 292 F.3d at 702; *see also Colodny*, 936 F. Supp. at 925 (concluding that a statement about fraud was an expression of non-actionable, pure opinion under the totality of the circumstances.)

Statements also were hyperbole when a court found that "no reasonable reader" would take them in their "literal sense." *Fortson*, 434 F. Supp. 2d at 1382-83. Terms like "thugged out," "vacant lot," "meaningless mass," "gangstas and wankstas," and "attempted murder" in *Fortson* were hyperbole when used to describe a basketball player and his actions. *Id.* at 1385. This Court described the statements as epithets and slang and noted the terms were "a form of hyperbole typical in sports parlance." *Id.* at 1382-83. This Court explained that the plaintiff's "assumption that reasonable people read words in a vacuum, according to their dictionary definition, is ill-founded. As the law recognizes, reasonable people read words contextually." *Id.* at 1385; *see also Colodny*, 936 F. Supp. at 925 (noting that the word "fraud" was "too imprecise, undefinable, and non-actionable" to "suggest to the ordinary reader that [the plaintiff] committed a crime").

> By detailing examples from cases, the writer not only illustrates the law in a meaningful and persuasive way but also sets up a strong argument in the Analysis section. The writer will analogize to these facts in the **Analysis**.

B. The Column In The Herald Tribune Describing Mahoney As A "Charlatan In Chanel" And A "Bankrupt Basket Case" Was Rhetorical Hyperbole.

> The **Analysis** begins with a short heading.

The statements in the Herald Tribune column were rhetorical hyperbole because the underlying facts were disclosed and because gossip columns are understood as hyperbole, not meant to be taken literally. First, the statements were "pure opinion," not a mixed opinion, because the column included the factual basis for the statements. *See From*, 400 So. 2d at 57. The column stated that the information came from "a source close to Mahoney." (Compl. ¶ 7, Ex. A.) Further, the facts that were the basis for the statements, including that Mahoney was about to file for bankruptcy and was being investigated for tax fraud, were disclosed to the reader. (*Id.*) The opinion was not based on implied or undisclosed defamatory facts. (*Id.*) The disclosure here is the same as in *Hay*, where the court held that a statement was pure opinion when it was based on facts that were disclosed in the article. *See Hay*, 450 So. 2d at 295.

> A thesis statement then summarizes the three major points in this **Analysis**. The rest of the paragraph describes the first major point.

> This **Analysis** paragraph shows that the general rule is satisfied by comparing the facts of the present case to the facts and outcome of another case.

5

Second, the medium in which the statement appeared—a gossip and entertainment column, rather than a news article—establishes that the statement was rhetorical hyperbole. Like "Hoop du Jour" in *Fortson*, the Loose Lips column in the Herald Tribune is a medium where readers expect to encounter opinions and hyperbole. *See Fortson*, 434 F. Supp. 2d at 1381. The column has a brash, impudent style that suits the topics it covers: reality television and celebrity gossip. *See id.* at 1382 ("[C]ourts have recognized that sports commentaries in particular are likely to contain statements of opinion, rather than fact, because they serve as a 'traditional haven for cajoling, invective, and hyperbole.'"). Although the tagline for the column refers to the subject matter of the column as "entertainment news," the column is on the same page as the horoscopes, cartoon strips, and Daily Jumble—not news articles. (Compl. ¶ 7, Ex. A.) Even taking the allegations in the Complaint as true, Loose Lips is not presented as news or fact-based reporting.

*This **Analysis** paragraph begins with a topic sentence explaining the second major point.*

The paragraph includes a detailed comparison to a relevant case. It uses an explanatory parenthetical to add support to the analogy.

This paragraph acknowledges a fact that helps the opposing side in a way that minimizes its impact.

Last, the context and language of the statement establish that it was rhetorical hyperbole. The statement must be read in context—as a column written in a jokey voice that uses harsh language to convey the writer's disdain for the column's badly behaving famous subjects. The same was true in *Feldt*, where context also established that the writer was stating an opinion and speaking figuratively. *See Feldt*, 304 F.3d at 1133 (noting that the writer's comments were "lusty and imaginative expression[s]" of her contempt toward the plaintiff). Readers of Loose Lips would not think that by calling Mahoney a "charlatan" and "bankrupt basket case," the Herald Tribune was stating actual facts regarding her financial and business activities or her mental health, just as the court concluded in *Fortson* that readers would not think that the plaintiff "engages in physically violent criminal activity" because the column claimed he was "thugged out." *See Fortson*, 434 F. Supp. 2d at 1382; *see also Rivera*, 292 F.3d at 702 (holding that no reasonable viewer would have concluded that Geraldo Rivera was "literally contending" that the plaintiff could be charged with a felony when he called him an "accomplice to murder").

*This **Analysis** paragraph also begins with a topic sentence. It describes the third major point.*

This close comparison to the facts and outcome of a relevant case establishes a third major point in support of Defendant's position.

The Loose Lips column used those terms figuratively, as exaggerated epithets, not factual statements. *See Fortson*, 434 F. Supp. 2d at 1385 ("[R]easonable readers...were no more likely to have believed that Fortson had actually tried to kill Cabarkapa than reasonable readers of the late 1920s were to have believed that 'Murderer's Row'—

*The final **Analysis** paragraph emphasizes a strong point in Defendant's favor and logically leads to the **Conclusion**.*

6

Ruth, Gehrig, and their Yankee teammates—had actually slayed opposing pitchers....
[T]he term 'murder' was obviously applied hyperbolically; and it was understood by the
reasonable reader in that manner."); *DeMoya v. Walsh*, 441 So. 2d 1120, 1120-21 (Fla.
Dist. Ct. App. 1983) (holding that calling plaintiff a "raving maniac" and "raving idiot"
was pure opinion). Thus, the Court should hold that as a matter of law the statements are
non-actionable rhetorical hyperbole and dismiss Mahoney's defamation claim. *See From*,
400 So. 2d at 58 (affirming grant of motion to dismiss because statement was pure opinion).

CONCLUSION

For the foregoing reasons, the Herald Tribune respectfully requests that the Court
dismiss Mahoney's Complaint.

DATED this 11th day of December, 2017.

Respectfully submitted,

/s/ Oscar Smalls

Oscar Smalls
Counsel for
Defendant Gold Coast
Herald Tribune

— The **Conclusion** section is
a single sentence that uses
customary language to
repeat the request for relief.

— This signature block is
properly formatted.

7

**UNITED STATES DISTRICT COURT
FOR THE SOUTHERN DISTRICT OF FLORIDA
CASE NO.: 18-3467-Civ-TUDOR/PHELIPPE**

Kieran G. Mahoney

    Plaintiff,

    v.

Gold Coast Herald Tribune

    Defendant.

Example
Motion 31.2

— The caption is properly
formatted according to
court rules.

DEFENDANT HERALD TRIBUNE'S MEMORANDUM OF LAW IN SUPPORT OF MOTION FOR SUMMARY JUDGMENT

INTRODUCTION

The Gold Coast Herald Tribune moves for summary judgment on Kieran G. Mahoney's defamation claim. Mahoney, despite having courted publicity relentlessly to promote herself and the show, "The Real Wives of Dade County," is attempting to use a defamation claim to chill the Herald Tribune's ability to comment and opine on her life.

But her claim fails for two reasons. First, the claim is based on statements in a Herald Tribune column that Mahoney's own testimony established to be true. Mahoney testified under oath that she was about to file for bankruptcy. And she was about to be investigated for tax fraud. Summary judgment can be granted on that basis alone. Second, beyond the truth of the statements, Mahoney admitted she is a public figure and that the Herald Tribune had no reason to doubt the truthfulness of the source for its story—a person whom Mahoney herself trusted with the intimate details of her life. Because there is no genuine dispute of material fact to be determined at trial, the Court should grant summary judgment to the Herald Tribune.

— The **Introduction** grabs the
court's attention, advances
the party's theme, and
summarizes the arguments
in the order they are made
in the **Argument** section. It
doesn't include citations to
factual documents or legal
authorities.

STATEMENT OF UNDISPUTED FACTS

A. The Gold Coast Herald Tribune

The Herald Tribune is one of the longest running newspapers in South Florida. (Lipkin Dep. 5:4-5.) It has won a Pulitzer, and its website gets more than 15 million page views per month. (*Id.* 5:8-10.)

— The **Statement of Undisputed Facts** weaves legally
significant, procedural, and
emotional facts into a persuasive story that advances
the party's theme. It doesn't
include any legal arguments
or facts that would be
disputed at trial.

The Herald Tribune has a popular celebrity gossip column written by Julie Lipkin. (*Id.* 3:8.) The column is called "Loose Lips." (*Id.*) Loose Lips often discusses reality television stars. (*Id.* 3:13.) The column's tagline is "Entertainment News with a View." (*Id.* 3:10.) The column appears on the paper's website under the "Entertainment" tab and on the comics page of the print version, next to the horoscopes, comic strips, and Daily Jumble. (*Id.* 3:14-17.)

— Every sentence is followed by a citation to a litigation document. Because this is a motion for summary judgment, the facts are from the depositions and exhibits.

B.   Kieran G. Mahoney And "The Real Wives Of Dade County"

Kieran G. Mahoney describes herself as a "reality television star" based on her appearance from April 2015 to May 2017 on "The Real Wives of Dade County," on the Brave Television Network. (Mahoney Dep. 5:12-17.) Mahoney is also a business owner with a 50% stake in a consulting business that she co-owns and operates with her sister. (*Id.* 21:14-25.) Mahoney has appeared frequently on television and radio and has been the focus of an untold number of newspaper, magazine, and online articles. (*Id.* 12:2-6.) She testified that she considers doing press and publicity part of her job and critical to her "brand." (*Id.* 13:7-12.)

— The facts are organized and characterized persuasively for Defendant. For example, the section begins with information about the Herald Tribune. And it is broken up into sections with subheadings.

Mahoney's consulting business suffered major difficulties in 2017. (*Id.* 22:1-25:1.) Mahoney testified at her deposition that in early 2017 she consulted with a bankruptcy attorney and the business filed for bankruptcy later that year. (*Id.* 22:11-24:12.) And she admitted that the business was investigated and audited by the IRS in the summer of 2017 for underreporting and tax fraud. (*Id.* 22:11-24:12.) The business filed amended returns and paid back taxes as a result of the investigation. (*Id.*)

On April 3, 2017, the Brave Network released a statement revealing its decision not to extend Mahoney's contract to appear on "Real Wives" for the next season. (*Id.* Ex. B.) The statement explained that "poor viewer response," a decline in ratings, and a desire to bring "fresh faces" to the cast were the reasons for its decision to not include Mahoney in the next season. (*Id.*)

C.   The Column

On March 3, 2017, the Herald Tribune ran a short item in its Loose Lips column about Mahoney. (Mahoney Dep. Ex. A.) The column stated as follows:

Mahoney a Charlatan in Chanel?
A source close to Real Wives diva Kieran Mahoney says Mahoney is about to file for bankruptcy and is about to be investigated for tax fraud. Despite this, the bankrupt basket case has been all over town pretending she can still handle the Miami lifestyle.

(*Id.*)

D. The Source

Mahoney testified that she was "certain" that the item in the March 3 column came from Lucy Rodriguez, Mahoney's former personal assistant. (*Id.* 32:11-33:9.) Mahoney described Rodriguez as being "extremely close" to Mahoney and her family. (*Id.* 32:11.) Mahoney admitted that she trusted Rodriguez so much that she gave her access to her "email, text messages, financial documents, personal life, credit cards, and really everything." (*Id.* 33:7-9.) Mahoney admitted that although she described Rodriguez as "disgruntled," she actually had no concern that she was untrustworthy and had agreed to be a reference for Rodriguez. (*Id.* 37:7; 38:18-20.)

— The facts are organized persuasively to highlight the helpful facts that will serve the arguments that appear later in the memorandum.

LEGAL STANDARD

Summary judgment under Federal Rule of Civil Procedure 56(a) is appropriate when "the pleadings...show that there is no genuine issue as to any material fact and that the moving party is entitled to a judgment as a matter of law." *Five for Entm't S.A. v. Rodriguez*, No. 11-24142-CIV, 2013 WL 4433420, at *5 (S.D. Fla. Aug. 15, 2013) (granting motion for summary judgment on defamation claim) (citing *Anderson v. Liberty Lobby, Inc.*, 477 U.S. 242, 247 (1986)).

— The **Legal Standard** section describes the procedural standard for a motion for summary judgment. Authorities from this Court and higher courts are cited for support, including a case that resulted in the outcome requested in the memorandum of law, which is noted in a parenthetical.

ARGUMENT

I. The Court Should Grant Summary Judgment On Mahoney's Defamation Claim.

— This point heading is a concise, persuasive sentence that states the motion's broad **Conclusion**.

Summary judgment should be granted because no genuine dispute of fact exists on two required elements of Mahoney's defamation claim. Under Florida law, a defamation claim fails unless the plaintiff proves the following five elements: (1) the statement was published; (2) the statement was false; (3) the statement was defamatory; (4) the defendant acted with actual malice, meaning knowledge or reckless disregard of the falsity on a matter

— The **Argument** starts with a brief Conclusion to begin the roadmap.

— This persuasive roadmap paragraph includes the overarching **Rule** stating the elements of defamation and cites an additional case with a favorable quotation in a parenthetical.

3

concerning a public figure; and (5) the plaintiff suffered actual damages. *Jews for Jesus, Inc. v. Rapp*, 997 So. 2d 1098, 1106 (Fla. 2008); *see also Colodny v. Iverson, Yoakum, Papiano & Hatch*, 936 F. Supp. 917, 925 (M.D. Fla. 1996) ("[T]o prevail at trial, Colodny must prove all the elements of defamation by clear and convincing evidence.").

The undisputed facts establish that the statements at the heart of Mahoney's claim were true and that the Herald Tribune did not act with actual malice. Thus, summary judgment is appropriate. *See Stewart v. Sun Sentinel Co.*, 695 So. 2d 360, 363 (Fla. Dist. Ct. App. 1997) ("Where the facts are not in dispute in defamation cases, however, pretrial dispositions are 'especially appropriate' because of the chilling effect these cases have on freedom of speech.").

A. The Undisputed Facts Show The Statements To Be Substantially True.

Mahoney admitted in her deposition that the statements she claims are defamatory were true, which defeats her defamation claim. A plaintiff cannot succeed on a defamation claim if the allegedly defamatory statements are true. *Turner v. Wells*, 879 F.3d 1254, 1267 (11th Cir. 2018) ("The challenged statements are true, and Turner's defamation claim falls short on this basis alone."); *Hallmark Builders, Inc. v. Gaylord Broad. Co.*, 733 F.2d 1461, 1464 (11th Cir. 1984) ("Since the statement is true, no reasonable person could interpret it as defamatory in any manner towards Hallmark."); *Byrd v. Hustler Magazine, Inc.*, 433 So. 2d 593, 595 (Fla. Dist. Ct. App. 1983) ("A false statement of fact is the *sine qua non* for recovery in a defamation action."). This Court has a "prominent function" in determining whether a statement is defamatory, and if a statement is true, "it should not be submitted to a jury." *Smith v. Cuban Am. Nat'l Found.*, 731 So. 2d 702, 704 (Fla. Dist. Ct. App. 1999).

Florida courts apply the substantial truth doctrine, which provides that a statement does not have to be "perfectly accurate" if the "gist" or the "sting" of the statement is true. *Id.* at 706 (noting that falsity exists only "if the publication is substantially and materially false, not just if it is technically false"); *Nelson v. Associated Press, Inc.*, 667 F. Supp. 1468, 1477 (S.D. Fla. 1987) ("Nor does the law require perfect accuracy—the law requires only that the publication be substantially true.").

A "statement is not considered false unless it would have a different effect on the mind of the reader from that which the pleaded truth would have produced." *Turner v. Wells*, 198 F. Supp. 3d 1355, 1365 (S.D. Fla. 2016), *aff'd*, 879 F.3d 1254 (11th Cir. 2018). In a

4

Margin annotations:

The persuasive roadmap paragraph then states the **Conclusion** on each issue in the order the issues appear in the **Argument**.

The roadmap ends with a transition that establishes that the relief requested is procedurally proper. The sentence is followed by a citation that includes a parenthetical that quotes favorable language.

This subheading states the **Conclusion** on the first issue.

The CREAC begins with a **Conclusion**.

The **Rule** section begins with the most general rule. All rules are stated as persuasively as possible. To add weight to the **Rule** section, there are explanatory parentheticals with quoted language from the cases. The cases are a mixture of mandatory and persuasive authorities, selected because they are legally and factually similar to the present case.

This sentence persuasively explains the first and only anchor.

This paragraph begins with a topic sentence that persuasively describes how the anchor has been interpreted. Then, it uses a case illustration of a very recent case from the same court and multiple citations with parentheticals to other favorable cases.

recent case, this Court granted summary judgment, which was affirmed on appeal, on a defamation claim after finding that statements in a movie describing the plaintiff as an alcoholic and drug addict were substantially true and had been confirmed by the plaintiff. *Schiller v. Viacom, Inc.*, No. 1:15-CV-22129-UU, 2016 WL 9280239, at *10 (S.D. Fla. Apr. 4, 2016) ("The Court concludes that while the scenes…could reasonably convey the defamatory meaning that Plaintiff was an alcoholic or drug addict, any such defamatory inference is non-actionable because it is substantially true."); *see also Nelson*, 667 F. Supp. at 1477 (granting summary judgment when truth of statements was confirmed by deposition testimony); *Smith*, 731 So. 2d at 708 (reversing and entering judgment in favor of defendant where statement was substantially true).

> The **Analysis** section is broken up with two subheadings—one for each statement. This is the first.

1. Mahoney Testified That She Was "About To File For Bankruptcy."

Here, the undisputed evidence shows that the statements that Mahoney was about to file for bankruptcy and be investigated for tax fraud were substantially true. First, Mahoney testified at her deposition that before the column was published on March 3, she had been consulting with a bankruptcy attorney. (Mahoney Dep. 22:11-23:8.) This admission makes the gist of the published statements true, just as in *Smith. See* 731 So. 2d at 706. The testimony is as follows:

> This **Analysis** paragraph begins with a topic sentence explaining why the anchor is satisfied.

> Next, this **Analysis** paragraph states the specific conclusion about why this statement is true. Then, it presents the relevant facts persuasively.

> Q. Before March 2017, had you ever contacted an attorney specializing in bankruptcy matters?
> A. Yes. I met with a bankruptcy lawyer three times in January and February 2017.

(*Id.*) (objections omitted).

Next, she was asked whether she had ever filed for bankruptcy and she testified as follows:

> Q. Did those meetings result in you filing for bankruptcy?
> A. Not immediately no. And not personally.
> Q. Can you explain what you mean?
> A. Well, a business that I co-own with my sister filed for bankruptcy. But not until much later. And I don't really consider myself to have filed for bankruptcy. My sister really ran the company and made the business decisions.
> Q. When did the business file for bankruptcy?
> A. October 2017.
> Q. And what is your share of the business?
> A. My sister and I own it 50-50.

(*Id.* 23:9-24:12.)

Thus, Mahoney has admitted the statement in the column that she was "about to file for bankruptcy" was, at the very least, substantially true: A business that she co-owns filed for bankruptcy just seven months later. *See Schiller*, 2016 WL 9280239, at *10 (holding the plaintiff could not disavow prior admission to support defamation claim).

— Last, the **Analysis** applies the rule to the facts and cites a relevant case with an explanatory parenthetical for legal support.

2. Mahoney Testified That She Was "About To Be Investigated For Tax Fraud."

— This is the second subheading in the **Analysis**. It focuses on the second statement.

Second, the published statement about the tax fraud investigation was substantially true because Mahoney admitted at her deposition that she was "investigated for tax fraud":

— Like the previous one, this **Analysis** paragraph states the specific conclusion about why this statement is true. Then, it presents the relevant facts persuasively. Last, it applies the rule to those facts and cites a relevant case with an explanatory parenthetical for legal support.

Q. Have you ever been investigated by the IRS?

A. Personally? No.

Q. Has any business in which you have an interest ever been investigated by the IRS?

A. Yes, but it was resolved very quickly.

Q. When was this investigation?

A. The summer of 2017.

Q. And what business was investigated?

A. A small consulting business that I co-own with my sister.

Q. Why was the business investigated?

A. We had a minor underreporting issue. After a short investigation and audit, we filed amended returns and paid a small amount of back taxes. And the issue was resolved.

(Mahoney Dep. 44:2-24.) Again, Mahoney's sworn testimony establishes the substantial truth of the challenged statements. When a plaintiff's deposition testimony confirms the alleged defamatory statement, courts easily find the statement to be true. *See Nelson*, 667 F. Supp. at 1477 ("The second sentence is the truth. Mr. Pulitzer admittedly testified to such in a deposition.").

And unlike cases where there is a dispute of fact regarding the statement's truth or context, in this case the undisputed evidence shows that Mahoney cannot prove the falsity of the statements because she admitted under oath that they were true. *See Rubin v. U.S. News & World Report, Inc.*, 271 F.3d 1305, 1307-08 (11th Cir. 2001) ("Rubin does not contend that he was misquoted in the article, or that any individual statement in the article is false. Because a statement must be false to be libelous, any damage to Rubin flowing from the article's uncontested statements…is not actionable."); *cf. Klayman v. Judicial Watch, Inc.*, 22 F. Supp. 3d 1240, 1254 (S.D. Fla. 2014).

— This paragraph affirmatively addresses a counterargument and distinguishes an unfavorable case. It is strategically located in the middle of this section.

6

Mahoney's statements that her business—which she owns with her sister 50-50— was about to file for bankruptcy and be investigated for tax fraud would have had no different "effect on the mind of the reader" than the statements that appeared in the column. *See Nelson*, 667 F. Supp. at 1481 (holding that a statement slightly different than the parties' stipulation "would not have had a different effect on the mind of the reader from that which the pleaded truth would have produced"). This sort of statement is protected from a defamation claim because a statement does not have to be "perfectly accurate" to be substantially true. *See Smith*, 731 So. 2d at 706; *Masson v. New Yorker Magazine, Inc.*, 501 U.S. 496, 516-17 (1991) ("[T]he defense of substantial truth...would absolve a defendant even if she cannot 'justify every word of the alleged defamatory matter; it is sufficient if the substance of the charge be proved true, irrespective of slight inaccuracy in the details.'"). Because there is no genuine dispute of material fact that the statements were substantially true, this Court should grant summary judgment.

B.   The Undisputed Facts Establish That Mahoney Is A Public Figure And Cannot Prove Actual Malice.

The Court should also grant summary judgment because Mahoney is a public figure who cannot prove that the Herald Tribune acted with actual malice. A defamation claim by a public figure will fail unless the plaintiff establishes "actual malice" on the part of the publisher by clear and convincing evidence. *Mile Marker, Inc. v. Peterson Publ'g, L.L.C.*, 811 So. 2d 841, 845 (Fla. Dist. Ct. App. 2002) (citing *N.Y. Times Co. v. Sullivan*, 376 U.S. 254 (1964)). "Under the actual malice test a public figure plaintiff must establish that the disseminator of the information either knew the alleged defamatory statements were false, or published them with reckless disregard despite awareness of their probable falsity." *Id.* Because the actual malice test is a high bar, "when a motion for summary judgment is brought by a defendant against a public-figure plaintiff...in a defamation action in which the actual malice test applies, summary judgments are to be more liberally granted." *Dockery v. Fla. Democratic Party*, 799 So. 2d 291, 294 (Fla. Dist. Ct. App. 2001).

1.   Mahoney Is A General Public Figure Because She Had Access To The Media And Volunteered To Be The Subject Of Public Scrutiny.

Mahoney is a general public figure. The Court decides as a matter of law whether a plaintiff is a public figure. *Mile Marker*, 811 So. 2d at 845. A general public figure is an

7

Margin annotations:

This paragraph ends the **Analysis** section with a strong argument that incorporates a quotation of key language. The paragraph uses favorable quotations as parentheticals.

This CREAC ends with a short **Conclusion** that ties the argument back to the legal standard for summary judgment.

The second subheading begins the second CREAC.

The second major issue contains two subissues and thus, two CREACs. This roadmap paragraph sets up the two subissues in the order they are argued below.

These are overarching rules that apply to both CREACs for this major issue.

This subheading states the **Conclusion** for the first CREAC.

The first CREAC begins here with a **Conclusion**.

individual who has achieved "pervasive fame or notoriety" in a community such that she "becomes a public figure for all purposes and in all contexts." *Gertz v. Robert Welch, Inc.* 418 U.S. 323, 351 (1974); *see also Don King Prods., Inc. v. Walt Disney Co.*, 40 So. 3d 40, 44 (Fla. Dist. Ct. App. 2010) (treating Don King as a general public figure).

— The **Rule** section persuasively describes the general rules.

Two qualities distinguish public figures from private figures: (1) public figures "usually enjoy significantly greater access to the channels of effective communication and hence have a more realistic opportunity to counteract false statements than private individuals normally enjoy," and (2) they have "voluntarily exposed themselves to increased risk of injury from defamatory falsehood concerning them." *Gertz*, 418 U.S. at 344-45.

— The **Explanation** section begins with a summary of the anchors relevant to this subissue.

Courts routinely treat individuals who have access to media channels and who use them for personal publicity as general public figures. *See id.* For example, Charles Rebozo was found to be a general public figure because he had access to the channels of communication, including major newspapers and television networks, and he had voluntarily exposed himself to public scrutiny through his high-profile relationship with President Richard Nixon and work on Nixon's reelection campaign. *Rebozo v. Wash. Post Co.*, 637 F.2d 375, 379-80 (5th Cir. 1981); *see also Curtis Publ'g Co. v. Butts*, 388 U.S. 130, 154–55 (1967) (holding that individuals were public figures because they "commanded a substantial amount of independent public interest" and "had sufficient access to the means of counterargument to be able 'to expose through discussion the falsehood and fallacies of the defamatory statements'"); *Little v. Breland*, 93 F.3d 755, 758 (11th Cir. 1996) (holding that plaintiff was a public figure because he had participated in "activities whose success depends in large part on publicity"); *Lampkin-Asam v. Miami Daily News, Inc.*, 408 So. 2d 666, 668 (Fla. Dist. Ct. App. 1981) (holding that author who sought "substantial" publicity was a public figure).

— The details of multiple cases are used in this paragraph to explain how courts have interpreted these anchors. Some of the cases are discussed in the text, while others are summarized in citations with explanatory parentheticals.

As a cast member of the Brave Network reality television program "Real Wives of Dade-County," Mahoney is a general public figure. Mahoney described herself as a "reality television star" in her deposition and admitted that she readily had access to the channels of communication and voluntarily sought to be the subject of public scrutiny. (Mahoney Dep. 5:12-17; 8:5-11.) Her actions show that she has "voluntarily exposed" herself and become a public figure, as the *Gertz* Court described. *See* 418 U.S. at 344-45.

— The **Analysis** begins with a concise thesis sentence. It follows the thesis with specific facts from the record and then connects those facts to a seminal case.

Mahoney testified that she appeared "constantly" on television, making public appearances to "get the word out" about her television show. (*Id.* 16:5-22.) Further, she said that she was written about in so many newspaper, magazine, and online articles that she "had lost count of how many." (*Id.* 12:2-6.) Like Charles Rebozo, who engaged in activities that were of great interest to the press, Mahoney chose to appear on a reality television show and promote that show in the media to garner public attention. *See Rebozo*, 637 F.2d at 379-80. Indeed, Mahoney brought this lawsuit because she alleges that she has suffered harm from not having her contract renewed to appear on the program. *See Lampkin-Asam*, 408 So. 2d at 668 (noting that the plaintiff sought substantial publicity, "including the very publicity which is the subject matter of this action"). Mahoney sought public exposure voluntarily; therefore, she is a general public figure as a matter of law.

The Analysis includes a detailed factual comparison to a relevant case to show how the anchors should be interpreted in the present case.

    2. Mahoney Admits The Article Was Not Published With Reckless Disregard.

This subheading states the **Conclusion** for the second CREAC.

There is no genuine dispute of material fact that the Herald Tribune did not act with actual malice. To prove actual malice, a plaintiff must show the publisher knew the statements were false or published the statements with reckless disregard as to whether they were false or not. *N.Y. Times Co.*, 376 U.S. at 279-80; *Lampkin-Asam*, 408 So. 2d at 668. A public-figure plaintiff must "present record evidence sufficient to satisfy the court that a genuine issue of material fact exists which would allow a jury to find by clear and convincing evidence the existence of actual malice on the part of the defendant." *Dockery*, 799 So. 2d at 294.

The second CREAC begins here with a **Conclusion**.

The **Rule** section persuasively describes the broadest rules.

The actual malice standard requires a plaintiff to prove the defendant had a "high degree" of awareness of the probable falsity of the information. *Lampkin-Asam*, 408 So. 2d at 668-69 (holding that the plaintiff must prove "the publication involved was deliberately falsified or published recklessly despite the publisher's awareness of probable falsity"). In a case where boxing promoter Don King sued ESPN for defamation, the court held that this standard was not satisfied even when the source of some of the statements had a "contentious" relationship with King and additional sources were not consulted to verify the statements. *Don King Prods.*, 40 So. 3d at 45-46 ("The law is well established that the failure to investigate, without more, does not constitute actual malice.").

This paragraph is the **Explanation**. The anchor is illustrated through the discussion of the details of one favorable case.

9

Even viewing the facts in the light most favorable to Mahoney, the author's reliance upon Mahoney's former assistant establishes that the Herald Tribune had a basis for believing the information was true and defeats Mahoney's claim of actual malice as a matter of law. Mahoney admitted at her deposition that the Herald Tribune did not publish the column with any degree of reckless disregard for its truth. Mahoney testified that she knew the column was based on information the author received from "a source who was extremely close" to Mahoney and her family. (Mahoney Dep. 32:11.) Thus, the Herald Tribune did not have a "high degree" of awareness of any potential falsity, as *Lampkin-Asam* required, but also, the Herald Tribune had no indication that anyone would take issue with the published statements. *See* 408 So. 2d at 668-69.

> The **Analysis** section begins with a thesis sentence. It then details the factual support for the argument with citations to the record.

Indeed, the undisputed facts show no evidence of any disregard on the Herald Tribune's part. Mahoney defeated her own claim when she testified that she was "certain" that the source was Lucy Rodriguez, her former assistant, who had access to Mahoney's "email, text messages, financial documents, personal life, credit cards, and really everything." (*Id.* 33:7-9.) Mahoney admitted that she had "never" known Rodriguez to be anything but truthful and honest. (Mahoney Dep. 39:6-10.) *See Dockery*, 799 So. 2d at 296 ("Reliance upon a reliable source insulates a defendant from a finding of actual malice as a matter of law."). And although Mahoney testified that Rodriguez is a "disgruntled" former employee, Mahoney did not claim that Rodriguez was untrustworthy. (*Id.* 37:7.) In fact, she testified to the opposite—that she had trusted Rodriguez with the intimate and mundane details of her life and had offered to serve as a reference for Rodriguez. (*Id.* 38:18-20.) Even if she could raise a genuine dispute of fact regarding whether her relationship with Rodriguez was contentious, which she cannot, that alone would be insufficient as it was for Don King. *See Don King Prods.*, 40 So. 3d at 45-46.

> The comparison to a relevant case occurs only in a parenthetical. This use of a parenthetical is a strategic choice that is appropriate here because it focuses the argument on the lack of evidence supporting Plaintiff's claim. It makes the argument appear simple and straightforward.

The undisputed facts also establish that there is no evidence that the Herald Tribune knew that Rodriguez was lying—which she wasn't—or acted with reckless disregard of a high likelihood that she was lying. (Compl. ¶ 10.) Instead, the author, Julie Lipkin, testified that she "absolutely" believed Rodriguez's information to be true. (Lipkin Dep. 12:15-20.) *See Dockery*, 799 So. 2d at 297 ("Plaintiff has failed to present any record evidence that would clearly and convincingly demonstrate that FDP knew, at the time that it published these statements, that Dockery was not under investigation by the federal government.").

10

Lipkin's decision to rely on a source she believed to be credible is similar to ESPN's reliance on sources who had been close to Don King, which the court held fell far short of the showing of reckless disregard. *See Don King Prods.*, 40 So. 3d at 46. Thus, there is no genuine dispute of material fact that the Herald Tribune did not act with actual malice, and Mahoney's claim fails as a matter of law.

CONCLUSION

For the foregoing reasons, the Herald Tribune respectfully requests that the Court grant Defendant's Motion for Summary Judgment.

— The Conclusion section is a single sentence that uses customary language to repeat the request for relief.

DATED this 12th day of March, 2018.

Respectfully submitted,

/s/ Oscar Smalls

— This signature block is properly formatted.

Oscar Smalls
Counsel for
Defendant Gold Coast
Herald Tribune

Appellate Briefs

An appellate brief is one of the most complex forms of persuasive legal writing. Appellate briefs are addressed to intermediate or highest-level courts, like the Michigan Supreme Court or U.S. Supreme Court. After a final decision or judgment by the trial court, the losing party files a notice of appeal. If a party loses at the intermediate appellate court, the party can ask the highest court to hear the next appeal in a writ of certiorari.

On an appeal, the parties file briefs on the merits. First, the losing party (now the "appellant" or "petitioner") files a brief asking the appellate court to review the decision of the court below and reach a different conclusion. Next, the prevailing party (now the "appellee" or "respondent") files a brief asking the court to affirm the lower court's decision. Last, the appellant files a reply brief. Once the briefs are submitted, the court may hold oral arguments.[1] After the intermediate appellate court renders its decision, the process may repeat, with the losing party asking the highest court to review the decision of the intermediate court.

Generally, new issues can't be raised on appeal. For an appellate court to decide an issue, that issue must have been decided in the lower court. Raising an issue at the trial court level so that it can be reviewed by an appellate court is called "preserving" the issue for appeal.

The format and substance of an appellate brief are governed by the appellate rules of procedure and local rules of court. This chapter provides general guidance for preparing an appellate brief, but you should always follow the specific court rules that govern the format and style for your document.

Writing an Appellate Brief

1. Create a template based on the requirements of the appellate rules of procedure and local rules.
2. Research and draft the Standard of Review.
3. Prepare a persuasive Issue Presented.

---

1. See Chapter 38 for a discussion of how to prepare for oral argument.

> 4. Draft a persuasive Facts section, including procedural history.
> 5. Write a forceful Summary of Argument.
> 6. Create a complete, cohesive document.
> 7. Set aside, then revise.

1. STEP ONE: CREATE A TEMPLATE BASED ON THE REQUIREMENTS OF THE APPELLATE RULES OF PROCEDURE AND LOCAL RULES

The appellate rules of procedure and local court rules determine the format for an appellate brief. These rules vary from court to court. A court can reject any document that does not comply with its rules, so you must follow them closely. Most appellate briefs include at least the following parts:[2]

Appellate Brief

1. Cover with caption
2. Table of Contents
3. Table of Authorities
4. Issues Presented
5. Facts section, including procedural history
6. Summary of Argument
7. Standard of Review
8. Argument
9. Conclusion section
10. Signature block

Put your appellate brief together by creating a template that follows the applicable font size, type, and spacing requirements, keeping in mind that the rules may be different than those for trial court documents. Also, take notice of the page or word limit, and calendar the deadline when the brief is due.

A. Create the Cover

Appellate briefs have a cover that is similar to the caption on a trial court memorandum of law. The cover typically includes (1) the court, (2) the case number, (3) the name of the case, (4) the title of the document, and (5) the name of the court below that rendered the decision being appealed. In some courts, the cover will also include the name and contact information of the lawyers representing the party filing the document.

Court rules differ regarding the spacing, orientation, and organization of the information on the cover. In federal court, the cover's color depends on which party files the brief. The appellant's brief has a blue cover, and the ap-

---

2. *See, e.g.,* Fed. R. App. P. 28. The names for these parts vary from jurisdiction to jurisdiction.

No. 06-14836-DD

———

In the United States Court of Appeals
for the Eleventh Circuit

———

LEAGUE OF WOMEN VOTERS OF FLORIDA, ET AL.,

Plaintiffs-Appellees,

v.

SECRETARY OF THE STATE OF FLORIDA, ET ANO.,

Defendants-Appellants.

———

**ON APPEAL FROM THE UNITED STATES DISTRICT COURT
FOR THE SOUTHERN DISTRICT OF FLORIDA**

THE HONORABLE PATRICIA A. SEITZ

———

**BRIEF OF PLAINTIFFS-APPELLEES LEAGUE OF WOMEN VOTERS
OF FLORIDA, ET AL.**

———

WENDY R. WEISER	ERIC A. TIRSCHWELL	ELIZABETH S. WESTFALL
RENÉE PARADIS	CRAIG L. SIEGEL	JENNIFER MARANZANO
The Brennan Center for	ERIN A. WALTER	Advancement Project
Justice at NYU School	Kramer Levin Naftalis &	1730 M St., NW Suite 910
of Law	Frankel LLP	Washington, DC 20036
161 Ave. of the Americas	1177 Ave. of the Americas	Phone: (202) 728-9557
New York, NY 10014	New York, NY 10036	
Phone: (212) 998-6730	Phone: (212) 715-9100	

Attorneys for Plaintiffs-Appellees

Figure 32.1

pellee's brief has a red cover.[3] Court websites often provide a template for a properly formatted cover. Figure 32.1 shows an example of a cover for a brief filed in the U.S. Court of Appeals for the Eleventh Circuit.

B. Fill in the Parts of the Brief

Next, you should create a heading for each part of the brief in the order required by the rules. Once you have a complete template, you should fill in the parts of the brief as you prepare them. You can begin by inserting into the Argument section your persuasive CREAC(s) and point headings. You may want to prepare the sections out of order; some sections will be easier and less time-consuming than others.

---

3. Fed. R. App. P. 32(a)(2).

2. STEP TWO: RESEARCH AND DRAFT THE STANDARD OF REVIEW

The standard of review is the level of deference an appellate court gives to the decision of a lower court. Because the standard of review frames the appellate court's analysis, an appellate brief must describe the applicable standard(s) of review before addressing the substantive arguments. Court rules establish where the standard of review appears in a brief. Typically, it is included at the end of the Facts section, in a separate section before the Argument, or at the beginning of each CREAC.

The standard of review that will apply to an issue depends on whether the issue is an issue of law, an issue of fact, a mixed question of law and fact, or an evidentiary ruling. The standard of review may also be determined by a case's procedural posture. Generally, appellate courts give less deference to lower courts on conclusions of law and more deference on findings of fact and rulings on evidentiary matters. The most common standards of review from the least deferential to the most deferential are de novo, clearly erroneous, substantial evidence, and abuse of discretion.

You should research the standard(s) of review that will apply to the specific issues in your brief. Look for a binding case that is procedurally and substantively similar to your case. For instance, if you were preparing an appellate brief challenging a grant of summary judgment on a claim for misappropriation of trade secrets, you would want to cite a case for the standard of review that involved an appellate court within your jurisdiction reviewing a summary judgment decision in a trade secret case.

You should present the standard of review persuasively for your side. Sometimes this task will be easy. A standard of review that is deferential to a lower court decision that you want the court to affirm is obviously helpful. But even when the standard is not so helpful, you can present it persuasively by selecting a case that applied the standard of review and reached a favorable outcome for your side. If you can find such a case, you should note the favorable outcome in a parenthetical.

The following examples show how the appellant and appellee could present the standard of review persuasively in an appeal after a grant of summary judgment in a trade secrets case:

Appellant's Standard of Review (asking appellate court to reverse summary judgment)

This Court reviews the district court's grant of summary judgment de novo, viewing the facts and drawing all reasonable inferences in favor of the non-moving party. *Kendall Holdings, Ltd. v. Eden Cryogenics, LLC*, No. 12-3258, 2013 WL 1363728, at *7 (6th Cir. April 5, 2013) (reversing summary judgment on claim for misappropriation of trade secrets). An appellate court does not "weigh the evidence and determine the truth of the matter," but instead decides only if "there is a genuine issue for trial." *Id.*

Appellee's Standard of Review (asking appellate court to affirm summary judgment)

This Court reviews a grant of summary judgment de novo. *Stratienko v. Cordis Corp.*, 429 F.3d 592, 597 (6th Cir. 2005) (affirming grant of summary judgment on claim for misappropriation of trade secrets).

3. STEP THREE: PREPARE A PERSUASIVE ISSUE PRESENTED

The Issue Presented, also called the "Statement of the Issues," sets out the issue or issues that the court will decide on appeal. The Issue Presented in an appellate brief is persuasive, unlike the Question Presented in an office memo. Your Issue Presented should be a leading question that communicates your client's position and persuasive theme to the court.

An Issue Presented can have a variety of formats, but one common format is similar to the under-does-when formula that you use to write the Question Presented in an office memo. For an Issue Presented, you can use the "did-when" format:

1. The Issue Presented begins with a clause starting with "did" that asks whether the lower court's decision was correct. For the appellant, this clause usually asks whether the court acted "improperly," and for the appellee, this clause usually asks whether the court acted "properly."
2. Then, it has a "when" clause that summarizes the most persuasive, legally significant facts.

For example, the following are Issues Presented for the opposing sides in the appeal of a trade secrets case:

Did the trial court improperly grant summary judgment when Gene Showers filed suit for trade secret misappropriation within four years of learning that Oscar Industries had wrongly acquired his detailed drawings of a self-cleaning juicer and used those drawings to manufacture a competing product? — The first part of the Issue Presented for the appellant asks whether the trial court improperly granted summary judgment.

The second part describes the legally significant facts that are persuasive for the appellant and advances the appellant's persuasive theme that Oscar Industries misappropriated Showers' trade secrets.

Did the trial court properly grant summary judgment when there was undisputed evidence that in 2013—more than five years before filing suit—Gene Showers was notified in writing that Oscar Industries may have been given access to conceptual artwork for Showers' juicer? — The first part of the Issue Presented for the appellee asks whether the trial court properly granted summary judgment.

The second part describes the legally significant facts that are persuasive for the appellee and minimizes facts that would be persuasive for the appellant.

These Issues Presented are persuasive because they induce the reader to answer "yes" in a way that favors the party who asked the question. You can include an Issue Presented for every major issue addressed in your brief. The major issues are often those with capitalized, Roman numeral headings— I., II., III., etc. These numbered headings often correspond with the CREACs following I., II., III., etc., in the Argument section of the brief.

4. STEP FOUR: DRAFT A PERSUASIVE FACTS SECTION, INCLUDING PROCEDURAL HISTORY

An appellate brief includes a persuasive statement of facts, which is also called "the Statement of the Case." The Facts section should be a persuasive story that includes legally significant, procedural, and emotional facts. Because the appellate court needs to know what happened to the case in the lower court and what rulings are being appealed, the Facts section should include a procedural history with dates.[4] The facts in this section must also be followed by citations to the Record on Appeal.

A. Use Persuasive Topical Subheadings

One technique that can be helpful when preparing a Facts section for an appellate brief is to include short subheadings to guide the reader. Topical subheadings break up a long statement of facts, organize the facts persuasively, and advance your theme. These subheadings are usually not complete sentences. Instead, they are fragments that highlight persuasive factual topics.

For example, in a summary judgment appeal on the statute of limitations in a trade secrets case, the following could be the subheadings for the Facts section in each party's brief:

Appellant's Brief (asking appellate court to reverse summary judgment)
A. Showers' Innovative Design for a Self-Cleaning Juicer
B. Oscar Industries' Misappropriation of Showers' Design
C. Showers' Suit for Trade Secret Misappropriation
D. Trial Court Proceedings

Appellee's Brief (asking appellate court to affirm summary judgment)
A. The Trial Court Grants Oscar Industries' Motion for Summary Judgment
B. Showers' First Notice of His Claim in May 2004
C. Showers' Delay in Filing Suit

Even though the facts are omitted in these examples, the reader can understand each party's persuasive theme from the subheadings alone. These

---

4. *See, e.g.*, Fed. R. App. P. 28(a)(6).

Facts sections are organized differently because the appellant organized the facts around his trade secrets and the alleged misappropriation, while the appellee organized the facts around the motion for summary judgment and the statute of limitations issue. Both parties used subheadings to highlight facts that are persuasive for their positions; neither party just listed the facts chronologically.

B. Include Citations to the Record

The facts in an appellate brief must appear in the Record on Appeal, which includes the documents filed in the lower court and the transcript of any proceedings.[5] Every sentence in the Facts section should be followed by a citation to the Record. One common citation format for the Record on Appeal is described in *The Bluebook*. In that format, record citations are enclosed in parentheses and include a pinpoint citation to the page in the Record where the fact appears. The following is a portion of a Facts section with citations to the Record on Appeal:

> On November 11, 2002, Gene Showers conceived the idea of a self-cleaning juicer. (R. at 18.) He described the idea in his "Invention Journal" as follows: "MAJOR INNOVATION! Juicer that cleans itself through a pulp recycling mechanism." (R. at 57.) He followed that written entry with a simple drawing of a pulp recycling mechanism. (R. at 60.)

5. STEP FIVE: WRITE A FORCEFUL SUMMARY OF ARGUMENT

A section called the Summary of Argument often precedes the Argument section in an appellate brief. Federal Rule of Appellate Procedure 28(a)(7) requires the Summary of Argument to be "a succinct, clear, and accurate statement of the arguments made in the body of the brief...." The Summary of Argument should be concise—usually no more than one page. In the Summary of Argument, you should distill your argument to its most important points, weave in your persuasive theme, and argue to the court why you should prevail.

The Summary of Argument in the brief prepared by Laurence Tribe, Kathleen Sullivan, and Brian Koukoutchos for Respondent Michael Bowers in the *Bowers v. Hardwick* case displays the type of concise and forceful writing that makes a Summary of Argument persuasive:

SUMMARY OF ARGUMENT

The State of Georgia would extend its criminal law into the very bedrooms of its citizens, to break up even wholly consensual, noncommercial sexual relations between willing adults. And the State contends before

—The first paragraph highlights the stark differences between the parties' positions and demonstrates the reasonableness of the respondent's argument.

---

5. *See, e.g.*, Fed. R. App. P. 10(a).

this Court that it may freely do so without giving any good reason. All that Respondent argues is that a Georgia citizen is entitled by the Constitution to demand not only a warrant of the Georgia police officer who would enter his bedroom, but also a substantial justification of the Georgia legislature when it declares criminal the consensual intimacies he chooses to engage in there.

No less justification is acceptable in a society whose constitutional traditions have always placed the highest value upon the sanctity of the home against governmental intrusion or control. Nor is the mere invocation of contestable moral views sufficient to defend a law that so thoroughly invades individuals' most intimate affairs.

Thus the law challenged here must be subjected to heightened scrutiny, and it may be upheld upon remand only if the State of Georgia offers a more powerful justification than the one it has offered here: namely, the tautology that the State has criminalized the private acts at issue because a majority of Georgia's legislators disapprove of them.[6]

> The second paragraph presents the respondent's theme regarding the sanctity and privacy of the home. This paragraph describes the important values at stake in the case and shows how they support the respondent's position.

> The third paragraph sets forth the relief requested by the respondent in the brief.

6. STEP SIX: CREATE A COMPLETE, COHESIVE DOCUMENT

Although you have now prepared most of your appellate brief, it is still incomplete. An appellate brief includes many discrete parts, but it should read like a cohesive document with a unified voice and theme. To create this cohesive document, you should prepare all of the required parts and then insert introductory roadmaps, transitions, and headings where necessary to guide the court.

For instance, an appellate brief begins with a Table of Contents that lists each required section as well as the Argument point headings and subheadings.[7] These point headings provide an outline of your Argument. When you create your Table of Contents, review this outline to make sure that your point headings are persuasive, readable, and logically organized. Consider also whether the point headings sufficiently convey the substance of your persuasive argument. The Table of Contents is one of the first parts of your brief that the court will read, so use it to persuade.

Additionally, your brief will need a Table of Authorities that lists every cited authority.[8] Compiling this Table of Authorities gives you an opportunity to assess whether you have included sufficient legal authorities in your brief and cited them correctly.

---

6. Brief for Respondent at 4, *Bowers v. Hardwick*, 478 U.S. 186 (1986) (No. 85-140), 1986 WL 720442.

7. *See, e.g.*, Fed. R. App. P. 28(a)(2).

8. *See, e.g.*, Fed. R. App. P. 28(a)(3).

You will also need a short Conclusion section and signature block at the end of your brief. And you may need to prepare a section establishing the basis for the appellate court's jurisdiction[9] and include a Certificate of Compliance stating that the brief is within the word limit.[10]

Do not underestimate how long it will take to complete these parts of the brief. Although these sections may seem simple, preparing them can be painstaking and time intensive. Further, prepare each section with the goal of making it persuasive and professional.

Once you have a complete document, you should read it from beginning to end. Look for long blocks of text of two or more pages and consider inserting subheadings as breaks. Then, add roadmaps or transitions where necessary to guide the court and create cohesion and a compelling, unified theme.

7. STEP SEVEN: SET ASIDE, THEN REVISE

Due to the complexity and importance of an appellate brief, you should leave enough time to set it aside before you begin the revising process. Your credibility as an advocate depends on how you have developed the substance of your arguments and how professionally you present those arguments to the court. Because an appellate brief has so many components, you will need considerable time to revise your brief.

Use the following checklist to ensure that your document is complete.

Checklist for your Appellate Brief

☑ Review the rules governing your document. Have you included every section that the rules require in the proper order?

☑ Does the cover follow the formatting rules that govern your document?

☑ Read the Table of Contents. Does it present a logical outline of your argument?

☑ Read the Issue Presented. Is it a leading question that persuasively suggests the answer you want the court to reach?

☑ Read the Facts section. Is it organized persuasively to advance your theme?

☑ Does the Facts section include a citation to the Record on Appeal for every fact it includes?

---

9. *See, e.g.,* Fed. R. App. P. 28(a)(4).
10. *See, e.g.,* Fed. R. App. P. 32(a)(7)(C).

☑ Read the Summary of Argument. Does it summarize your major points and forcefully advance your theme?

☑ Read the Standard of Review. Is it presented persuasively for your side by, if possible, citing a case with a favorable outcome?

☑ Read the brief from beginning to end. Does it have a cohesive voice and persuasive theme?

The following is an example of an appellate brief.

No. 18-11112-PL

IN THE UNITED STATES COURT OF APPEALS
FOR THE ELEVENTH CIRCUIT

———————

Kieran G. Mahoney,

Plaintiff-Appellant,

v.

Gold Coast Herald Tribune,

Defendant-Appellee.

———————

APPEAL FROM THE UNITED STATES DISTRICT COURT
FOR THE SOUTHERN DISTRICT OF FLORIDA

APPELLANT KIERAN G. MAHONEY'S INITIAL BRIEF

Gus T. Geline
Fla. Bar No. 992828
GELINE, PORCH, & SMIGEL, P.A.
1300 S. Bayshore Dr., Suite 86
Miami, FL 33132
Telephone: (305) 444-8888
gtf@fpslaw.com

Counsel for Plaintiff-Appellant
Kieran G. Mahoney

Example
Appellate Brief
32.1

— The **Cover** is properly
formatted according to
court rules.

TABLE OF CONTENTS

— The **Table of Contents** lists every part of the brief and all of the persuasive headings and subheadings that appear in the Facts section and the Argument. Checking that the pages listed are correct should be one of the final proofreading tasks.

i

TABLE OF AUTHORITIES

—— The **Table of Authorities** organizes and lists every legal authority cited in the brief with a properly formatted citation. This is a time-consuming section of the brief to prepare and should be proofread many times.

STATEMENT OF THE ISSUES

I. Did the trial court improperly grant the Gold Coast Herald Tribune's Motion to Dismiss when Kieran G. Mahoney stated a facially plausible claim for defamation on the basis that the Herald Tribune's article was a mixed expression of fact and opinion that was explicitly and implicitly based on false and defamatory facts?

II. Did the trial court improperly grant the Herald Tribune's Motion to Dismiss when Ms. Mahoney adequately alleged actual malice because the Herald Tribune acted with reckless disregard when it purposefully avoided learning that its single unnamed source was lying?

STATEMENT OF THE CASE

This is a defamation case against the Gold Coast Herald Tribune for false statements published about Kieran G. Mahoney.

I. The Herald Tribune's Defamatory Statements

On March 3, 2017, the Herald Tribune included an article in its entertainment news section, "Loose Lips," that reported on Ms. Mahoney's financial and mental health:

> Mahoney a Charlatan in Chanel?
> A source close to Real Wives diva Kieran Mahoney says Mahoney is about to file for bankruptcy and is about to be investigated for tax fraud. Despite this, the bankrupt basket case has been all over town pretending she can still handle the Miami lifestyle.

(R. at 3, ¶ 4.)

The information in the article is false. (R. at 4, ¶ 10.) Ms. Mahoney did not file for bankruptcy, was never investigated for tax fraud, and is not a "basket case." (*Id.*) The Herald Tribune did not attempt to confirm the story with Ms. Mahoney before publishing the article. (R. at 4, ¶ 12.)

Although the source of the false information is unnamed in the article, Ms. Mahoney alleged that she believes the source to be her former personal assistant, Lucy Rodriguez. (*Id.*) Ms. Mahoney had a falling out with Ms. Rodriguez days before the article appeared in the Herald Tribune. (*Id.*)

II. Ms. Mahoney's Contract Is Not Renewed.

In the month following publication of the Herald Tribune article, the Brave Network decided not to renew Ms. Mahoney's contract to appear on its reality program

1

Annotations (right margin):

— The **Statement of the Issues** includes a persuasive **Issue Presented** for every major issue—meaning every issue at the Roman numeral level of the outline—argued in the brief. The issues are presented as leading questions that communicate the party's position and persuasive theme. They use the "did-when" format.

— The **Statement of the Case** contains the factual and procedural history and the rulings presented for review. This **Facts** section tells the persuasive story of the case from Ms. Mahoney's perspective, using legally significant, procedural, and emotional facts.

— The **Facts** section begins with a fact that is helpful to Ms. Mahoney, and the facts are characterized persuasively for her throughout. For example, Loose Lips is described as an "article" in the "entertainment news section," rather than a gossip column.

— Every fact is followed by a citation to the Record on Appeal.

— Negative facts are minimized by being placed in the middle of facts that are persuasive for Ms. Mahoney.

— The facts are organized under persuasive topical subheadings.

"The Real Wives of Dade County." (R. at 7, ¶ 22.) "Real Wives" followed the daily lives of six wealthy women living in South Florida. (R. at 2, ¶ 2.) The Brave Network claimed that Ms. Mahoney's contract was not renewed out of a desire to add "fresh faces" to the cast, but the real reason the contract was not renewed was that the article made it appear that Ms. Mahoney could no longer afford the glamorous, expensive lifestyle that is the focus of the show. (R. at 8, ¶¶ 23, 25.)

*Because the **Facts** section is from Ms. Mahoney's point of view, it presents the facts as true rather than couching them as allegations.*

Ms. Mahoney is a divorced mother of two. (R. at 3, ¶ 6.) Before appearing on the show, she was a stay-at-home mom who had never been on television or performed publicly. (*Id.*) She is not an actress or celebrity. (*Id.*) Since the article was published, Ms. Mahoney has suffered considerable financial harm, including the loss of income from the show and related promotional appearances. (R. at 9, ¶ 35.)

*The **Facts** section concludes with a fact that is persuasive for Ms. Mahoney.*

III. Procedural History And Rulings Presented For Review

On February 18, 2018, Ms. Mahoney filed a Complaint against the Herald Tribune stating a cause of action for defamation. (R. at 1.) The Herald Tribune responded to Ms. Mahoney's Complaint by moving to dismiss under Fed. R. Civ. P. 12(b)(6). (R. at 15.) The district court granted the motion on July 17, 2018. (R. at 52.) The district court dismissed the defamation claim on the basis that (1) the challenged publication was pure opinion and rhetorical hyperbole, and (2) the Complaint failed to allege the actual malice required because Ms. Mahoney is a public figure. (R. at 55.)

This section provides the procedural history of the case from Ms. Mahoney's point of view. To humanize her, the brief refers to her as Ms. Mahoney. Every sentence is followed by a citation to the Record on Appeal.

Ms. Mahoney timely filed her Notice of Appeal on August 8, 2018. (R. at 70.) Ms. Mahoney appeals the decision of the district court on the bases that the defamatory statements were not pure opinion and the Complaint sufficiently alleged actual malice.

SUMMARY OF ARGUMENT

Ms. Mahoney's Complaint for defamation states a claim for relief and should not have been dismissed. Defamation is intended to redress precisely the harm Ms. Mahoney suffered in this case. Ms. Mahoney was the subject of a newspaper article based on information from a single unnamed source that stated that she was going to file for bankruptcy and was being investigated for tax fraud. The article also described her as a "charlatan" and a "basket case." All of these facts are false and defamatory, and the district court's decision should be reversed.

*The **Summary of Argument** distills the persuasive theme and arguments in the brief into a succinct and clear statement. It uses simple and direct language to explain to the court why Ms. Mahoney should prevail. It does not include citations to the Record or legal authorities.*

First, the district court improperly held that the Herald Tribune's article was rhetorical hyperbole. The article is both explicitly and implicitly based on false and

*The **Summary of Argument** uses "first" and "second" to mirror the organization of the arguments in the **Argument** section.*

defamatory allegations regarding Ms. Mahoney's financial situation. The reasonable reader would have taken these statements literally, and the statements are therefore not protected pure opinion. At a minimum, the article contains a mixed expression of opinion and fact, and the jury should decide whether the harmful content is defamatory.

Second, the district court improperly held that Ms. Mahoney has not adequately pleaded actual malice, which is required because she is a public figure. In fact, the Complaint alleges that the Herald Tribune acted with actual malice by purposefully avoiding the truth that its single unnamed source was a disgruntled former employee who was motivated to lie. Viewing the allegations in the Complaint in the light most favorable to Ms. Mahoney, this Court should hold that the Complaint states a facially plausible claim for defamation and should not have been dismissed.

— The **Summary of Argument** concludes with a transition to the Argument.

STANDARD OF REVIEW

— The **Standard of Review** is presented persuasively for Ms. Mahoney. It cites mandatory authorities and notes any positive outcomes in explanatory parentheticals.

This Court reviews de novo the grant of a Rule 12(b)(6) motion to dismiss. *Speaker v. U.S. Dep't of Health & Human Servs.*, 623 F.3d 1371, 1379 (11th Cir. 2010) (reversing grant of motion to dismiss). The Court accepts the allegations in the complaint as true and construes them in the light most favorable to the plaintiff. *Id.*

To state a facially plausible claim, a plaintiff needs to plead only "factual content that allows the court to draw the reasonable inference that the defendant is liable for the misconduct alleged." *Id.* at 1380 (citing *Ashcroft v. Iqbal*, 566 U.S. 662 (2009)). "The Court has instructed us that the rule 'does not impose a probability requirement at the pleading stage,' but instead 'simply calls for enough fact to raise a reasonable expectation that discovery will reveal evidence of' the necessary element." *Id.* (quoting *Watts v. Fla. Int'l Univ.*, 495 F.3d 1289, 1295-96 (11th Cir. 2007)).

— Words like "only" make it appear easy for Ms. Mahoney to satisfy the pleading standard and survive a motion to dismiss.

ARGUMENT

This Court should reverse the district court's decision granting the motion to dismiss Ms. Mahoney's defamation claim. The Complaint adequately pleads the elements of defamation: the statement was published, false, and defamatory; the defendant acted with actual malice; and the plaintiff suffered actual damages. *See Jews for Jesus, Inc. v. Rapp*, 997 So. 2d 1098, 1106 (Fla. 2008). When the allegations are viewed in the light

— The **Argument** section begins with a persuasive roadmap paragraph. The paragraph starts with a general **Conclusion**. Then, it states the overarching rule of the elements of a defamation claim. It ends with a specific **Conclusion** that states the two major issues that will be argued in the **Argument** section.

most favorable to Ms. Mahoney—as is required when reviewing a dismissal—they establish that the challenged statements were defamatory, and the Herald Tribune acted with actual malice.

I. The Complaint Stated A Claim for Defamation Because The Challenged Statements Were False, Defamatory Statements Of Fact, Not Rhetorical Hyperbole.

> — The Roman numeral point heading concisely states the **Conclusion** on the first issue.

The Court should reverse the district court's decision because the Herald Tribune's false statements were not rhetorical hyperbole. Instead, they were mixed expressions of fact and opinion that relied upon defamatory facts and created a false factual assertion. To be defamatory, a statement must be a false statement of fact. *Keller v. Miami Herald Publ'g Co.*, 778 F.2d 711, 715 (11th Cir. 1985). Mixed expressions of fact and opinion are also actionable. *Johnson v. Clark*, 484 F. Supp. 2d 1242, 1247 (M.D. Fla. 2007) ("The law, however, distinguishes between pure expressions of opinion, which are constitutionally protected, and mixed expressions of opinion, which, like factual statements, are not."). A mixed expression of opinion occurs when the challenged statement is based on defamatory facts. *Id.*

> — The CREAC begins with a **Conclusion** that includes more detail than the **Conclusion** in the point heading.
>
> — The rules are organized from general to specific. The **Rule** section uses a mixture of paraphrasing and quoting to present the rules persuasively. Explanatory parentheticals add detail.

Whether a mixed expression of opinion is defamatory is a question for the jury. *Id.* ("Where the court finds that the statement in question is of mixed opinion and fact and reasonably capable of defamatory interpretation, then a jury issue is presented."); *E. Air Lines, Inc. v. Gellert*, 438 So. 2d 923, 927 (Fla. Dist. Ct. App. 1983) ("If Ashlock's statement would likely be reasonably understood by ordinary persons as a statement of an undisclosed existing defamatory fact, then it was properly the jury's function to determine whether a defamatory meaning was attributed to it by recipients of the communication...."), *abrogated on other grounds by Ter Keurst v. Miami Elevator Co.*, 486 So. 2d 547, 550 (Fla. 1986).

> — Explanatory parentheticals quote key language from cases that describe and apply the narrow rule.

A. A Statement Is A Mixed Expression Of Fact And Opinion When It Is Explicitly Or Implicitly Based On False Factual Allegations.

> — This subheading signals the beginning of the **Explanation** section. It emphasizes the anchors that are persuasive for Ms. Mahoney.

A statement is a mixed expression of fact and opinion when "the underlying facts of the situation" are not presented along with the defamatory remarks. *Zambrano v. Devanesan*, 484 So. 2d 603, 606-07 (Fla. Dist. Ct. App. 1986). Liability arises "where the speaker or writer neglects to provide the audience with an adequate factual foundation prior to engaging in the offending discourse." *Id.* at 607; *see also E. Air Lines, Inc.*,

> — The **Explanation** begins with a topic sentence that persuasively summarizes the anchors.

4

438 So. 2d at 927 (citing Restatement (Second) of Torts § 566, cmt. c) ("It is the court's function to determine from the context 'whether an expression of opinion is capable of bearing a defamatory meaning because it may reasonably be understood to imply the assertion of undisclosed facts that justify the expressed opinion about the plaintiff or his conduct.'").

A statement is not protected as pure opinion when it creates a "false assertion of fact." *Anson v. Paxson Commc'ns Corp.*, 736 So. 2d 1209, 1211 (Fla. Dist. Ct. App. 1999) (quoting *Milkovich v. Lorain Journal Co.*, 497 U.S. 1, 18-19 (1990)). The United States Supreme Court has stated, "[e]ven if the speaker states the facts upon which he bases his opinion, if those facts are either incorrect or incomplete, or if his assessment of them is erroneous, the statement may still imply a false assertion of fact." *Milkovich*, 497 U.S. at 18-19.

A statement also is not protected as pure opinion when it implies the existence of undisclosed, defamatory facts. *LRX, Inc. v. Horizon Assocs. Joint Venture*, 842 So. 2d 881, 885 (Fla. 4th DCA 2003). The statements in *LRX, Inc.* were not protected as pure opinion because they impliedly charged the plaintiffs with the unauthorized practice of law. *Id.* The newspaper's statements in *Johnson* also were not protected as pure opinion because they implied undisclosed facts that the plaintiff "acted unethically or even illegally and that he should be subject to punishment." 484 F. Supp. 2d at 1251 (M.D. Fla. 2007).

Thus, statements that imply the existence of false and defamatory facts—especially facts regarding the plaintiff's ability to perform his or her profession—are actionable. *See Zambrano*, 484 So. 2d at 607; *E. Air Lines, Inc.*, 438 So. 2d at 928. The defendants' statements in *Zambrano* were not protected as rhetorical hyperbole because they contained factual allegations about the plaintiff that did not accurately present the underlying facts. *Zambrano*, 484 So. 2d at 606. These damaging statements were that a doctor "had deserted his responsibilities and duties; that he had walked away from his private practice, and his hospital on-call schedule, without prior notice; and that he had acted in an unprofessional and unethical manner." *Id.* Similarly, statements accusing a pilot of being "paranoid" and claiming that he was still flying jets only because it was "awfully hard to fire anyone these days" were defamatory because they implied "that the plaintiff suffers from a mental affliction incompatible with his

---

This paragraph provides a more specific description of a key anchor relating to false factual statements and uses key language from a major case to explain it persuasively. It also sets up the first major point in the **Analysis**—that the article includes false factual statements.

This paragraph continues to advance the reader's understanding of "pure opinion" by persuasively describing a second anchor—that undisclosed facts can make a statement defamatory.

This paragraph uses details from favorable cases, including the facts, holdings, and key language, to describe examples that help set up analogies in the **Analysis** section.

ability to carry out the responsibilities of his occupation." *E. Air Lines, Inc.*, 438 So. 2d at 927-28.

— This subheading signals the beginning of the **Analysis** section. It asserts that the rule described in heading A. is satisfied in this case.

B. The Article Was A Mixed Expression Of Fact And Opinion.

The Herald Tribune's article was actionable defamation, not rhetorical hyperbole. The statements in the article were mixed expressions of fact and opinion that both stated and implied that they were based on false and defamatory facts.

— This paragraph states the broad thesis and incorporates the brief's persuasive theme.

1. The Article Includes False Factual Statements.

— This subheading briefly applies the first anchor to the present case.

First, the Loose Lips article is not rhetorical hyperbole because "the statements on their face contain factual allegations." *See* 484 So. 2d at 607. The article contains two false factual allegations: (1) that Ms. Mahoney filed for bankruptcy and (2) that she was investigated for tax fraud. (R. at 4, ¶ 10.) These false factual statements about Ms. Mahoney are actionable defamation, not pure opinion, much like the factual statements in *Zambrano* that the plaintiff had left his medical practice and the hospital's on-call schedule without notice. *See* 484 So. 2d at 607; *see also Keller*, 778 F.2d at 717 (finding that statements are actionable when they are "false and consist of a statement of fact"); *LRX, Inc.*, 842 So. 2d at 885 ("The Horizon letter, as a matter of law, was not pure opinion, where it contains false assertions of fact.").

— The paragraph begins with a topic sentence summarizing how the first, most persuasive anchor supports the **Conclusion**.

— This paragraph analogizes the facts in this case to the facts of a factually and legally similar case with a favorable outcome.

— Explanatory parentheticals provide additional support by showing the present case is similar to cases with a favorable outcomes.

The "Real Wives" show depicts the daily lives of wealthy women. (R. at 2, ¶ 2.) To claim—falsely—that Ms. Mahoney lacks the financial resources to maintain the lifestyle required by the show is defamatory. *See Madsen v. Buie*, 454 So. 2d 727, 730 (Fla. Dist. Ct. App. 1984) ("[T]he statements made by appellee in her letter clearly attack appellant's ability to perform adequately within his profession and therefore . . . constitute libel per se."). By falsely representing that Ms. Mahoney was having financial problems, the Herald Tribune attacked her ability to perform her profession, like the defamatory statements in *Eastern Airlines* that falsely claimed the plaintiff lacked the ability to perform as a pilot. *See* 438 So. 2d at 927-28.

— Again, an explanatory parenthetical provides additional support by showing the present case is similar to another case with a favorable outcome.

— An analogy to another case from the **Explanation** provides more legal support.

2. The Article Is Based On Undisclosed, Defamatory Facts.

— This subheading briefly applies the second anchor to the present case.

Second, the Loose Lips column is not rhetorical hyperbole because it contains accusations about Ms. Mahoney that are based on undisclosed defamatory facts. The article cannot be pure opinion because while it describes Ms. Mahoney as a "charlatan"

— The paragraph begins with a topic sentence persuasively summarizing how the analysis of the second anchor supports the **Conclusion**.

6

and a "basket case," it presents no facts to support or explain these descriptions. The article, thus, implies undisclosed, defamatory facts and cannot be protected, just as the statements in *LRX, Inc.* and *Johnson* were not protected. *See Johnson*, 484 F. Supp. 2d at 1251 (finding that while the defendant had the opinion "that Mr. Johnson had engaged in 'spin,' lying, and 'betrayal' of the heirs...the 'facts' upon which the opinion is based themselves might reasonably be determined to be either untrue, incomplete, or incorrectly interpreted"). The implication that undisclosed facts show Ms. Mahoney to be a fraud or mentally unstable is defamatory. *See Milkovich*, 497 U.S. at 18 (stating that "expressions of 'opinion' may often imply an assertion of objective fact").

— This explanatory parenthetical demonstrates that the facts of a case with a favorable outcome are similar to the facts in the present case.

The Herald Tribune cannot couch its false defamatory statements as "opinions" or "hyperbole" to avoid a defamation claim. *See Anson*, 736 So. 2d at 1210-11. The statements calling Ms. Mahoney a "charlatan" and a "basket case" are defamatory because they imply the existence of undisclosed facts regarding her conduct and mental health. These statements are similar to the statements in *Anson*, where the court held that statements describing the plaintiff as a "drug using teenage homosexual prostitute" could be defamatory even if they were opinions or "talk radio schtik." *See id.* at 1211 ("[L]abeling the statements as opinion does not necessarily shield the defendants from an action for defamation.").

— This paragraph affirmatively refutes a counterargument.

— Analogizing to a case with a favorable outcome adds legal support to help refute the counterargument.

3. The Article's Medium, Context, And Language Establish That It Is Actionable Defamation, Not Rhetorical Hyperbole.

— This subheading briefly refutes a counterargument.

Last, the Herald Tribune's statements are not rhetorical hyperbole based on the medium, context, or words used in the article. The medium of the article was the "entertainment news" section of a newspaper, not a letter to the editor or the opinion page. *See Colodny v. Iverson, Yoakum, Papiano & Hatch*, 936 F. Supp. 917, 924 (M.D. Fla. 1996); *cf. Johnson*, 484 F. Supp. 2d at 1251 (holding that statements in a letter to the editor were mixed expressions of opinion and fact, not pure opinion).

— The paragraph begins with a topic sentence preemptively refuting the strongest counterargument. Later, the paragraph cites a helpful case after referencing a case that opposing counsel used.

The article was not printed in the context of an emotional debate concerning an issue of public concern but was instead a short gossipy piece about a reality television program. *See Horsley v. Feldt*, 304 F.3d 1125, 1132 (11th Cir. 2002) ("The context of Gandy's statements and their flavor convince us that they are rhetorical hyperbole. Gandy and Horsley were engaged in heated debate on the highly controversial topic of abortion and the emotionally-charged [sic] subject of the Nuremberg Files and the

— This paragraph provides factual and legal support to refute the counterargument.

— This paragraph uses explanatory parentheticals to distinguish mandatory authorities with unfavorable outcomes.

murder of abortion providers."); *Horsley v. Rivera*, 292 F.3d 695, 702 (11th Cir. 2002) ("Horsley and Rivera were engaged in an emotional debate concerning emotionally-charged [sic] issues of significant public concern.").

The language in the article is straightforward and literal, and thus, it is actionable. The article states that Ms. Mahoney is going to file for bankruptcy and is being investigated for tax fraud. It does not use the kind of over-the-top invective that would not be taken literally by any reasonable reader. *See Fortson v. Colangelo*, 434 F. Supp. 2d 1369, 1381-83 (S.D. Fla. 2006) ("[C]ourts have recognized that sports commentaries in particular are likely to contain statements of opinion, rather than fact, because they serve as a 'traditional haven for cajoling, invective, and hyperbole.'"). The article describes Ms. Mahoney as a diva, a charlatan, and a basket case, but it also states alleged facts about Ms. Mahoney in the typical style of a newspaper article. This language is far more straightforward and much less extreme than the insults in *Fortson* that described a basketball player as a "meaningless mass" and characterized his actions as "attempted murder." *Id.* at 1385.

> *This paragraph makes an affirmative argument to preemptively refute a counterargument and distinguish a factually and legally similar case with an unfavorable outcome.*

Thus, when viewed in their totality and in the light most favorable to Ms. Mahoney, the statements in the Herald Tribune article are not rhetorical hyperbole. The Court should reverse the district court's decision granting the Herald Tribune's Motion to Dismiss.

> *The CREAC ends with a* **Conclusion** *on the major issue and a reprise of the request for relief.*

II. The Complaint Alleges Actual Malice Because It Pleads That The Herald Tribune Purposefully Avoided The Truth By Relying On A Single Untruthful Source.

> *The Roman numeral point heading concisely states the* **Conclusion** *on the second issue.*

Ms. Mahoney's Complaint adequately alleges that the Herald Tribune acted with actual malice because it recklessly published false information from a source it knew had a reason to lie. A public figure has a claim for defamation when the publisher acted with actual malice. *N.Y. Times Co. v. Sullivan*, 376 U.S. 254, 279-80 (1964). "If a false and defamatory statement is published with knowledge of falsity or a reckless disregard for the truth, the public figure may prevail." *Harte-Hanks Commc'ns, Inc. v. Connaughton*, 491 U.S. 657, 688 (1989) (affirming that newspaper acted with actual malice).

> *The CREAC begins with a* **Conclusion** *that includes more detail than the* **Conclusion** *in the point heading.*

> *The* **Rule** *section uses a mixture of paraphrasing and quoting to present the rules persuasively. An explanatory parenthetical describes a favorable outcome.*

Reckless disregard is established when the defendant had a "high degree of awareness of probable falsity." *Id.*; *see Dunn v. Air Line Pilots Ass'n*, 193 F.3d 1185,

> *The rules are organized in the* **Rule** *section from general to specific. This paragraph describes the narrower rules.*

1197-98 (11th Cir. 1999). Reckless disregard can be established by showing that the publisher purposefully avoided learning the truth. *Harte-Hanks Commc'ns, Inc.*, 491 U.S. at 691 ("Although failure to investigate will not alone support a finding of actual malice, the purposeful avoidance of the truth is in a different category.").

    When a defendant publishes the false information of an informant, "recklessness may be found where there are obvious reasons to doubt the veracity of the informant or the accuracy of his reports." *Id.* at 688. The United States Supreme Court held that a newspaper had acted with actual malice when it "used a single source as the basis for a highly improbable story" and purposefully avoided evidence that would reveal the truth. *Levan v. Capital Cities/ABC, Inc.*, 190 F.3d 1230, 1243 (11th Cir. 1999) (distinguishing a case where all of the evidence supported the published statements as "precisely the opposite" of *Harte-Hanks*) (citing *Harte-Hanks Commc'ns, Inc.*, 491 U.S. at 691-92). Similarly, the evidence created a jury issue on actual malice when a television news program aired a program that relied upon an "unidentified informer," despite knowing that the informer's credibility was "greatly suspect." *S. Air Transp., Inc. v. Post-Newsweek Stations, Fla., Inc.*, 568 So. 2d 927, 928 (Fla. Dist. Ct. App. 1990).

    Here, the Herald Tribune acted with actual malice when it purposefully avoided learning the truth regarding the statements it printed from an unnamed source. Ms. Mahoney has sufficiently alleged that because the unnamed source was likely a disgruntled former employee—a personal assistant she had a falling out with days before the story ran—the Herald Tribune had "obvious reasons" to doubt the source's veracity. *See Harte-Hanks Commc'ns, Inc.*, 491 U.S. at 691.

    The Herald Tribune did not even attempt to confirm the story with Ms. Mahoney, likely because it knew she would establish its falsity. (R. at 4, ¶ 12.) The Herald Tribune is just like the defendant in *Harte-Hanks*: Both newspapers reported stories based on information from one unreliable source while avoiding obvious information to the contrary. *See Harte-Hanks Commc'ns, Inc.*, 491 U.S. at 691. Just like the defendant's reliance on an "unidentified informer" who was "greatly suspect" created a jury issue in *Southern Air Transport, Inc.*, the Herald Tribune's reliance here on an unreliable, unidentified informer shows recklessness and precludes dismissal. *See* 568 So. 2d at 928. This purposeful avoidance constitutes actual malice, and because Ms. Mahoney has adequately pleaded this claim, the Court should reverse the district court's decision granting the Herald Tribune's Motion to Dismiss.

Annotations (right margin):

The **Explanation** section begins with a topic sentence that persuasively describes an anchor.

The details of an important case are used to persuasively explain the anchor.

A mandatory authority with an unfavorable outcome is minimized by being discussed in a parenthetical in the middle of a paragraph.

Details from an additional case with a favorable outcome set up an argument in the **Analysis**.

The **Analysis** begins with a sentence that states the thesis on this issue.

This sentence uses facts to show how the anchor supports the **Conclusion** on this issue. It also integrates a quotation of key language from a case with a favorable outcome.

This paragraph provides legal support for the anchor by analogizing the facts of the present case to the facts of a case with a favorable outcome.

The CREAC ends with a **Conclusion** on the second issue and a reprise of the request for relief.

CONCLUSION

The Court should reverse the district court's decision to grant the Herald Tribune's — The **Conclusion** uses customary language to repeat the request for relief.

Motion to Dismiss.

Date: September 7, 2018

Respectfully submitted, — The signature block is properly formatted.

/s/ Gus T. Geline

Gus T. Geline
Counsel for Appellant
Kieran G. Mahoney

Other Legal Communication

Introduction to Other Forms of Legal Communication

Attorneys communicate with judges, clients, colleagues, and opposing counsel in many ways. In addition to writing memos and motions, attorneys write correspondence, including letters, emails, and text messages. Judges, with the assistance of their clerks and interns, write judicial opinions. And after all the necessary documents have been written, attorneys present oral arguments to the court.

Each type of legal communication has principles and conventions for the new legal writer to learn—these are discussed and demonstrated in the following chapters. But like the legal writing formats you have already learned, these other forms of legal communication provide an opportunity to demonstrate your competence, credibility, professionalism, and attention to detail. Understanding these new and still evolving forms of legal communication will make you into a legal writer who is ready for the challenges of the day-to-day practice of law.

chapter 34

Letters

Attorneys write letters to judges, opposing counsel, clients, clerks, witnesses, and many others. For instance, many attorneys prepare client advice letters to convey the same objective legal analysis that is found in an office memo. Attorneys also frequently prepare persuasive letters to opposing counsel regarding discovery disputes or other issues. And many attorneys apply for jobs by writing cover letters that describe their skills and experience.

A letter can be more formal than an email message. And the format and conventions of proper letter writing may be unfamiliar to you because we rarely write letters for personal correspondence these days. But as an attorney, any letter you send will reflect your professionalism. Your letters should be written thoughtfully and display a careful attention to detail. Moreover, because letters can be legally significant documents, a letter must be an accurate record of when, where, and how it was sent, as well as being accurate and precise about the matters it discusses.

Professional letters are typically printed on letterhead and structured as shown in Figure 34.1 on the next page.

Usually, the text of a letter is single spaced with non-indented, block paragraphs that are separated with a blank line between each paragraph, as shown in the examples beginning on page 276. Letters that are longer than one page should have a heading on subsequent pages that includes the page number. Often, this page number is formatted as "Page 2 of 8" to help the reader keep track of all the pages of the letter.

The Components of a Professional Letter

1. The correct date
2. The method of transmission
3. A properly formatted recipient name and address
4. A useful re: line
5. An appropriate greeting
6. A professional style that is tailored to the recipient
7. A customary closing

LETTERHEAD [1]

Date

<u>VIA METHOD OF TRANSMISSION</u>

Recipient Name
Recipient Address

Re: Line
PRIVILEGE DESIGNATION, IF APPLICABLE

Salutation:

Body of letter in non-indented, single-spaced paragraphs with a blank
line between each paragraph.

Closing,

Signature

Enclosure
cc: Names of cc recipients

Figure 34.1

1. THE CORRECT DATE

A professional letter must be dated correctly. Often, an attorney will begin drafting a letter days before she sends it. If the attorney enters the date that she starts working on the letter, rather than the date that she mails it, the letter will not be an accurate record of when it was sent.

A letter's date can be legally significant. For example, the date of a letter may establish when a party received notice of a legal right or when a party fulfilled a legal obligation. Letters exchanged during a case are usually stored chronologically in a correspondence file, and they create a timeline of litigation events. A letter with the wrong date can create practical and ethical problems because it misrepresents when the communication occurred.

Develop a practice to ensure that letters are always dated correctly. Some attorneys avoid entering the date until the letter is finalized and sent, others

---

1. If you are preparing a professional letter that is not on letterhead, the sender's address should appear above the date.

manually update the date each day that they work on the letter, and others insert the date as a field so that the date updates automatically.

2. THE METHOD OF TRANSMISSION

The VIA line on a professional letter describes the method used to send the letter. Because letters can be legally significant, every letter must accurately state how it was transmitted. A letter sent by U.S. Mail would have the following VIA line:

<u>VIA U.S. MAIL</u>

Attorneys routinely send letters using methods other than the U.S. Postal Service, and they may send a single letter using multiple methods. For example, an attorney may write an enclosure letter for a box of documents. The letter will be included in the box that will be sent by FedEx, but the attorney may also send the letter as an attachment to an email to inform the recipient that the box is on its way. In that case, the VIA line would state as follows:

<u>VIA EMAIL & FEDERAL EXPRESS</u>

By accurately reflecting how a letter was transmitted, you preserve the letter as a trustworthy record.

3. A PROPERLY FORMATTED RECIPIENT NAME AND ADDRESS

Every letter must include the recipient's name and address. In a formal professional letter, the letter should also include the recipient's job title.

For example, in a letter addressed to a judge, the recipient's name should be written as "The Honorable __[name]__," and the next line should identify the full name of the court before the court's address. For example,

The Honorable Thelton E. Henderson
U.S. District Court for the Northern District of California
Phillip Burton Federal Building & United States Courthouse
450 Golden Gate Avenue
San Francisco, CA 94102

Other appropriate titles include Clerk of Court, Esq., General Counsel, Dr., and business titles like Senior Vice President of Development.

4. A USEFUL RE: LINE

Similar to the subject line of an email, a professional letter should have a re: line that informs the recipient of the general subject of the letter. Typically, letters written during litigation put the case name and docket number in the re: line. For example,

Re: *Sato v. Schmidt*, No. C18-288228

The re: line can include a more detailed description of the subject of the letter, as long as it is concise and helpful to the recipient. For example,

Re: Scheduling Nyongo Deposition in *Sato v. Schmidt*, No. C18-288228

If the letter is protected by the attorney-client privilege, that information should be noted after the re: line, as follows:

PRIVILEGED ATTORNEY-CLIENT COMMUNICATION

5. AN APPROPRIATE GREETING

The appropriate greeting depends on the level of formality in the letter. Typically, letters are used for more formal correspondence. A professional letter will usually use the highest level of formality and have a greeting that includes a salutation, an honorific, and a colon. For example,

Dear Mr. Nasiri:	Dear Ms. Baily:
Dear Judge Hur:	Dear Chief Justice Rodriguez:

When a letter is addressed to a judge, the appropriate honorific is Judge or Justice, unless the person is the Chief or Presiding Judge or Justice, in which case that title should be used.

6. A PROFESSIONAL STYLE THAT IS TAILORED TO THE RECIPIENT

When you sign a letter as an attorney, you put your reputation and credibility on the line. For this reason, you should never send a letter that is inaccurate or intemperate. Every letter has the potential to become a matter of public record. Letters exchanged in litigation are often attached to court filings. When that happens, the court, the clients in the case, and the public all have access to the letter.

A. Avoid Legalese

The principles of good writing apply especially to formal letters. Like any legal document, a professional letter should use concise, plain English—not legalese. A letter should also reflect the voice, personality, and professionalism of its author. And it should be written in a readable style appropriate to its audience. When writing to a judge, the style should be deferential; when writing to opposing counsel, the style should be civil; and when writing to a layperson, the style should be accessible.

A professional letter can include pleasantries that are appropriate to the situation and the relationship between the writer and the recipient. But a letter should not adopt mannered or stilted phrases just because they are common in professional correspondence. Weak wording, like "we write to inform you that," "it is important to note that," "in light of the fact that," and "with regard to," do not belong in a professional letter any more than they belong in a legal memo or brief.[2]

B. Consider the Recipient's Knowledge of the Law

Attorneys should tailor the tone and style of a professional letter to the recipient's sophistication and knowledge of the law. A letter that is written to a nonlawyer should use language that is comprehensible to a layperson. This type of letter should use quoted language from legal sources sparingly, if at all, and it should probably not include citations, which will not be useful or understandable to a nonlawyer. In contrast, a letter to a lawyer or judge should use the relevant language from legal sources and should include correctly formatted citations.

Any professional letter, like any legal document you write, should be scrupulously accurate regarding the facts and law it describes. Further, any letter that provides legal advice or states a legal conclusion should describe the facts and law that are the basis for the advice. By doing so, the letter memorializes what the attorney knew at the time the letter was prepared.

C. Use Pronouns Thoughtfully

A letter should use pronouns thoughtfully. Use the preferred pronouns for the recipient and any person mentioned in the letter. And notice how pronouns describing the relationship between the writer and recipient can impact the letter's tone. A letter addressed to a client will sound cooperative when it uses "we" to describe the actions being taken as part of the representation.

For example, writing to a client, "we need to prove the following elements," sounds like the attorney and the client have a common goal. But "you need to prove the following elements" sounds like the attorney is giving the client a difficult assignment. Also, letters often use the plural "we" and "our" when they are written by an attorney who works for a firm or in an office with other lawyers to show that the letter reflects the position of all the lawyers working on the matter.

D. Adopt a Readable Format and Organization

An effective professional letter is readable and its purpose is clear. The most important information in a letter should usually appear at the beginning and

---

2. See page 150 for other examples of wordy warm-ups and more tips on how to use plain language.

may be repeated at the end—much like how the CREAC framework repeats the Conclusion at the beginning and end of the legal analysis. For instance, a client advice letter should usually state the attorney's conclusion in one of the first few paragraphs.

Professional letters should use short sentences and paragraphs whenever possible because they are easier to read. Letters should also include bulleted and numbered lists when they will assist the reader. Longer letters should include headings and signposts to guide the reader and to break up the text.

E. Proofread

A letter must be proofread carefully. Although typographical and proofreading errors are not acceptable in any legal document, recipients may have some understanding regarding errors that appear in email messages sent quickly from mobile devices. The same understanding does not extend to formal letters. Never send a letter that has misspellings, typos, grammar problems, or other correctable errors.

7. A CUSTOMARY CLOSING

Just as letters usually have formal greetings, they also have formal closings. Professional letters typically end with a sentence or two that wraps up the letter on a positive note, often encouraging the recipient to contact the writer with any questions. Then, the letter includes a formal closing. The most common closings used in legal letter writing are as follows:

Sincerely,
Very truly yours,
Respectfully,

When a letter is addressed to a judge, it should close with "Respectfully" or a similarly deferential closing. Otherwise, any polite, formal closing is appropriate.

After the closing and signature, the letter should indicate whether it includes any enclosures or carbon copy ("cc") recipients. Again, these details ensure that the letter is an accurate record of what was sent and to whom.

8. EXAMPLES OF PROFESSIONAL LETTERS

The following examples show three types of professional letters. The first two are advice letters to a client that present the same legal analyses that appear in Example Memos 17.1 and 17.2 in Chapter 17 and Example Emails 35.5 and 35.6 in Chapter 35. The third is a letter to opposing counsel regarding a discovery dispute.

Example
Letter 34.1

STERN, SOGARD & MURANO, LLP

5 CALIFORNIA STREET, 34TH FLOOR | SAN FRANCISCO, CA 94111 | PHONE: 415-333-4444

June 15, 2018

— Correct date and method of transmission reflecting when and how the letter was sent

VIA EMAIL & U.S. MAIL

Ms. Willis
3625 Oakwood Forest Lane
Lima, Ohio 45801

Re: Analysis of strategy for upcoming status conference on aggravated robbery charge in *State v. Willis*, 18-6215-cr

— Helpful re: line indicating letter's specific subject

PRIVILEGED ATTORNEY-CLIENT COMMUNICATION

— Privilege designation

Dear Ms. Willis:

I am writing as a follow-up to our meeting last week. As we discussed, my team and I reviewed your case and researched Ohio aggravated robbery law. We developed a recommended legal strategy, and this letter summarizes our analysis. In sum, we believe we should pursue a plea agreement with the State because the carving fork found in your car would likely qualify as a "deadly weapon." That means the likelihood of an aggravated robbery conviction is high.

— The opening paragraph states the purpose and develops a collaborative tone, using the passive voice when describing the potential conviction to soften the accusation. It ends with a **Conclusion**.

A "deadly weapon" is "any instrument, device, or thing capable of inflicting death," according to Ohio Code Section 2923.11(A). Previous cases in Ohio have found that an object is a deadly weapon for aggravated robbery purposes when its use or contemplated use could inflict great bodily harm. For example, one case found that a wrench taped to black socks to resemble a gun was a deadly weapon, even though it couldn't shoot bullets, because it could be used as a bludgeon. And in another case, a 5- to 6-inch piece of metal resembling a screwdriver was a deadly weapon because it could cause great harm if used to stab a person.

— The **Rule** includes an informal citation.

— Next, the **Explanation** summarizes the law and includes detailed examples from case law, without citations, because the client here would be unfamiliar with them.

In our case, the carving fork will likely qualify as a deadly weapon because its manner of use and contemplated use mean that it could inflict great bodily harm. Here, the fork was used as a weapon to stab Gus Bitner once and swat him repeatedly, so its manner of use likely makes it a "deadly weapon" under Ohio law. Moreover, the fork—with its sharp steel points—is comparable to the screwdriver because it can be used as a stabbing device and cause great harm. So its contemplated use also likely makes it a "deadly weapon." For these reasons, we recommend pursuing a plea agreement.

— The **Analysis** references "our" case to foster a cooperative tone. It incorporates the facts, instead of describing them in a separate facts section. Passive voice throughout softens the accusations against the client.

Page 2 of 2

But the decision on how to proceed is yours. If you choose instead to go to trial, we could argue that the fork's design shows that it is incapable of inflicting death. First, unlike a gun, which is designed to kill, the fork is designed to hold meat on a cutting board, not to cause harm. And at 5 ounces, the fork might be viewed as less dangerous than a wrench or screwdriver.

Even so, the fact that the fork was used to swat and stab at Mr. Bitner and the fact that it has sharpened, metal edges weigh heavily against us. That's why we're recommending the plea bargain option.

We've scheduled a meeting with Assistant State Attorney Lucia Jemisin to discuss these options. The meeting is 9:30 a.m., Friday, June 22, at her office at 204 N. Main Street. Please plan to attend. If you'd like to discuss our legal strategy further before then, don't hesitate to reach out. I look forward to helping you reach the best possible resolution in your case.

With best regards,

/s/ Prudence Chavez

Prudence Chavez

— Page number

— The writer also summarizes the counteranalysis so the client can make an informed decision. In both the core analysis and counteranalysis, the writer compares and contrasts specific facts in this case with facts from the case law.

— The resolution uses passive voice to avoid an accusatory tone.

— Next, the writer repeats and emphasizes the **Conclusion**.

— The closing discusses the next steps.

— The signature is formal.

Example
Letter 34.2

Stern, Sogard & Murano, LLP

5 California Street, 34th Floor | San Francisco, CA 94111 | Phone: 415-333-4444

January 22, 2019

— Correct date reflecting when letter was sent

VIA U.S. MAIL

— Method of transmission

Ms. Despina Blackhurst
278 Queensbridge Way
San Jose, CA 95002

— Properly formatted recipient's name and address

Re: Analysis of open and notorious element for adverse possession claim

— Useful re: line including concise summary of the subject of the letter

PRIVILEGED ATTORNEY-CLIENT COMMUNICATION

— Privilege designation

Dear Ms. Blackhurst:

— Formal greeting with Dear, honorific, and a colon

As we promised last week, we have analyzed your adverse possession claim and concluded that it will likely be successful. Specifically, your use of the small parcel of land likely satisfies the requirement that it is "open and notorious" to give notice to the owner.

— The letter begins by stating its purpose.

— The **Conclusion** is stated early in the letter.

As described below, your shed and "No Trespassing" signs provided the owner of the parcel with constructive notice of your adverse possession. This letter is limited to our analysis of this one element. At this stage, we believe this element is the only one in dispute, but for an action to quiet title to succeed, we would have to prove all five elements required of an adverse possession claim.

— The use of "we" reflects that this letter is from all of the lawyers working on the matter.

Facts

You purchased a piece of property in North Lake Tahoe from your uncle in June 2011, believing that the property included both a large parcel and a smaller parcel across an alley from the larger parcel. You live in a house on the large parcel. On the small parcel, you installed a shed where you store snow removal equipment. You used a combination lock to secure the shed. In October 2016, you discovered that teenagers were hanging out in the shed. You chased them away and changed the lock's combination. You also posted "No Trespassing" signs on the small parcel.

— Headings guide the reader and break up the text.

— The letter describes the facts that are the basis for the legal analysis.

In June 2018, Aaron Krieger, the owner of the property adjacent to the small parcel, claimed that, according to county records, he owned the small parcel. He told you that he had been living in Norway for the past seven years and had been renting out the property, though he said he

— Page number

could not provide a copy of any lease agreements. You are unaware of any tenants. Now, you seek to quiet title by proving that you acquired the parcel through adverse possession.

California Adverse Possession Law

— This heading signals the **Rule** and **Explanation** sections.

To establish adverse possession in California, we need to prove five elements:

(1) actual occupation that is sufficiently open and notorious to give the owner reasonable notice;

— The letter uses a numbered list to make the rule easier to understand.

(2) possession hostile to the owner's title, which includes possession that occurred through mistake;

(3) a claim that you have title to the property;

(4) continuous and uninterrupted possession for five years; and

(5) payment of all property taxes.

The purpose of the open and notorious element is to give the owner actual or constructive notice of the adverse possession. To be open and notorious, the use of the property must be visible to the true owner and others. When a use is open and notorious, it raises the presumption that the owner had notice of the adverse possession. But the owner is not required to have actual notice of the adverse use. And an owner cannot defeat an open and notorious use by ignoring it.

— The rules are described in plain language without using quoted language or legalese.

An adverse use is sufficiently open and notorious to provide notice when the claimant has enclosed, maintained, or improved the land in some way. For example, in a case called *Nielsen v. Gibson*, where the adverse claimants fenced, irrigated, improved, and built a go-cart course on a property, the possession was sufficiently open and notorious. Similarly, in the case *Lobro v. Watson*, where for 25 years the adverse claimants occupied the property and made improvements at their own expense, including fencing the lot, replacing the roof, and planting trees and flowers, the court held that the use was open and notorious.

— For the **Explanation**, the letter describes relevant cases but does not include citations because they would not be helpful to the client who is not a lawyer.

In contrast, possession of a vacant lot was not sufficiently open and notorious where the land was not improved or regularly cultivated and where there was conflicting evidence about how much the claimants used the property. In that case, *Klein v. Caswell*, one claimant testified that she occasionally visited the property over a 22-year period for picnics, and at one time, she asked a neighbor to keep the lot cleaned up. But several neighbors who frequently passed the lot said that it always appeared neglected, the same as other unoccupied, vacant lots in the area. The court held that this "slight use" was not sufficient.

Page 3 of 3

<u>Analysis of Whether the Use Was Open and Notorious</u>
By installing and maintaining a locked shed on the small parcel and hanging "No Trespassing" signs on the shed after you discovered that teenagers were using it without your permission, you likely used the property in a way that was sufficiently open and notorious to provide reasonable notice to Krieger of your adverse possession. Like a fence or a go-cart course, your shed and signs were visible to Krieger. The shed and signs showed him that you were occupying, maintaining, and improving the parcel, as in the *Nielsen* and *Lobro* cases, where the claimants installed fences, planted flowers, and otherwise improved the properties they were adversely possessing.

— This heading signals the Analysis.

In addition, your use of the property was active and not occasional. Your use of the small parcel goes beyond the occasional picnic in *Klein* that was held to be an insufficient use. Further, there will not be conflicting evidence about your use of the property as there was in that case.

Krieger may argue that he did not have actual notice of your use because he was in Norway during the five years that you used the property. He could argue that the shed falls short of the level of improvement necessary to give notice. The shed and signs are not as significant as the improvements made by the claimants in *Lobro*, who replaced the roof, made additions, and installed a fence.

— The letter includes a discussion of contrary authority and a potential counterargument.

Even so, actual notice is not required. Krieger cannot defeat your open and notorious use by willfully ignoring it. In *Nielsen*, the court rejected a similar argument by an owner who had been in Ireland during the period of adverse possession. Based on this analysis, we conclude that a court would likely hold that your use of the property satisfied the open and notorious element for adverse possession.

<u>Next Steps</u>
You will hear from us soon summarizing the next steps that we can take to pursue an action to quiet title. As always, please let us know if you have any questions or would like to discuss this in person or on the phone. You can call me directly at (415) 888-9999.

— This heading signals a discussion of what will happen next.

— The letter concludes on a positive note and encourages the client to contact the attorney with any questions. As a courtesy, it includes the attorney's direct phone line.

Very truly yours,

/s/ Sarit Levi-Goodman

Sarit Levi-Goodman

— Formal closing

STERN, SOGARD & MURANO, LLP

5 CALIFORNIA STREET, 34TH FLOOR | SAN FRANCISCO, CA 94111 | PHONE: 415-333-4444

January 22, 2019 — Correct date reflecting when letter was sent

VIA EMAIL & U.S. MAIL — Method of transmission

Ms. Adara Wiking — Properly formatted recipient's
The Rivers Law Group   name and address
278 San Carlo Way, Suite 800
San Jose, CA 95002

Re: Discovery issues in *Sato v. Schmidt*, No. C10-288228 — Useful re: line

Dear Ms. Wiking: — Formal greeting

Thank you for granting an extension of time through today for Sarah — Polite tone, reflecting civil rela-
Schmidt to respond to Plaintiff's First Set of Interrogatories and First   tionship with opposing counsel
Set of Requests for Production. Ms. Schmidt's responses are enclosed. — Short sentences are used when possible.

As I mentioned in the voicemail that I left for you yesterday, we would — The use of "we" reflects that this
like to schedule Frederik Nyongo's deposition as soon as possible. We   letter is from all of the lawyers
have been happy to work with you on a deposition schedule that is   working on the matter.
convenient for everyone involved, but five months have passed since we — The letter is concise and
noticed this important deposition. And it has yet to be scheduled. If Mr.   direct but uses passive voice
Nyongo is not made available in the next month, we will be forced to   here to avoid sounding too
move to compel. Please let me know by 5 p.m., Friday, January 25, when   confrontational.
Mr. Nyongo's deposition can go forward.

I look forward to hearing from you. Please let me know if you have any — Positive wrap-up
questions.

Very truly yours, — Formal closing

Rebecca McCarthy

Enclosures — Notification of enclosures
cc: Brandon Murano — Carbon copy recipient

Email

In many law offices, email is the primary mode of communication. Most attorneys spend much of their time reading and writing email messages. Although many of us regularly use email for personal correspondence, a professional email should have certain qualities that distinguish it from a personal email message.

The Qualities of a Professional Email

1. A "to" line that includes only the correct and necessary recipients
2. A subject line that is brief, substantive, and specific
3. A greeting that is professional
4. A format and writing style that is simple and direct
5. An appropriate closing and signature block
6. Attachments that are properly titled and attached
7. A concern for privilege and privacy

---

1. A "TO" LINE THAT INCLUDES ONLY THE CORRECT AND NECESSARY RECIPIENTS

The first step in preparing an effective professional email is to email only the proper recipients. Attorneys often send emails that discuss sensitive, confidential, or privileged information. Because the emails that attorneys send are important, sending them to the wrong recipients can have outsize consequences. An attorney who includes an unintended recipient on an email to a client could destroy the attorney-client privilege for that message and make it discoverable. And an attorney who incorrectly addresses an email is likely to cause confusion and feel embarrassed. Be careful when using the "reply all" command in email; it often leads to unintended recipients.

2. A SUBJECT LINE THAT IS BRIEF, SUBSTANTIVE, AND SPECIFIC

Every professional email should have a subject line that concisely describes the substance or purpose of the message. An effective subject line notifies the recipient of the message's contents and allows the sender and recipient to sort the email into a folder and search for it later.

The subject line should be brief. Attorneys often read emails on their phones, and a long subject line is hard to understand when viewed on a small screen. A concise subject line has the best chance of catching the recipient's attention.

The subject line should describe the substance of the email with enough detail to distinguish it from other messages. Identifying the case or matter that a message concerns in the subject line is helpful. By doing so, the sender and recipient can file the message with other messages about the same case. Because colleagues may exchange thousands of emails about a single case, an email with a subject line that includes only the case name can easily be lost. Thus, the better practice is to include the case or matter name and a brief description of the specific topic covered by each message.

For instance, suppose you are working on the case *Myneni v. Hall* and need to send an email to another attorney working on the case concerning edits to a motion to compel. The following subject line is too vague to be effective:

Subject: Myneni v. Hall

A better subject line would be as follows:

Subject: Myneni v. Hall: Edits to motion to compel

This subject line is effective because it identifies both the case and the specific issue discussed in the email.

3. A GREETING THAT IS PROFESSIONAL

Many acceptable greetings can begin an email. The relationship between the sender and recipient, the subject of the email, and the circumstances surrounding the correspondence determine what greeting is most appropriate. Table 35.1 describes the most common email greetings and when to use them.

4. A FORMAT AND WRITING STYLE THAT IS SIMPLE AND DIRECT

Although attorneys send emails on an infinite number of topics, the following principles of organization and style can make any email more effective.

Table 35.1

Greeting	Usage
Dear Mr. Jones: Dear Ms. Ali:	This greeting uses a salutation, an honorific, and a colon. This is the most formal greeting format and the standard for professional letters. An email that uses this format is akin to a formal letter being transmitted electronically. Use this greeting when you are writing a formal email and need to show deference to the recipient. For instance, this greeting would be appropriate if you are writing an email to a judge's clerk or a new client. Note that the honorific Ms. should be used instead of Mrs. or Miss for female recipients, unless you have been advised that the particular recipient prefers something other than Ms.
Dear Sam, Dear Farrah,	This greeting uses a salutation, the recipient's first name, and a comma. This greeting is common in email correspondence. It reflects that email messages often require less formality than professional letters because they are exchanged between people who are familiar with each other. This greeting would be appropriate when emailing opposing counsel. It preserves some formality by using "Dear" but acknowledges that the sender and recipient are on a first-name basis.
Sam, Farrah,	This greeting uses the recipient's first name and a comma. This greeting is common in email correspondence when the sender and recipient know each other well and often exchange emails. It would be appropriate when emailing a colleague.
No greeting	An email without a greeting is appropriate when the sender and recipient exchange multiple emails in the same chain. The lack of repeated greetings makes the email chain shorter and easier to read. For formal emails requiring deference to the sender, however, the better approach is to repeat the greeting even for later emails in a chain.

A. Lead with the Most Important Information

The main point of an email should appear in the first few sentences of the message. Often, a recipient will not read an email closely at first. Instead, the recipient will skim the message quickly to get the gist and plan to come back to the message at a later time if it requires more attention. So the most important information in the email should be located in the first paragraph or the first sentence of a paragraph to guarantee that the recipient notices that information during the initial skim.

B. Distill the Substance of the Email into Short Components

A professional email should be compact and easy to read on a small screen. The best format for the body of an email is usually short, single-spaced, non-indented paragraphs that are separated by a blank line. In addition, when an email needs to list information, use bullets or numbers.

An email that uses short sentences and paragraphs to convey information will be more effective than an email that is written with long, complex sentences and paragraphs. If an email is long and unwieldy, it may be more efficient to discuss the issues in person or on the phone. And if an email needs to communicate a complicated legal analysis, it may be more helpful to write the analysis in a formal memorandum and attach that document to a short email message that briefly summarizes the memo's contents.

C. Make It Easy for the Recipient to Respond

If an email requires the recipient to answer a question, it should ask the question in a way that makes it easy for the recipient to answer. The question should be direct and, when possible, ask for a simple answer. Further, the question should not be buried in the middle of a message where the recipient may not notice it. Short questions in short messages are more likely to elicit quick responses, as are messages that include only a question or two, rather than a long list.

For instance, imagine that you are emailing a senior attorney about a hearing in the case you are working on together. The following question is too vague and open ended to allow for a simple response:

How should we handle staffing for the upcoming hearing?

In contrast, the senior attorney can easily answer the following question with a yes or no:

Should I plan to appear at the upcoming hearing?

Often, the key to writing an effective email is to put yourself in the position of the recipient. By doing so, you will make it more likely that you receive a prompt and direct response.

D. Be Careful About Tone

Email messages often have a less formal tone than business letters because email allows us to exchange messages quickly. But as with any written communication, conveying the appropriate tone in an email can be difficult. Emails cannot include gestures, facial expressions, or vocal cues (and professional emails should not include emojis, emoticons, or textese like LOL, TTYL, BRB). Thus, emails can be easily misinterpreted. In the professional context, it is safer for the new legal writer to err on the side of formality. Although you can certainly include personal touches in professional emails—for instance, by wishing the recipient well—avoid sarcasm, exclamations, and overly emotional responses. In particular, exclamation points appear frequently in emails because they help lighten the tone of a message. But be careful about overusing them as a new attorney—too many exclamation points can make an email seem immature or unprofessional.

The tone of an email reflects how formal, familiar, and friendly the message appears to the recipient. Aside from its content and the greeting and closing, the tone of an email is most affected by word choice, pronoun use, and sentence structure. An effective email calibrates its tone to accurately reflect the purpose of the message and the relationship between the sender and recipient.

The words used in an email have an obvious impact on tone as they describe the substance of the message. Before using an incendiary or provocative word in an email, consider whether it is appropriate. Often, an email written in the heat of the moment will seem too strong once you have had some time to consider the proper tone. Moreover, certain words can make an email feel more or less formal. For instance, although contractions should appear sparingly in formal legal documents like memos or motions, they are appropriate for email messages.

Similarly, the use of pronouns impacts the tone of an email by characterizing the relationship between the sender and recipient. For instance, when writing an email to opposing counsel regarding a discovery dispute, the use of "you" can give the message an appropriately accusatory or adversarial tone. In contrast, when writing an email to a client, it may be preferable to use "we" to convey that the sender and recipient are working toward a common goal. And take care to always use the personal pronoun that the recipient prefers.

Consider the following two examples, which provide the same information, but have different tones because of their word choice:

As I mentioned in my email last Monday, we need to discuss the best day for the Cruz deposition. — This sentence has a friendly tone. It describes something that "we" need to "discuss," which sounds collaborative. The use of the word "best" sounds positive and non-threatening. This sentence would be appropriate in an email to a client.

You have failed to respond to the email I sent last Monday regarding scheduling the Cruz deposition.

— This sentence has a harsher tone. It accuses the recipient of failing to do something. It also creates a sharp distinction between "you" and "I." This sentence could be appropriate in an email to an opposing counsel.

Short sentences make an email easy to read on a small screen, but short sentences can also sound terse and give a message a harsh tone. For instance, responding to a question with the one-word answer "No" can sound unintentionally brusque to the recipient. An email should balance the need for brevity with a concern for how that brevity will appear to the recipient out of context.

E. Proofread

Like all legal writing, email messages should use proper grammar and punctuation and be free of spelling and other typographical errors. An error in the subject line or body of an email is unprofessional and hurts the sender's credibility. In addition, a spelling or typographical error may make it harder to use the search function to find the email later.

F. Use a Professional Format

Email messages should use a font that is conservative and professional in type, size, and color. In particular, the font type should be one typically used in professional writing, including Arial, Calibri, Georgia, Times New Roman, Verdana, or something similar. The font size should be between 10- and 12-point. The color should be black or dark blue.

5. AN APPROPRIATE CLOSING AND SIGNATURE BLOCK

At the end of an email message, inviting the recipient to call with any questions is often a good idea. Like the salutation, the closing and signature block should be tailored to the relationship between the sender and recipient.

The closing needs to be appropriate for the purpose and tone of the message. Common appropriate closings are as follows:

Best regards,   Thank you,
Regards,   Very truly yours,
Sincerely,

When the sender and recipient have exchanged multiple emails in a single chain, the closing does not need to be repeated for each message.

An email signature block should be short, simple, and professional. Its purpose is to provide the recipient with the sender's basic contact information, not to convey the quirks of the sender's personality. Generally, the most important information to include in a professional signature block is the sender's full name, employer, business address, and direct phone number. A professional signature block should also use a conservative font type, size, and color.

The following is an example of an appropriate signature block:

Vishal Lee
Parker, Van Nort, and Granville, LLP
2416 Nobel Drive
Miami, FL 33133
(555) 123-4567

As with salutations and closings, when the sender and recipient have exchanged multiple messages in a single chain, repeated signature blocks can be omitted to avoid making the chain longer than necessary. Similarly, an attorney's signature block should not include an inspiring or amusing quotation. Adding a quotation to a signature block makes every message longer and creates the risk of irritating the recipient. Last, an attorney should not include "Esq." after his or her name in the signature block. Esquire is an honorific to show deference or respect to someone else, rather than a title to adopt for yourself.

6. ATTACHMENTS THAT ARE PROPERLY TITLED AND ATTACHED

Attorneys often send email attachments. Before attaching a document, give the document a useful, descriptive title that will mean something to the recipient. Then, make sure that the document has the correct file extension (.docx, .pdf, etc.) to allow the recipient to open it and make edits as appropriate. Most important, always attach the attachment. To avoid sending a message without the attachment, consider attaching the document first, before writing the rest of the message. If you do send a message without its attachment, quickly send a short follow-up message—with the attachment—stating that the document is attached.

7. A CONCERN FOR PRIVILEGE AND PRIVACY

Any email has the potential to become a public document. Email messages can easily be forwarded to unintended and unforeseen recipients. And even emails covered by the attorney-client privilege or attorney work-product protection could be discoverable in later litigation between the attorney and the client or accidentally disclosed to opposing counsel or other parties. For this reason, be extremely careful about discussing sensitive topics over email. Never send an email that your gut tells you is inappropriate or unwise.

When sending an email that is protected by the attorney-client privilege, include a privilege label, such as "PRIVILEGED ATTORNEY-CLIENT COMMUNICATION," at the top or bottom of the message. In addition, before sending a privileged message, take care to check that no recipients included on the message would destroy the privilege. For instance, including an expert witness on an email to a client will mean that the message is no longer privileged because there is no privilege between an attorney or client and an expert.

When corresponding with recipients with whom there is no privilege, an attorney should be aware that the email could become a public document. For example, emails exchanged between opposing counsel are routinely attached to motions that are filed with the court during discovery disputes. Such emails will impact an attorney's professional reputation with the recipient, the court, and anyone else who reads the message.

Many law offices have boilerplate language that they include on all messages regarding how an email should be treated if it is inadvertently received by the wrong person. To the extent possible, make sure that any such disclaimers are professionally formatted and designed to take up no more room than necessary.

8. EXAMPLES OF EFFECTIVE EMAILS

The following examples of professional emails show the different levels of formality that attorneys use when preparing email messages. The first is an email to a clerk of court. The second is an email to opposing counsel. The third is an email to a client. The fourth is an email to a colleague. The last two examples are advice emails to clients conveying the same legal analyses that appear in Example Memos 17.1 and 17.2 in Chapter 17 and Example Letters 34.1 and 34.2 in Chapter 34.

Email to a judge's calendar clerk

Example
Email 35.1

To: clerk@court.com

Subject: Myneni v. Hall (Case No. 12-1113): Response to request to reschedule — The subject line identifies the case by name and number and briefly describes the purpose of the email.
telephone hearing on motion to compel

Dear Ms. Ali: — The formal greeting uses an honorific and a colon.

Thank you for your message regarding rescheduling the telephone hearing on — The body of the email is short simple sentences in a single-spaced, non-indented paragraph.
the motion to compel in Myneni v. Hall.

The attorneys for Defendant Travis Hall are available on August 1, 2018, at both
11 a.m. and 3:30 p.m. for the hearing.

Please let me know if you have any questions. My direct line is (555) 123-4567. — The last paragraph offers to have the recipient contact the sender directly and includes a phone number.

Best regards, — The email ends with a formal closing with a complete signature block.
Vishal Lee
Parker, Van Nort, and Granville, LLP
2416 Nobel Drive
Miami, FL 33133
(555) 123-4567

Email to opposing counsel

Example
Email 35.2

To: sam@opposinglawfirm.com

Subject: Myneni v. Hall: Plaintiff's interrogatory responses

— The subject line identifies the case name and subject of the email.

Dear Sam,

— The less formal greeting uses Dear, the recipient's first name, and a comma.

I am writing regarding Plaintiff's insufficient responses to Defendant's First Set of Interrogatories. You have not provided substantive responses to any of the interrogatories. Instead, your answers are vague and composed almost entirely of inappropriate objections.

— The writer creates an adversarial tone by using the pronoun "you" and "inappropriate."

Please serve your revised responses by 5 p.m. on Thursday, October 31. If we do not receive your revised responses by that time, we will plan to file a motion to compel.

— Information requiring action on the part of the recipient is placed in the first sentence of a paragraph.

If you wish to discuss Plaintiff's responses in more detail, please call me directly at (555) 123-4567.

Best regards,
Vishal Lee
(555) 123-4567

Email to client

To: farrah@client.com

Subject: Motion to compel analysis

PRIVILEGED ATTORNEY-CLIENT COMMUNICATION

Dear Farrah,

We have analyzed whether we should file a motion to compel Plaintiff to provide revised interrogatory responses. We think that the Court is likely to grant the motion, and even if the motion is denied, it will educate the Court about Plaintiff's discovery abuses.

The Court is likely to grant the motion for two reasons:
(1) Three of Plaintiff's responses include only objections. The Court has held in previous cases that such responses are inappropriate; and
(2) Plaintiff's responses to all 10 interrogatories total only 14 pages. Given that Defendant's responses to Plaintiff's interrogatories were more than 60 pages long, we have a strong argument that Plaintiff's responses are insufficient.

Please let me know if you would like to discuss this analysis further in person or on the phone. You can always call me directly at (555)123-4567. We would like to begin drafting the motion as soon as possible.

Best regards,
Vishal Lee
Parker, Van Nort, and Granville, LLP
2416 Nobel Drive
Miami, FL 33133
(555) 123-4567

— The subject line identifies the purpose of the email. If the attorney worked on multiple cases for this client, it would be helpful to also include the case name.

— Privilege label

— The greeting's formality depends on the relationship.

— The first sentence gives the email a friendly tone. The next sentence states a conclusion using "we" to create a connection between the attorney and the client.

— A numbered list makes the substance of the email easy to read.

— The email ends with an offer to discuss further in person or by phone and includes a direct phone number.

Email to colleague

Example
Email 35.4

To: denise@lawfirm.com

Subject: Myneni v. Hall: Edits to motion to dismiss

—— The subject line identifies the case name and subject of the email.

Denise,

—— The informal greeting uses the recipient's first name and a comma.

When will you be finished inputting the edits to the motion to dismiss?

—— The body of the email is a simple, direct question.

Thank you,
Vishal

—— The email ends with an appreciative closing and no signature block.

Advice email to client

Note: This is the same legal analysis that appears in Example Memo 1 in Chapter 17 and Example Letter 1 in Chapter 34.

Example
Email 35.5

To: sara.willis@email.com

From: prudence.chavez@ssmllp.com

Subject: Summary of Legal Strategy; Meeting with Asst. State Attorney

— Specific and helpful subject line

PRIVILEGED ATTORNEY-CLIENT COMMUNICATION

— Privilege designation

Dear Sara,

As we discussed last week, my team and I reviewed your case and researched Ohio aggravated robbery law. We believe we should pursue a plea agreement with the State because the carving fork found in your car would likely qualify as a "deadly weapon." That means the likelihood of an aggravated robbery conviction is high.

— The opening paragraph states the purpose and develops a collaborative tone, using the passive voice when describing the potential conviction to soften the accusation. It ends with a **Conclusion**.

Ohio Law

A "deadly weapon" is "any instrument, device, or thing capable of inflicting death," according to Ohio Code Section 2923.11(A). Previous cases in Ohio have found that an object is a deadly weapon for aggravated robbery purposes when its use or contemplated use could inflict great bodily harm. For example:

- a wrench taped to black socks to resemble a gun was a deadly weapon, even though it couldn't shoot bullets, because it could be used as a bludgeon; and
- a 5- to 6-inch piece of metal resembling a screwdriver was a deadly weapon because it could cause great harm if used to stab a person.

— The **Rule** includes an informal citation.

— Next, the **Explanation** summarizes the law and includes detailed examples from case law, without citations, because the client here would be unfamiliar with them.

— The **Explanation** uses bullets to break up the text.

Our Analysis

The carving fork will likely qualify as a "deadly weapon" because its manner of use and contemplated use mean that it could inflict great bodily harm. The fork was used as a weapon to stab Gus Bitner once and swat him repeatedly, so its manner of use likely makes it a "deadly weapon." And the fork—with its sharp steel points—is comparable to the screwdriver because it can be used as a stabbing device and cause great harm. So its contemplated use also likely makes it a "deadly weapon."

— Headings throughout help guide the reader.

— The **Analysis** references "our" and "we" to foster a cooperative tone. It incorporates the facts, instead of describing them in a separate facts section. Passive voice throughout softens the accusations against the client.

For these reasons, we recommend pursuing a plea agreement. But the decision is yours. If you choose to go to trial, we could argue that the fork's design shows it is incapable of inflicting death. First, unlike a gun, which is designed to kill, the fork is designed to hold meat on a cutting board, not to cause harm.

— The writer also summarizes the counteranalysis so the client can make an informed decision. In both the core analysis and counteranalysis, the writer compares and contrasts specific facts in this case with facts from the case law.

And at 5 ounces, the fork might be viewed as less dangerous than a wrench or screwdriver.

Even so, the fact that the fork was used to swat and stab at Mr. Bitner and the fact that it has sharpened, metal edges weigh heavily against us. That's why we're recommending the plea bargain option.

The resolution uses passive voice to avoid an accusatory tone.

Next, the writer repeats and emphasizes the Conclusion.

Meeting with Assistant State Attorney
We've scheduled a meeting with Assistant State Attorney Lucia Jemisin to discuss these options. The meeting is 9:30 a.m. on Friday, June 22, at her office at 204 N. Main Street, and we will attend together. Please let us know if you have any questions or would like to discuss this matter in person or by phone before the meeting.

The closing discusses the next steps.

With best regards,
Prudence

The signature is less formal and includes a short signature block.

Shareholder
Stern, Sogard & Murano, LLP
Prudence.Chavez@ssmllp.com
(415) 888-9999

Advice email to client

Note: This is the same legal analysis that appears in Example Memo 2 in Chapter 17 and Example Letter 2 in Chapter 34.

Example
Email 35.6

To: despina.blackhurst@email.com
Subject: Analysis of open and notorious element
Attachment: August28_Letter.pdf

— The attachment is attached and properly titled.

PRIVILEGED ATTORNEY-CLIENT COMMUNICATION

Dear Despina,

As we promised last week, we have analyzed your adverse possession claim and concluded that it will likely be successful. Specifically, your use of the small parcel likely satisfies the open and notorious element for adverse possession. A court would probably determine that because your shed and "No Trespassing" signs provided the owner with constructive notice of your adverse possession, your use was sufficiently open and notorious.

— The first substantive paragraph of the email provides the attorney's **Conclusion**. The email uses "we" to reflect that this is advice from the team of attorneys working on the case.

Facts
- You purchased a piece of property in North Lake Tahoe from your uncle in June 2011, believing that the property included both a large parcel and a smaller parcel across an alley from the larger parcel.
- You live in a house on the large parcel.
- On the small parcel, you installed a shed where you store snow removal equipment. You used a combination lock to secure the shed.
- In October 2016, you discovered that teenagers were hanging out in the shed. You chased them away and changed the lock's combination. You also posted "No Trespassing" signs on the small parcel.
- In June 2018, Aaron Krieger, the owner of the property adjacent to the small parcel, claimed that, according to county records, he owned the small parcel.
- He told you that he had been living in Norway for the past seven years and had been renting out the property. But he could provide no records at that time.

— Headings guide the reader and break up the text of this long email.

— The facts that are the basis for the **Analysis** are presented as a bulleted list, which is easy to read.

California Adverse Possession Law
Adverse possession has five elements:
1. actual occupation that is sufficiently open and notorious to give the owner reasonable notice;
2. possession hostile to the owner's title, which includes possession that occurred through mistake;

— For the **Rule** section, the elements are presented in a numbered list written in plain language.

3. a claim that you have title to the property;
4. continuous and uninterrupted possession for five years; and
5. payment of all property taxes.

The purpose of the open and notorious element is to give the owner actual or constructive notice of the adverse possession. To be open and notorious, the use of the property must be visible to the true owner and others. When a use is open and notorious, it raises the presumption that the owner had notice of the adverse possession. But actual notice is not required. And an owner cannot defeat an open and notorious use by willfully ignoring it.

An adverse use is sufficiently open and notorious to provide notice when the claimant has enclosed, maintained, or improved the land in some way.

Relevant cases

Our analysis is based on three cases that are factually and legally similar to your situation. They are summarized below:

Nielsen v. Gibson: The adverse claimants fenced, irrigated, improved, and built a go-cart course on a property. The court held the possession was sufficiently open and notorious.

Lobro v. Watson: For 25 years the adverse claimants occupied the property and made improvements and additions at their own expense, including fencing the lot, replacing the roof, and planting trees and flowers. The court held that the use was open and notorious.

Klein v. Caswell: The court held that possession of a vacant lot was not sufficiently open and notorious where the land was not improved or regularly cultivated and where there was conflicting evidence about the extent that the claimants used the property. One claimant testified that she occasionally visited the property over a 22-year period for picnics, and at one time, she asked a neighbor to keep the lot cleaned up. But several neighbors who frequently passed the lot said that it always appeared neglected, the same as other unoccupied, vacant lots in the area. The court held that this "slight use" was not sufficient.

Analysis

By installing and maintaining a locked shed on the small parcel and hanging "No Trespassing" signs on the shed after you discovered that teenagers were using it without your permission, you likely used the property in a way that was sufficiently open and notorious to provide reasonable notice to Krieger of your adverse possession.

*— For the **Explanation**, the relevant cases are summarized in separate, short paragraphs. Citation information is omitted because it would not be helpful to the client.*

*— The **Analysis** is presented in short, non-indented paragraphs.*

Like a fence or a go-cart course, your shed and signs were visible to Krieger. The shed and signs showed the owner that you were occupying, maintaining, and improving the parcel, like in the *Nielsen* and *Lobro* cases, where the claimants installed fences, planted flowers, and otherwise improved the properties they were adversely possessing.

In addition, your use of the property was active and not occasional. Your use of the small parcel goes beyond the occasional picnic in *Klein* that was held to be an insufficient use. And there will not be conflicting evidence about your use of the property like there was in that case.

Krieger may argue that he did not have actual notice of your use because he was in Norway during the five years that you used the property. He could argue that the shed falls short of the level of improvement necessary to give notice. The shed and signs are not as significant as the improvements made by the claimants in *Lobro*, who replaced the roof, made additions, and installed a fence.

— The email includes a summary of the counteranalysis, discussing contrary authority and a potential counterargument.

Even so, actual notice is not required, and Krieger cannot defeat your open and notorious use by claiming he did not have actual notice.

— The resolution resolves the discrepancy between the core analysis and counteranalysis.

Based on this analysis, we think that a court would likely hold that your use of the property satisfied the open and notorious element for adverse possession.

*— The email ends the legal analysis by restating the **Conclusion**.*

Next steps

Please note that this analysis is limited to one element required for adverse possession. For an action to quiet title to succeed, we would have to prove all five elements. You will hear from us soon summarizing the next steps that we can take to pursue an action to quiet title.

The letter we received last week from Krieger's attorney, which we discussed yesterday on the phone, is attached.

— The email describes the attached document.

As always, please let me know if you have any questions or would like to discuss this in person or on the phone.

Very truly yours,
Rebecca McCarthy
Stern, Sogard & Murano, LLP
(415) 888-9999

— The sender's direct phone number is included in the signature block.

Messaging and New Technology

The technology available to attorneys to communicate with their clients, adversaries, and colleagues is constantly evolving. Many attorneys now correspond over text message from their phones or watches and instant message from their computers or tablets. Because communication is one of an attorney's primary tasks, attorneys should be enthusiastic about these expanding forms of communication.

As you use these new technologies, and any others that may soon be invented, you should remember that your written correspondence, in any format or medium, is a reflection of your credibility and professionalism. Consider the following three principles of professional correspondence when using new messaging technology.

> **Principles of Professional Correspondence When Using New Technology**
> 1. Err on the side of formality.
> 2. Pause before pressing "send."
> 3. Be vigilant regarding confidentiality.

1. ERR ON THE SIDE OF FORMALITY

Messaging makes it easy to communicate quickly and informally, which can be helpful to a busy attorney. But you should hesitate before dispensing with the typical formalities of written correspondence, including the use of capitalization and complete sentences. These formalities help to establish the boundaries of the professional relationship. Communicating with your clients or colleagues in the same style that you communicate with your friends may undermine your professional credibility.

When you are writing in your professional capacity, err on the side of maintaining the formalities that demonstrate your prudence, maturity, and reliability. Do not feel that you have to match the informality of the person on the other side of the conversation. Even if you receive a very informal message (for example, one that uses text abbreviations or emojis), you should respond with the level of formality appropriate to the legal profession.

2. PAUSE BEFORE PRESSING "SEND"

Messaging allows for written correspondence to happen in real time with very little lag. The efficiency of communicating over text and instant message has many benefits for attorneys. But it also it makes it easy to send a message in haste that you may regret.

Attorneys are expected to exercise good judgment. Part of this good judgment is taking a moment, when necessary, to weigh the options before making a decision. Do not let the speed of messaging technology force you to act more quickly than you would like. Instead, if you need more time to respond, you can usually say that. There is nothing to gain from responding quickly with an answer that you later decide was incorrect.

3. BE VIGILANT REGARDING CONFIDENTIALITY

An attorney has an ethical duty to maintain a client's confidential information.[1] You should, therefore, make sure that any technology you use for correspondence does not jeopardize the confidentiality of your clients' information. Be as vigilant regarding the privacy of your professional communications over text and instant message as you are for emails and letters.

---

1. *See, e.g.*, ABA Model Rule of Professional Conduct 1.6.

Judicial Opinions

At this point in law school, you have likely read judicial opinions from courts of all levels and many jurisdictions. A judicial opinion sets forth the reasons and the authorities for a decision. Judges write opinions for two main purposes: to explain the court's rationale and to provide consistency in the law by following and setting precedent. Judges also write opinions to communicate with the parties, their attorneys, and the public. Although judges are the authors of opinions, they frequently receive assistance in drafting the opinions from their judicial clerks and judicial interns. As a result, you could have the opportunity to help write an opinion early in your law school career.

Judicial opinions share many of the characteristics of a legal memorandum. Both should present a fair and objective view of the facts and the law, both present a sound legal analysis, and both typically follow the logical CREAC organization.[1] As a result, the process for writing a judicial opinion and a legal memo are similar.

But memos and opinions have one major difference: While a legal memo predicts the most likely answer to a legal question, a judicial opinion provides the answer authoritatively. As a result, an opinion will not use qualifying language, such as "probably" or "likely," in its Analysis or Conclusion. Instead, an opinion will definitively state the answer to the legal question as it renders a decision in a legal dispute.

Writing a Judicial Opinion

1. Identify the issue(s) for analysis.
2. Outline and draft each part.
3. Proofread to perfection.

---

1. STEP ONE: IDENTIFY THE ISSUE(S) FOR ANALYSIS

The first step toward drafting a judicial opinion is making sure that you understand the specifics of the case before you. When you write an opinion for

---

1. Review the *Hamilton v. Walker* opinion in Chapter 5 for one example of an opinion that follows the CREAC format.

an intermediate appellate court or supreme court, you will have persuasive briefs from the parties and an extensive record to review. For an order or opinion at the trial level, you will have a complaint and persuasive motions, possibly with affidavits, declarations, and other factual documents, to review.

The appellate record will have numerous documents from the lower court, such as deposition transcripts, affidavits, a trial transcript, and lower court orders. These documents provide a starting point for understanding the case, and you will need to carefully read and reread each page of the record to grasp the nuances of the case before you. You also will need to conduct your own research and analysis—using the parties' briefs as a starting point—to ensure that you apply the law fairly and reach an impartial decision.

For cases at the trial court level, you can start to identify the issue or issues you need to analyze by reviewing the point headings from the parties' motions. A good point heading should explicitly state the legal issue. For example, a Defendant's Motion to Dismiss in an adverse possession case could have the following two point headings:

I. The Motion To Dismiss Should Be Granted Because Plaintiff Cannot Establish That She Occupied Defendant's Land In An Open And Notorious Manner.

II. Plaintiff's Motion to Dismiss Should Be Granted Because Plaintiff Rarely Trespassed On Defendant's Land And Therefore Cannot Establish That She Continuously Possessed The Land As California Law Requires.

After reviewing the point headings and independently researching and reviewing the law, you would discover that California law requires five elements for an adverse possession claim, including "open and notorious possession" and "continuity of possession." After fully reviewing the record to make sure no other issues need to be analyzed, you would conclude that your opinion needs to address these two elements in a Discussion with two separate CREACs.

But suppose the point headings above were less clear regarding the issues to be analyzed. Your task might be more challenging, but you would reach the same result. After reviewing the allegations in the complaint, the parties' motions, and the applicable law, you would discover that an adverse possession rule has five elements. After research and analysis, you could then rule out three elements that are not in dispute and narrow your focus to the two elements identified in the specific point headings above.

For cases at the appellate court level, the point headings could also provide you with the starting point to identify the issues for analysis. But you will have an even better indicator of the precise legal issue before you: the issue presented. All briefs begin with an issue presented of some form. The exact style and title for the issue presented varies between courts—some court rules require an "Issue Presented" or "Statement of the Issues." But whatever the name, this statement should set forth the precise issue for review.

For example, consider the following "Legal Issue" statements from the State and Defendant in a Minnesota criminal case.[2]

APPELLANT'S LEGAL ISSUE

Did the police officer seize Wiggins—when she had him put his hands behind his head and told him to move his legs? And then did the police officer search Wiggins—when she pulled up his sagging pants and found a gun—all without the requisite reasonable and articulable suspicion to seize and search?[3]

RESPONDENT'S LEGAL ISSUE

A police officer saw marijuana in an automobile. Before searching the car, she had appellant get out and put his hands behind his head. As appellant got out, his pants were at his knees. The officer pulled the pants up and noticed something hard in appellant's pocket. Appellant said he did not know what it was. The officer reached into the pocket and seized a loaded pistol. Was the pistol seized lawfully?[4]

A careful reading of these two issue statements reveals two precise issues: whether the search of the appellant was lawful and whether the seizure of the pistol was lawful. A review of the applicable law confirms that courts analyze these two issues separately under the Fourth Amendment. And a review of the record shows that both issues are in dispute. So each issue would merit a separate CREAC in the opinion's Discussion.

2. STEP TWO: OUTLINE AND DRAFT EACH PART

A. Review Samples to Create a Template

Courts use different formats for their orders and opinions depending on their level and jurisdiction. In general, each opinion will provide a case caption, an Introduction, a Facts or Background section, a Discussion with a CREAC-style analysis of each issue, and a Decision. Depending on the complexity of each of these sections, an opinion may include headings, along with subheadings within the sections. When preparing to draft a judicial opinion, review several examples from your judge and your court to create an exact template for the opinion—from the case caption to the final Decision. Opinions are public records, and you can find opinions from many courts—for free—on the courts' websites.

---

2. *State v. Wiggins*, 788 N.W.2d 509, 509 (Minn. Ct. App. 2010).

3. Based on Appellant's Brief at 3, *Wiggins*, 788 N.W.2d 509 (No. A09-1987), 2010 WL 3779216.

4. Respondent's Brief at 1, *Wiggins*, 788 N.W.2d 509 (No. A09-1987), 2010 WL 3779218.

As an example, the following represents a basic outline of a Minnesota search and seizure opinion that is discussed throughout this chapter of the *Handbook*.

- Case caption
- Introduction
- Facts or Background
- Issue Statement
- Discussion/Analysis beginning with roadmap
  - CREAC on seizure issue
  - CREAC on search issue
- Decision

B. Introduction

The Introduction at the start of a judicial opinion briefly describes what the case is about. This section should introduce the parties, procedural history, key facts, precise legal issue(s), and the outcome of the case. The Introduction is often only a paragraph or two, so the challenge is to summarize the key information in a concise yet complete way. The following example by Judge Vance E. Salter of the Florida Third District Court of Appeal is succinct and straightforward as it introduces the case's key details.

> ⌐——— Nature of the case

> Marisol Alonso appeals an order denying a motion for new trial based on alleged misconduct by certain jurors. Ms. Alonso is the personal representative for the estate of Kristine Fernandez, original plaintiff in a severe (and ultimately fatal) motor vehicle collision and rollover case. After a three-week trial, the jury returned a verdict in favor of appellee Ford. We affirm the denial of the motion for new trial.

— The parties include plaintiff-appellant Alonso and appellee Ford.

— The case history and the Conclusion are described in these two sentences.

> The issues raised by the appellant are (1) an allegation of premature deliberations by certain members of the jury, (2) an allegation that one member, Juror S., suffered a "high blood pressure headache" and "went along with a defense verdict in this case only because he was fearful of having a stress-induced stroke caused by his severe hypertension," and (3) an allegation by Juror S. that another juror, Juror K., "smelled like a batch of beer," and seemed to Juror S. to have been intoxicated at one or more points during the trial. Of these, only the third issue merits extended analysis as a basis for the motion denied by the trial court.[5]

— Here, the court details the issues that the appellant raised on appeal with specific quotes from the record.

— The court then states that it needs to fully analyze only one of the issues.

The above example provides a traditional opening to an appellate opinion. But judges—unlike law students—do not have to follow a strict format for their writing assignments. Chief Justice Roberts' Introduction to a dissent from a denial of certiorari on pages 126-27 has drawn attention for its crime-noir-style creativity. Even so, the Introduction provides all the necessary

---

5. *Alonso v. Ford Motor Co.*, 54 So. 3d 562, 563-64 (Fla. Dist. Ct. App. 2011).

information: the nature of the case, the parties, the key facts, the issue, the procedural history, and Roberts' conclusion.

C. Facts or Background

In cases where the facts are not too complex, a judge may choose to weave all the legally significant facts into the Introduction and Discussion. But when the relevant facts of a case are particularly involved, you may need to include a separate Facts or Background section with a heading.[6] Whichever format you choose, keep in mind a judge's obligation to remain impartial. So while you should take into account the parties' version of events, the Facts section must present the story of the case objectively.

An opinion must set forth all the legally significant facts. Because the holding in a case depends on the facts, omitting a key fact could affect the way that courts apply and interpret the precedent. So a judicial opinion should include every legally significant fact and any fact that is necessary to provide context.

A Facts section also must be organized logically. Like a Facts section for an office memo,[7] the Facts section can be organized by chronology or by topic. It should also consist of short, focused paragraphs with topic sentences and transitions that guide the reader through the story of the case. Longer Facts sections may also use short headings to break up the text and describe the main topics.

D. Discussion

The Discussion section sets forth the law and rationale for a decision. This section may begin with a separate issue statement, and it will include a CREAC-style analysis for each legal issue. If the opinion addresses more than one legal issue, the Discussion should include a roadmap paragraph and headings to help the reader follow the analysis of each issue.

i. Issue Statement

The Discussion in the opinion for the Minnesota search and seizure case began with the following issue statement:

ISSUE

Did the police officer seize or search Wiggins unconstitutionally when she ordered him out of the car and pulled up his sagging pants?

---

6. Headings vary based on the judge's preference and may include "Facts," "Factual Background," or "Background," depending on the type of case. An opinion deciding a Motion to Dismiss would use the heading "Background" because it assesses the allegations in a complaint, while the heading in an opinion reviewing the granting of a Motion for Summary Judgment might use "Factual Background." See part 2 of Chapter 31 for more guidance.

7. Refer to Chapter 15 for a review.

This issue statement introduces the idea that the opinion will analyze the search and seizure issues separately. Because the opinion addresses two distinct issues, Judge Kevin G. Ross of the Minnesota Court of Appeals provided a roadmap at the start of the Discussion, before sections with the headings, "The Seizure" and "The Search."[8]

ii. Roadmap

A roadmap in a judicial opinion introduces the CREAC analyses that follow. A roadmap can be one or more paragraphs, and it typically begins with a general Conclusion. It then states the overarching Rule for the minor issues analyzed in each CREAC and shows how the issues relate to each other. For example, the roadmap in the search and seizure opinion details the state and federal constitutional provisions that protect against unreasonable searches and seizures.

iii. Standard of Review

Appellate opinions typically describe the standard of review. Once a case reaches an appellate court, the question before the appellate panel of judges is often not the same as it was when the trial court decided it. The standard of review determines how much deference the appellate court should give to the lower court's judgment. In some cases, the appellate court is required to defer to the trial court's judgment because the trial court is the finder of fact.

For example, under the abuse of discretion standard, the appellate court will reverse only if the decision below was based on an erroneous conclusion of law or where the record contains no evidence on which the judge could have rationally based the decision.[9] The de novo standard, in contrast, requires the appellate court to show no deference to the lower court's finding and review the judgment anew.[10] To determine the standard of review in your case, begin by reviewing the parties' briefs. Then, even when the parties do not dispute the standard of review, conduct your own research to confirm that the standard cited by the parties is correct.

Because the standard of review determines how the court analyzes the facts and law in a case, describing the standard of review at the start of the opinion makes sense. The roadmap is often a logical point for addressing the standard of review. If an opinion does not have a roadmap, then include the standard of review in a separate section before the Discussion or in the Rule section of your CREAC.

iv. CREAC-Style Analysis

After the roadmap, the Discussion in a judicial opinion will discuss each legal issue using a CREAC-style analysis. The CREAC in a judicial opinion does

---

8. *Wiggins,* 788 N.W.2d at 509.

9. *See, e.g., Deitchman v. E.R. Squibb & Sons, Inc.,* 740 F.2d 556, 563-64 (7th Cir. 1984).

10. *Ams. for Prosperity Found. v. Becerra,* 903 F.3d 1000, 1007 (9th Cir. 2018).

not look exactly the same as the traditional CREAC that you will use for an office memo.

The major difference is that judicial opinions cannot use any qualifying language, such as "probably" and "likely," because they need to decisively render a judgment. As you draft the CREAC for each issue in your opinion, make sure that your Conclusions are stated authoritatively. For example, the first Conclusion for the seizure analysis in the Minnesota case begins definitively:

> Wiggins was seized when the officer ordered him from the car and instructed him to raise his hands.

The Analysis in a CREAC in an office memo not only includes qualifying language but it also includes a counteranalysis, where the writer objectively describes the legal arguments that do not support the Conclusion. Similarly, a judicial opinion can and should describe the losing party's arguments. But the court must address the failed arguments in a way that authoritatively dismisses them. Under the analysis of the search in the Minnesota case, Judge Ross details a few arguments that the defendant unsuccessfully made or could have made. Judge Ross then decisively describes why those arguments fail:

> Wiggins argues that affirming the district court would encourage officers to trample the privacy of young people who participate in the baggy-pants fashion trend. The concern is unwarranted. Our holding arises from the unique facts here. . . .

> Wiggins has not made and the facts would not support the claim that the officer's raising of his pants was a pretext to explore for contraband in his pockets; the officer had no motive to look for justification to search because she had already concluded that a pat-search was justified and she intended to conduct one immediately after Wiggins' pants were suitably rearranged. . . .

> Wiggins raises other arguments that mistakenly assume that the officer's touching of his pants constituted a search. We do not address these arguments.[11]

The Analysis points above fairly summarize the failed arguments while explaining why the arguments fail under the law.

E. Decision

The CREAC for each issue under review will typically have two Conclusion statements, one at the beginning and one at the end, to follow the CREAC organization. A judicial opinion will then have a Decision section that for-

---

11. 788 N.W.2d at 515.

malizes the Analysis and Conclusion by stating the court's holding. Because the holding sets precedent, it must clearly describe the scope of the court's decision. The Decision below from the search and seizure case describes the key facts that support the court's final ruling:

DECISION

> Police lawfully detained Wiggins after reasonably suspecting that he and others were exchanging illegal drugs. The officer reasonably ordered Wiggins to raise his hands and reasonably decided to adjust his excessively sagging pants. The adjustment did not constitute a search and was not conducted in a manner that raises any constitutional concerns.[12]

3. STEP THREE: PROOFREAD TO PERFECTION

A judicial opinion represents not only the work of the judge or justice who authors the opinion, but also the work of the court. The quality of both the analysis and the writing reflects on the credibility of the judiciary. As a result, making sure that the analysis, writing, and style are flawless is of paramount importance.

The editing process for a judicial opinion is intense. Several judicial clerks and judges may work together on numerous drafts to refine the analysis before declaring it sound. Once the editing phase is complete, a careful proofreading will commence. The proofreading will check every detail—ensuring that every letter, space, comma, and period is in its proper place. A thorough proofreading will include checking citations for format and accuracy, and it will include reviewing every word, sentence, and paragraph for spelling, grammar, and style. Finally, the proofreading phase will check for any remaining typographical and formatting errors. The goal is to turn out an accurate, sound, and well-written opinion that helps maintain the integrity of the judicial process.

4. EXAMPLE OF AWARD-WINNING OPINION WRITING[13]

In the search and seizure case discussed throughout this chapter, Judge Ross found that a police officer did not violate a defendant's constitutional rights. The officer discovered a handgun in the defendant's pocket after "she hoisted up his sagging pants that had dropped to hang around his knees."[14]

---

12. *Id.*

13. The Green Bag, http://www.greenbag.org, recognized the opinion for "exemplary legal writing" in 2010.

14. *Wiggins,* 788 N.W.2d at 509.

STATE v. WIGGINS
788 N.W.2d 509 (Minn. Ct. App. 2010)

Opinion

ROSS, Judge.

This case requires us to determine the constitutionality of a novel police procedure which, as far as we can tell, has never been reviewed on appeal by this court or any other. An officer investigating a suspected drug deal directed appellant Frank Wiggins from a car, ordered him to raise his hands high overhead, and then discovered a handgun in his pocket when she hoisted up his sagging pants that had dropped to hang around his knees. Wiggins appeals from his conviction of possession of a firearm by an ineligible person. We must decide whether the unique wardrobe assist was a search subject to constitutional regulation and, if not, whether it was the kind of seizure-related contact otherwise prohibited by the Fourth Amendment. Because we hold that the officer's tactic was neither a search nor an unreasonable touching during a lawful investigative detention, we affirm.

— This **Introduction** paragraph describes the defendant and the search and seizure that led to this appeal. It also sets forth the precise legal issue before the appellate court.

— The holding is stated in clear, decisive terms.

Facts

St. Paul police officer Kara Breci and her partner were on patrol on a November 2008 afternoon in a high drug-activity area when they noticed a car parked with its engine idling in a White Castle parking lot. Officer Breci had seen many drug deals, and several things in addition to the location aroused her suspicion that she was witnessing another one. The driver and a man later identified as appellant Frank Wiggins sat in the front seat, and a third man approached and entered the back seat without any food from the restaurant. No one in the car appeared to be eating. The back-seat occupant began to look down at his lap. As the officers walked to the car they saw the rear occupant drop a plastic bag to the floor. They asked the man what the bag contained, and he replied, "Some weed." Wiggins seemed nervous to Officer Breci while her partner was questioning the rear occupant.

— The **Facts** section tells the story of the case chronologically, first explaining why officers stopped the defendant and asked him to step out of his car. The section sets forth the facts in an impartial and straightforward manner.

The officers ordered the men out of the car. Officer Breci directed Wiggins to raise his hands above his head. Wiggins wore loose-fitting jeans, which, when he stood, were hanging down around his knees. Officer Breci decided to pat-frisk Wiggins for weapons. But first, she pulled his pants up. As she lifted Wiggins' pants, she felt a hard object in his front pocket. She asked Wiggins what it was, and he responded that he did not know. The officer surmised that it was a handgun and removed a .380 caliber pistol from Wiggins' pocket.

— Next, the story continues the chronology by describing why and how one police officer interacted the defendant.

Because Wiggins had prior violent-crime convictions, the state charged him with possession of a firearm by an ineligible person. Wiggins moved the district court to suppress the gun evidence, arguing that the seizure of the car and its occupants was unsupported by reasonable suspicion and that the officer conducted an unconstitutional frisk when she hoisted his pants. The district court denied Wiggins' motion to suppress, reasoning that the officers lawfully approached the car and ordered the occupants out based on their seeing the marijuana, that Officer Breci reasonably chose not to direct Wiggins to reach for his own pants out of concerns for her own safety, and that Officer Breci did not search Wiggins but instead found the gun by accident as she was "help[ing] him get his pants into a decent position."

Wiggins waived his right to a jury trial and submitted the case to the district court on stipulated facts, preserving for appeal his challenge to the stop and alleged search. *See State v. Lothenbach*, 296 N.W.2d 854, 857-58 (Minn. 1980); Minn. R. Crim. P. 26.01, subd. 4. The district court found Wiggins guilty of possession of a firearm by an ineligible person. Wiggins appeals, challenging the district court's denial of his pretrial suppression motion.

— The **Facts** section then details the state's criminal case against the defendant and the procedural history that led to the appeal.

Issue

Did the police officer seize or search Wiggins unconstitutionally when she ordered him out of the car and pulled up his sagging pants?

— The **Issue Statement** references both the search and seizure issues.

Analysis

Wiggins argues that the district court failed to vindicate his state and federal constitutional rights by denying his motion to suppress the gun evidence that resulted from the officer's alleged search. The United States and Minnesota constitutions guarantee the right of persons not to be subjected to "unreasonable searches and seizures." U.S. Const. amend. IV; Minn. Const. art. I, § 10. Evidence seized in violation of this guarantee generally must be suppressed. *State v. Jackson*, 742 N.W.2d 163, 177-78 (Minn. 2007). Wiggins correctly argues that in limited circumstances the supreme court has interpreted the state constitution to provide greater protection than the Fourth Amendment provides. *See In re Welfare of B.R.K.*, 658 N.W.2d 565, 577 (Minn. 2003) ("[W]e are free to interpret the Minnesota Constitution as affording greater protection against unreasonable searches and seizures than the United States Constitution, but do not do so cavalierly."). But Wiggins does not contend that this is such a circumstance, and we will analyze his constitutional claims under a single standard. When reviewing a district court's pretrial suppression ruling on undisputed facts, we consider the facts independently and decide de novo whether the undisputed facts warrant suppression as a matter of law. *State v. Othoudt*, 482 N.W.2d 218, 221 (Minn. 1992).

— The roadmap devotes two paragraphs to introducing the legal issues of search and seizure.

— First, the roadmap provides the broadest search and seizure **Rules** from the highest authorities: the federal and state constitutions.

— By providing the broad rules first, the roadmap puts the search and seizure issues that are analyzed below in context.

— The roadmap sets forth the de novo standard of review here.

Wiggins retreats somewhat from his argument to the district court, conceding now that the police lawfully approached the parked car and looked inside and that, on observing the bag of marijuana in plain view in the rear passenger compartment, they could also order the three occupants out to search the car. Wiggins challenges only the police conduct that occurred after he left the car. He argues that police unlawfully seized and pat-searched him without having a reasonable, articulable suspicion that he was involved in criminal activity and that he was armed and dangerous. His arguments do not persuade us.

The Seizure

Wiggins was seized when the officer ordered him from the car and instructed him to raise his hands. A person has been "seized" when, "in view of all of the circumstances surrounding the incident, a reasonable person would have believed that he was not free to leave." *In re Welfare of E.D.J.*, 502 N.W.2d 779, 781 (Minn. 1993). A reasonable person would not have believed that he was free to leave after a police officer discovered illegal drugs in his car and ordered him to get out and to raise his hands. So Wiggins was seized and we must decide whether the seizure was lawful.

To lawfully seize a person temporarily to investigate a crime, a police officer must have a reasonable, articulable suspicion that the person was or will be engaged in criminal activity. *Terry v. Ohio*, 392 U.S. 1, 21-22 (1968); *State v. George*, 557 N.W.2d 575, 578 (Minn. 1997). This is not a high standard, *State v. Timberlake*, 744 N.W.2d 390, 393 (Minn. 2008), and we apply it in view of the totality of the circumstances from an objectively reasonable officer's perspective, *Appelgate v. Comm'r of Public Safety*, 402 N.W.2d 106, 108 (Minn. 1987). In doing so, we recognize that trained law enforcement officers may interpret circumstances using inferences and deductions beyond the competence of untrained persons. *State v. Richardson*, 622 N.W.2d 823, 825 (Minn. 2001).

Wiggins argues that the bag of marijuana found in the passenger compartment cannot justify his detention because spotting the drugs would not reasonably lead an officer to suspect that Wiggins was involved with them. Wiggins casts the episode with himself as the uninvolved occupant of a car in which someone else's contraband just happened to be discovered in the back seat. But his characterization misses the bigger scene: police came upon a stopped and idling car in a fast-food restaurant's parking lot in an area known to them as a place of drug dealing; they observed that the car was occupied by three men having no apparent business with the restaurant, including a man who wandered up to the car and into the back seat; and they watched Wiggins sitting nervously

---

Margin annotations:

The roadmap ends by stating the appellant's arguments, which the appellate court must resolve. The summary serves as a thesis for the **Analysis** that follows.

This paragraph begins and ends with the court's **Conclusion**, which includes a description of the precise legal issue.

The seizure **Rule** from a state supreme court case provides the context necessary to explain the legally significant terms in the **Conclusion**.

The **Explanation** uses federal and state cases to describe how to interpret whether a seizure is unlawful.

The court states the **Rule** and the **Explanation** objectively, describing the anchor that reasonable suspicion depends on the circumstances.

The **Analysis** begins by briefly summarizing Wiggins' arguments to show how he views the circumstances.

The transition "but" marks the start of the court's objective analysis of how police view the circumstances. The details here show why police had reasonable suspicion to seize the defendant.

when the back-seat occupant told the officers that the bag he had tried to hide on the floor contained "some weed." These circumstances would lead a reasonable officer to suspect that Wiggins was engaging in a drug deal. The seizure and brief investigative detention that arose from that suspicion therefore did not violate the Fourth Amendment or article I, section 10 of the Minnesota Constitution.

— The court ends its seizure analysis by restating the Conclusion.

The Search

[CREAC analysis omitted.]

Decision

Police lawfully detained Wiggins after reasonably suspecting that he and others were exchanging illegal drugs. The officer reasonably ordered Wiggins to raise his hands and reasonably decided to adjust his excessively sagging pants. The adjustment did not constitute a search and was not conducted in a manner that raises any constitutional concerns.

— The **Decision** section authoritatively summarizes the specific Conclusions on the search and seizure issues before providing the overall Conclusion. The court provides a fact-based reason for each Conclusion.

Affirmed.

Oral Arguments

Oral argument gives you the opportunity to convince the court that your argument should prevail. This practice—of standing at a court podium and having a formal conversation with the judge or judges deciding your case—allows you to emphasize and elaborate on the best arguments in your motion or brief. Oral argument also gives you a chance to respond to and rebut opposing counsel's arguments and to address specific questions that a judge may have about your position.

Whether you are arguing before a trial court judge or Supreme Court justices, oral argument also provides you with an opportunity to build your professional reputation. Through oral argument, you can develop and display your personal style and voice as an advocate—there isn't just one mold for an effective oral advocate. But whatever your approach, at oral argument you should demonstrate to the court, your client, and your colleagues that you are meticulously prepared. A well-prepared advocate knows the facts, the record, and the law and can seamlessly cite each throughout an argument. A well-prepared advocate also can communicate a credible argument without any embellishment of the facts or law.

Additionally, a well-prepared advocate should zealously defend a client's position—but with the restraint necessary to show the proper respect for the judicial process. A respectful advocate will show deference to the judges, civility to opposing counsel, and reverence to the customary rules of decorum.

Specific practices for oral argument will vary depending on the court. A trial court argument on a motion could take just a few minutes and draw only a few questions from the judge. An argument before the U.S. Supreme Court typically lasts 30 minutes and includes multiple questions from most of the justices. For every argument, you should acquaint yourself with the particular court's rules and practices. To prepare for oral argument, you can start by developing a plan and following the strategy outlined in this chapter.

> ### Oral Arguments
> 1. Develop a plan.
> 2. Prepare for a conversation, not a speech.
> 3. Follow rules of decorum.

1. STEP ONE: DEVELOP A PLAN

Start preparing for oral argument by developing a strategy. Review your persuasive document and opposing counsel's—whether that includes a motion and response or a brief and an answer brief. Think about how you can fine tune your theme and arguments. Consider what arguments you want to emphasize and what points your opposing counsel made that you need to address. Then, develop an outline for your argument that includes your (1) greeting, (2) opening roadmap, (3) an outline of your major arguments and authorities, and (4) conclusion. If you are the movant or appellant, you also will need to plan for a rebuttal. Your outline will serve as the notes you need to present an effective oral argument.

A. Greeting

The greeting that starts your oral argument will provide a formal introduction to you and your case. The customary greeting begins, "May it please the Court." This formal opening shows deference to the court. Next, you should provide your name and your client's name. Deputy Solicitor General Gregory Garre's argument in *Hepting v. AT&T* before the United States Court of Appeals for the Ninth Circuit in 2008 provides a typical greeting, which is transcribed below:

> Thank you, Judge Pregerson, and may it please the Court. My name is Gregory Garre, and I'm appearing here today on behalf of the United States.

In some cases, you might appear with co-counsel for oral argument with each of you arguing a distinct issue. The first speaker should introduce both attorneys and explain the issue that each of you will address. The greetings for both attorneys could follow this format:

> First attorney (Jones):
>
> Good morning, your Honors, and may it please the Court. I am Melody Jones, and I'm here with co-counsel John Day on behalf of the appellant, pharmacist Jody Levinson. I will argue that Dr. Levinson fulfilled her duty to the customer. And Mr. Day will argue that there is no duty extended to remote plaintiffs.
>
> Second attorney (Day) (following first attorney's completed oral argument):
>
> Thank you, and may it please the Court. I am John Day, here on behalf of Dr. Levinson.

Note that this example uses the plural "your Honors" because the greeting is for an appellate argument before a panel of judges or justices. For an argument before a trial court judge, simply make the greeting the singular, "your Honor."

B. Opening Roadmap

After the greeting, you should move into your argument with an opening roadmap that provides an overview of the major points you want to make. The roadmap should begin with a conclusion referencing the relief that you seek. Then, the roadmap should briefly describe the essential arguments that you plan to make in the order you plan to make them.

The roadmap should be concise yet thorough. Keep in mind that while you should be prepared to address each of your arguments in detail, you may run out of time because of the judges' questions. As a result, the roadmap gives you the first and best opportunity to summarize the major reasons why the court should grant the relief you seek. A basic outline for the roadmaps in a motion to suppress hearing before a trial court judge could look like this:

DEFENDANT'S COUNSEL

The motion to suppress should be granted because the Defendant, Carrie Zinsser, was subjected to a custodial interrogation without receiving *Miranda* warnings. Two reasons show this constitutional violation.

First, Ms. Zinsser was subjected to distinctly accusatory questions, specifically stating that she committed a money laundering crime, and these questions turned the interrogation custodial.

Second, Ms. Zinsser was physically coerced by being placed in handcuffs and in a locked room, to the extent that no reasonable person would have felt free to leave. Thus, she was in custody.

GOVERNMENT'S COUNSEL

The motion to suppress should be denied because the Defendant was asked only routine questions and was delayed only a short time as part of a typical inquiry at the border. Three reasons support the Government's position.

First, border security officers asked the Defendant only routine questions relating to the amount of money that she was carrying and that she failed to report on customs forms.

Second, border security officers did not restrain the Defendant for any length of time throughout a short, general inquiry.

And finally, border security officers have more leeway to conduct interrogations at the border because of the nation's interest in protecting its borders. And the officers' actions and questions here were typical for anyone entering the country.

The following is an example of a roadmap for an appellate case relating to whether a pharmacist has a duty to warn customers of drugs' side effects.

This case is about a pharmacist, Dr. Levinson, who fulfilled her duty as a pharmacist by correctly filling a customer's prescription and answering all the customer's questions. This Court should affirm summary judgment in favor of Dr. Levinson because the trial court correctly determined that no genuine issue of material fact exists relating to Dr. Levinson's careful fulfillment of her duty as a pharmacist. Three points demonstrate why Dr. Levinson fulfilled this duty.

First, Dr. Levinson did everything she was required to do under the Missouri statute, pharmacy regulations, and case law. And according to these authorities, there is no duty to warn pharmacy customers about side effects.

Second, the duty to warn patients about side effects belongs to the physician.

Third, requiring pharmacists to warn customers about every possible adverse reaction would be unduly burdensome and unnecessarily extend the pharmacists' duty.

This roadmap provides a concise overview of the advocate's three best arguments. The first two points are based on statutory and case law; the third invokes a policy consideration that begins to incorporate the theme that extending the duty to warn would have unworkable consequences.

In the opening to *Hepting v. AT&T*,[1] Deputy Solicitor General Garre provides a clear roadmap that also emphasizes three major points and incorporates a theme: protecting national security. *Hepting* was a class action lawsuit that alleged constitutional violations relating to the government's alleged warrantless surveillance programs.[2] Here is a transcript of Garre's opening:

> Your Honors, the nation's top officials', whose job it is to assess and protect foreign intelligence, have determined that litigating this action could result in exceptionally grave harm to the national security of the United States. They've reached that judgment because litigating this action would require the adjudication of three central facts, each of which directly implicates state secrets: first, whether or to what extent any secret intelligence gathering relationship exists between AT&T and the government; second, whether or to what extent any alleged surveillance activities have taken place; and third, whether or to what extent any particular communications have been intercepted.
>
> As the director of national intelligence and the director of the National Security Agency have explained in the public and non-public declarations filed with this Court, litigating those central facts could compromise the sources, methods, and operational details of our intelligence gathering

---

1. To watch a YouTube video of the oral argument in *Hepting v. AT&T*, go to http://bit.ly/149L99W.

2. *See Hepting v. AT&T*, 439 F. Supp. 2d 974 (N.D. Cal. 2006).

capabilities, and equally important, could disclose potential gaps in those capabilities.

C. Argument

i. Create an Outline of Your Arguments

Immediately following the roadmap, you should be prepared to elaborate on your first major argument. You should also be prepared to be interrupted by a stream of questions—relating to your first argument or any other issue you or opposing counsel raised in your documents. The following strategy for developing an outline will allow you to do both.

Your oral argument will describe and elaborate on the points you made in the Analysis section of your motion or brief—and summarized in your roadmap. Your outline will provide you with the notes you need to make an effective presentation on these points. The outline should not follow the same overall organization you used in your motion or brief. For instance, you do not need to begin by reciting your Facts section, describing the Legal Standard, or by reading the Rule and Explanation sections that you wrote. The judges have read your arguments, and they are familiar with the facts and the law.

Your roadmap will have provided the necessary overview of the case, so the main part of your oral argument should focus on elaborating on the arguments from your Analysis section. Your oral argument outline should not be a series of sentences and paragraphs similar to what you have in your motion or brief. This format would inhibit eye contact and your ability to have a conversation with the judges about your case. Instead, use bullets or another readable format to list the major points you want to make. And include only those notes that are necessary for you to describe your argument.

The extent of notes that attorneys use for oral argument varies widely. Some attorneys will jot down only a few phrases and case names. Others will have a comprehensive, bulleted outline that details the facts and holdings of key cases and the specific points to address for each argument. They key is to practice with your notes and develop a system that allows you to describe your arguments effectively and move easily between your major points without reading your argument word for word.

As a starting point, create an outline that lists each of your major arguments. Then, below each argument, provide a list of the points you want to make, along with supporting factual and legal authority. For example, an outline for an oral argument could follow this basic format:

Argument 1
- Point A
  - Supporting authorities
- Point B
  - Supporting authorities
- Point C
  - Supporting authorities

Argument 2
- Point A
  - Supporting authorities
- Point B
  - Supporting authorities

Suppose a judge asks you a question about Argument 1, Point B when you are addressing Point A. This outline would allow you to move to your notes for Point B to answer the question. Then, you could transition back to Point A or move on to Point C, depending on the progression of your argument.

Try to take a balanced approach as you fill in your outline, providing only the details necessary for you to describe your arguments. The following example provides a detailed outline for four points under the first argument on the pharmacist's duty to warn. The notes summarize the argument and then provide a list of legally significant facts and authorities as support.

First, Dr. Levinson fulfilled the duty required by Missouri law because there is no duty to warn pharmacy customers about side effects.
- Did everything required under Missouri law:
  - Correctly filled customer's prescription
  - Personally offered to discuss medication with her
  - Confirmed the dosage
  - Answered all her questions
  - Addressed all her concerns
- Missouri statute § 388.010: Practice of pharmacy requires that pharmacists counsel customers "about the safe and effective use of drugs."
  - Does not reference side effects
- Missouri board of pharmacy regulation 20 C.S.R. 2220-2.190(1) requires pharmacists to "personally offer to discuss matters" and to discuss issues deemed significant in the pharmacist's professional judgment.
  - Cannot practically include discussing every possible adverse reaction with every customer
- *Horner* and *Krug* cases both demonstrate no duty to warn pharmacy customers about side effects.
  - *Krug*: Physicians are learned intermediaries who act between the drug manufacturer and the patient, and physicians have the duty to warn patients about side effects.
  - *Horner*:
    - Distinguishable facts b/c customer died of overdose
    - Referenced side effects, interactions in one footnote, relating to Washington state case (which held that imposing a duty to warn about side effects would interfere with the physician-patient relationship)

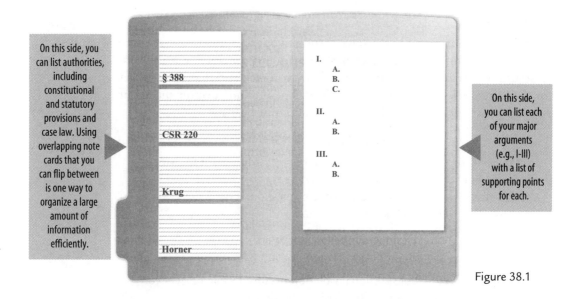

On this side, you can list authorities, including constitutional and statutory provisions and case law. Using overlapping note cards that you can flip between is one way to organize a large amount of information efficiently.

§ 388

CSR 220

Krug

Horner

I.
  A.
  B.
  C.

II.
  A.
  B.

III.
  A.
  B.

On this side, you can list each of your major arguments (e.g., I-III) with a list of supporting points for each.

Figure 38.1

ii. Create an Outline of Your Authorities

In addition to creating an outline for each major argument you want to address, you should create an outline with additional details about each authority you want to use. This list of authorities should include your best cases as well as any unfavorable authorities that opposing counsel may use or that the judges may ask you about. The list should include quotations of relevant constitutional and statutory provisions and brief summaries of the relevant facts and law of pertinent cases.

For instance, the previous argument outline probably does not give the speaker enough information about the *Horner* or *Krug* cases to answer tough questions about the cases. Having a separate outline of authorities would allow the attorney to check the notes for the cases, respond to questions, and move back to the major argument.

Preparing your notes to look orderly and professional will allow you to appear organized before the court. An attorney who has to rifle through a disheveled stack of papers to respond to a judge's question on a particular argument or a particular case does not appear well prepared and may be unable to find the necessary information. To organize their materials for oral argument, some attorneys like to use a folder with their authorities listed on one side and their arguments listed on the other. This method allows you to keep your notes and your thoughts organized and to move seamlessly between your points (see Figure 38.1). Other attorneys use binders with side tabs or color coded folders. You should try different methods to develop a system that allows you to appear organized, well prepared, and professional during your argument.

D. Conclusion

Keep track of your time as you move through your argument to make sure that you have time to complete your argument and conclude. For the conclusion, ask the court again for the relief that you seek and thank the judges for their time. Here's how counsel for the defendant and government might conclude their arguments in the motion to suppress hearing:

DEFENDANT'S COUNSEL

For these reasons, we respectfully request that this Court grant the Motion to Suppress because Ms. Zinsser's constitutional rights were violated both by the distinctly accusatory nature of the questioning and the coercive actions of the officer. Thank you.

GOVERNMENT'S COUNSEL

For these reasons, we respectfully ask that this Court deny the Motion to Suppress because no constitutional violation occurred while officers conducted a routine and mundane border inquiry. Thank you.

And an example of a closing statement in the duty to warn case at the appellate level is the following:

For these reasons, we respectfully request that this Court affirm the grant of summary judgment in favor of Dr. Levinson and find that she fulfilled her duty as a pharmacist and that no extension of this duty is required. Thank you for your time.

If you run out of time before you reach your conclusion, make sure you show respect for the court's schedule and conclude as quickly as possible. A simple conclusion could suffice: "We ask that you affirm summary judgment. Thank you, your Honors." The key is to provide a formal, respectful closing to your argument.

E. Rebuttal

If you are the movant or appellant, you will get the last word in oral argument. How much time you should devote to rebuttal is a strategic decision. Most attorneys spend the bulk of their time on their argument and reserve a few minutes to respond to opposing counsel's argument. The general practice is to tell the judges at the start of the oral argument that you would like to reserve time for rebuttal. After your greeting, provide a short statement describing the time allocation you desire, such as: "I would like to reserve two minutes for rebuttal."

DEFENDANT'S COUNSEL GREETING AND ROADMAP

Good morning, your Honor, and may it please the Court. I am Jon Mubarek, here on behalf of the Defendant. I'd like to request two minutes for rebuttal.

The motion to suppress should be granted because the Defendant, Carrie Zinsser, was subjected to a custodial interrogation without receiving *Miranda* warnings. Two reasons show this constitutional violation. . . .

Then, make sure you honor this time allocation. If you have a total of ten minutes and reserve two minutes for rebuttal, you should wrap up your oral argument within eight minutes. If you fail to reserve time for rebuttal or if your argument runs too long, you may forfeit the opportunity to make a rebuttal.

Your rebuttal should respond to opposing counsel's oral argument. Take notes on opposing counsel's major arguments and on the judges' questions, and try to identify your weakest point. Then, use your rebuttal to provide your best response based on the facts and law. If time permits, offer an additional ground for the court to grant the relief you seek. Finally, make sure to offer a brief conclusion, and thank the judges—again—for their time.

2. STEP TWO: PREPARE FOR A CONVERSATION, NOT A SPEECH

Having an organized set of notes should help you prepare to have a conversation with the judges. Oral argument is not an opportunity to give a speech or lecture. Instead, you should prepare to answer a wide array of questions from the judges. Make sure that you know your record, facts, and law well enough to be able to cite specific facts in the record when answering questions. And make sure that you can cite specific authorities, the relevant language in each, and their citations. To prepare to answer questions, consider any weak points in your argument and try to anticipate what the judges might ask. Make a list of potential questions and practice answers that you could use in response.

A. Expect Tough Questions, Hypotheticals, and Friendly Questions

Generally, judges' questions fall into one of three basic types. First, judges will likely ask you tough questions that delve into weak points in your argument. Be prepared to highlight key facts, to distinguish unfavorable authorities, and to describe your position fairly and persuasively. Second, judges may ask hypothetical questions. For instance, in the duty to warn example, a judge could ask a hypothetical exploring the consequences of extending pharmacists' duty to warn.

Third, a judge might ask you a friendly question that allows you to state one of your most persuasive arguments or cite one of your most helpful cases. Take care to recognize this type of question as a lifeline. A judge might ask a friendly question to explore a point that was interrupted earlier, or a judge might want you to offer a particular argument to communicate the point to a colleague on the bench. To help you recognize this type of question, keep in mind that the judges are not your adversaries. Oral argument provides you the chance to have a conversation with the judges and to help them see your view of the case.

In the *Hepting* oral argument reviewed earlier, Deputy Solicitor General Garre responds to an array of questions. The first question, which comes directly after he provides his roadmap, is a friendly one. Garre responds with a direct answer and uses citations and explanations of multiple cases in support. Throughout the 30-minute argument, Garre responds to a variety of questions, each time offering a direct answer supported by authority. In this way, he engages in an effective conversation with the judges that advances his position.

The following transcript excerpt provides examples of tough, friendly, and hypothetical questions in *Florida v. Jardines*, the U.S. Supreme Court case addressing whether police violated the Fourth Amendment when they took a trained drug-detection dog to the door of a private home.[3] The advocate for the government is again Gregory Garre.

> *Justice Ginsburg:* Suppose—suppose the house had on the lawn, no dogs —Hypothetical Question
> allowed?
> *Mr. Garre:* I think that would be different, Your Honor. It would be—and that's a way in which the house is different than a car. Homeowners can restrict access to people who come up to their front door by putting gates or a sign out front.
> *Justice Scalia:* Well, that's right. And there's such a thing as what is called —Friendly Question
> the curtilage of a house. As I understand the law, the police are entitled to use binoculars to look into the house if—if the residents leave the blinds open, right?
> *Mr. Garre:* That's right.
> *Justice Scalia:* But if they can't see clearly enough from a distance, they're —Friendly Question
> not entitled to go onto the curtilage of the house, inside the gate, and use the binoculars from that vantage point, are they?
> *Mr. Garre:* They're not, Your Honor.
>
> * * *
>
> *Justice Kagan:* Mr. Garre, this is what we said in *Kyllo*. And I'm just going —Tough Question
> to read it. We said, "We think that obtaining by sense-enhancing technology any information regarding the interior of the home that could not otherwise have been obtained without physical intrusion into a constitutionally protected area constitutes a search, at least where, as here, the technology in question is not in general public use." So what part of that do you think separates your case from this one? In other words, what part of that language does not apply in this case?
> *Mr. Garre:* Well, first of all, Franky's nose is not technology. It's—he's using—he's availing himself of God-given senses in the way that dogs have helped mankind for centuries.

---

3. *Florida v. Jardines*, 569 U.S. 1 (2013).

Justice Kagan: So does that mean that if we invented some kind of little —Hypothetical Question
machine called a, you know, smell-o-matic and the police officer had
this smell-o-matic machine, and it alerted to the exact same things
that a dog alerts to, it alerted to a set of drugs, meth and marijuana
and whatever else, the police officer could not come to the front door
and use that machine?

Mr. Garre: Your Honor, I think the contraband rationale would be the
same. It would be different in that you don't have technology in this
case. And I think that's an important distinction because, as we read
Kyllo, the Court was very concerned about advances in technology, and
that's just not true for a dog's nose.[4]

B. Prepare a Response

When asked a question, take a moment to consider your answer before
launching into your response. Then, start your response with a direct "yes"
or "no" answer. Next, provide the facts and authority necessary to support
your answer. If you don't understand a question, ask the judge to repeat the
question, or offer your understanding: "Your Honor, I believe you are asking
me _____." Then, pause and allow the judge to agree or rephrase the
question before offering your answer.

Be mindful of your time when answering questions. If you run out of time
in the middle of a question, ask for a moment to respond: "Your Honor, I see
my time is up. May I have a moment to answer your question and conclude?"
Then, if allowed, provide a concise answer and an abbreviated conclusion.

C. Practice Seamless Transitions Between Arguments and Questions

An oral argument is a conversation with the judges. To have an effective conversation, you can neither read your notes aloud for the entire argument nor
give a memorized speech. Instead, you should think about your argument as
a set of distinct points or subarguments—all of which lead to your ultimate
conclusion.

For example, in the outline for the argument on the pharmacist's duty
to warn, the attorney details four major bullet points for her first argument.
She has a major bullet point listing helpful facts and three more bullets referencing authorities with notes on how each authority helps her position.
Each of these arguments is distinct but contributes to supporting the major
argument that the pharmacist had no duty to warn customers about side
effects.

---

4. Transcript of Oral Argument at 6, 16-17, *Florida v. Jardines*, 569 U.S. 1 (No. 11-564),
https://www.supremecourt.gov/oral_arguments/argument_transcripts/2012/11-564.pdf.
Transcripts and audio from oral arguments before the U.S. Supreme Court are available on the
Court's website: http://www.supremecourt.gov.

First, Dr. Levinson fulfilled the duty required by Missouri law because there is no duty to warn pharmacy customers about side effects.

- Did everything required under Missouri law:
  - Missouri statute § 388.010: practice of pharmacy requires that pharmacists counsel customers "about the safe and effective use of drugs."
  - Missouri board of pharmacy regulation 20 C.S.R. 2220-2.190(1) requires pharmacists to "personally offer to discuss matters" and to discuss issues deemed significant in the pharmacist's professional judgment.
  - *Horner* and *Krug* cases both demonstrate no duty to warn pharmacy customers about side effects.

This organization allows the attorney to transition seamlessly between her major points. For example, suppose the attorney has just started describing the helpful facts when a judge asks a question about the *Horner* case, which the attorney needs to distinguish. The attorney could glance at the fourth bullet point before answering the question.

Because all of the points are related, the attorney could then transition to any one of the four major bullet points in her outline to continue to support her argument. For example, after answering the question about *Horner*, she could transition with the following: "In addition, the *Krug* case supports the argument that pharmacists have no duty to warn customers of side effects because...." Or she could move back to her second point with this transition: "The *Horner* case deals with Section 388.010, which states . . . ." By organizing your argument outline into a set of distinct—but related—points, you can prepare yourself to seamlessly transition between each.

Not all transitions are effective, however, particularly when they fail to show the proper deference to the court. Keep in mind that you want to follow the judge's lead when making your argument. You should invite questions because you want to make sure that you have adequately satisfied any concerns a judge may have about your position. Do not become frustrated if you are interrupted. For example, if a judge interrupts your first argument to ask a question, you might want to return to your first point by stating: "As I was saying...." But this transition reflects a mild annoyance at the interruption. Instead, use transitions to show how your arguments build upon one another to support your conclusion. A term like "also," "additionally," or "moreover" can help you seamlessly move to your next point.

D. Memorize Your Opening and Closing

Having a conversation with the judges requires eye contact. Try to memorize most or all of your greeting and opening roadmap so that you can establish eye contact with each of the judges from the start. Try also to memorize your conclusion so you can finish your argument in the same effective fashion. Even if you need to write out the opening and closing verbatim in your outline to feel comfortable for your oral argument, practice reciting most of your opening and closing without looking down at your notes.

E. Practice to Refine Style

To ensure that you maintain eye contact throughout the presentation, practice using your notes and looking up toward the judges. Watching yourself in a mirror or recording yourself with your phone, tablet, or computer will show you how much—or how little—eye contact you make. It also will help you become mindful of this important oral argument technique. Repeated practice and review of your oral argument will help you gain confidence and reduce nervousness.

Practicing with a colleague also will help your preparation and confidence. Use the list of potential questions you created and ask a colleague to practice drilling you as you practice your oral argument. Work on your transitions between different arguments and between your answers to questions and your different arguments. Consider how each of your distinct arguments is related so you can easily transition between them and create a seamless presentation.

As you practice for your oral argument, be open to trying different approaches as a way to find your own voice. Seek out opportunities to watch oral arguments in person and use the audio and video recordings available on the internet to appreciate the different types of oral advocacy. Notice the broad range of personas, strategies, and styles that experienced attorneys use. And then think about how you can develop an approach to oral argument that is professional and appropriate for the lawyer you want to be.

F. Prepare for the Unexpected

Remember that any topic raised in the parties' motions or briefs is open for debate during oral argument. Although your goal is to be prepared for any question, the court may ask you a question that you did not expect, or opposing counsel may make an argument or give an answer that you did not anticipate. In such instances, you want to have the ability to respond accurately and with confidence.

Thus, along with the outlines of your arguments and authorities, you should bring to your argument copies of the parties' motions or briefs, any relevant factual documents, and the cited statutes and cases. You should arrange these materials so that they appear organized and are easy for you to reference in case you need them. These materials will help you provide a thoughtful response if an unexpected issue arises during your argument.

3. STEP THREE: FOLLOW RULES OF DECORUM

Every court has its own rules of professional conduct. But in general, these rules require that you show deference to the court, civility to opposing counsel, and respect for the judicial process. The checklist below provides a good starting point for conducting yourself according to the customary rules of decorum.

Checklist for your Oral Argument

☑ Arrive early. Be ready to begin when the judges are ready, whether that time is 15 minutes early or one hour late.

☑ Adhere to timekeeping requirements without being reminded by the judge.

☑ Dress in court attire appropriate for your jurisdiction.

☑ Be meticulously prepared.

☑ Be respectful by addressing the judge as "Your Honor."

☑ Be civil toward opposing counsel.

☑ Show an appropriate level of seriousness; jokes are seldom proper.

☑ Stand up straight at the podium, with organized notes and no pen in hand; limit hand gestures.

☑ When a judge starts talking, stop talking immediately.

☑ Invite questions from the judges.

☑ At the close of argument, thank the judges for their time.

part VIII

Research and Citation

Introduction to Legal Research and Citation

Lawyers must be skillful researchers. Before you can prepare a memo, motion, brief, letter, email, or judicial opinion containing legal analysis, you must first conduct accurate and thorough legal research. Then, for that research to be useful to the document's audience, the legal sources must be cited correctly. The following chapters explain how legal research and the related skill of legal citation provide the foundation for the objective and persuasive documents you are learning to prepare.

In practice, legal research and citation tasks are frequently assigned to junior lawyers. Thus, employers expect law students and recent graduates to be practice ready in research and citation. The following chapters present principles of legal research and legal citation that will enable you to become effective at these important skills. These chapters are a guide to researching and citing legal authorities as you write the documents discussed throughout this book.

Legal Research Basics

Research Basics for the New Legal Writer

1. The process of legal research
2. The sources for legal research
3. Legal sources in print and online

1. THE PROCESS OF LEGAL RESEARCH

As a legal researcher, you must balance the pressures of accuracy, thoroughness, efficiency, and economy. When doing legal research, you do not get credit for trying. You must always find the correct answer and understand that answer completely. Further, you must conduct your research efficiently and economically. Lawyers are expected to juggle multiple projects at once, and charges for your research time and resources will often be passed along to cost-conscious clients. Thus, your approach to every research question should be thoughtful and well organized.

The only way to become an effective legal researcher is through practice. There is rarely just one way to research a legal question. Some lawyers develop strong preferences for certain sources, formats, and methods. But if your research is accurate, thorough, efficient, and economical, your supervisors and clients will likely not be concerned with the details of how you did it. In law school, you have the opportunity to practice your research skills without the pressure of a paying client. So you need to do enough legal research to discover which methods, techniques, and approaches work best for you. During this period of experimentation as your research skills develop, you should aim to understand the process of legal research, not just look for the "right" answer to each particular question.

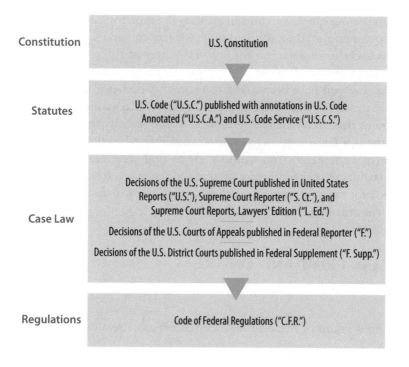

Constitution	U.S. Constitution
Statutes	U.S. Code ("U.S.C.") published with annotations in U.S. Code Annotated ("U.S.C.A.") and U.S. Code Service ("U.S.C.S.")
Case Law	Decisions of the U.S. Supreme Court published in United States Reports ("U.S."), Supreme Court Reporter ("S. Ct."), and Supreme Court Reports, Lawyers' Edition ("L. Ed.") Decisions of the U.S. Courts of Appeals published in Federal Reporter ("F.") Decisions of the U.S. District Courts published in Federal Supplement ("F. Supp.")
Regulations	Code of Federal Regulations ("C.F.R.")

Figure 40.1

2. THE SOURCES FOR LEGAL RESEARCH

Recall from Chapter 4 that there are two types of legal authorities: primary authorities and secondary sources. The goal of any research task is to find the primary authorities that will determine the outcome of your legal question. And although you will not usually quote or cite secondary sources in your legal documents, you should use them to help you to identify and understand the relevant primary authorities.

There are four types of primary authorities: constitutions, statutes, cases, and regulations. Constitutions are the foundational governing documents for the nation and the states. Statutes are the laws passed by legislatures, which are organized and published as a code. Cases are the written opinions of courts, which are published in chronological order in books called case reporters. Regulations are rules promulgated by agencies, which may also be codified and published. Figure 40.1 shows a chart of these primary authorities under federal law.

There are many types of secondary sources, including legal encyclopedias, American Law Reports, treatises, Restatements, law review and journal articles, annotated codes, headnotes, and digests. The formats for secondary sources include books, periodicals, and electronic publications.

Some questions will require you to find only one form of primary authority—usually case law. But your research will often involve more than one type of primary authority. If you identify a constitutional provision, statute, or regulation that is relevant to your question, you will also have to look for case law that interprets that provision, statute, or regulation. Moreover, you may need to use secondary sources to understand the subject matter of the relevant primary authorities and to find all of the relevant primary authorities.

For example, imagine that you have been asked to research whether it is constitutional for a city to pass a law that makes it illegal to carry a gun within 50 feet of any establishment that serves alcohol. First, you would identify the Second Amendment to the U.S. Constitution as a relevant authority. But that would not be the end of your research. You would want to find secondary sources that discuss the evolution of the interpretation of the Second Amendment. And you would look for cases interpreting and applying the law in cases involving limitations to the amendment.

3. LEGAL SOURCES IN PRINT AND ONLINE

A. Print Sources

Law libraries contain print versions of the legal sources that lawyers use most often: statutes and cases.

i. Statutes

Federal and state statutes are collected and organized into codes that are published as a set of books. When doing legal research, attorneys use annotated codes because the annotations include helpful information about cases and secondary sources that have interpreted and discussed the statutes that make up the codes.

The U.S. Code is the official version of the federal statutes. U.S. Code Annotated (West) and U.S. Code Service (LexisNexis) are annotated versions of the federal statutes. States vary in how they title and organize their codes. Every state has at least one annotated version of its state statutes, and in some states, an annotated version is also the official version.

ii. Cases

Cases are printed in books called reporters, which are published in sets and series. Reporters are organized by jurisdiction and court tier.[1] There are federal reporters, regional reporters, and state reporters. The volume and page of the reporter where a case is published provides key information for the citation for the case. Because cases are identified by where they are published in the print reporters, even attorneys who look at most cases online need to understand what the reporters are and what they contain.

The same case can be published in more than one reporter. For many courts, there is an "official" government-published reporter and an unofficial

---

1. A few reporters also are organized by subject matter, including bankruptcy and tax.

reporter published by West or LexisNexis. For instance, decisions of the U.S. Supreme Court appear in the United States Reports (official), the Supreme Court Reporter (West), and the United States Supreme Court Reports, Lawyers' Edition (LexisNexis). For some courts, including the federal courts of appeals and certain state courts, there is no government-published reporter.

a. Federal Reporters

There are separate reporters for each tier in the federal court system, but the federal reporters do not separate cases by circuit or district. The federal reporters are as follows:[2]

Federal Case Reporter	Court Tier
U.S. Reports (U.S.)	U.S. Supreme Court cases
Federal Reporter (F., F.2d., F.3d.)	U.S. Courts of Appeals cases
Federal Supplement (F. Supp., F. Supp. 2d, F. Supp. 3d)	U.S. District Court cases

Table 40.1

b. Regional Reporters

West's National Reporter System groups state cases by geographic region. The regional reporters include decisions from state highest courts and some decisions of state intermediate appellate courts. The regions are divided as follows:

West Regional Reporter	States Included
Atlantic Reporter	Connecticut, Delaware, D.C., Maine, Maryland, New Hampshire, New Jersey, Pennsylvania, Rhode Island, Vermont
South Eastern Reporter	Georgia, North Carolina, South Carolina, Virginia, West Virginia
Southern Reporter	Alabama, Florida, Louisiana, Mississippi
North Eastern Reporter	Illinois, Indiana, Massachusetts, New York, Ohio
South Western Reporter	Arkansas, Kentucky, Missouri, Tennessee, Texas
North Western Reporter	Iowa, Michigan, Minnesota, Nebraska, North Dakota, South Dakota, Wisconsin
Pacific Reporter	Alaska, Arizona, California, Colorado, Hawaii, Idaho, Kansas, Montana, Nevada, New Mexico, Oklahoma, Oregon, Utah, Washington, Wyoming

Table 40.2

---

2. The Federal Reporter and Federal Supplement are published by West. West also publishes the Federal Appendix, which includes decisions of the federal courts of appeals since 2001 that weren't selected for publication in the Federal Reporter.

West's reporters include headnotes and Key Numbers that correspond to the West Key Number System. As explained in Chapter 42, the headnotes and Key Numbers, and the digests that collect them, are useful research tools.

c. State Reporters

Many state cases are also published in state-specific reporters. State reporters may divide cases by tier, publishing highest court opinions separately from intermediate appellate court opinions. For instance, Ohio Supreme Court opinions are published in Ohio State Reports, intermediate appellate court opinions are published in Ohio Appellate Reports, and select trial court opinions are published in Ohio Miscellaneous Reports. Ohio Appellate Reports and Ohio Miscellaneous Reports are printed together in a single volume but are considered two separate publications.

B. Online Sources

Legal research used to be a process that involved using multivolume sets of leather-bound books, which were housed in grand law libraries. Now, legal researchers primarily use three fee-based internet services: Westlaw, LexisNexis, and Bloomberg. And every day there are new internet-based research services that aim to make the process of legal research easier and more efficient.

These online services seek to provide online access to virtually all legal research sources. Along with these fee-based services, there are many free online sources for legal research, which are discussed in Chapter 42. Also, many of the legal sources available on Westlaw, LexisNexis, and Bloomberg are available in print form in law libraries. In fact, many legal sources were designed to be used in print, so their physical versions can be more intuitive to use than their electronic versions. Almost all legal research is now done online, but as you practice your legal research skills, you should experiment with sources in different formats to see what makes the most sense to you.

Creating a Research Plan

Legal research can feel similar to internet searching because both involve using search terms to look for information. And your internet search skills will be helpful when you are doing legal research. But most people take a scattershot approach to internet searching—entering terms at random and reviewing the results haphazardly. This undisciplined approach is not an effective legal research technique.

Instead, to ensure that your research is accurate, thorough, efficient, and economical, you must be organized. To organize your research approach, you should make a plan before you start.

> ### Creating a Research Plan
>
> 1. Formulate a research question.
> 2. Identify the relevant jurisdiction.
> 3. Generate search terms.

1. STEP ONE: FORMULATE A RESEARCH QUESTION

The first step in planning your research is to formulate the research task as a question. Every research problem is different. And it is extremely difficult to research efficiently when you don't understand what you are looking for.

Some research tasks will require you to find a discrete answer to a simple question. For example, how many days does a party have to file a notice of appeal after a decision by a federal district court? Or, what are the elements of battery under Texas law?

Other research tasks will require you to survey the authorities that cover a legal issue and select those that are likely to have the most relevance to your case. This type of research usually precedes preparing a legal document where you will analyze a legal question. If you have been assigned this type of research, your question will describe the legal issue that you have been asked to analyze for your client. For example, does your client's use of a music sample constitute copyright infringement? Or is a houseboat a conveyance under the New York trespass statute?

With these more complex research tasks, you may actually have a series of questions that you need to answer. You should isolate each question that you can identify. For example, the question above regarding copyright infringement has other questions nested within it.

- Does the client's use of a music sample constitute copyright infringement?
  - What are the elements of copyright infringement?
  - How have those elements been applied to the act of music sampling?
  - What are the defenses to copyright infringement?
  - How have those defenses been applied to the act of music sampling?

You may not be able to identify all possible questions before you begin your research. So continue to keep track of the legal questions that arise as you do your research.

2. STEP TWO: IDENTIFY THE RELEVANT JURISDICTION

The second step in planning your research is to identify the relevant jurisdiction for your research. Jurisdiction has three distinct meanings: (1) the category of law (state or federal) that governs the issue; (2) the specific geographic area that provides the controlling law for the issue; and (3) the level of courts that have the power to bind the court that will decide the issue.

Identifying the relevant jurisdiction for your research is a three-step process:

1. Determine whether state or federal law governs your question.
2. Determine the particular state or federal circuit law that will apply in your case.
3. Determine the level of the court that will decide the issue in your case.

For example, imagine that you have been asked to research whether your client, a musician, can be found liable for copyright infringement by the District Court for the Northern District of California based on her sampling the song "Smokestack Lightning" for 15 seconds. First, you would determine that federal law, and in particular, a federal statute, governs copyright infringement. Second, you would determine that the law of the United States Court of Appeals for the Ninth Circuit will apply to your case because that is the federal judicial circuit where the District Court for the Northern District of California is located. Third, you would determine that decisions of the Ninth Circuit Court of Appeals and the U.S. Supreme Court are binding and that decisions of the District Court for the Northern District of California are "highly" persuasive.

3. STEP THREE: GENERATE SEARCH TERMS

The third step in planning your research is to brainstorm possible search terms. Search terms are at the heart of any research task. No matter what sources or methods you use, at some point you will need to use search terms. Just as when you search for information on the internet, the search terms you use determine the results you get. The following three steps will help you to brainstorm search terms:

1. Look for key words.
2. Think of synonyms.
3. Add breadth and depth.

First, you should harvest key words from the documents or information that you already have regarding your legal issue. Look for words that describe legal claims, relationships, and legally significant actions. Legal claims include the words that describe causes of action in civil cases, like "breach of contract," "negligence," and "copyright infringement," and crimes in criminal cases, like "murder," "burglary," and "drug possession." Legal relationships include the words that describe how the parties to a case are related, like "employer/employee," "landlord/tenant," and "parent/child." Legally significant actions include the words that describe the facts of a case, like "use of a 15-second music sample," "occupation of a parcel of land for six years," and "entry into a fenced yard."

After you have looked for key words, you should think of possible synonyms for those words. Different courts may use different terms to describe the same claims, relationships, and actions, and you want your research to capture all relevant results. For example, if you identify the legal claim as "gender discrimination," possible synonyms would be "sexual discrimination," "sexual harassment," and "sex-based discrimination." A legal dictionary and secondary sources can help you find synonyms for legal terms. And some research platforms now suggest synonyms as you enter your search terms.

Last, you should expand the breadth and depth of your search terms. You can make your search terms broader by making them more general. For example, if your case involved assault with a knife, you could expand the breadth of your search by also using "assault with a deadly weapon" or just "assault" as search terms. Conversely, you can make your search terms deeper by making them more specific. If your case involved false advertising, you could expand the depth of your search by using as a search term the specific product that had been advertised—for example, "false drug advertising," "false prescription drug advertising," or "false prescription drug acid reflux advertising."

Your goal is to have a plan for your research that makes the process efficient and accurate. To do so, you need to know what you are looking for, where you will search for it, and how you will try to find it.

Smart Research Strategies

Because the types of questions you will be expected to research can vary so much in scope and complexity, no uniform research approach will work for every question. Instead, you will need to develop a plan that is appropriate to each research question based on the following research strategies.

Smart Research Strategies for the New Legal Writer

1. Move from general to specific.
2. Use free sources first.
3. Don't start from scratch.
4. Browse.
5. Build in redundancy.
6. Run searches of the right size on fee-based platforms.
7. Validate and update.
8. Cite correctly.

---

1. MOVE FROM GENERAL TO SPECIFIC

As a law student or new lawyer who does not have an extensive background of legal knowledge, it is best to start your research with a general inquiry and make it more specific as you gain knowledge of your topic. Starting general will provide a strong foundation for the analysis of your legal question. More-over, your general research will point you to the more specific sources, like statutes and cases, that will determine the outcome of your particular legal question.

Often, the best place to do your general research is in secondary sources. Secondary sources are commentaries and summaries of the law. Because secondary sources are not law and can never be binding on a court, you will rarely cite them in your legal documents. But secondary sources are often the most efficient way to locate the primary authorities that will govern the outcome of your legal question.

Commonly used secondary sources include the following:

Legal encyclopedias: Legal encyclopedias are collections of brief summaries of legal topics arranged alphabetically. Legal encyclopedia entries include citations to primary authorities. There are two general, national legal encyclopedias, *American Jurisprudence* ("AmJur") and *Corpus Juris Secundum* ("C.J.S."). Many states also have their own legal encyclopedias. These state-specific encyclopedias include, among others, *Florida Jurisprudence*, *New York Jurisprudence*, and *Pennsylvania Law Encyclopedia*.

American Law Reports ("ALR"): ALR is a collection of in-depth articles, called annotations, which summarize and analyze specific legal issues. ALR annotations include numerous citations to primary authorities, including citations to cases organized by jurisdiction.

Treatises: A treatise is a book that provides an in-depth treatment of a broad legal subject by an expert. A treatise may be a single volume or multiple volumes. Examples of well-known treatises include Phillip E. Areeda & Herbert Hovenkamp, *Antitrust Law: An Analysis of Antitrust Principles and Their Application*; David Nimmer, *Nimmer on Copyright*; and Wayne R. LaFave, *Substantive Criminal Law*.

The category of treatises also includes practice guides, which offer pragmatic advice and often include forms and checklists. Practice guides can be particularly helpful for procedural questions. Commonly used practice guides include *Moore's Federal Practice*; Wright & Miller, *Federal Practice and Procedure*; *Trawick's Florida Practice & Procedure*; and The Rutter Group Practice Guide, *Federal Civil Procedure Before Trial*. Treatises and practice guides include citations to primary authorities.

Restatements of the Law: Restatements are a synthesis of the common law prepared by the American Law Institute, an organization of professors, judges, and attorneys. Restatements summarize the consensus on the state of the common law on a variety of legal topics, including contracts, torts, agency, and property. Restatements include an appendix listing the cases that have cited the Restatement.

Law review and journal articles: Law review and journal articles are scholarly publications written by law school professors, judges, lawyers, and law students that usually discuss emerging or cutting-edge legal issues. These articles are often detailed and include numerous references to both primary and secondary sources.

As you use your search terms to learn general information about your question in these secondary sources, you will find references to primary authorities that are relevant to your question. Pay careful attention to these references because they will allow you to transition your research from general background information to the specific, primary sources that will determine the outcome of your question.

For example, if you were researching the question of whether your client was liable for copyright infringement, you could begin your research by looking up copyright in the legal encyclopedia *American Jurisprudence*. The entry regarding copyright infringement describes the elements required to prove copyright infringement and includes references to the relevant sections of the copyright statute and cases that interpret the elements of copyright infringement. Your general inquiry in a secondary source, therefore, quickly provides you with specific sources that are potentially relevant to your legal question.

2. USE FREE SOURCES FIRST

Legal research can be expensive. In addition to the cost of your time and the price of a subscription to a fee-based service, every search you do can have a charge that may get passed along to the client. When you begin your research, you may not know enough information to formulate effective searches. To avoid unnecessary costs for your client, you should start your research using free sources, and then transition to fee-based sources once you have developed more specific research questions.

The most obvious free research source is the internet via Google or similar search engines. Typing your research question into a search engine is a fine way to start your research because it can help you get a general understanding of an issue and point you in the direction of relevant sources.

Be careful, however, to verify and validate any information that you find on the internet before relying on it for your legal analysis. There is no guarantee that information on the internet is accurate or up to date. Secondary sources like Wikipedia can be helpful at the beginning of your research, but you cannot trust them and you cannot cite them in a legal document. Instead, you should use them to find a primary authority that you can verify, read, and cite.

Before you rely on any information from the internet to advance your research, you must evaluate the following three properties:

1. Authority: The information must be from a reputable and reliable source.
2. Accuracy: The information must be correct.
3. Currency: The information must be up to date.

For legal information, you should rely on free internet sources only when they have some official sanction that guarantees their information is accurate and current. Further, you should use a citator to validate that any authority you plan to rely on is still good law.[1]

Some of the most useful and reliable free sources on the internet are described here:

> Government websites: The text of constitutions, statutes, court rules, and regulations are available on government websites. When you need

---

1. Citators are also discussed in sections 3 and 7 of this chapter.

to read only the text of a primary authority, you should look it up on an official government website. For example, the U.S. Code is available at http://uscode.house.gov.

Legal Information Institute: The Legal Information Institute ("LII"), http://www.law.cornell.edu, provides free access to, among other things, the U.S. Code ("U.S.C."), the Federal Rules, and the Code of Federal Regulations ("C.F.R"). Like government websites, LII is a free and reliable place to get the full text of federal primary authorities.

Google Scholar: Google Scholar, http://scholar.google.com, is a free way to search for cases and scholarly articles. Google Scholar allows you to search for cases and then filter the results by date and issuing court. Once you identify a potentially relevant case in Google Scholar, you can read the full text of the opinion and see a list of cases that have cited that case and other related cases.

Google Scholar also allows you to search for scholarly articles, including law review articles. Unlike the case law on Google Scholar, however, you may not be able to access the full text of the articles retrieved in response to your search if those articles appear in subscription databases like JSTOR and HeinOnline.

Findlaw, Justia, and Public Library of Law: Findlaw, http://lp.findlaw.com, Justia, http://www.justia.com, and Public Library of Law, http://www.plol.org, are free sources that provide access to the text of some cases and statutes for both state and federal law.

In addition to free internet sources, remember that the books in the library are free. And print sources are not just available while you are in law school—many law offices have libraries with print versions of annotated codes and secondary sources. Using these print versions can be a cost-effective way to begin your research.

3. DON'T START FROM SCRATCH

Rather than attempting to find relevant sources from scratch, you should use each source you find as a link to more sources. Although you may be tempted to jump into your research by immediately running searches for statutes or cases online (and you usually will do this type of searching later in your research process), you will likely find much of what you are looking for and find it more quickly by letting other relevant sources guide you to it.

In addition to the secondary sources described on page 339, the best resources to use to avoid starting from scratch are as follows:

Annotated codes: Annotated codes are statutory compilations that include not only the statutory text but also references to relevant authorities, including cases, regulations, and secondary sources. When you have identified a statute that governs your legal issue, the annotated code is often the most efficient way to find cases that interpret and apply that statute. The federal statutes in the U.S. Code appear in annotated codes called U.S. Code Annotated ("U.S.C.A.") and U.S. Code Service ("U.S.C.S."). States also have annotated versions of their statutes. For example, the New York statutes are annotated in McKinney's Consolidated Laws of New York Annotated and New York Consolidated Laws Service.[2]

Example Statute 42.1 shows an example of a statute as it appears in the U.S.C.A.[3] After the text of the statute, this annotated version provides "Context and Analysis" in the form of West Key Numbers, an ALR article, and secondary sources. It also lists and briefly describes a case under "Notes of Decisions."

Headnotes/Key Numbers: For cases published by West, editors write headnotes that summarize the major points of law in the case, and they categorize these points and other specific legal concepts according to the West Key Number System. The Key Number System is a massive outline of American law, where nearly every legal concept has been assigned a unique number. Headnotes also are assigned a number (available as a link online) that corresponds to the place in a case where the point of law is discussed. Headnotes do not have the force of law, so they cannot be quoted or cited in a legal document. To make searching for a particular legal topic easier, West compiles all the headnotes assigned to each key number. Using Westlaw, you can click on any key number to find other cases that address that same point of law.

For example, Figure 42.1 shows the first of eight headnotes in *Light-Hawk v. Robertson*,[4] the case listed in the annotated code example as a "Note of Decision."[5] This headnote describes one point of law in that case—that content-based regulations or restrictions are presumptively inconsistent with the First Amendment. Using this headnote, you could identify other cases that discuss the same or similar points of law and other cases that cite this case for this point.

Other fee-based platforms similarly offer headnotes that distill the points of law in a case to make it easier to skim the case and identify the rules.

---

2. For federal statutes and many state statutes, the annotated code is not the official code for citation purposes. You should always cite the official code in your legal documents.

3. Reprinted with the permission of Thomson Reuters from the U.S. Code Annotated as available on Westlaw.

4. 812 F. Supp. 1095 (W.D. Wash. 1993).

5. Reprinted with the permission of Thomson Reuters from the Federal Supplement as available on Westlaw.

Example
Statute 42.1

For Educational Use Only

§ 580p-4. Injunction against unauthorized manufacture, use, or…, 16 USCA § 580p-4

United States Code Annotated
  Title 16. Conservation
    Chapter 3. Forests; Forest Service; Reforestation; Management
    Subchapter I. General Provisions

16 U.S.C.A. § 580p-4

§ 580p-4. Injunction against unauthorized manufacture, use, or reproduction

Currentness

— Context of where statute appears in U.S. Code

⌐ Text of the statute

(a) Whoever, except as provided by rules and regulations issued by the Secretary, manufactures, uses, or reproduces the character "Smokey Bear" or the name "Smokey Bear", or a facsimile or simulation of such character or name in such a manner as suggests "Smokey Bear" may be enjoined from such manufacture, use, or reproduction at the suit of the Attorney General upon complaint by the Secretary.

(b) Whoever, except as provided by rules and regulations issued by the Secretary, manufactures, uses, or reproduces the character "Woodsy Owl", the name "Woodsy Owl", or the slogan "Give a Hoot, Don't Pollute", or a facsimile or simulation of such character, name, or slogan in such a manner as suggests "Woodsy Owl" may be enjoined from such manufacture, use, or reproduction at the suit of the Attorney General upon complaint by the Secretary.

CREDIT(S)

(Pub.L. 93-318, § 4, June 22, 1974, 88 Stat. 245.)
16 U.S.C.A. § 580p-4, 16 USCA § 580p-4
Current through P.L. 115-182

Context and Analysis (7)

Library References (3)
  United States ●─3, 40.
  Woods and Forests ●─5.
  Key Number System Topic Nos. 393, 411.

— Key Number references

ALR Library (1)
  51 ALR 6th 359, Constitutionality, Construction, and Application of Statute or Regulatory Action Respecting Political Advertising — Print Media Cases.

⌐ ALR references

Treatises and Practice Aids (3)
  Callmann on Unfair Compet., TMs, & Monopolies § 2:9, The Lanham Trademark Act Limitations.
  Callmann on Unfair Compet., TMs, & Monopolies § 26:2, History and Constitutionality of United States' Trademark Statutes.
  Callmann on Unfair Compet., TMs, & Monopolies App 40 § 40:3, Excerpts from 18 U.S.C.A.

— Secondary source references

Notes Of Decisions (1)

Constitutionality

Statute and regulation relied upon by the United States Forest Service to prohibit environmental organization's use of caricature of Smokey Bear in advertisement criticizing Forest Service's forest management policies violated organization's First Amendment rights; organization's use of chainsaw-wielding caricature of Smokey Bear was unlikely to cause confusion or to dilute the value of Smokey Bear to help prevent forest fires. LightHawk, the Environmental Air Force v. Robertson, W.D. Wash.1993, 812 F.Supp. 1095, 25 U.S.P.Q.2d 2014. Constitutional Law ●─1652

— Summary and citation of a case that cites the statute

> [1] **Constitutional Law**
> ●─Content-Based Regulations or Restrictions
>
> 92Constitutional Law
> 92XVIIIFreedom of Speech, Expression, and Press
> 92XVIII(A)In General
> 92XVIII(A)1In General
> 92k1516Content-Based Regulations or Restrictions
> 92k1517In General
> (Formerly 92k90(1))
>
> Statute or regulation that places burden on speakers due
> to content of their speech is presumptively inconsistent
> with First Amendment. U.S.C.A. Const.Amend. 1
>
> Cases that cite this headnote

Figure 42.1

Citators: Citators help you determine whether a case or statute is still good law.[6] Attorneys used to use citators in print, but the process was cumbersome. Westlaw, LexisNexis, and Bloomberg each include a citator that provides a list of all subsequent primary and secondary authorities that have cited a particular case or statute.

Citators are one of the best ways to find other relevant authorities. Once you have identified a relevant case, you can use a citator to locate cases that are part of the case's history and cases that have cited the case positively and negatively. Citators use symbols to indicate the depth and type of treatment the case received in a later case. For example, Key-Cite, the Westlaw citator, uses a red flag to indicate negative treatment; Shepard's, the LexisNexis citator, uses a red stop sign; and Bloomberg Law Citator uses a minus sign in a red box.

Cases: Cases always cite other cases. Thus, if you have found one relevant case, you may find other cases that are relevant to your legal question by looking up the cases cited within your case and by using a citator to find all the later cases that cited your case.

4. BROWSE

Although you will do much of your legal research using electronic sources on the internet, you should consider, whenever feasible, browsing through sources as though you were looking at them in print. Any source that includes a table of contents or an index is a candidate for this kind of browsing.[7] Online platforms provide electronic versions of tables of contents and indexes for sources that have them in their print versions.

---

6. Citators are also discussed in section 7 of this chapter.

7. Case reporters, which are organized chronologically rather than topically, cannot be browsed in this way.

Encyclopedias, treatises, and statutes all have tables of contents that you should browse. A statute often has multiple sections that relate to a particular topic. By looking at the table of contents, you can identify all the sections that may be relevant to your question.

For example, 18 U.S.C. § 2333(a) describes civil remedies for terrorism. It states,

> Any national of the United States injured in his or her person, property, or business by reason of an act of international terrorism, or his or her estate, survivors, or heirs, may sue therefor in any appropriate district court of the United States and shall recover threefold the damages he or she sustains and the cost of the suit, including attorney's fees.

By browsing the table of contents of the U.S. Code, you would learn that 18 U.S.C. § 2331 defines the terms "international terrorism," "national of the United States," and "person" that appear in § 2333(a). You would also see that 18 U.S.C. § 2335 provides a ten-year statute of limitations for actions under § 2333(a). To have an accurate and thorough understanding of § 2333, you would need to browse and read the other related sections that surround it.

Similarly, many sources, including encyclopedias, treatises, ALRs, and statutes have an index. By looking up search terms in the index, you can find all of the places in a source where your issue is discussed.

5. BUILD IN REDUNDANCY

Because your research needs to be efficient and economical while also being accurate and thorough, you should build redundancy into your research strategy. Redundancy means searching for the same information in different ways to make sure that you have found all the relevant sources. For example, even though you should attempt to find primary authorities through links in primary and secondary sources, you should also run key word searches to make sure that you capture all relevant primary authorities in your research.

As you repeat your searches, using different terms, methods, and sources, you might feel like you are researching in circles. Doing searches in different ways is the best way to make sure you've found everything available to answer your legal question. Some research platforms now use algorithms to offer additional sources that may be relevant based on your searches. You should review these suggestions, but don't let them replace your own efforts to build redundancy into your research.

One easy way to build redundancy into your research strategy is to use a checklist. The following questions will help you determine whether you have identified all the primary authorities relevant to your question:

1. Are there any constitutional provisions relevant to your legal question?
2. Are there any statutes relevant to your legal question?
3. Are there any cases decided by courts higher than the court in your jurisdiction that are relevant to your legal question?

4. Are there any cases decided by courts at the same level as your court in your jurisdiction that are relevant to your legal question?
5. Are there any cases that are more recent than the most recent case you have found that are relevant to your legal question?
6. Are there any regulations that are relevant to your legal question?

Building redundancy into your research strategy will help you know when you are finished researching. The best evidence that you have sufficiently researched a question is when you repeatedly find the same results that you have already found. If the links from relevant sources and the results of new searches all bring up authorities that you have already seen, your research has likely found everything relevant to your question.

6. RUN SEARCHES OF THE RIGHT SIZE ON FEE-BASED PLATFORMS

Tailoring the scope of your electronic searches correctly is essential to researching efficiently and economically. Whenever you run a search on a fee-based platform, you want to be sure that your search is not too wide or too narrow. Running a search of the right scope ensures that you won't capture an overwhelming number of irrelevant results or inadvertently exclude relevant results.

Tailor the scope of your searches on fee-based platforms using these four techniques:

1. Correctly limit your search to the relevant jurisdiction.
2. Avoid overly broad search terms.
3. Use Boolean searching when possible.
4. Filter or limit your results before reviewing them.

Make sure to identify the jurisdiction relevant to your legal question and select that specific jurisdiction when searching. For example, if you were researching a federal copyright infringement question for a case in the District Court for the Northern District of California, you would want to search for decisions from the U.S. Supreme Court and federal courts in the Ninth Circuit. Similarly, if you were researching a question involving adverse possession under Florida law for a case in the Florida Third District Court of Appeal, you would want to search for decisions from Florida state and federal courts applying Florida law.

Whenever possible, you want to avoid using search terms that are so broad that they retrieve many irrelevant results. For example, if you were looking for cases where summary judgment was granted on a gender discrimination claim, the search term "summary judgment" by itself would bring back many irrelevant cases. To limit your search, include more specific terms. And to find information about general topics like summary judgment, you would want to use other research methods, like free and secondary sources, rather than running case searches on fee-based platforms.

Boolean[8] searching, also called terms-and-connectors searching, uses search terms and connectors, like "and," "or," and "not," to describe the relationship between search terms. Rather than relying on an algorithm's interpretation of a natural language query, searching with Boolean connectors allows you to control the relationship between your search terms. For example, by using connectors such as "and" and "or," you can control whether your search results include all your search terms or any of your search terms. You can also control how closely the terms appear in the result. For example, you can search for cases that use the terms "copyright" and "sampling" within the same sentence to create a more targeted search using the connector "/s" in Westlaw, "w/sent" in LexisNexis, and "S/" in Bloomberg. Because Boolean searching gives you more control over your search, this kind of searching often excludes irrelevant results. The specifics of how to compose Boolean searches differ based on which online platform you are using, so refer to the guides on each platform for how to compose effective Boolean searches.

After you have run a search on a fee-based platform, you can further narrow the results or run another search within the results. Filtering your results allows you to exclude irrelevant results that were captured by your original search. For example, you can narrow the results by categories including type of document, date, and deciding judge, or you can search your original results using a new search term.

7. VALIDATE AND UPDATE

The law is always evolving. Before you rely on any source in a legal document, you must validate that source using a citator. As described in section 3 of this chapter, the Westlaw citator is called KeyCite, the LexisNexis citator is called Shepard's, and the Bloomberg citator is called Bloomberg Law Citator. No research is complete until you have used a citator to check that your sources are still good law. At any time, a court could issue an opinion that invalidates a case, or a legislature could amend a statute that you intend to rely on for your analysis. By linking to the procedural history and citing references for every case and statute, these citators tell you whether there is negative history or treatment that may affect the validity of a case or statute that you plan to use in a legal document.

Then, even after you have validated the sources that are relevant to your question, you must continually update your research. Courts are constantly

---

8. Boolean search is named after George Boole, a 19th century mathematician. Shauntee Burns, *What is Boolean Search?*, New York Public Library Blog (Feb. 22, 2011), https://www.nypl.org/blog/2011/02/22/what-boolean-search.

deciding new cases, and you must be vigilant to make sure that your research remains up to date.

8. CITE CORRECTLY

Ultimately, for your research to be successful, you must correctly cite the sources you rely on in your legal documents. Your readers, who may include judges, clerks, supervising attorneys, and opposing counsel, will not be able to verify your analysis if they can't find the sources you cite. Failing to cite your sources correctly will undermine the usefulness and credibility of your research. The next chapter provides detailed instructions on how to cite sources correctly.

Citation

1. CITATION IS A LANGUAGE

Citation is a language designed to communicate a great deal of information in a concentrated way. This language has one simple and important purpose: to concisely identify the relied-upon authorities with enough specificity that the reader can find and evaluate them. The rules of citation can be both trivial and overwhelming. But to understand how the language of citation works, it helps to remember its purpose. Every part of a citation is included for a reason, and if a part is missing or incorrect, the reader will be confused. A citation isn't useful unless it precisely identifies the source so that the reader can determine its weight, age, and relevance.

> **Citation Principles for the New Legal Writer**
> 1. Citation is a language.
> 2. Master the most common formats and be consistent.
> 3. Use the index, tables, and quick reference guides for everything else.
> 4. Learn the rules that arise frequently.
> 5. Cite correctly as you write.

You will encounter judges, supervisors, professors, and colleagues who are exacting about legal citation. For them, a writer's ability to format citations correctly demonstrates that writer's credibility, attention to detail, and professionalism. You will also encounter judges, supervisors, professors, and colleagues who believe that as long as the authorities are cited so the reader can understand what is cited and where to find it, the minute details of citation format are a distraction from a legal writer's more important tasks of research, drafting, and analysis.[1] Given these differing perspectives, knowing the expectations of your audience is critical. And if you can't know what your audience expects, assuming that your reader values the uniformity and reliability of impeccable citations is the safest choice.

---

1. *See, e.g.*, Richard A. Posner, *The Bluebook Blues*, 120 Yale L.J. 850, 853 (2011).

2. MASTER THE MOST COMMON FORMATS AND BE CONSISTENT

A golden rule in citing is to be consistent. That's not easy considering how many different citation formats exist. Much of the legal writing world follows *The Bluebook*[2] and will expect citations to follow the exhaustive list of formats that the manual details. Another acceptable and well-known citation system, developed by the Association of Legal Writing Directors, is the *ALWD Citation Manual*.[3] Other citation manuals add additional colors to the mix and include the online *Indigo Book*[4] and *The Maroonbook*.[5]

To figure out what citation format to follow, check local court rules, which may specify preferred citation formats. Montana federal court rules, for example, allow either *The Bluebook* or *ALWD* citation formats.[6] California state courts dictate that citations should follow *The Bluebook* or the *California Style Manual*.[7] Other sources also may provide citation guidance. Cornell University Law School has compiled a helpful chart of the citation practices and rules for all 50 states, with examples from each.[8]

Many courts have their own citation rules that trump general citation manuals in documents submitted to those courts. The citation formats for cases and statutes under local rules can differ dramatically from other citation formats. Thus, follow the local citation practices for your jurisdiction when preparing any legal document.

Because citation practices can vary by court, you may need to toggle between citation styles for different cases. A New York attorney who practices in both state and federal court may use New York citation formats from the *New York Law Reports Style Manual*[9] for state court documents and *Bluebook* citation formats for federal court documents. But within each document, the citation format and style should be consistent.

The rest of this chapter focuses on the citation format in *The Bluebook*, which has rules for how to cite every imaginable type of authority. *The Bluebook* has an extensive index, which you can use to find the specific rules that

---

2. *The Bluebook: A Uniform System of Citation* (Columbia Law Review Ass'n, et. al. 20th ed. 2015).

3. *ALWD Citation Manual: A Professional System of Citation* (Colleen M. Barger, ed., 6th ed. 2017).

4. Christopher J. Sprigman et al., *The Indigo Book: A Manual of Legal Citation*, Public Resource (2016).

5. *The Maroonbook: The University of Chicago Manual of Legal Citation* (U. Chi. L. Rev., ed., 2018).

6. D. Mont. L.R. 1.5(d) (2017).

7. Calif. Ct. R. 1.200 (2018); Edward W. Jessen, *California Style Manual: A Handbook of Legal Style for California Courts and Lawyers* (4th ed. 2001).

8. Legal Information Institute, § 7-500. Table of State-Specific Citation Norms and Practices (2017), https://www.law.cornell.edu/citation/7-500.

9. New York Law Reports Style Manual (2017), http://www.nycourts.gov/reporter/style-manual/2017/2017-SM.htm#2.0.

clarify the intricacies of proper citation. But most practicing attorneys cite two types regularly: cases and statutes. If you master the long- and short-citation formats for cases and statutes in the federal and state jurisdictions where you practice, you will be able to easily cite most of the authorities in most legal documents.

To master these formats, you need to understand the basic organization of the information in the citation and the format for long and short citations. A long-form citation is the complete cite for an authority. You will use long citations the first time you cite an authority in a document. For every successive citation to that same authority, you will use a short-citation format.

A. Cases: Long-Form Citations

The organization of the information in long-form citations for federal and state cases published in printed reporters is the same (see Figure 43.1):

> case name—comma—volume number—reporter abbreviation—first page—comma—pinpoint page—left parenthesis—court [if necessary]—year—right parenthesis—period

Figure 43.1

The organization of the information in citations for cases that have only been published electronically in online databases is more detailed than that for cases published in printed reporters (see Figures 43.2 and 43.3):

> case name—comma—docket number—comma—Westlaw or Lexis citation—comma—"at"—asterisk—pinpoint page—left parenthesis—court—full date—right parenthesis—period

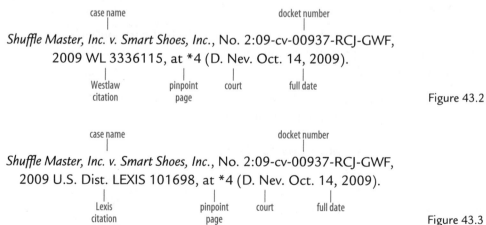

Figure 43.2

Figure 43.3

A case that is not published in a reporter may have both a Westlaw and Lexis citation; you may choose which one you use in your document. Electronically published cases all begin on page *1, so this citation format only includes the pinpoint page number, which is indicated by *4 in the examples on the previous page.

The Bluebook has rules for citing cases within the text of a sentence and as a stand-alone citation sentence that follows a sentence. Generally, stand-alone citation sentences are preferred because they don't interrupt the writer's prose the way a citation in the text of a sentence does. When using stand-alone citation sentences, the citation should end with a period, just like a normal sentence. While many specific rules govern how to properly cite cases, your overall goal is to accurately, efficiently, and consistently convey the citation information the reader needs so she can evaluate the case's relevance, weight, and age and find it herself if she wishes to read it in full.

The following four steps will help you write proper long-form case citations:

Long-Form Case Citations

i. Italicize and abbreviate case names.
ii. Abbreviate the reporter.
iii. Include the first page and pinpoint page.
iv. Abbreviate the court.

---

i. Step One: Italicize and Abbreviate Case Names

Every case name should be italicized.[10] *The Bluebook* also offers the option of underlining case names, but most writers prefer italics because they look cleaner and are easier to read.

The following rules regarding the proper abbreviation of case names are the most important:

- If the caption includes multiple parties, list only the first party on each side of the "v." If the party is a person, include only the last name of the party. For example,

Jacob Newmeyer and Stan Smith, et al., v. Golds Candlemakers
and Goldstar Insurance

↓

Newmeyer v. Golds Candlemakers

---

10. *See generally Bluebook* Rules B10 and 10.2.

- Abbreviate common words in case names.[11] For example,

Environmental Systems Technology, Incorporated v. Marketing
Service Corporation
↓
Envtl. Sys. Tech., Inc. v. Mktg. Serv. Corp.

American Manufacturing Company v. Regional University Society
↓
Am. Mfg. Co. v. Reg'l Univ. Soc'y

- Abbreviate locations when the location is not the full name of the party.[12] For example,

Bank of Nova Scotia v. Pennsylvania
↓
Bank of N.S. v. Pennsylvania

Not

Bank of Nova Scotia v. Pennsylvania
or
Bank of N.S. v. Pa.

ii. Step Two: Abbreviate the Reporter

Every case reporter has an abbreviation.[13] Writing that a case appears in the Federal Supplement Second Series would take up too much space. Instead, that case reporter is abbreviated in citations as F. Supp. 2d. Learning the abbreviations for the reporters you will cite most often will save you time.

The federal reporters you will cite frequently are abbreviated as follows:

Full Name	Abbreviation
U.S. Reports (U.S. Supreme Court cases)	U.S.
Federal Reporter (U.S. Courts of Appeals cases)	F. F.2d F.3d
Federal Supplement (U.S. District Court cases)	F. F. Supp. 2d

---

11. *See generally Bluebook* Table T6.
12. *See generally Bluebook* Table T10.
13. *See generally Bluebook* Table T1.

State cases often appear in more than one reporter. Local citation rules often require citation to the official reporter. But *The Bluebook* format is to cite state cases to the regional reporter where they appear. The abbreviations for the regional reporters are as follows:

Full Name	Abbreviation
Atlantic Reporter (Connecticut, Delaware, D.C., Maine, Maryland, New Hampshire, New Jersey, Pennsylvania, Rhode Island, Vermont)	A. A.2d A.3d
South Eastern Reporter (Georgia, North Carolina, South Carolina, Virginia, West Virginia)	S.E. S.E.2d
Southern Reporter (Alabama, Florida, Louisiana, Mississippi)	So. So. 2d So. 3d
North Eastern Reporter (Illinois, Indiana, Massachusetts, New York, Ohio)	N.E. N.E.2d
South Western Reporter (Arkansas, Kentucky, Missouri, Tennessee, Texas)	S.W. S.W.2d S.W.3d
North Western Reporter (Iowa, Michigan, Minnesota, Nebraska, North Dakota, South Dakota, Wisconsin)	N.W. N.W.2d
Pacific Reporter (Alaska, Arizona, California, Colorado, Hawaii, Idaho, Kansas, Montana, Nevada, New Mexico, Oklahoma, Oregon, Utah, Washington, Wyoming)	P. P.2d P.3d

iii. Step Three: Include the First Page and the Pinpoint Page

A long-form case citation should include the first page that the case appears on in the reporter and a pinpoint page where the specific cited information appears in the case. The first page and the pinpoint page are separated by a comma and a space.

Including the first page enables the reader to find the case. Including the pinpoint page allows the reader to find the specific information being relied upon. Without both, the citation is incomplete and unhelpful to the reader.

iv. Step Four: Abbreviate the Court

A long-form case citation ends with a parenthetical that typically includes the abbreviated name of the court that issued the decision and the year of the decision.[14]

Court	Abbreviations
U.S. Courts of Appeals	1st Cir., 2d Cir., 3d Cir., 4th Cir., 5th Cir., 6th Cir., 7th Cir., 8th Cir., 9th Cir., 10th Cir., 11th Cir., D.C. Cir., Fed. Cir.
U.S. District Courts *See Bluebook Table T10 for abbreviations for geographical terms.*	United States District Court for the Central District of California • C.D. Cal. United States District Court for the District of Massachusetts • D. Mass. United States District Court for the Southern District of New York • S.D.N.Y.
State Courts *See Bluebook Table T1 for abbreviations of state court names.*	Supreme Court of Arkansas • Ark. Tennessee Court of Appeals • Tenn. Ct. App.

When the reporter unambiguously conveys the court that decided the case, you do not include the court in the citation. The federal and regional reporters include cases decided by a variety of courts, so the court must be included. The U.S. Reports, however, includes only decisions of the U.S. Supreme Court. Thus, when citing a U.S. Supreme Court case, you should not include the court in parentheses:

Brown v. Bd. of Educ., 347 U.S. 483, 487 (1954).

— No court is included in the parentheses because the reporter unambiguously conveys that this is a decision of the U.S. Supreme Court.

B. Cases: Short-Form Citations

After providing the long citation for a case on the first reference, you should use the short-citation format for all subsequent citations to that case. Short citations are more concise than long citations, while still giving the reader all of the necessary information about the cited source.

The following examples show the four different types of short-citation formats for cases.[15] The short form will vary depending on how much infor-

---

14. *See generally Bluebook* Tables T1, T7, and T10.
15. *See generally Bluebook* Rule B10 and Rule 4.

mation the reader needs to identify the case and the page being cited. The following are the short formats for the citation to *Brown v. Board of Education*:

> Use this short format when the case has been cited in full earlier in the document, and the preceding citation is to a different authority.
>
> one party name—comma—volume number—reporter abbreviation—"at"— pinpoint page number—period
>
> > *Brown*, 347 U.S. at 488.

> Use this short format when the case has been cited in full earlier in the document, the preceding citation is to a different authority, and the case name appears in the sentence.
>
> volume number—reporter abbreviation—"at"—pinpoint page number—period
>
> > 347 U.S. at 488.

> Use this short format when the case has been cited in full earlier in the document, and the preceding citation is to a different page of the same case. *Id.* is an abbreviation of the Latin word idem and means "the same." As such, *id.* is always italicized and should be capitalized like any other word—only when it begins a citation sentence.
>
> *Id.*—"at"—pinpoint page number—period
>
> > *Id.* at 488.

> Use this short format when the case has been cited in full earlier in the document, and the preceding citation is to the same page of the same case. Remember that *id.* is always italicized and should be capitalized only when it begins a citation sentence.
>
> *Id.*
>
> > *Id.*

For cases that have been published only on Westlaw or LexisNexis, the same rules apply for short-form citations. The short-form citations use the following formats:

> *Shuffle Master*, 2009 WL 3336115, at *4.
>
> *Shuffle Master*, 2009 U.S. Dist. LEXIS 101698, at *4.

You can also use the *id.* formats above, if appropriate, for Westlaw or Lexis citations.

C. Federal Statutes: Long-Form Citations

A federal statute citation reflects where the statute is located in the official U.S. Code.[16]

> The information in the citation is organized as follows:
>
> title number—abbreviated name of U.S. Code—section symbol—specific section—left parenthesis—year of cited code edition—right parenthesis—period
>
> 16 U.S.C. § 1332(b) (2018).

There are three steps to writing a proper long-form statute citation:

> ### Long-Form Statute Citations
>
> i. Cite the official code.
> ii. Include all subsections.
> iii. Use the most recent year the code was printed.

i. Step One: Cite the Official Code

Usually, you will use an annotated version of the U.S. Code to do your research. But in your legal documents, you should always cite the official U.S. Code. Thus, your citations for federal statutes should always use the abbreviation for the official Code—U.S.C.—not the abbreviation for an annotated code.

ii. Step Two: Include All Subsections

Statute citations must be specific. Just as case citations must include a pinpoint page, statute citations must include a specific subsection. If the code section you are citing is divided into subsections, sub-subsections, or even more small parts, include them all in your citation. For example, if you were relying on 35 U.S.C. § 271(e)(2)(C)(ii)—a statute with four layers of subsections—it would not be helpful to the reader to cite only 35 U.S.C. § 271. The reader needs to know the specific part of that section that you are citing.

iii. Step Three: Use the Most Recent Year the Code Was Printed

According to *The Bluebook*, a long-form federal statute citation should include the most recent year that the U.S. Code was printed in parentheses. The U.S. Code is printed every six years. The most recent printing was in 2018. In practice, attorneys frequently omit the year from statute citations.

---

16. *See generally Bluebook* Rule B12 and Rule 12.

D. Federal Statutes: Short-Form Citations

After the first long citation for a statute, you can use short citations through-out the rest of your document.[17] The short-citation formats for federal stat-utes are as follows:

Use this short format when the statute has been cited in full earlier in the document.

title—code abbreviation—section symbol—specific section—period

16 U.S.C. § 1332(b).

Use this short format when the statute has been cited in full earlier in the document, and there is no risk that the reader will be confused about which title is being referred to.

section symbol—specific section—period

§ 1332(b).

Use this short format when the statute has been cited in full earlier in the document, and the preceding citation is to a section in the same title. Remember that *id.* is always italicized and should be capitalized only when it begins a citation sentence.

Id.—section symbol—specific section—period

Id. § 1332(b).

Use this short format when the statute has been cited in full earlier in the document, and the preceding citation is to the identical section of the statute. Remember that *id.* is always italicized and should be capitalized only when it begins a citation sentence.

Id.

Id.

E. State Statutes

The long-citation formats for state statutes vary greatly because each state's code is organized differently.[18] Some state codes are organized around numer-

---

17. *See generally Bluebook* Rule B12 and Rule 12.
18. *See generally Bluebook* T1.

ical titles or sections while others are divided by subject area. And some states don't have an official, unannotated code. Here are a few examples:

> **STATE CODE ABBREVIATION EXAMPLES**
>
> Arkansas Statute (only annotated code available)
> ↓
> Ark. Code Ann. § 13-3-201 (2018).
>
> California Statute
> ↓
> Cal. Bus. & Prof. Code § 17206(a) (2018).
>
> Maine Statute
> ↓
> Me. Stat. tit. 8, § 222(1) (2018).
>
> New York Statute
> ↓
> N.Y. Civ. Rights Law § 50-A(3) (McKinney 2018).

Any short form that clearly identifies the specific statute being cited is acceptable after the statute has been cited in long form in the document.

3. USE THE INDEX, TABLES, AND QUICK REFERENCE GUIDES FOR EVERYTHING ELSE

When you encounter a new citation issue, use the index, tables, or quick reference guides to find the correct format. *The Bluebook* has an extensive index that will guide you to the most helpful places in the text. In addition, the tables in the back of *The Bluebook* provide jurisdiction-specific information for federal, state, and foreign authorities. Last, inside the front and back covers, quick reference guides provide examples of the most common formats.

4. LEARN THE RULES THAT ARISE FREQUENTLY

The Bluebook has certain rules that are not intuitive, but they arise frequently for a law student or lawyer preparing common legal documents. You should learn these rules early because you will apply them often. You can find these rules, and others like them, by using the index in *The Bluebook*.

Citation Rules to Learn

A. Spacing in abbreviations
B. Ordinal numbers
C. Page ranges
D. Federal Rules
E. Signals
F. String cites
G. Parentheticals

A. Spacing in Abbreviations

Single capital letters that appear next to each other in an abbreviation are not separated by a space: S.D.N.Y. Ordinal numbers are treated like single capitals for purposes of this rule: F.3d. But any abbreviation that is not a single capital letter should be separated by a space on both sides: F. Supp. 2d.

B. Ordinal Numbers

Ordinal numbers should not use superscript: 11th Cir., not 11th Cir. *The Bluebook* abbreviations for second and third are unusual. They are abbreviated 2d and 3d, not 2nd and 3rd.

C. Page Ranges

To cite more than one page, give the first and last pages of the range separated by a dash. For the last page, retain the last two digits and drop any other repetitious digits: *Brown*, 347 U.S. at 490–93.

D. Federal Rules

The citation formats for the Federal Rules of Procedure and Evidence are as follows: Fed. R. Civ. P. 12(b)(6); Fed. R. Crim. P. 24(a); Fed. R. App. P. 32(c)(2)(A); Fed. R. Evid. 802.

E. Signals

Signals are short words or phrases that precede a citation and tell the reader how the cited authority relates to the proposition for which it is cited. You should not use a signal when the authority directly states the proposition, is the source of a quotation, or is referred to directly. All other citations should be introduced with a signal. Signals should be italicized, and when a signal begins a citation sentence, it should be capitalized.

The most common signal is *see*. Use *see* when the cited authority supports the proposition but does not state it directly. For instance, *see* is appropriate when you are inferring something about the meaning of a case, synthesizing a rule that is not stated explicitly, or using an authority to support a conclusion about your own case.

The following opinion from *Facebook, Inc. v. Pacific Northwest Software, Inc.*, shows each of the ways to use *see* as an introductory signal:

> A party seeking to rescind a settlement agreement by claiming a Rule 10b-5 violation under these circumstances faces a steep uphill battle. *See* Petro-Ventures, Inc. v. Takessian, 967 F.2d 1337, 1341-42 (9th Cir. 1992).

— *See* indicates that the writer has inferred this proposition from the outcome of the cited case.

> An agreement meant to end a dispute between sophisticated parties cannot reasonably be interpreted as leaving open the door to litigation about the settlement negotiation process. *See Petro-Ventures*, 967 F.2d at 1342 (discussing the parties' "intent to end their various disputes... once and for all" (ellipsis in original)).

— *See* indicates that the writer has synthesized this rule from the reasoning of the cited case.

> This agreement precludes the Winklevosses from introducing in support of their securities claims any evidence of what Facebook said, or did not say, during the mediation. *See Johnson v. Am. Online, Inc.*, 280 F. Supp. 2d 1018, 1027 (N.D. Cal. 2003) (enforcing a similar agreement).[19]

— *See* indicates that the writer has used the cited case to support a conclusion about this case.

Other signals that show either support or contradiction are described in *The Bluebook*, including *see also, see generally, c.f., but see,* and *see, e.g.*

F. String Cites

A citation sentence that includes more than one citation with the same signal is called a "string cite." String cites should be used rarely, but they can be useful when the writer wants to show that multiple authorities support the stated proposition.

The citations within a string cite are separated by semicolons and ordered according to the hierarchy of authority, with the citations for higher courts appearing before the citations for lower courts. When multiple citations are from the same level of court, the citations are listed in reverse chronological order, with the most recent case first.

For example, in a brief to the U.S. Supreme Court, the petitioner used a string cite of binding and non-binding cases to illustrate the principle that a search of the curtilage of the home requires a warrant.

> *See also Taylor v. United States*, 286 U.S. 1, 5-6 (1932) (holding it "inexcusable" and "unreasonable" for police to search a garage "adjacent to the dwelling" without a warrant); *United States v. Wells*, 648 F.3d 671, 679 (8th Cir. 2011) (observing that "because we treat curtilage as part of the home... [the] same rules apply" with regard to warrants); *United States v. Breza*, 308 F.3d 430, 433 (4th Cir. 2002) (noting that the "curtilage of [the] home... typically is afforded the most stringent Fourth Amendment

— Binding precedent from the U.S. Supreme Court is cited first.

— Non-binding cases are cited in reverse chronological order.

---

19. *Facebook, Inc. v. Pac. Nw. Software, Inc.*, 640 F.3d 1034, 1039–41 (9th Cir. 2011).

protection"); *Daughenbaugh v. City of Tiffin*, 150 F.3d 594, 601 (6th Cir. 1998) ("[W]e conclude that the garage was located within the curtilage of [the] house. The officers consequently violated [the owner's] constitutional rights by conducting a warrantless search of the garage.").[20]

G. Parentheticals

A parenthetical appears at the end of a citation sentence and gives the reader useful substantive information about the cited authority. The most common types of parentheticals are (1) those that explain the authority cited, (2) those that indicate that the authority cites or quotes an additional authority, and (3) those that describe the weight of the authority. For more guidance on the style for parentheticals, see pages 146-48 in Chapter 20.

i. Explanatory Parentheticals

Explanatory parentheticals provide substantive information about the cited authority in a sentence or a phrase. These parentheticals are useful because they allow the writer to concisely convey relevant information about a cited authority as part of the citation sentence.

An explanatory parenthetical appears after the citation and usually begins with a present participle (a verb ending in "ing"). These explanatory parentheticals tell the reader how or why the cited authority supports the proposition that is being cited. In explanatory parentheticals for case citations, the verb describes an action of the court, with words like "holding," "explaining," "noting," or "finding." For statutes, the verb usually describes the purpose or effect of the statute, with words like "requiring," "mandating," "describing," or "listing." This form of explanatory parenthetical doesn't begin with a capital letter or include a period within the parentheses because it isn't a full sentence.

> The veterinarian's rule applies because Defendant owed no duty to Plaintiffs under the dog bite statute based on the parties' contractual relationship. *See Rosenbloom v. Hanour Corp.*, 78 Cal. Rptr. 2d 686, 689 (Cal. Ct. App. 1988) (holding that the defendant owed no duty to the plaintiff when the defendant contracted for the services of the plaintiff and entrusted a shark to the plaintiff's care and control).

— This parenthetical begins with "holding" and describes the court's reasoning in support of the outcome in the cited case.

Explanatory parentheticals can also contain quoted language from the cited authority. Including quoted language in a parenthetical gives the citation heft by showing how the cited authority supports the proposition through the authority's own language. If the quoted language reads as a full sentence, the parenthetical should begin with a capital letter and end with a period. This format includes a period within the parentheses to mark the

---

20. Brief for Petitioner at 12-13, *Collins v. Virginia*, 138 S. Ct. 1663 (2018) (No. 16-1027), 2017 WL 5508777.

end of the sentence and a period outside the parentheses to mark the end of the citation.

> The hazard of being bitten and injured by dogs is an inherent risk associated with dog walking. *Priebe v. Nelson*, 47 Cal. Rptr. 3d 553, 568 (Cal. 2009) ("We therefore conclude that Priebe, by virtue of the nature of her occupation as a kennel worker, assumed the risk of being bitten or otherwise injured by the dogs under her care and control while in the custody of the commercial kennel where she worked pursuant to a contractual boarding agreement.").

— This parenthetical quotes language from the cited case that echoes the proposition in the main sentence; it begins with a capital letter and ends with a period.

Explanatory parentheticals can also be short phrases, if a short phrase is all that is needed for the reader to understand the relevance of the citation. Often, this type of explanatory parenthetical is used when the writer cites multiple authorities together and needs to highlight only one aspect of each authority.

> The veterinarian's rule has been applied to a variety of professions that provide services for dogs. *See Priebe*, 47 Cal. Rptr. 3d at 556 (kennel workers); *Nelson v. Hall*, 211 Cal. Rptr. 668, 671 (Cal. Ct. App. 1985) (veterinary assistants); *Jordan v. Lusby*, 81 S.W.3d 523, 524-25 (Ky. Ct. App. 2002) (dog groomers); *Reynolds v. Lancaster Cnty. Prison*, 739 A.2d 413, 427-28 (N.J. Super. Ct. App. Div. 1999) (independent contractor who agreed to care for dogs in connection with his employment as a manager of a guard dog company).[21]

— These parentheticals use short phrases to illustrate a single fact from each case.

ii. Quoting or Citing Parentheticals

Quoting or citing parentheticals indicate that the authority quotes or cites an additional authority. These parentheticals are useful when the source quoted or cited by an authority has some weight, relevance, or interest that would be meaningful to the reader. For example, if the cited case relies on a case from a higher court or from another jurisdiction, or if the cited case quotes an unexpected secondary source, including information in a quoting or citing parenthetical can be helpful. Only one level of quoting or citing parentheticals should be included, meaning that a citation should never include more than one quoting or citing parenthetical. Additional sources can always be included as separate citations.

A quoting or citing parenthetical follows the same format as an explanatory parenthetical that begins with an "—ing" verb.

> We conclude our discussion the way we began it—with the guiding principle of Texas tort law: *"The thing to be kept in view is that the party shall be compensated for the injury done."* *Luna v. N. Star Dodge Sales, Inc.*, 667 S.W.2d 115, 119 (Tex. 1984) (quoting *Craddock v. Goodwin*, 54 Tex. 578,

---

21. This string cite was for an issue that would be decided under California law, so the California cases are listed first according to the hierarchy of jurisdiction. Then, the non-binding cases are organized alphabetically by jurisdiction. *See generally Bluebook* Rule 1.

588 (1881) (emphasis added))).... Permitting loss-of-use damages in to-tal-destruction cases, however, is not a license for unrestrained raids on defendants' coffers. As with all consequential damages, the availability of loss-of-use damages is necessarily circumscribed by commonsense rules. To begin with, the damages claimed may not be "too remote." *Arthur Andersen & Co. v. Perry Equip. Co.*, 945 S.W.2d 812, 816 (Tex. 1997) (citing *White v. Sw. Bell Tel. Co.*, 651 S.W.2d 260, 262 (Tex. 1983); *Henry S. Miller Co. v. Bynum*, 836 S.W.2d 160, 164 (Tex. 1992) (Phillips, C.J., concurring)).[22]

iii. Weight of Authority Parentheticals

Weight of authority parentheticals provide information that affects the weight of the cited authority. These parentheticals must be included when citing a concurring or dissenting opinion. The format for parentheticals for concurrences and dissents has the judge or justice's last name followed by J. (or C.J. for Chief Justice) and the nature of the opinion, all separated by commas.

Ledbetter v. Goodyear Tire & Rubber Co., 550 U.S. 618, 644 (2007) (Ginsburg, J., dissenting).

5. CITE CORRECTLY AS YOU WRITE

Citing often intimidates new legal writers, and some unwisely choose to put in "filler" citations as they write their documents, intending to come back and fix all of the citations at the end of the writing process.

Learning to incorporate correct citations into the flow of your writing has many advantages. In particular, it helps you to learn how to cite efficiently and avoid putting off a task that can be unexpectedly difficult and time consuming, especially if you are close to your deadline. It also ensures that you don't have to retrace your steps to find the authorities or pages that you meant to cite, which can be frustrating and create the risk of citation errors. By citing as you write, correctly citing the most common sources will become a seamless part of your legal writing process. And your early attention to detail will help you create a flawless and credible document.

---

22. *J & D Towing, LLC v. Am. Alt. Ins. Corp.*, 478 S.W.3d 649, 676-77 & nn. 198 & 200 (Tex. 2016).

Index